Demetrius Charles de

THE
HISTORY OF BELGIUM

Part I
Cæsar to Waterloo

Elibron Classics
www.elibron.com

Elibron Classics series.

© 2005 Adamant Media Corporation.

ISBN 1-4021-6714-8 (paperback)
ISBN 1-4212-8216-X (hardcover)

This Elibron Classics Replica Edition is an unabridged facsimile of the edition published in 1902 by the Author, London.

Elibron and Elibron Classics are trademarks of Adamant Media Corporation. All rights reserved.

This book is an accurate reproduction of the original. Any marks, names, colophons, imprints, logos or other symbols or identifiers that appear on or in this book, except for those of Adamant Media Corporation and BookSurge, LLC, are used only for historical reference and accuracy and are not meant to designate origin or imply any sponsorship by or license from any third party.

BODUOGNAT
CHIEF OF THE NERVII.
COURAGE AND PATRIOTISM—BELGIUM UNDER CÆSAR.
(THE STATUE AT ANTWERP).

THE HISTORY OF BELGIUM

PART I.—CÆSAR TO WATERLOO

BY

DEMETRIUS C. BOULGER

Author of
" *The History of China,*" " *Life of Gordon,*" *etc., etc.*

PUBLISHED BY THE AUTHOR
AT 11 EDWARDES SQUARE, KENSINGTON, W.
London.
1902

CONTENTS.

Chapter.		Page.
1.	The Roman Occupation	1
2.	The Franks to the Death of Charlemagne	22
3.	The Early Feudal Period	41
4.	The Crusades	68
5.	The Decline of Feudalism	96
6.	The Growth of the Communes	128
7.	The Communes lose Political Power	160
8.	The House of Burgundy	186
9.	The First Union of Belgium	213
10.	The Transition to Spanish Rule	259
11.	The Spanish Rule	291
12.	The Last Century of Spanish Rule	338
13.	Austrian Rule	369
14.	The Brabant Revolution	398
15.	French Rule in Belgium	422
16.	The Waterloo Campaign	446

LIST OF ILLUSTRATIONS.

FULL-PAGE ILLUSTRATIONS.

	Page.
Boduognat	*Frontispiece*
The Battle with the Nervii	7
The Battle of Tolbiac	25
The Battle of Cassel	57
Godfrey of Bouillon	75
Battle of Guinegate or Courtrai	113
Battle of Woeringen	121
Edward III. and James van Artevelde	149
Philip van Artevelde haranguing the People	175
Charles the Bold at Ghent	233
Abdication of Charles the Fifth	285
Margaret of Parma receiving the Gueux	309
The Count de Nény	387

TEXT ILLUSTRATIONS.

	Page.
Punishment of Brunhilda	28
Charlemagne visiting a School	37
Death of Charlemagne	39
Capture of Jerusalem	81
Origin of Arms of Flanders	85
Baldwin's Coronation	91
Flemings abandoning Siege of Calais	215
Arrival of Joanna of Spain	268
Egmont and Horn	317
Entry of Albert and Isabella	338
Brussels after French Bombardment	360
Entry of Prince Charles of Lorraine	385
Battle of Turnhout	408
General van Merlen	456
The Prince of Orange at Waterloo	466

PREFACE.

THE following pages represent the research and work of more than three years, during the greater portion of which period I resided in Belgium.

This volume concludes with the battle of Waterloo, and is mainly intended as a preliminary study to the history of Belgium in the 19th century, first as a portion of the Kingdom of the Netherlands, and secondly, as an independent state.

It is for this reason that I have employed the name Belgium as applying to the Low Countries or Netherlands before the name came into use at the Waterloo period when projects of independence were freely entertained, and before it was formally adopted for the country after the revolution in 1830. In its adjectival form Belgic or Belgian, the name goes back to early mediæval history, which thus handed on the language of Cæsar to modern times. If a final reason is needed for the use of the word Belgium before it was coined, the plea of convenience must be urged. It is short, and concise as separating the ten (now nine) Provinces of the South from the seven Provinces of the North that constitute the present Kingdom of the Netherlands, which we call Holland.

DEMETRIUS C. BOULGER.

7th April, 1902.

THE HISTORY OF BELGIUM.

CHAPTER I.

The Roman Occupation.

THE history of the Belgian races forms a remarkable and perhaps unique picture in the life of Europe. At every epoch they have maintained, often without independence and sometimes even without a country as defined by regular boundaries, an individuality that commanded recognition, and that preserved the national type as something distinct from either of their two great neighbours in such a manner as to furnish plausible arguments for those who assigned them both a German and a Gallic origin.* Numerically inferior to either, contracted within limits that precluded expansion in numbers and wealth

*Much ink has been and will continue to be spilt on the subject whether the Belgæ of Cæsar's time had a German or a Celtic origin. With regard to the Nervii there can apparently be no doubt that, as Cæsar states, they were Germans, and probably the tribes allied with them had a similar origin. But one's inclination rather than the evidence—which is nil— favours the supposition that the Menapians who inhabited the forests of the lower Scheldt and Meuse were Celts, and perhaps the Treviri of the great Ardenne forest were so also, as it is only reasonable to assume that when the German invasion of the second century before our era took place the original Celtic inhabitants retired into the regions most difficult of access. It will be remembered that the Treviri abandoned the league formed by the Nervii in anticipation of the invasion of Cæsar, while the Menapian colonies in Brittany (mentioned by Cæsar) and in Ireland (mentioned by Ptolemy) were in all human probability Celtic. The ancient name of Dublin was Menapia. If it cannot be asserted then that all the Belgian tribes were German it may, however, be affirmed that the most numerous and powerful of them were. The subject has formed the theme of scores of erudite and laborious writers, of whom, if it cannot be said that they have attained perfect agreement among themselves or carried complete conviction to the minds of their readers, it may at least be affirmed that their distinctions and differences have been so fine as to suggest to a new set of seekers after truth the thesis that Germans and Gauls were identical in a common Cymric origin—which, even if ethnologically true, will not disturb the facts of history or provide the basis of a new fraternity.

B

sufficient to enable them to cope on equal terms with the Germans or the French, the stout-heartedness of the race has enabled it to survive the storms and the stress of twenty centuries, so that to-day a Walloon and a Fleming are not to be confounded with the two powerful nations at their doors. With some affinities to them both they possess characteristics as clearly opposite as those which differentiate the peoples east and west of the Rhine from each other. The Belgian races were not able to carry their authority permanently over the surrounding regions, whether towards the Seine or the Rhine, or to impress the mark of their special institutions and character on the towns of the adjacent provinces, but they succeeded in perpetuating their own separate existence under Duke, Emperor, and King, and in forming, on many critical occasions of history, a barrier, passive but effective, against tyrants and conquerors who, without their opposition, would have established solid hegemonies along the coast of the German Ocean.

When Julius Cæsar decided, in the year B.C. 57, to invade without pretext that part of Gaul which was in the hands of the Belgæ, the territory assailed extended as far south as the Seine and the Marne. The Atrebates and Veromandui, for whose aid the Nervii formed their celebrated league, occupied Picardy and the northern parts of the Ile de France and Champagne, but of the twenty-four tribes named by the Roman conqueror the most powerful were settled along the Sambre and the Meuse and in the fertile region now known as Brabant and Hainaut. Of these tribes the Nervii are by far the most famous, although it may be said that the imperishable lustre of their name was gained by the heroism of a single day. Their courage and fortitude constitute, as it were, the epic round which Belgian nationality took its earliest form.

The celebrated description of the Germans and their mode of life given by Tacitus applies with more or less exactitude to the Belgian tribes of Cæsar's time and more especially to the Nervii. They were monogamists, scorned trade and agriculture, and devoted themselves exclusively to the pursuits of the hunter and the warrior. A line in Cæsar's description suggests that after all they were agriculturists, at least by deputy, because he states that they had been attracted by "the fertility of the soil." Wine was forbidden as tending to diminish the physical force of the body, and so rigorously was this prohibition enforced that among some of the tribes there was the practice of measuring the girth of the stomach and imposing a fine when it exceeded fixed dimensions. The system of government was popular rather than monarchical. Ambiorix, king of the Eburones, one of the five chief clans or nations, told Cæsar that the people had as much power as the King, and in support of this statement mentioned that every hundred warriors deputed a member or senator to the tribal parliament. The Nervii counted 60,000 men capable of bearing arms, and the government, such as it was, was carried on by 600 senators. Perhaps the only question of importance they ever had to decide was that of peace or war, and when the Romans crossed the Seine this question was discussed by all the assemblies and unanimously decided in favour of combat. Cæsar enumerates the tribes joining the national league and he gives them a fighting strength of nearly a quarter of a million—of these the Nervii counted for 60,000 and the Atrebates, their close allies, for 15,000. The whole of this force consisted of infantry, and the only tribes known to possess cavalry were the Treviri, who held aloof from the Belgian League, and the Batavians who, occupying part of modern Holland, could not be considered to form part of it. The mass of men had as arms nothing better than an axe or a bundle of javelins, while their defensive armour was represented by a cloak and hood of skins. The chiefs and perhaps some of the elder warriors were better equipped with sword and spear, and shield, helmet, and even cuirass. These men were placed in the exposed points of the battle or at the angles of the triangular formation in which the nation advanced to the attack. Neither their arms nor their discipline placed them on a level with the Romans, but their physical strength, untamed spirit and dauntless courage made them opponents whom even Cæsar could not affect to despise.*

*The Belgians used also a two-horsed chariot (Virgil mentions it under the name Belgica in his Georgics) but this was reserved for the chief or still

The immediate causes of the Roman invasion of the country which we call Belgium* were the incursions of the Germans into Gaul, and the fear of the Gauls, as represented by the Sequani and Aedui, that they would lose their possessions. The ulterior fear of the Germans was quickened by the memorable invasion of the Helvetii under Orgetorix whose movement was probably caused by the same apprehension. When Cæsar defeated the Helvetii he compelled the survivors to return to their homes so that the gap they had left on the frontier might not be filled up by the Germans. He then turned to deal with the more serious peril represented by the Germans under Ariovistus, King of the Suevi. To the Roman summons to quit Gaul and restore the hostages he had in his possession, Ariovistus returned a defiant answer. Cæsar, warned by the Treviri of the German advance, hastened to meet them, and in a battle fought near Belfort routed the army of the Suevi. This signal success put an end for that period to German pretensions to dispute with Rome the mastery in Gaul.

The overthrow of the Suevi carried a warning to the kindred Belgian tribes who had themselves emerged from the Hercynian forest not so long before. Filled with alarm they formed the league that has been referred to, and Cæsar, whose mission was to establish the authority of Rome throughout all the provinces of Gaul, did not delay in justifying their fears.

<small>more frequently for the tribal standard, generally the snout of a wild animal fixed on a pole. Round the chariot the tribe rallied if the day was going against them. Little more is known of the religion or the superstitious rites of the Belgian tribes than what they had in common with the Germans, but they worshipped Mercury as the God of the soil under the name of Theutates, and Mars (Esus), and Jupiter (Taranus) stood next in their esteem. With regard to what has been said above about trade, other tribes were not as strict as the Nervii. The Menapians and Morini certainly traded with Britain and Ireland, sending copper and receiving tin in exchange. While all authorities agree in dilating on the exceptional ferocity of the Nervii in battle, they also bear tribute to their hospitality and good faith, calling special attention to their fêtes among which was the practice of sword dancing, similar to that existing in the Highlands, and at the town of Alost, in Flanders, to-day. Finally among the faults and weaknesses of the Nervii is cited a marked passion for gambling which suggests affinity with the Huns.

*A name derived from Belgium, a small canton of Flanders. It will be recollected that Switzerland has a very similar origin, being called after Schwyz, the least important of its divisions.</small>

Raising two fresh legions, which brought his regular force up to ten legions or 100,000 men, Cæsar crossed the Seine in the year 57 B.C. The outlying Belgian tribes either surrendered like the Remi or offered a slight and futile resistance like the Amieni, while the Atrebates and the Veromandui retired on his advance and effected a junction with the Nervii on the Sambre. The Nervii themselves had prepared for the struggle before them by sending their old men, women, and children into the forests through which the Scheldt forced a way to the sea. Having done this they and their allies took up their position on the banks of the Sambre and fortified a camp on the slopes of a wooded hill. In this place* they awaited the arrival of the Roman army.

When Cæsar reached this point he does not appear to have been aware of the proximity of the enemy, or at least of his being in such great force, for we are assured that 80,000 Belgians were collected here to resist the Roman army which itself numbered from 50,000 to 60,000 men. While Cæsar gave orders to form his camp on the bank of the river he sent his cavalry across it to reconnoitre the hill on the opposite side. At this sight the impetuous Nervii could no longer be

*The exact position of this camp and the ensuing battle, which Shakespeare has helped to immortalise in the reference to "that day against the Nervii" in Mark Antony's oration, has been the subject of much discussion. As the only evidence is furnished by the facts that there was a "wooded hill" close to the river and that the river Sambre here was three feet deep, it is highly improbable that the site will ever be discovered beyond controversy. Napoleon favoured the claims of Maubeuge—once the capital of Hainaut, but long a French possession—and General Renard of the Belgian army, a most competent authority, has supported the same view. On the other hand Napoleon III., in his edition of the Commentaries, states that the height of Hautmont, between Berlaimont and Hautmont, in the district of Avesnes alone accords with the particulars given by Cæsar. This opinion is based on the researches of the French Commission on the topography of Gaul, and perhaps its members were over anxious to discover the site on French soil. The Belgian popular view is that the battle was fought at Prêsles, six miles south of Charleroi. In favour of this is, first, the name which may be plausibly derived from Prælium, battle, and secondly its more reasonable proximity to Aduaticum, the fort on the Meuse which was associated with Cæsar's second exploit in the Belgian war. Had the battle been fought at Maubeuge, and still more if at Hautmont, the Commentaries would have contained some reference to the comparatively long march in an unknown country to the districts of the Aduatici who, moreover, almost arrived in time for the battle.

restrained, and quitting the position they had fortified they charged down the hill under their chief Boduognat,* overwhelmed the light Numidian cavalry, and, pursuing them across the river, assailed the Roman army. In this impetuous and probably unpremeditated onset it is not to be supposed that any regular order was maintained, but the Atrebates were assigned the right, the Veromandui the centre and the Nervii themselves the left of the national army. So sudden and vigorous was the charge of these stalwart but poorly armed hunters and warriors that the Roman army gave ground, and one legion, the Twelfth, showed signs of breaking. At this critical moment the personal courage of Cæsar restored the day. He seems to have been in his tent when the action began, and the few minutes that elapsed before the Nervii reached the Roman lines did not admit of his putting on all his armour. Snatching a shield from one of his soldiers he hastened to the point of greatest danger, and rallied the troops by his presence and example.

In all such encounters the moment of peril is the first. The Nervii came on like a raging and apparently resistless torrent, which if it could have effected several entrances within the lines of the Roman army would have overwhelmed it. They were on the point of gaining that advantage when the arrival of Cæsar at the front of the battle restored the wavering line, and discipline placed an effective barrier in the path of the fierce clansmen. Foiled in the only attempt that gave the Nervii any chance of victory a wise leader would have called off his men, and thus saved the bulk of his force for further resistance in conjunction with the other allies who had not yet reached the scene of action. But the Nervii were obstinate and proud fighters who did not know when they were beaten, and their elementary tactics had not impressed upon them the advantages to be sometimes derived from a judicious and well-timed retreat. When the Roman army regained its steadiness and presented the solid front of shimmering steel which made the legions so impressive in the eyes of naked or skin-clad barbarians, the Nervii continued the struggle with unabated

*Most probably Buddig-nat, Son of Victory.

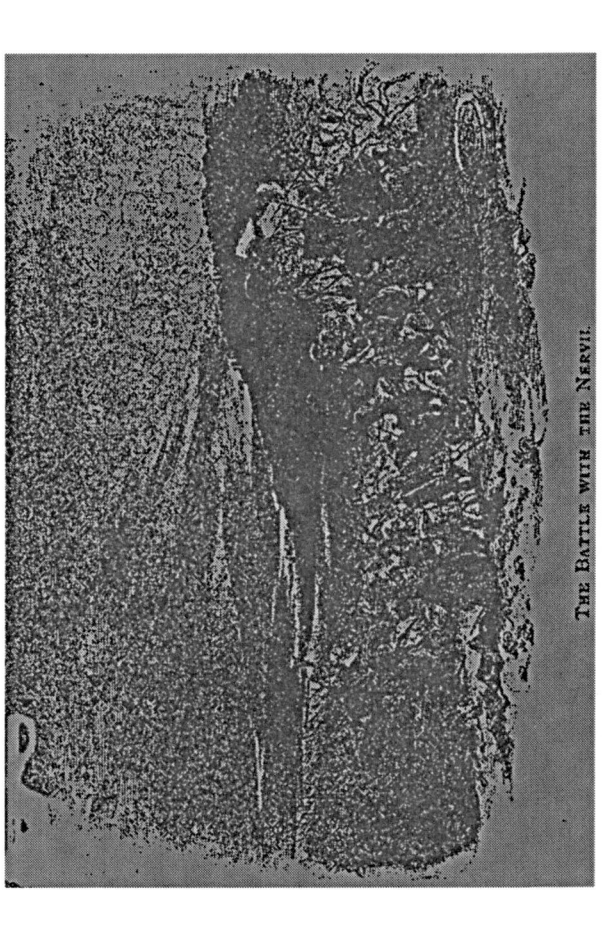

The Battle with the Nervii.

'rage and intrepidity. The numbers of the contending forces were almost equal and the encounter was fought out, body against body, by men on either side who flinched not at the death blow. The slaughter which ensued, and which far exceeded anything known in modern battles despite the adoption of scientific means of destruction, is explained by these facts. The Nervii, inspired by their own courage, and the heroic example of their chief, Boduognat, fought to the last man. We are told that the slaughtered soon formed a rampart behind which the survivors continued to fight and that the dying raised themselves to hurl their last javelins at the invaders of their soil. When the struggle or butchery ended the manhood of the Nervian race had disappeared. Of 60,000 warriors only 500 survived, of 600 senators only three. The old men and women in the recesses of the forests sent in their submission to Cæsar, who graciously accorded them not merely personal safety but the protection of Rome. In admiration of the unexampled courage and fortitude of the fallen warriors the Nervii were granted the status of a Free People, exempted from taxation, and styled allies instead of the subjects of the Mistress of the World. Perhaps a still higher tribute was paid in the fact that not fewer than fifteen days of sacrifice were ordained for this victory in the temple of Capitolian Jove.

The practical annihilation of the Nervii and presumably of their two allies also was the first step in the Roman conquest of Belgic Gaul. The Aduatici, whose forces for war numbered nearly 30,000 men, were marching to join the Nervii when they learnt of their defeat, and they at once retired to their own territory. Instead of retreating before the invaders or seeking shelter in the forests this tribe collected all its members in the fort of Aduaticum which, in ignorance of what the Roman engineers could do, was believed to be impregnable. When Cæsar reached this place he proceeded to lay seige to it in regular form. He erected round it a rampart 12 feet high and 5000 yards in length, and on it he placed in the customary manner at intervals towers from which he proceeded to bombard the fortress with his catapults. The Aduatici are said to have been frightened by this mode of warfare, and they asked for terms. They were told that they must give up their arms, and in apparent compliance they threw many of them over the walls. But during the night they formed a sudden and unfortunate resolution. They attempted to surprise and storm the Roman entrenchments. The Romans were found on their guard, the attack was defeated with ease, and the next morning the legions entered the fortress. Cæsar ordered the sack of the place, or to express the situation more correctly he directed that everything in it should be sold by auction. On the morrow he was informed that the total of heads reached 53,000.*

Cæsar's first campaign had thus resulted in the practical annihilation of the two most warlike tribes of the Belgæ, and the other members of the League hastened to send in their submission to the conqueror. There were, however, two exceptions. The Menapians and the Morini, holding the marshy tracts along the coast from Boulogne to Antwerp and covered by a screen of impenetrable forest, rightly concluded that the Roman soldiers would be unable to force a way to their retreats. They accordingly remained defiant, and when Cæsar attempted to coerce them they had the satisfaction of repulsing his efforts. The Roman leader, sooner than admit that he was baffled, gave orders to cut down the forests that obstructed his progress, but he soon realised that the task was beyond his resources. He however, overcame that section of the Morini who occupied the more open country on the coast of Normandy, and thus acquired means of executing his cherished expedition to Britain.† During his absence his lieutenants, Sabinus and Cotta, gained some further successes, and on his return Cæsar obtained from the

*The position of the fort of Aduaticum has been as much discussed as that of the battle of the Nervii. The most general opinion, perhaps, is that it occupied the site of the citadel of Namur, while others place it still in this neighbourhood, but on the plateau of Hastédon. Napoleon III. favoured the claims of Namur generally, and the discovery of the remains of a great camp of the Roman period that had been destroyed by fire at Hastédon furnishes some evidence in its favour. The topographical commission mentioned in the earlier note declared for Mount Phalize near Huy on the Meuse between Namur and Liége. The great Napoleon shared none of these views, fixing the locality at Fallais on the Mehaigne north of Huy. Perhaps Hastédon has the best claims.

†The King or principal chief in South Britain at this time was Divitiacus, a chief of the Suessones—that is, a Belgic tribe.

Menapians, impressed by his expedition across the Channel, the recognition of his authority. The Morini were placed under the sovereignty of Cæsar's friend Commius, king of the Atrebates, and when Cæsar, dissatisfied with the nominal surrender of the Menapians, devoted his attention during his fifth campaign to their effective coercion, bridging the Scheldt and assailing them from three sides, they also, in the settlement that ended the operations, were assigned as subjects to Commius.

The absence of Cæsar on his second expedition to Britain seems to have inspired the principal remaining tribes with a hope that they might recover their independence. On this occasion the Treviri, who had joined the Romans before the invasion of Belgic Gaul, took the lead, or rather, Indutiomar, one of their great chiefs, did so, for another chief, by name Cingetorix, remained attached to Cæsar. Here the racial differences may be detected, for Indutiomar was a German and Cingetorix a Celt.* But if Indutiomar was the first to throw off the yoke of Rome, Ambiorix, chief of the Eburones, was by power and ability the true leader of the rising. Cæsar had stationed a garrison of one legion and half another at Aduatuca—probably Wittem between Maestricht and Aix-la-Chapelle—and entrusted the command to two of his lieutenants, Cotta and Sabinus. The position was on the extreme limits of Roman authority, and its defenders could only look to themselves. When Ambiorix revolted and surrounded the place, the garrison had no other hope than in their own valour, yet Sabinus weakly listened to the suggestion made by Ambiorix of allowing them a safe retreat. Cotta was in favour of resistance to the bitter end, but he was overruled, and the Romans marched out of their camp in blind confidence in the oath of a chief whose race had many wrongs and heavy losses to avenge. The Roman soldiers and their leaders were attacked in the forest and butchered to the last man. Rendered confident by success, Ambiorix hastened westward, gathering

*The ingenious Schayes puts in a theory that the Gauls and Germans were neither strangers nor brothers, but "relations of an unascertainable degree of proximity." Strabo has something to the same effect when he says that there were German Celts and pure Germans.

to his force the intermediate tribes and hoping to surprise the Roman garrison under Quintus Cicero at a place somewhere in the neighbourhood of Charleroi. This second enterprise might have fared as well as the first if Cæsar had not returned from Britain and hastened to the scene of danger in person. Before he could reach the beleaguered camp he succeeded in restoring the sinking spirits of its garrison by one of his famous laconic messages. In five words he wrote "Cæsar (to) Cicero. Courage. Expect aid." He was not far behind his messenger. With one legion of 8,000 men he forced his way through the army of Ambiorix, numbering 60,000 men, rescued Cicero, and on learning of the massacre of the force under Cotta and Sabinus swore that he would neither shave nor have his hair cut until he had wiped out that loss by exterminating the Eburones.

In the meanwhile, Indutiomar and the Treviri had fared worse than their allies. The scene of their operations was further south, probably on the Semois, the most beautiful tributary of the Upper Meuse, and the object of their attack was the camp of Labienus which may have been the historically interesting position of Bouillon.* This commander was on his guard, and when the enemy incautiously approached the camp his cavalry made a sudden sortie through two gates and put the Treviri to the rout. Not content with defeating the army Labienus aspired to capture the leader and he incited his cavalry in the pursuit by offering a reward for Indutiomar's person, dead or alive. That chief was slain by his pursuers while attempting to swim across the Meuse. Cæsar then turned against the Eburones, and with an army of 100,000 men he marched across the country to the modern towns of Maestricht and Liege. In the neighbourhood of the latter place Ambiorix was nearly captured, but more fortunate than Indutiomar he escaped to the Germans. The fifth of Cæsar's campaigns in Gaul which began with the coercion of the Menapians concluded with the subjugation of the Eburones, the most numerous and powerful of the Belgic tribes after the Nervii.

*Rocroi and Sedan are also suggested.

The final triumph of the Roman arms had not yet been attained, for, in the year following the flight of Ambiorix, Commius, on whom Cæsar had bestowed his confidence, raised the national standard, and proclaimed his independence. He seems to have been encouraged to take this step by the league formed in Gaul by Vercingetorix, a chief in the modern Burgundy country. He was also joined by Correus, chief of the Bellovaci, but Cæsar proved once more equal to the occasion. Vercingetorix when beleaguered in his capital at Alesia* made a voluntary surrender by riding into the Roman camp and exclaiming to Cæsar "You have conquered." Correus was killed in battle, and Commius himself surrendered on condition that he need never appear before any Roman. With these incidents of the years 51-50 B.C. the Roman occupation of the state which we call Belgium became complete. In six campaigns out of the eight required for the conquest of all Gaul Cæsar carried his eagles through this northern division, annihilated the most warlike tribes, and effectually humbled the remainder. His triumph was due not merely to his military genius, but to the terribly effective manner in which he dealt with those who resisted him. At the same time, it is difficult to find evidence of the perfidy with which his enemies at Rome and his detractors since have accused him.

If Julius Cæsar has the exclusive credit for the conquest of Belgium, its civil organisation under the Roman Government was the work of Augustus. The uncle did indeed include the Belgæ in the order utilising the military qualities of the Gauls, and some of his old adversaries in the Ardennes fought on his side no doubt in the battle of Pharsalia, but it was the nephew who established the Roman administration on the basis which endured for five centuries from Augustus to Augustulus. Owing to the depopulation that had accompanied some of Cæsar's operations, fresh colonies were established. The Nervii were mixed with immigrants, and the new race was distinguished as the læti Nervii, but the name of the Eburones passed out of use with the manhood of the tribe, and in their place appeared the people known as the Tungri.

*Mont-Auxois in Burgundy.

When Augustus, after the defeat of Mark Antony, took up seriously the task of governing the empire that had been so largely founded by the military genius of his predecessor, he turned his chief attention to Gaul. He began by dividing the empire into two classes of provinces, provinciæ Cæsaris governed by the Emperor's sole decree, and provinciæ senatus vel populi in which the authority still continued to be dispensed by the representatives of the Roman people. Gaul came under the former category and Belgium formed one of the four provinces into which Augustus divided it. In order to show the spirit in which he took up the task, he appointed Licinius, an ex-slave whom Julius Cæsar had freed, his Procurator in Gaul. But the Emperor did not act only by deputy. He visited Gaul and resided there for the greater part of three years. It is also probable that he visited the Belgic portion of the province after Agrippa's successes on the Rhine had rendered the eastern frontier secure by the establishment of the great camp of Ubiorum Oppidum on the site of the modern city of Cologne. Drusus, the next Roman commander, built fifty camps on the Meuse and the Rhine. His canal to the Yssel gave the Rhine a third bed, his Castellum Flevum commanded the navigation of both streams and deprived the foe of all hope of obtaining supplies from England.

The prisoners taken in the long border strife with the Germans were established as colonists along the Meuse and Sambre, and thus the German element was again strengthened. In fact, Belgium's population was always fed from Germany, and not from Gaul. The importance of Belgium in the eyes of the Romans was essentially military. Through it passed the great road to the Lower Rhine. This road led from Arras to Cologne past Cambrai, Bagacum (Bavai near Mons), Vaudrez, Gembloux, Tongres, and Juliers. At first the places named were merely postal stations with relays of chariots and horses, but in time, several of them, as well as other points of importance like Maestricht, became walled villages,* and Tongres and Tournai eventually attained the size and position of towns. Tournai (which was the capital of the Suevian and

*Among other Roman stations may be named Nasogne, Dinant, Huy, and Namur.

Menapian colonies after they were united into one community by Agrippa under Augustus) owed its importance to its proximity to Boulogne, the port for Britain. The residence of the Roman Præses or Legatus for Belgium was, however, at none of these places but at Rheims. He sometimes resided at Bavacum, the second town of the department specially known as Belgium. Upper and Lower Germany were two other departments in that division of Gaul, which was expressly termed Belgic, with their capitals at Tongres and Cologne respectively.

Notwithstanding these efforts the assimilation of Belgium with the Roman Empire made slight progress. Gaul became Latin in language, customs, and civilisation. But Belgium retained the ruder but more robust habits of the German. The tribes spoke German, Roman writers like Tacitus and Strabo attest it with regret. They retained their warlike character, and their aversion to live in houses. The Menapians continued their maritime adventures, landing on the Irish coast and permanently associating themselves with the early history of that country under the name of Fir-Bolgs. The Roman garrisons were kept along the main roads, the chiefs were left undisturbed in the outer districts, and the character of the Roman conquest was expressed in the phrase that the Belgians were *plus victi quam domiti*. They could not stand up to the legions on the field of battle with any chance of victory, but on the other hand the Roman authorities were well content to procure their tranquillity by a large measure of indulgence.

The Roman authority extended, however, to the further limits of the Menapian territory on the southern banks of the lower Meuse. In the estuary formed by that river and the Rhine, and especially where the Waal forms a connecting link between them, dwelt a tribe known as the Batavi or Batavians. They had succeeded to the reputation that the Nervii possessed in the time of Julius Cæsar, for Tacitus calls them the bravest of the Germans. They were, however, only one of the warrior clans grouped together under the common name of the Catti,

*There seems every reason to believe that the Bolgs and the Belgæ have names of a common origin—meaning the skin-clad people.

who left the Hercynian forest a little later than the Nervii, but still before the Roman invasion. Of this race, Tacitus has left an imperishable account in the 30th and 31st chapters of his Germania. Their courage and energy were not less clearly demonstrated in the successful struggle they carried on against the natural difficulties of the region in which they elected to find a new home than on the field of battle. Strangely enough, considering the marshy character of the country that the Batavians inhabited, their most formidable fighting force consisted of cavalry. Augustus recruited 5,000 of the cavalry of his Guard from this tribe, and the Batavian Horse played a prominent part in the wars and military plots of the Empire. Their military prowess gained for them the name of the friends and brothers of the Roman People.

The destruction of the legions of Varus by Arminius signified a great deal more than the loss of the fighting men for whom Augustus called in vain. It produced a recrudescence of national spirit among all the members of the German race. One of its immediate consequences was the disarmament of the Batavian cohorts, but Tiberius restored them their arms with the object of gaining their support. The success of the German leader increased their self-confidence, and strengthened their opinion that they were the equals of the Romans. The military triumphs of the son of Drusus, known as Germanicus, on and beyond the Rhine did not shake this belief. Yet that great captain and ruler of men restored the reputation of the legions, the method and resources of Rome triumphed over the patriot Arminius who withdrew further into the great forest, there to experience the fickleness of popular applause and the injustice of the men whose courage he had stimulated.

The danger from Arminius passed away and so also passed his conqueror Germanicus from the scene of his triumphs to meet his fate in distant Antioch. But the peril from the Germans had been only warded off and not dispelled, and that from the Batavians formed not the smallest part of it. Tiberius himself escaped the worst portion of it although he came into collision with the Frisians, and when his troops suffered some reverses at their hands, he thought it safest to accept the situation and refrain from heroic measures. It was not surprising that at such a moment two of their chiefs, on visiting Rome, should have insisted on receiving as honourable a place in the tribune of the Senators at the Coliseum as other strangers admitted on account of their courage and fidelity to Rome, because there were none braver and more faithful than the Germans. The trouble with the Frisians flickered out, but in its place soon arose the graver difficulties with the Batavians.

In the reign of Nero, Claudius Civilis, a Roman name concealing whatever may have been the correct cognomen of a Batavian chief of undoubted position and reputation, received harsh treatment. He had served the Romans for twenty-five years in the Batavian contingent. In education and training he and his brother, Julius Paulus, were Romans, and when the latter was imprisoned and executed by Nero, the former swore to have revenge. Other chiefs would have retired to their own territory and raised a revolt, hopeless of victory and barren of result. But Civilis was no ordinary man, and he threw himself into the disputes at Rome of rival candidates for the Imperial fillet. Nero had sapped the foundations of the Empire, Galba had failed to realise the expectation of his soldier days, and the rivalry of Vitellius and Vespasian gave Civilis the needed opportunity. He declared himself for Vitellius, who was on the spot while Vespasian was in the East, and he obtained from him a commission to recruit Batavian levies. He kept up the pretence of loyalty to Rome, while he was bent on destroying its authority. He recruited Batavians for the legions, but his real object was to achieve independence and to revive the German spirit. He invited the boldest and most influential of his countrymen to a secret banquet, at which he made a speech calling upon them to achieve their independence and put an end to the tyranny of Rome. It is said that the feast concluded amid scenes that recall the more famous oath of the Beggars fifteen centuries later. The insurrectionary movement among the Batavians became general, and the neighbouring and kindred clan of the Caninefates, under their chief Brinnon, also declared themselves the enemies of Rome.

The confederates did not delay in carrying their intentions

C

into acts. A detached garrison of several cohorts was destroyed, the Roman merchants scattered throughout the province of Belgium were all murdered, and, finally, the Roman garrison of Mayence was defeated in a battle on the Rhine with the loss of twenty-four vessels, not so much by the valour of the Batavians as by the defection of Batavian and Belgic levies, the latter of whom, in particular, formed a considerable part of the fleet. Other successes followed, and the Belgic tribes generally abandoned the side of Rome whose force was at last reduced to the garrison of two legions in the camp of Castra Vetera, the modern Xanten near Cleves. Notwithstanding the magnitude of his success Civilis, knowing the power of Rome, hesitated to measure himself with it. He accordingly conceived it to be politic to declare himself in favour of Vespasian whose rivalry to Vitellius had become the great question of that day. This proclamation may have been merely intended as a ruse to obtain possession of Castra Vetera, for Civilis requested the garrison to declare for Vespasian, and to combine with him. The only response he received was a haughty one to the effect that he was a traitor.

A desultory campaign, in which fortune wavered between the two contending parties, ensued, but it is unnecessary here to furnish all the details. The garrison of Castra Vetera were at last starved into surrender, and although promised their lives, they were set upon by the Germans and annihilated. In the meantime, the Gauls, encouraged by the example and success of the Germans, had risen in revolt, and established what they called the Empire of the Gauls. Then first appeared the coinage, having the face of Gallia on the one side, and on the other the clasped hands and the motto *fides*; and if an alliance could have been formed between the two races, perhaps the final chapter of the Roman Empire might well have begun before it reached its zenith. But Civilis, the German, could not enter into a hearty alliance with Classicus, the Gaul. He wished for complete independence, and not a change of masters. The prophetess or witch, Velleda, whose alliance had been invaluable to Civilis on account of her happy predictions, was also wholly in favour of a Pan German confederacy. The suitable moment for action passed by unutilised. The Romans recovered their courage and self-confidence. Civilis was beaten in a battle outside Castra Vetera, the scene of his most signal success. He retired to the Isle of the Batavians, and continued to show a good front to the enemy, but the German chiefs abandoned the confederacy and made their peace with Rome. The prophetess Velleda, moving with the times, changed the character of her utterances and foretold the triumph of Rome. The Batavians themselves were shaken. and Civilis, seeing his hopes dispelled and himself abandoned, demanded an interview with the Roman general on the broken bridge across the Yssel. There is no record of that interview, nor of the terms agreed upon, because the record perished with the lost volume of Tacitus. Nor can it even be asserted that the life of Civilis was spared, but we can affirm that the Batavians were restored to their ancient privileges, that they possessed the status of a free people, and that during the following centuries they formed a prominent part of the Prætorian Guard.

There is nothing much to be said of the history of Belgium under the Romans in the second, third, and fourth centuries of our era. The Emperor Hadrian visited the country in 120 A.D., only 50 years after the rising of Civilis, and declared it to be very flourishing. A similar opinion was expressed three centuries later by Eumenes as Rhetor, and he dwelt especially on the wealth and agricultural prosperity of the Belgians in the reign of Constantine. His evidence is all the more noteworthy because he specially singles out the Nervii for honourable mention. In the intervening period the Emperor Probus, at the end of the 3rd century, had introduced the cultivation of the vine along the banks of the Moselle, and although Luxembourg forms only a natural and not a political part of modern Belgium, it was as closely linked with the ancient province as Flanders or Brabant. If it may be maintained that the Roman civilisation never obtained the firm hold on the Belgian tribes, who were Germans, that it did on the Gauls, it may safely be declared that it turned a very large portion of the population, who were originally averse to agriculture, into agriculturists, and that it established among them an organised civil administration and respect for the principles of justice.

At the end of the 4th century the three divisions into which Augustus had divided the country were increased by the addition of a second German province. The first Belgium had its capital at Treves, and comprised Lorraine and a great part of Luxembourg; the second Belgium, which included the two Flanders, Hainaut, as well as Artois, and Champagne, had its capital at Rheims, with, however, an important subsidiary seat of Government at Tournai. The first Germany had its capital at Mayence, and was outside Belgium, but in the second, with its capital at Cologne, were included Tongres, Brabant, and Antwerp. In each of these provinces the supreme authority was vested in a Duke, from whom the military commanders of the different garrisons received their orders. Such was the political division of Belgium when the Franks, a German confederacy formed for purposes of national defence and even preservation, made their first appearance. Although their name had appeared before the decline of the Empire had become marked, and although their actions contributed to bring about its fall, they are chiefly interesting in Belgium as the successors of the Roman possessors of its soil.

The conclusions to be drawn from the consideration of the Roman rule in Belgium are few perhaps, but they are clear. The information about the period, whether contained in the scanty literary records that have come down to us, or in archæological and palæontological remains, gives but a fragmentary description of the country and its inhabitants, and tells us little as to the exact extent of the civilisation and prosperity attained. But, if fragmentary and incomplete, it leaves no doubt on certain main points of essential importance. It enables us to see clearly enough that the Belgians preserved, under Roman domination, their rude and vigorous German customs and attributes. They would have none of the softer and enervating fashions of civilisation. They would not build towns, and it is probable that very few of them lived in houses. They were proud of their German ancestry, and flaunted it in every one's face. The tribes of Cæsar's time were of no different stock from the later colonies established by Augustus, Vespasian, and subsequent Emperors, for the colonists were openly brought from the other side of the Rhine. The people were proud of calling themselves War-men, and when the Hun inroad brought the German nation to its knees, as well as the Roman Empire, it was in the forest of Ardenne, in the marshy retreats of the Batavians, that the Franks found the refuge place among kindred and friendly tribes which enabled them to preserve their liberties, and as the storm swept by to emerge once more on the arena of the world's history, and to reassert the superiority of their race. The Belgians have a share in the glories of early German history. The heroism of the Nervii, the courage and address of Civilis, were national exploits in which Belgians may reasonably take as much pride as Britons do in the deeds of Cassivelaunus and Boadicea. They form a good basis on which to rear the spirit and sentiment of an independent state and free people. Many centuries separate the present citizens of Belgium from these early occupants of their country, there are gaps between that seem almost to obliterate all trace of identity, but the connection is not to be seriously denied.

CHAPTER II.

The Franks to the Death of Charlemagne.

THE history of the Franks belongs strictly to that of the great country whose name preserves their place in the record of European progress, but although the name Belgian or Belgic rarely occurs during these centuries, this race played a prominent part under Merovingian and Carlovingian, and a brief sketch must be given of the period terminating with the death of Charlemagne, because out of it emerged the feudal system that struck its roots so deeply in Burgundy, Lorraine, Flanders, and the other provinces of the Low Countries. Moreover, it must be recollected, although students seldom think of them in that light, that the Mayors of the Palace, and Charlemagne, the greatest member of the house of Pepin of Landen, were by race and family of the clearest Belgian origin. It will be sufficient for the purpose we have in hand if, out of the chaos of Merovingian and Carlovingian annals, a streak of historical fact can be established as a connecting link between the Belgians of the Roman time and the same race in the feudal period of Lorraine and Flanders.

The Franks were a league, not a race. They were German and Belgian warriors who declared their intention to be " free " men. At least one of the Belgian tribes, the Catti, joined them *en masse*. The name of Frank appears as early as the year 240, but it was not for another century that they took a prominent place as one of the powers rising on the ruins of Rome. Even when defeated by some of the rare later Emperors of capacity, or their successful generals, they knew how to preserve their independence as læti or military colonists. Their numbers increased so much that they were divided into two distinct peoples, the one purely German, the other Belgian, German at the root with an untraceable mixture of Celtic blood, and also, it cannot be doubted, leavened by connection with the Roman garrisons during three centuries. The former were known as the Ripuarian Franks because they held the banks of the Rhine, the latter as the Salian or Salic Franks from their dwelling on the Yssel, the arm of the lower Rhine which helped to render secure their home and retreat in the Batavian isle. The Germans of the Rhine provinces on both banks of the river are the descendants of the former, whereas the latter may be regarded as the ancestors of the Dutch and the Belgians. The inhabitants of Luxembourg and the Namur provinces seem, however, to have retained the separate name of Belgians, and when the Vandals crossed the Rhine and invaded Gaul, the Emperor owed his victory at Cateau Cambresis to the military aid of the Franks and the Belgians, both of whom are specifically mentioned by name.

After the capture of Rome by Alaric, and the transfer of the capital of the Western Empire from Rome to Ravenna for the brief period before its final fall in 475, Clodion,* chief of the Salic Franks, extended his authority over western Belgium to Tournai and Soissons. The further success of this warrior was arrested by Aetius, the Roman Governor of Gaul, but, although his progress was checked, he retained his conquests on giving a hostage for future good conduct. This hostage was Merovæus, probably the son and certainly the successor of Clodion, and the founder of the Merovingian dynasty, in the sense that it took his name. After receiving his education in Italy he returned, on Clodion's death, to rule the Salic Franks and, as the ally of the Romans,† took a prominent part in the battle of Chalons, when Aetius defeated the Huns under Attila, in probably the most sanguinary battle of all history.

*Clodion was King of Taxandria or Brabant. Pharamond, himself the son of a chief named Marcomir, and the father of Clodion, had been proclaimed king in the usual way by elevation on the shields of his warriors. Pharamond is often called the first of the Merovingians, but the dynasty really began with Clovis.

†It has been said of this period that the barbarous Franks were civilised and the civilised Romans barbarians.

Childeric, the son and successor of Merovæus, combined the two branches of the Franks in a single league, and possessed undisputed authority from the North Sea to the Black Forest. Childeric died in 481, six years after the fall of the Empire of the West.

Clovis, the son and successor of Childeric, is famous for having been the first of the Franks to adopt Christianity. It was at the battle of Tolbiac against the Allemanni in 496, that, in imitation of Constantine, he made the vow to adopt Christianity if what seemed a certain defeat were turned into a victory. But it must also be noted that the way had been cleared for this conversion by his marriage with Clotilda, niece of Gondebald, King of the Burgundians. The victory was won, and Clovis and 3000 of his warriors were baptized at Rheims. It is recorded that on this occasion the Archbishop, St. Remi, said: "Bow thy head, gentle Sicambrian!* worship what you have burned, burn what you have worshipped." Clovis, although in name no more than the King of Tournai, was unquestionably the head of the Franks, and to make it clear that his position was something different from his predecessors, the Emperor at Constantinople sent him a patent with the right to bear the old Roman titles of Patrician, Consul and August. But Clovis did not care for high sounding names alone, he wanted the substance of power. He resolved to make his authority supreme over all the Frank kings. His new religion did not prevent him from murdering one rival with his own hand, and getting rid of others in a sinister and summary manner. A very large portion of his subjects were Gauls or Celts, but they had nothing whatever to do with the government, which was essentially German. Still it is an accepted practice to call Clovis a French King, although the heart of his dominions was in Belgium, his capital at Tournai, and his administrators Graves or Grafs, the German word for Count. Clovis died in the year 511.

The death of Clovis was followed by the division of his

---

*This would make the Merovingians more German than Belgian, for the Sicambri were essentially a Rhine people and joined the Frankish league in 240.

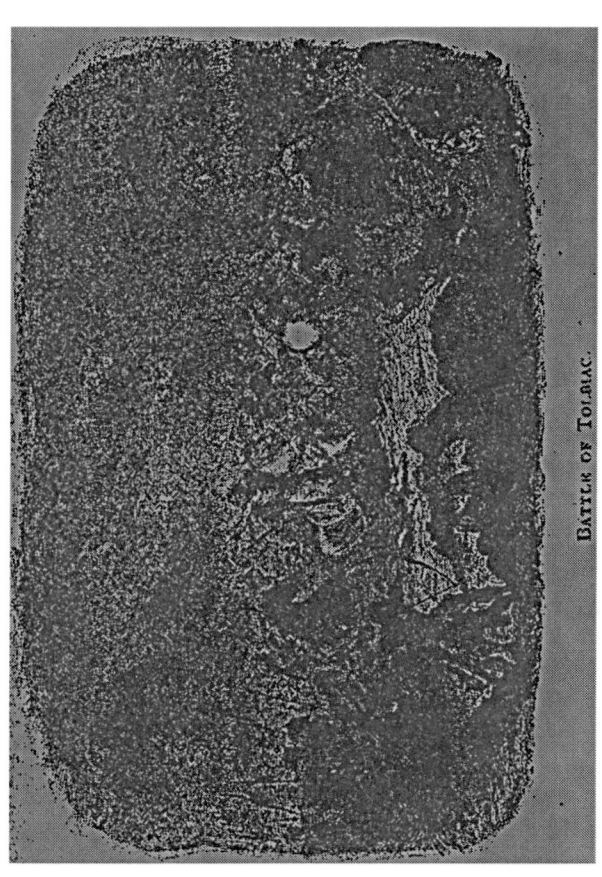

Battle of Tolbiac.

states among his four sons in accordance with Frank law, and this practice proved the cause of the want of stability in Merovingian power and the fall of the dynasty. Two of these sons, Clotaire and Thierri or Theodoric, divided Belgium between them, while Childebert ruled at Paris, and Clodomir at Orleans. The deaths of his brothers, which he followed up by the murder of his nephews, enabled Clotaire, the most Belgian of the four so far as his territories went, to again unite the Frank dominions, but although he united them in his own person he did not know how to ensure their union, for after his death they were again distributed among his own four sons. Of these Sigebert and Chilperic were the two more important. The former was the King of Austrasia which, besides the greater part of Belgium included Lorraine and parts of Germany, but Chilperic was also possessor of the western provinces of the former state known as Neustria. These kings and their immediate successors played, however, only a secondary part on the stage of their time. They were quite eclipsed by the rivalry of two women. Sigebert had married Brunhilda, the younger daughter of Athanagilde, King of the Visigoths. His brother Chilperic was in the hands of his mistress, Fredegonde, when jealousy of his brother led him to seek a legal wife at the same Court. Fredegonde was dismissed from the Palace, and Chilperic wedded Galswinthe, the elder sister of Brunhilda, but her reign proved short. Fredegonde regained her ascendency over Chilperic, and Galswinthe died suddenly, it was presumed of poison.

Fredegonde personified the Gallic influence at the Frank courts, and Brunhilda the German, and it may be no unsound theory to allege that the bitterness of Franco-German animosity dated from the feud of these two women. Brunhilda,[*] not unnaturally, resolved to avenge her sister's murder. The wrong she deemed was the greater in that the royal blood of Alaric had been spilled by one who had been a kitchen-maid. A war then ensued between the brother kings of Austrasia and Neustria, and Brunhilda easily gained the day by obtaining the alliance

[*]Wagner has worked this theme to great advantage in his operas.

of Gontrand, King of the Burgundians. It is unnecessary to follow the fortunes of this civil war, in the course of which both Sigebert and Chilperic were assassinated, but Brunhilda continued the struggle on behalf of her son Childebert, while Fredegonde fought equally well, or rather ferociously, in the name of her son Clotaire II. The long struggle continued during another generation, and, Childebert dying by poison, Brunhilda maintained the rights of Austrasia in the name of his sons, or her grandchildren. The fortune of war then turned in favour of Fredegonde, but her death in 597 arrested her

PUNISHMENT OF BRUNHILDA.

triumph. Unfortunately for Brunhilda, a rising among her own great vassals prevented her profiting by the death of her rival, and her own grandson Theodebert drove her out of his territory. She succeeded in returning, and in triumphing over Theodebert, who was killed by her orders, but her long career was by this nearly run. The Austrasian chiefs would not tolerate her rule on any terms, and invited the Neustrian king, Clotaire II., son of Fredegonde, to rule them. Brunhilda was seized and put to death by the son of her old enemy, her sister's murderess, in a most cruel fashion. Although nearly eighty years of age she was tortured and then fastened to the tail of

an unbroken horse—the principal charge against her being that
she had murdered ten Frank kings. Clotaire II. completed his
work by extirpating the brood of Sigebert and Brunhilda, and
ruling alone over the realm of the Franks.

His son Dagobert benefited by this reunion, but, unmindful
of the teachings of the past, revived the vicious system of
dividing his states between his two sons Sigebert and Clovis,
the second bearers of their names. Their successor, Childeric
II., completed the process by further sub-divisions, and it was
only in the time of Clovis III. that Neustria and Burgundy were
formed into a single state.* But before that Austrasia had
asserted its autonomy, and, what was more durable, its racial
distinction. As the Salic Franks had gradually moved south-
ward, and concentrated more and more their political influence
in the valleys of the Somme and the Seine, the Ripuarian
Franks had moved westwards from Cologne and Treves, and
had asserted their purely Teutonic influence over the whole of
Austrasia. The Merovingians were the representatives of the
Salic Franks, and for three centuries they, as the chiefs of
Roman France, enjoyed predominance over those of Teutonic
France, but with the subdivisions of the later Clovis and
Childeric, the term of their power had been almost reached.

In the Frank system there was, almost from the beginning,
a functionary known as the *Major domus*, whose title, with the
growth of the kingdom, was amplified into that of Maire du
Palais. The duties first assigned to this individual were not
important, and did not extend beyond the household, but the
office was given for life and continued to be held even after
a change of sovereigns. It can readily be imagined how this
permanent official gradually drew into his hand matters quite
distinct from his domestic duties, and when the office was made
hereditary in a single family, the Mayor of the Palace became

---

*In 638 on Dagobert dividing his territories, Austrasia was defined as
consisting of "the first Germany" with the two cities of Mayence and
Strasburg, "the second Germany" with Cologne, Maestricht and Tongres,
the first Belgium, with Metz as the capital of the whole of Austrasia, and
also a great part of the second Belgium with the towns of Rheims, Laon
and Cambrai. Neustria comprised the territory west of Austrasia to the
Channel and North Sea with the Loire as a southern boundary.

scarcely less imposing, and on many occasions far more important, than the King. The remarkable talents of the family of Pepin of Landen, continued during four generations, ensured for it a pre-eminence that more vigorous rulers than the *rois fainéants* of the period of Merovingian decadence would have found it difficult to throw off.

The Merovingians, as has been pointed out, passed from their original German origin through Belgian nationality to the throne of France, but as they fixed their homes in southern regions they neglected Belgium. The race on which, as it were, they turned their backs, produced in revenge the Mayors of the Palace, from whom, in due course, emerged the Carlovingians. It is worth while considering these movements with some little care because they explain why the Belgians, who often in our eyes appear so insignificant, are one of the proudest races of Europe, and, let it also be added, not without reason. The Merovingians sprang from the loins of their ancestors, and so too did the vigorous mayors of the Palace, of whom the first was Pepin of Landen, a small town in the province of Liége. Little or nothing is known of this chief before he distinguished himself by the successful defence of his district against a band of Frisian invaders. This appears to have been in the year 620, and the fame of the exploit induced all the Franks to combine in choosing him as *Major domus* to Clotaire II. For nearly 20 years he served in this capacity at the Court, and it was in his able hands that the office gradually assumed its higher character. He died in 639, and his wife, St. Iduberge or Itta, retired with her daughter, also canonized, Gertrude, to the Abbey of Nivelles in the midst of the forest of Soignies. Little as we know of the first of the Pepins, there are various reasons for stating that he was a loyal servant of the Merovingians, and that he had no idea of supplanting them. The fate of his son and successor, Grimwald, demonstrated his prudence. Taking advantage of what he thought was the death of the Merovingians Grimwald made a bid for the succession, but his peers resented his presumption, and, handing him over to the second Clovis, he perished with his only son in a Paris dungeon.

CHARLES MARTEL.

In the male line the stock of Pepin of Landen had run its brief course, but his daughter Begge had wedded the heir of an Austrasian Duke, afterwards Bishop of Liége, and by him she had a son, born at Herstal near Liége, who was named Pepin, and who is distinguished from his grandfather by being called Pepin of Herstal. With this individual the real greatness of the family began, and in his time the title of Mayor of the Palace became hereditary. While Neustria was the prey of internal dissensions, during which deposed kings deemed themselves fortunate if they escaped assassination by obtaining permission to enter the cloister, Austrasia stood aloof, carefully and even scornfully vigilant. The chiefs of that kingdom repudiated all the Merovingian princes* as unworthy, and made Pepin of Herstal their Duke. After some reverses Pepin succeeding in capturing the person of Theodoric III. in 687, and in removing the Merovingian capital to his own place of residence, which fluctuated between Cologne and Herstal.

For twenty-seven years Pepin was the real ruler of the Franks. He coerced the Frisians, the first step towards the conquest of Germany. He was a great patron of the Church, religious communities first receiving grants of land from him, but on his death at the end of 714 he left his power and the destinies of his family in the feeble hands of his widow, Plectrude, and his grandson, a child named Theobald.

Besides Plectrude, Pepin left behind him a mistress, Alpaïde, whom he had discarded and even cast into prison, and by her he left also a son known to fame as Charles Martel. The Austrasian chiefs wished for no feeble leader. Charles Martel had already given his proofs, and, ignoring the bar sinister, they declared him Duke of Austrasia. The sequence of descent

---

*One instance of this may be given because it furnishes additional proof of the early intercourse between Ireland and Belgium that has been referred to in the cases of the Firbolgs and the Menapians. The young Dagobert II., son of Sigebert II., the great-grandson of Fredegonde, was sent as a child for safety to an Irish monastery by the Bishop of Poitiers. He returned in 679 in the hope of recovering his inheritance, but he was waylaid in the Ardenne forest and assassinated by order of Pepin: on the other hand Pepin entrusted the conversion of the Frisians to Willibrod, a priest of the monastery of Colm Hill in Ireland. Under the name of Clemens he became Bishop of Utrecht, and laboured for 40 years in what is now the kingdom of Holland.

is not as perfect as in the family of Amurath, but these Mayors of the Palace showed an equally continuous record of energy, power and success. Charles Martel had first to make sure of his position. He did so in three striking campaigns between the years 716 and 720, and in the latter year his triumph was ratified by the person of the Merovingian king, Clotaire IV., being placed in his charge as Mayor of the Palace.

Charles Martel played on a larger stage than either of his predecessors in office. There was always peril on the side of Germany from the warlike races which were ever impelled westward by the same necessity that had brought the Belgians themselves into Gaul. While on the south a new danger had arisen in the Saracens who, having conquered Spain, had traversed the Pyrenees. When the latter trouble became acute, Charles had fortunately pacified the Germans, and he was thus the better able to hasten to the assistance of the Duke of Aquitaine when that prince lost his territories to the Arabs. In a battle fought between Tours and Poitiers, and known indifferently by both names, Charles vanquished and practically destroyed the Saracen army under the Emir Abd-ur-rahman. An almost contemporary chronicle, that of Moissac, gives the following terse description of this campaign: "Having collected all the immense booty seized in Spain and Aquitaine by the Saracens which we found in their camp, and having received the homage of Eudes of Aquitaine, Charles returned to France in the full glory of his triumph. After this everyone began to call him Martel, because, as the hammer breaks every kind of iron, so Charles, with the aid of the Lord, breaks his enemies in every battle." Fresh from this triumph, Charles Martel attacked the Frisians and completely reduced the tribes which his father had only coerced. He was on the point of marching to save Rome from the attack of the Lombards—in return for which service Pope Gregory III. had promised to crown him Emperor of the West —when death arrested the great ruler's steps in 741, at the early age of 50. Charles Martel never possessed any higher titles than those of Duke of Austrasia, and Mayor of the Palace, but there is no doubt that he was the first to revive the possibility of a new Empire of the West.

PEPIN THE SHORT.

Immediately after the death of Charles Martel, Childeric the Third, the last of the Merovingians, ascended the throne of the Franks which still continued to preserve a nominal existence. But Charles had left behind a possible cause of strife by making his two sons, Carloman and Pepin, the offspring of his first wife, his heirs while he had disinherited Grifon, the son by the second wife, a daughter of the Duke of the Bavarians. If Carloman and Pepin had been Merovingians they would have fought and plotted against each other, and the fruits of their ancestors' labours would have been thrown away. But they joined hands and discomfited their enemies. During six years Carloman ruled in Austrasia as Duke and Prince of the Franks, while Pepin was content to play the smaller part in Neustria of Mayor of the Palace to the last of the Merovingians. An end was put to this dual authority when Carloman, oppressed by the terrors of a superstitious age, decided to retire from active life and to pass the evening of his days in a monastery. On this event the Austrasians hastened to proclaim Pepin as their Duke, and he, to improve the occasion, deposed the last of the Merovingians, and mounted the throne of the Franks as the first of the Carlovingian dynasty, a name derived from Charles Martel who was rightly thus proclaimed the true founder of its regal power.

Pepin, the third of his name among the Mayors of the Palace, was distinguished from his predecessors by the epithet of le Bref, or the short, on account of his stature. With him the hour had at last arrived when no possible end was served by the continuance of the nominal rule of the Merovingians. He did everything, however, in regular form, even to consulting the Pope, who very wisely decided that the royal power had best be assigned where it was practically exercised. Whereupon, the last of the Merovingians took shelter in the cloister, and Pepin was proclaimed King in the good old German fashion by being raised on the shields of the warriors who supported his authority. A more formal ceremony took place sometime afterwards in the Abbey church of St. Denis, when the Franks swore allegiance to him and his sons with an oath, twice repeated, that they would elect no other king than his descendants.

It is said that some of his courtiers sought to turn his short stature into a joke, but they soon discovered that he was not to be trifled with. His courage and energy seem to have exceeded those even of his resolute father. He had not been many months on the throne when, during one of the savage games in which the Franks continued the practice of the Romans, a lion killed a bull, and Pepin called out asking who would venture into the arena. No one replied, whereupon Pepin himself jumped into the arena and slew the lion in single-handed fight. During the sixteen years that his reign covered he conducted campaigns in every direction that were crowned with remarkable success. He conquered Saxony* on one side and Brittany and Languedoc on the other. He twice crossed the Alps to save Rome from the Lombards. He confirmed the theory that the Mayors of the Palace showed a crescendo order of ability and success, and he would have been hailed as the greatest of them all, if he had not been the father of Charlemagne.† He died in 768.

The greatest of the Carlovingians, whose fame and achievements only insular prejudice could deny dwarf those of the Saxon Alfred, and who, if tested by the magnitude of his work and the extent of its consequences, is the greatest historical figure between Cæsar and Napoleon, was born in April, 742. Many cities claim to be his birthplace, and it is by no means certain that the pretensions of Aix-la-Chapelle, his favourite residence and afterwards the Imperial city of the Holy Roman Empire, are better than those of several other places.‡

Pepin, by his will, divided his dominions between his two sons, Charles and Carloman. Charles either selected, or received by his father's will, Austrasia, and he fixed his chief residence at Liége, while he passed the winter at Herstal. His

---

*Saxony was then the whole country between the Lower Rhine and the Elbe.

†A Monk of the 13th century was ordered to place an epitaph on the monument of Pepin. He wrote merely four words, "Peppin pater Caroli Magni," Pepin the father of Charlemagne.

‡His secretary, Eginhard, declared that nothing was ever known for certain as to the place of his birth.

chief amusement was hunting, and the pursuit of game in the vast forest of the Ardennes. Whenever the cares of his government and the conduct of his campaigns allowed him, he always betook himself to the banks of the Meuse for rest and recreation. When he became Emperor he was still essentially an Austrasian, and that meant practically a Belgian. His brother Carloman died in 771, and although he left two sons they were put on one side, and Charles, by the unanimous popular vote, was raised to the sole sovereignty over the Franks. The chiefs, and the people whom they represented, had seen enough of the evils of disunion and division. They decided for a single ruler. The dangers of the age were too serious and too many for them to entrust the fortunes of what was rather a large confederacy with many ramifications and not a few internal points of weakness than a nation, to the hands of inexperienced boys or feeble children. The moment called for a Charles Martel. The Franks found him in the second Charles who earned the title of the Great.

Charlemagne was in the first place a warrior and a conductor of great campaigns. The age was one of constant warfare, and the Franks had to hold their own on two menaced frontiers, on the side of Germany and on that of Spain. Had they shown themselves unequal to the occasion they would have succumbed to the Pagan warriors pouring through the Hercynian forest from Scandinavia and Lithuania on the one side, and the fanatical hosts of the Koran on the other. The fall of the Franks would have signified the extinction of Christianity and civilisation in Western Europe, and the advent of a long night to which there might have been no dawn. In the 46 years that the reign of Charlemagne covered from the death of his father, he conducted fifty-three military expeditions on a large scale in person—a number that puts in the shade anything accomplished by Napoleon, or the great Mongol conquerors.

Perhaps the greatest of his military successes was the conquest of the Saxons under their famous chief Witikind, the ancestor of the Royal Houses of Saxony and of Brunswick, or in other words, of the present sovereigns of Belgium and Great

Britain. He not only conquered the Saxons, but he compelled them to become Christians, thus bringing them within the pale of civilisation. His success was so complete and assured that Germany and her warlike races, gradually came to constitute a bulwark for Western Europe against the nomadic and predatory tribes that Asia continued to belch forth, until the tide of conquest finally turned against her in the 17th century.

One curious consequence of Charlemagne's triumph on land was that the Scandinavians and Northmen, finding the Elbe closed to them, and that it was hopeless for them to think of coping with the Frank power, turned their energies to maritime enterprise, and made descents along the coasts of Holland, Belgium,* and Normandy. Charlemagne publicly admitted his inability to deal with them, as the heavy slow-moving boats which he built at Ghent and Boulogne, his two naval arsenals, were no match for the rapid snekkars or serpent boats of the Normans. Among his many campaigns in Spain against the Saracens, history has best preserved the memory of that of 778, because the Paladin Roland was slain during the return march at Roncesvalles, not by the Arabs, but by the treacherous Gascons—thieves as they are called in the chronicle of Eginhard.

The most memorable passage in Charlemagne's career occurred in the year 800. In the previous year the Pope, Leo III., had barely escaped with his life from a conspiracy at Rome, and hastening to Ratisbon threw himself on the protection of Charlemagne, who at once took up his cause, and, marching with an army to Rome, restored the Pontiff to his throne. The Pope showed his gratitude in a very striking, and, according to the story, wholly unexpected manner. While Charlemagne was kneeling in prayer at the altar the supreme Pontiff came behind him and placed a crown of gold on his head, and proclaimed in a loud voice: "Life and victory to Charles, the great and pacific Emperor of the Romans, crowned

---

*Popular legend in Belgium preserves the story of the Quatre Fils d' Aymon and their famous horse Bayard, which helped them to escape across the Meuse from the Emperor's pursuit. The Roche à Bayard near Dinant marks the supposed scene of the exploit.

by the hand of God!" Not only the priests and the choristers but the people in the edifice took up the reclaim. Thus was restored in name, and under the special protection of the Catholic Church, that Western Empire which had fallen with Augustulus, and which now, in its revived form of the Holy Roman Empire, was to endure for over a thousand years, until it, too, passed away as the consequence of that too brilliant "sun of Austerlitz" at the end of 1805.

In this manner the Mayors of the Palace, after passing through the intermediate stage of Carlovingian kings, became Emperors of the West, and, as the natural consequence, the chiefs under them became fiefs of the Empire, and took unto themselves, as hereditary attributes, the titles of dukes and

CHARLEMAGNE VISITING A SCHOOL.

counts. Both the Roman duke and the German grave or count were terms in cómmon use before the proclamation of the Empire. The descendants of Pepin of Herstal were, *par excellence*, the Dukes of Austrasia, and, to give only one other instance, Roland was a Count of the Palace. But none the less these dignities acquired a higher form, a more durable basis and even a wider acceptance in the years following the proclamation of Charlemagne as Emperor. It is necessary to remember this fact when we come to consider the origin and rise of that feudal period during which Belgium became a regular state, and its chiefs appeared before the rest of the world as Belgian princes.*

But Charlemagne was a great deal more than a mere soldier and conqueror. He knew how to establish a stable government, as well as how to provide for the security of his country. Not merely in the administrative qualities did he shine, but also as a patron of literature and architecture. As the promoter of education among the masses, he may be said to have marked a new era. He established schools in every province, and he enjoined on the priests the necessity of making the education of the young their first care. He even attached to his court, or camp, a Palatine Academy, in imitation of some of the later Emperors, and he frequently conducted the examinations in schools and colleges himself. In one of his schemes he failed, or at least had to change his original purpose. He wished to make German the language of the Government and the schools, but he found the Latin tongue and influence too deeply established for his scheme to be put in practice. He had the good sense to recognise the difficulties attending such an alteration, and failing the support of the Church, to abandon it on the very threshold of the undertaking. But although Charlemagne† abandoned the hope of making the Western Empire a strictly German institution, he none the less grafted many of his national customs on the Roman system which he found himself constrained to adopt as being identified with

---

Belgicæ principes are definitely mentioned in the Carlovingian period.

†The following description of Charlemagne is that given by his secretary Eginhard: "Charles was stout, robust and tall, but well proportioned withal, as his height did not exceed seven times the length of his foot. The top of his head was round, his eyes large and full of life, his nose slightly long, the hair fine, the countenance open and gay; whether sitting or standing his whole person commanded respect and denoted dignity. The Emperor's ordinary dress was that of his fathers, and like that of the Franks. He was never without his sword. He was sober both in eating and drinking, and during meals he listened to recitations or to the reading of histories or religious works. Not confining himself to his mother tongue, he learnt to speak Latin fluently, and he also knew some Greek, but he was never able to write well in any language. He could also chant very well, and finally he was very inquisitive, having shutters through which he could see who entered and who left his Palace."

the only existing form of civilisation. The influence and power of the Church were also arrayed on the same side, but it must be noted that the ruling classes in France, the feudal chiefs and the nobility of a later age, were originally a German caste. The recollection of this fact has induced some historical writers to put forward the theory that the old French noblesse represented a German system, and that the French Revolution of 1789 was a Gallic triumph.

In the splendid personality of Charlemagne, the Carlovingians reached their highest capacity, and the apogee of their political power. Constrained by the practice of the Franks,

DEATH OF CHARLEMAGNE.

Charlemagne also felt obliged to divide, while still living, his extensive territories among his sons. By a public proclamation at Thionville in 806 he assigned to Louis, Aquitaine; to Pepin the Hunchback, Italy and part of Germany; and to Charles, Austrasia, including Belgium and the rest of Germany. But this project was upset by the death of the two last-named in the lifetime of their father, so that when Charlemagne died at Aix-la-Chapelle, in the year 814, the whole of his dominions passed into the hands of Louis of Aquitaine. To have borne that burden, Louis would have needed to be a man of the type of Charles Martel, Pepin the short, or Charlemagne, and instead he seems to have been a very poor creature, despite his good looks and his popular name of the Debonnaire. The dissolution of the Carlovingian monarchy marks the appearance of feudalism, under which the Provinces of the Belgic division of Gaul, of the Frank territories known as Austrasia and Neustria, took their places definitely as the counties and duchies of the Middle Ages, and with that event the true separate history of Belgium* may be said to have begun.

*Namèche in his *Histoire Nationale* gives the following explanation of the origin of the two languages spoken in Belgium. "The oaths of 842 constitute the most ancient known monument of that Romance tongue which was to serve as the transition between the dying Latin and the French that was about to be born. This tongue was born directly from Latin; German and Celtic elements have in it only a very secondary part. Walloon is a branch of the primitive French or *langue d' oil*. A Tudesque idiom, Flemish, has remained in use in our northern provinces. Whence comes this difference? We will indicate the most likely causes (1) the Latin tongue became, under the Roman domination, a vulgar language in Gaul, but the more northern peoples by their geographical position, and their contact with the unsubdued Germans, did not submit themselves sufficiently completely to the Roman yoke, and experienced in a far less degree the influence of Roman civilisation and language. (2) Numerous German peoples established themselves successively in the north of Belgic Gaul, with or without the consent of the Romans, and preserved there the use of their Tudesque language. (3) After the conquest of Clovis, the greater part of his comrades in arms fixed their residence in the northern part, on the banks of the Rhine and Meuse. (4) Finally, it is proved that Charlemagne transported thousands of Saxon families across the Rhine into Flanders and Brabant, which must have greatly contributed to the continued use in those countries of the Tudesque tongue."

CHAPTER III.

The Early Feudal Period.

THE death of Charlemagne marks the true commencement of the feudal period. He was the last of the great autocrats who were able, in some form or other, to maintain a semblance of union between the fragments of the Roman Empire in the West, and to establish a common obedience, if not complete harmony, among its various component nationalities, Latin, Gallic, and German. Deeper causes than would occur to the monk chroniclers, who are our sole authorities for the period, prevented the fusion of these races into one people, an amalgam of elements ethnologically incompatible. The Frank chief, whether as Mayor of the Palace or as Austrasian Duke or King, or even as Emperor of the West, was the central object of public attention, admiration, and confidence, because his success as a war leader was conspicuous and unbroken, but the subjects he controlled remained as separated from each other, and as instinctively hostile, as when the Gauls called upon Cæsar to save them from the Germans. The magnitude of the frontier successes of Charles Martel, Pepin, and Charlemagne, indeed, may be said to have precipitated the struggle, or, more correctly, the diffusion of the nationalities. As long as a greater fear controlled their personal and inner relations, the three great generic branches of the Caucasian stock stood and fought together. But in Charlemagne's time this common fear had passed away. The frontiers were secure. The Arabs had been driven behind the Pyrenees. The German forests, always fecund of warriors, had been absorbed, and, after ten centuries of ceaseless excursions, it seemed as if the recesses of Asia had at last been rendered void of those formidable hordes which had carried fire and sword across Europe, and debased the majesty of Rome.

There were more than ethnic causes to explain why a single central authority was impossible. The practical difficulties in the path of a supreme ruler were sufficient to explain the repeated sub-divisions of Frank power. The means of intercommunication were both limited in number and imperfect of kind. The main roads of the Romans endured, but they were few in number, and the only routes that existed beyond them were the tracks cut by armies during the innumerable warlike expeditions of the Merovingians and Carlovingians. . The greater part of the region north of the Seine still consisted of virgin forest. Agriculture had made but a modest appearance, and the House of Pepin had only added to the list of towns of Austrasia and Belgium, Aix la Chapelle, and the special residences associated with their names at Landen and Herstal in the Liége country. Tournai had also become a place of the first importance by the decline of Bavai, Ghent had begun its municipal existence as a naval station, and the proud name of Antwerp had emerged from the records of the time. But with these exceptions the country remained difficult of access, an appropriate home for independence, the secure refuge of turbulent and robber chiefs. The King or Emperor had no available power to enable him to assert his authority at their doors, but for centuries circumstances had allowed him to draw them out of their homes by a superior attraction in which the hope of plunder formed not the least potent part. And now a change comes over the scene. The chiefs enriched by the expeditions of Charlemagne and his predecessors—by the plunder, for example, of Spain transferred from the hands of the Saracens to their conquerors—began to weary of far-distant wars, and to think more of strengthening their positions in their native districts. They built castles in inaccessible spots, they strengthened those already existing, and they tightened the bonds of union and dependence between them and the inhabitants of the tract of country over which they extended the protection afforded by their military training, experience, and the possession of weapons of offence and defence. In this manner did the local authority gradually supersede, as the effective administrative government, the central and nominally supreme authority of the Emperor, and in no division of the newly revived Empire of the West did this system of feudalism take firmer root, or display more vigour, than in the country to which for convenience sake its modern name of Belgium may be given.

It was not, indeed, until after the death of Louis the Debonnaire in 840, that these sub-divisions became in any way general or noteworthy. They were part, as it were, of the sub-division of the Frank Monarchy itself which was finally resolved, by an almost natural process, into three great territories by the Treaty of Verdun in August, 843. The three sons of Louis divided, after a little fighting and more negotiation, his heritage among themselves, one taking Gaul which gradually became France; another Germany, and the third, Lothaire, founding an intermediate state in what was known as Austrasia, and which was gradually called from his name Lotharingia or Lorraine. The three brothers met on an island in the Saone near Macon, and took a common oath that they would not only aid each other against any foreign assailant, but that they and their descendants would never make war on each other. How often and how completely were those oaths to be violated! The possession of that third intermediate state has for ten centuries been the cause of endless contention and strife between the two other inheritors of Charlemagne's wide Empire, and even now no one can regard the existing situation as permanent, or assume that the same prolific cause of strife will not again entail the rude arbitrament of war. The newly revived Empire was too large for one hand, and not large enough for three. The part of the third became the object of greed to the two others, and the fortunes of war first diminished its extent, and then cast its fragments from one side to the other.*

* The derivation of the name of Lorraine seems as clearly established as it is easy. The Germans called it Lotheringhe-rike, the kingdom of the children of Lothaire, the Latin (monkish) name was Lotharingia, and the French name soon became Lorraine. When the subdivision took place it is curious to note what a prominent part the question of the languages had in making the final arrangements and in attaching the population to one reigning house or the other. In the treaties which preceded that of Verdun the German feuds were addressed in Teuton and the Gallic in Roman. There are those who insist that the Roman referred to was the corrupt Latin which we call Walloon, and which, in the Flemish tongue, is known as Welsh. The oaths taken before the Verdun agreement and after it by Lothaire, are cited as the first occasion on which Walloon was written in an official proclamation or document.

It was in the year following the death of Louis, the grandson of Lothaire, that feudalism made its definite commencement, and obtained what has been called its Great Charter, by the Edict of Quiercy-sur-Oise—14 June, 877—which established all governors and representatives of the King in their stations as a personal right, and one that could be transmitted to their posterity, while it decreed that the sons of counts should also be counts. The principle of heredity was essential to the prolonged continuance of feudalism, and, as the causes which prevented its working well in a widestretching and loosely-knit empire did not apply to what were, after all, local and limited territorial jurisdictions, the system became generally adopted, and a source of strength and stability. At the same time the magnates of the Church asserted themselves in the domain of politics, adding secular privileges to religious, and holding ignorant laymen in terror by the awful penalty of excommunication. The period which witnessed the decline and disappearance of the Carlovingian family was one during which the transfer of power was effected rather in the council chamber than on the field of battle, and thus the clerkly priest enjoyed the advantage over the mail clad but illiterate warrior. In the family quarrels, depositions and tragedies of the successors of Lothaire and Charles the Bald to the third and fourth generations, the representatives of the Church played the leading part, and gradually acquired a complete ascendancy.*

In Lorraine† the reigning power soon passed from the legitimate line of Lothaire to Arnulph of Carinthia, the natural son of Carloman, grandson of Charles the Bald. He took a special interest in Belgium, successfully defending the coast against the Norman, and mindful, perhaps, of his own doubtful origin, he associated with himself his illegitimate son, Zwentibold, as king of Lorraine. But feudalism, in the sense of the sub-division of power, had taken too deep a root there

* Hallam.

† We cannot attempt to give the details of Lorraine history in the 9th century, or to describe the alternations of fortune and the dearth of heirs which transferred it for a time to the descendants of Charles the Bald.

for this irregular proceeding at the expense of others to be tolerated. He was defeated and either murdered or slain in a second attempt to maintain his position. Prominent among the nobles who overthrew Zwentibold was Regnier, the long-necked, son of Ermengarde, daughter of the Emperor Lothaire. He had many titles but that of Duke of Hasbagne* is the best known.

When Charles the Simple was recalled from England, whither his mother Edgiva, the sister of Alfred, had taken him for safety, Regnier of Hasbagne was rewarded, for what was at most passive aid, with the Dukedom of Lorraine. On the death of this great chief, his eldest son, Giselbert, was confirmed in the Lorraine title, while his second son, Regnier, was created Count of Hainaut. This, the first great family of the feudal period, was Belgian to the core. The phrase Belgian princes (*Belgicæ principes*) is expressly applied to them in the nearly contemporary chronicle of Richer.

Duke Giselbert aspired, however, to be something more than a feudatory, and having a strong and probably merited contempt for Charles the Simple, he plotted among the other feudatories, rallied them to his side, and prepared the way for the extension of his authority across the Netherlands to the sea. But Charles was not so simple as his name implied. He marched with an army into Lorraine, the barons deserted Giselbert, who was obliged to seek safety in Germany, where Henry of Saxony gave him protection and took up his cause. Charles was, however, induced to restore a great portion of his estates to Giselbert who, taking advantage of the other troubles which compelled Charles to withdraw from the throne into private life, resumed his original designs. He took a prominent part in the troubles arising out of the question as to who should succeed Charles on the French throne, but, finding no stability in that direction, he turned from France to Germany. In 925 he, and the great barons of Lorraine, placed that province as a vassal state under the authority of Henry of Saxony, King of Germany, who, to

---

* The modern district of Hesbaye between Liége and Brabant. Its inhabitants were famous for their strength and turbulence; hence the saying "Who enters the Hesbaye is fought on the morrow."

rivet the connection, gave Giselbert his daughter Gerberga in marriage. But Giselbert had no more love of a German than of a French overlord, he was playing solely for his own hand. He engaged in a bitter but unequal struggle with his brother-in-law, Otho the Lion, and at last ended his stormy life by being drowned in the Rhine, after suffering a signal defeat at the hands of his relation. The result of all these measures and struggles was that Lorraine became more firmly attached to Germany than to France, and a German prince, Conrad of Franconia, Otho's son-in-law, was raised to the Dukedom in supersession of all the surviving members of Giselbert's family. His rule was, however, never popular and, after a period of inextricable confusion, the chief authority in Lorraine was restored to the House of Giselbert in the person of his nephew Regnier, third of his name, Count of Hainaut. His administration proved unsatisfactory and Otho interfered, placing Lorraine under the charge of his brother, Bruno, the Archbishop of Cologne. The archbishop showed his appreciation of the difficulty of the task by dividing the old kingdom of Lorraine into two duchies, distinguished from each other by the names of Upper and Lower Lorraine. The former, watered by the Moselle, was entrusted to Frederick, Count de Bar, and the latter to Godfrey, Count of Verdun, or, as he was more generally called, of Ardenne. The Archbishop reserved to himself the controlling power as Arch-Duke of Lorraine, and during his lifetime a considerable improvement was effected, not merely in the peace and good order of the two provinces, but even in the lot of the unfortunate cultivators of the soil, who were no better than slaves. His efforts in the cause of civilisation were ably seconded by several Bishops of Liége, of whom Notger was the most famous. Notwithstanding the strenuous efforts of the French under the last of the Carlovingians and the first of the succeeding dynasty of the Capets, Lorraine leant more and more on the support of Germany, where King Otho had revived the Imperial style by causing the Pope to crown him Emperor of the Romans.

While events progressed in this fashion in the duchy of Lorraine, another feudal family had taken root in Flanders, and, as it was never tempted to play an exaggerated rôle through vying with Emperors and Kings, its position proved more stable, and it remained more strictly Belgian than the German and Belgian contestants in Lorraine. The germ of national feeling and life lay with Flanders, while the shadow of that higher supremacy, which controlled and checked national development under Lorraine, Burgundy, Spain, and Austria during ten centuries, was cast over the land by that third division of the Carlovingian empire in which we have seen local magnates and Imperial delegates attempting to set up a separate administration. The name, Flanders, was originally applied only to the town which at a slightly later date became Bruges. Under Charlemagne and his son, the valley of the Lower Scheldt and the marshy country in which the tribes had defied Cæsar were entrusted to the charge of royal officers to whom the name of Foresters seems to have been given. Their centre of government was fixed at Harlebeke, a little north of Courtrai, and soon after the death of Louis the Debonnaire, one of these administrators was known as Count Ingelram. His son Baldwin, Bras de Fer, was more famous because he defeated the Normans and successfully defended the Flemish coast, so far at least as rendering it impossible for those raiders to make a settlement. To the success of this and other Flemish chiefs must be attributed the fact that the Northmen were compelled to proceed further south, and establish themselves along that part of the French coast, which became known, from their name, as Normandy. Baldwin allied himself by force with the Carlovingian family, abducting Judith, daughter of Charles the Bald, and widow of the Anglo-Saxon Prince Ethelwulf. So great was his reputation that the Pope himself interceded in his favour, and Charles conferred on him the higher grade of Count which we know under the title of Marquis.* In 877 the title of Count of Flanders was made hereditary, and this, the first hereditary title in the Frank Empire, may perhaps be regarded as the oldest in Europe. Baldwin's son, the second Baldwin, married Elstrud, daughter of Alfred the Great, and thus began, as it were, the close connection with Great

* Marchio = Mark-grave = Count of the Frontier.

Britain, which has reacted in many directions on the destinies of the two countries and associated them in the same cause during several critical epochs of mediæval and modern history.

Baldwin II. is chiefly famous for fortifying Bruges, Ghent, Courtrai, and Ypres, and he may be said to have commenced that city or burgh life which made the flat plains of Flanders a focus of liberty, intelligence, and social development when more favoured regions were sunk in barbarism, and when the castles of Lorraine were no more than robber strongholds. For this reason, if for no other, this son-in-law of Alfred deserves to live in history as the originator and beginner of a new, memorable, and productive system. His son, Arnulph, continued his good work, and during the war between Otho and Louis d' Outremer, when the Giselberts lost their rights in Lorraine, the Flanders family retained theirs in undiminished force. Arnulph even obtained from the German ruler the surrender of the strong castle at Ghent which Otho had caused to be constructed for the protection of his own frontier, and the gift seems to have been earned by a somewhat dramatic service. The success of the Normans on the coast of France, and their failure on that of Flanders have been referred to, and out of that contest had arisen a family feud between the two ruling houses of Flanders and Normandy, and the fact that their territories marched on the land side did not allow it to sleep. Hrolf or Rollo had allowed himself to be converted to Christianity, and had accepted, at the hands of the French king, the title of Duke of Normandy. His son and successor, William Longsword, had taken a prominent part in the murder of Ralph, Count of Cambrai, uncle of Arnulph of Flanders. The situation was thus rendered more than ever strained.

The Norman Duke was the chief if not the only support of the French ruler in his struggle with Germany, and when Otho arranged an interview with Louis d' Outremer in the royal residence at Attigny, William Longsword went there to attend the conference. Thither also proceeded Arnulph of Flanders, and the other great feudatories. There seems to have been an understanding to humiliate the Norman, for he was not summoned to the Council chamber when the meeting took place.

He waited a little time in the expectation that the omission would be repaired, and then finding that such was not intended he forced open the doors of the chamber and slammed them after him. What he saw within the room increased his anger. Otho occupied the seat at the head on the couch or bed of state, Louis was placed opposite him in a position of marked inferiority, while Arnulph of Flanders, and the others were seated around. William at once went up to Louis, and asked him to rise for a moment. He then sat down himself in his place, and exclaimed that there was no one present who should occupy a higher place than Louis of France. The chronicler tells us that Otho rose from his seat, and that Louis took his place, while Otho, concealing his rage as well as he could, remained standing throughout the rest of the business. When the meeting was over Otho complained to his allies of the insult offered him, and Arnulph of Flanders, mindful of his own injuries, resolved with others to get rid of the over-confident Norman. They, however, resorted to treachery, and concealed their designs under the pretence of a desire for reconciliation. A meeting was accordingly arranged on the island of Péquigny, in the Somme near Amiens. Everything had been amicably concluded, and William was leaving by boat, when he was taken off his guard and stabbed by Arnulph's secretary or chancellor, a man named Blason. After this the prosperity of Flanders steadily increased under the sons and grandsons of Arnulph. The cloth manufacture began to be established in 960, markets* were formed at Ghent, Courtrai, and Bruges, and the people were incited to see in commerce, as much as agriculture, a source of wealth as well as a basis of security.

Leaving Flanders for the moment attention must now be turned to that division of the country known as Lower Lorraine, to which patriotism at an early date gave the prouder and more distinctive name of Brabant. The fact has already been recorded in this chapter that Bruno entrusted it to Godfrey,

---

* The markets were placed round the church or cathedral, hence the name Kerk (church) Messe (market) from which comes kermesse, the popular fête of the Belgian races. When commerce began to flourish in the middle of the 10th century barter was still in force and money rare, if not absolutely non-existent.

Count d' Ardenne, a man powerful by reason of his connections, for his brothers were the Marquis of Antwerp and the Count of Valenciennes. Baldwin IV. of Flanders, the great-grandson of Arnulph, thought the occasion auspicious for his own aggrandisement, and crossing the Scheldt, captured Valenciennes from the brother of Godfrey. Valenciennes was a fief in common to the crowns of France and Germany, and the enterprising Count found that he had brought himself into a hornets' nest, for he was very soon besieged in his new possession by the forces of France and Germany, as well as by a contingent provided by Richard, Duke of Normandy. He beat off all his assailants, yet, wisely bending to the storm, he proceeded in person to Aix, made his peace with the Emperor, and accepted Valenciennes as a fief. In this manner the connection between Flanders and Germany was strengthened, while the former entered upon the anomalous phase in its fortunes of being, at the same time, the fief of France and Germany. While Godfrey of Ardenne thus lost, in the person of his brother, Valenciennes, he succeeded in effectually pacifying Brabant, and at the battle of Florennes in 1015, he routed the Count of Louvain, the representative of the old Giselbert family. However, none of these successes were pushed too far, and sufficient territories were always left to the survivors or to the heirs of the slain to preserve their dignity as counts of the Empire, and as administrators of considerable districts. Prominent among these chiefs, or noblemen, was Regnier of Hainaut, who had married one of Godfrey's nieces. By her he had only one child, a daughter named Richilde, whose adventures form a turning point in Belgian history at this period, A.D. 1050.

Godfrey of Ardenne was succeeded by his brother, Gothelon, Marquis of Antwerp, who succeeded in again joining the two Lorraines into a single duchy, and in earning, by his wise measures and consideration for the people, the title of the Great. But the youngest of the three brothers, Hermann, Count of Eenham, is the most interesting of these Brabant brothers, for his daughter married Regnier the Fifth of Hainaut, and their only daughter and child, Richilde, was ultimately married to Baldwin the Sixth of Flanders, thus commencing that matrimonial union of the provincial dynasties which were finally merged in the House of Burgundy. The fertile province of Hainaut, a considerable part of which is now included in France, may be generally described as the tract of territory lying between the middle course of the Scheldt and the Sambre, with its capital at Mons, although Valenciennes was perhaps its chief stronghold. In language the inhabitants were more akin to those of Brabant than of Flanders, so that a matrimonial alliance between their ruling family and that of the Flemish Baldwins might signify a step towards union. Richilde's first husband was Hermann of Saxony, whose mother was Gertrude of Flanders. He died in 1051, and Richilde with the fair domain of Hainaut became the object of the boldest and most successful bidder. The able Baldwin, the Fifth of Flanders, at once proposed that his neighbour should espouse his eldest son, and when it became clear that the marriage was not regarded with wholly favourable eyes by the people of Hainaut, he resorted to force, and invaded their state at the head of a considerable army. But there is no doubt that while he thus appeared to constrain the young countess, he had secretly ascertained that her own wishes were favourable to the marriage, and that she would offer no stubborn resistance. The Flemish army laid siege to Mons, but in a skirmish outside the walls, Richilde allowed herself to be captured, and was promptly married to young Baldwin in the camp. After this Hainaut did not hold out, and for a time the two provinces were under the same administration.

The marriage of Richilde and Baldwin was not effected without some graver opposition than the reluctance of the people of Hainaut to see themselves merged in the more numerous Flemings. They were second cousins, both being great-grandchildren of Hugh Capet, and the Church had set itself against the marriage of relatives within the fourth degree, and even this was extended at one period. It may be conceded that under the Carlovingians the marriage of cousins had become a crying evil, and one of the causes of the degeneracy of the race, but political motives also underlay the decrees of the Pope, who did not wish to see the secular power and estates concentrated in a few hands. Moreover, the decrees were soon made too far reaching—forbidding marriage within the seventh degree of blood or alliance—as the reigning and princely families of the West were so intermingled that their literal application would soon have rendered any marriage impossible. The difficulty was well exemplified in the case of Henry the First of France, who about this time found it impossible to obtain a wife nearer than in Russia.* The Pope threatened Baldwin and Richilde with the pains of excommunication, and the Emperor, Henry the Third, marched at the head of a large army to teach his vassal the lesson that the desire to be too great has its perils. But Baldwin the Fifth showed himself equal to the occasion. He took effective military measures for the defence of his territory, and he secured the alliance of Godfrey, the Courageous, of Lorraine, who had also aroused the ire of the same enemies by marrying his cousin. Even with his support, Baldwin might have failed to hold his own against the Imperial power when an end was put to the struggle by the death of the Emperor himself. The thunders of the Church also died away, and the pains and penalties were never inflicted. Perhaps something of this was due to the intercession of Henry of France himself, the most faithful son of the Church, but a great admirer of his neighbour and vassal Baldwin, to whom he left, on his death in 1060, the guardianship of his son Philip.

Reference has on several occasions been made to the connection between England and Flanders, and to the fact that several Saxon princesses had married counts and chiefs in that part of the continent. But Baldwin the Fifth gave an entirely new turn, and perhaps, impetus to the connection by the active and prominent part he took in the Norman invasion. The success with which the first Baldwin repelled the Normans from the Flemish shores has been noted, but the antipathy of the two ruling families had long abated, and William of Normandy, soon to be known as the Conqueror, had married Mathilde or Matilda, daughter of Baldwin. The Flemish

* He married the Princess Anna, daughter of Jaroslaf of Kief.

prince threw himself heart and soul into his son-in-law's enterprise, and his squadron formed a considerable and efficient part of the fleet that reached Pevensey. Among those who fought at Hastings were several Flemish knights. Gerbod, son of Mathilde, Gilbert of Ghent, Walter of Flanders, Ralph of Tournai are perhaps the four most conspicuous names on the list, and the magnitude of their rewards is the best proof of how highly their services were regarded by their great leader. Gerbod was Earl of Chester, and Walter of Flanders was Earl of Northumberland. The grandson of Gilbert was Earl of Lincoln, and Ralph married William's niece. No doubt the material support rendered by Baldwin in this great and successful enterprise contributed to raise his reputation, and to ensure peace in his own dominions, which passed, in the year following the Norman expedition, to his son Baldwin VI., the husband of Richilde.

The new ruler proved himself, for the few remaining years of his life, an able and pacific administrator, paying more attention to the welfare of his people than to his relations with his neighbours. The period between 1067 and 1070 was so calm and prosperous that Baldwin the Sixth was accorded the title of the Good, while the traces of the terrible famine and pestilence of 1045 were finally obliterated from the land. It was he who greatly strengthened the civic life of Belgium, and the memorable Charter of Grammont in 1068 is the first of a long series of documents which gave the burghers a security against the nobles that enabled them to work and to prosper, and that ultimately raised the country to its proud and unique position among European communities. The chroniclers described his period of power in the following terms " He might be seen riding across Flanders with a falcon or hawk on his wrist; he ordered his bailiffs to carry a white staff, long and straight, in sign of justice and clemency; no one was allowed to go out armed; the labourer could sleep without fear with his doors open, and he could leave his plough in the fields without apprehension of being robbed." It is not remarkable that so enlightened a prince should have wished to give the maximum of security to the inhabitants of the towns on whose growth the progress of the country mainly depended, and the Charter of Grammont is a memorable instance of the practical application of beneficent intentions.

Baldwin selected what he considered a good position for a new town on the banks of the Dendre, by buying the residence and estate of a baron named Gerard. It was situated on a hill, and thence called Gerardus-Montis, whence in time came the name of Grammont. Well placed by its topographical advantages, the situation derived a peculiar political importance from the fact that it stood on the confines of the three provinces of Flanders, Hainaut, and Brabant. With the view of making his creation secure Baldwin, therefore, summoned a meeting of the barons of the three provinces, and having explained to them what should be the rights of the town he exacted from them an oath to observe and uphold them. This charter, the chief points of which are given below,* has been called "the most ancient written monument of civil and criminal laws in Flanders."

---

* M. Le Glay in his *History of the Counts of Flanders* gives the following summary of the contents of the charter: "Everyone of whatsoever rank or condition who shall have bought a heritage in the town of Gerard-mont shall be free, on the condition of observing these laws according to the judgment of the sheriffs; he can leave the town if it seems good to him, but only after first meeting his debts and obligations; no one is to be forced to have recourse to the judicial duel, or to submit himself to the proof of fire and water; a layman in dispute with a layman for a debt, an agreement, an inheritance cannot be summoned before the dean or the bishop, if he wishes to submit the case to the sheriffs; but in matters concerning ecclesiastical law such as belief, marriage, and similar matters, he must reply to them before the Church. If any one has no heirs he has the right to give his fortune in charity either to the Church or to the poor. If a legitimate child dies immediately after birth his inheritance shall belong to the survivor of the father or mother. If the sons or the daughters receive the money or the goods of their parents, when one of the parents dies they shall place in the common fund what they have received in order to be then redivided. If any one will not pay what he owes to a citizen, and provided that the matter has been reported to the sheriffs, the debtor shall be forced, with the assistance and power of the court, to satisfy his obligation. If any one kills another, or breaks a limb beyond the right of legitimate defence, he shall lose head for head, and limb for limb. He who shall wound or throw down another, or catch hold of another by the hair, shall pay the court sixty sous; if he repeats the offence the fine shall be six pounds. He who shall utter slanderous words of the sheriffs, or of any servants of the court in the town shall pay sixty sous to the court, for the second offence the penalty will be increased to six pounds." This charter reveals one of the first successful attempts to resist the encroachments of the Church, and to establish civic law in the domain of business and transference of property.

Having contributed his share to the greatness of his people Baldwin the Sixth died prematurely, dividing his estates between his two young sons. To the elder, Arnulph, he left the title and the estates of Flanders, and to the younger, Baldwin, fell the same rights in Hainaut. But both were too young to rule for themselves, so he appointed his brother, the adventurous pilgrim and knight errant, Robert of Flanders, guardian over Arnulph, and he placed the charge of Baldwin in the hands of his widow, Richilde. The arrangement was the best that could be made, but it did not please Richilde. Her dissatisfaction became more marked after her third marriage with William of Osbern, one of the most prominent combatants at Hastings, but she did not improve her chances of success by resorting to despotic measures which alienated her subjects. However, her chance of acquiring Flanders was undoubtedly improved by the embarrassment of Count Robert, who, having married the widow of the Count of Holland, found himself involved in hostilities with the Frisians for the defence of her children's territory. A still more formidable enemy revealed himself in the person of the Bishop of Utrecht, who declared that the Counts of Holland had robbed his see of many rights and extensive tracts of land. The Duke of Brabant, or Lower Lorraine, took up the Bishop's cause, and Robert of Flanders was soon a fugitive on the other side of the Rhine. During the same period Richilde occupied Flanders, and having concluded a fresh and firm treaty with the King of France, conceived that she was secure against all attack, and resorted to a system of government as harsh as that of her husband had been lenient.

But the Flemish townsmen had tasted the sweets of freedom, and the race sprang from a stubborn stock, so that before long Richilde found that she had, under her authority, rebels rather than subjects. Still she would not abate one jot of what she called her rights and punished those who disobeyed or disregarded her decrees with ruthless severity. One instance of this will suffice. The burghers of Ypres, the capital of West Flanders, and one of the most prosperous commercial centres in the country, sent her a deputation. Its members spoke with great freedom, roundly declaring that she was governing in defiance of justice. Richilde's reply was to order the burghers to instant execution. On their side the Flemings concerted measures for a general revolt, and sent a request to Robert of Flanders to return from Germany and act as their leader. That chief was nothing loth to undertake the adventure, and returned to Flanders with some German mercenaries while the whole of the Flemish people rose in rebellion. Richilde, on her side, was not inactive, and in addition to the Hainaut forces she obtained the active aid of the King of France, so that the struggle became one of languages as well as liberties. The Flemings were, however, in a position of manifest inferiority, and Robert of Flanders, prudently recognising the fact, resorted to the defensive and established a strong camp on the hill of Cassel.* Here he was attacked by the combined forces of Richilde and the King of France. The Flemish army was mainly composed of infantry, the burghers of Ypres, Courtrai, Tournai, and, probably, the newly constituted town of Grammont, while the opposing force consisted of the men-at-arms and other retainers of the baronial chiefs. The battle of Courtrai, 230 years later, is generally considered the first demonstration of what a solid infantry could achieve against the heavy armed knights and men-at-arms, but at Cassel the Flemish burghers, in the youth of their municipal existence, gave a foretaste of their future strength and efficiency.

The battle of Cassel covered the whole of two days (22nd and 23rd February, 1071). On the first, the Flemings standing firmly to the defensive had the advantage, repulsing all attacks and crowning their success by the capture of Richilde, who fought in the ranks of her army. But carried away by his victory, Robert pursued the French too far, and was himself taken prisoner close to St. Omer. An arrangement was soon come to to exchange Richilde for Robert, and on the second day the struggle was renewed with fresh fury. However, the contest again turned in favour of the Flemings. William of Osbern was killed early in the day, and also the youth Arnulph, titular Count of Flanders. The French King drew off his

* In Normandy almost due west of Ypres.

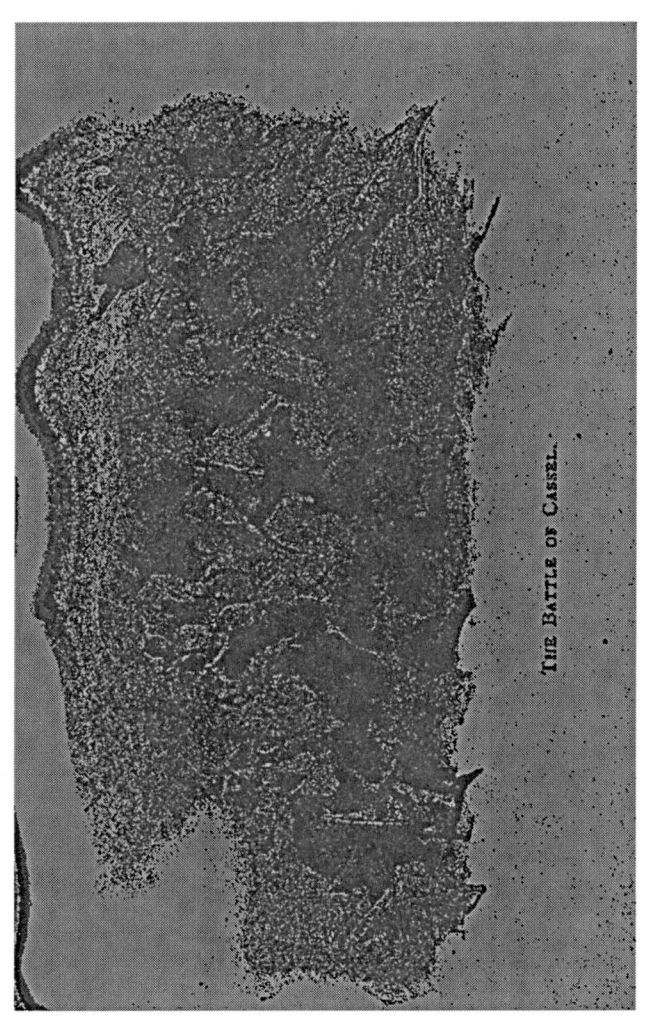

The Battle of Cassel.

forces, and the Flemings were left masters of the hill which they had so well defended. In gratitude for his services and the victory, the Flemings with one voice proclaimed Robert their Count, but Richilde, skilful in expedients, had not abandoned hope. The King of France had proved a weak reed to lean on, but she turned to the Bishop of Liége, and by pledging to him the whole province of Hainaut, and constituting the castle of Mons his fief, she gained his support. Aid was also promised by the Duke of Brabant, and the Counts of Louvain and Namur, and her last son, Baldwin, was entrusted with the command of the army. But Robert, with admirable decision, resolved to dispel the storm gathering on his frontiers before it had gathered force. While the allies were collecting their forces and completing their plans, Robert made a descent on Mons and crushed the army of Richilde in its position above the Abbey of St. Denis. The slaughter was so great that the battle was named "the hedge of the dead." Even then, Richilde would not confess to being beaten, but after a further reverse at Denain, she was constrained to abandon the contest, and retired into the convent of Messines, where she died ten years later. Robert of Flanders completed the success he had thus gained in his own country by recovering Holland for his step-son, and then, with characteristic enterprise, he decided on undertaking the pilgrimage to the Holy Land, from which he returned after many years absence, only to die and leave an example that undoubtedly inspired and facilitated the efforts of Peter the Hermit a few years later.

The consequences of these internal struggles had been disastrous to the suffering people. The Flemings had fought for hardly earned privileges, the preservation of which repaid their sacrifices, but in the other provinces disorder and civil strife were rampant, and one of the largest contributions to the town revenues were the sums paid in compensation for murder. To such a pass had the evil come, that the Bishop of Liége summoned a meeting of the chief ruling counts and barons and exacted from them under a solemn oath the promise to maintain "a law of peace," and to establish "a tribunal of peace," with the view of investigating all offences against public order and tranquillity. One of the principal regulations made was in limiting the right to carry arms in public. All the inhabitants were forbidden to carry weapons from the dawn of Friday until the same time on the following Monday, also for the whole of the period between Advent and Epiphany, and from Septuagesima day to the eighth day of Pentecost. In this way some restriction was placed on the inclination of the turbulent to adjust all differences by recourse to violence. The Bishop of Liége (Prince Henry of Verdun) proved that he was so far a statesman in that, by adding a leaf to the book of progress, first opened by the sixth Baldwin, he secured for the Church its share in the maintenance of internal peace and the suppression of lawlessness. On the tribunal of peace the bishop sat beside the aldermen, and the representatives of the burgh were assigned their places in the choir of the cathedral. There justice was dispensed after a set form very much in the following manner—

The citizens were admitted into the naves of the church, and the Mayor thus addressed them: " Citizens of Liége, and other inhabitants of the diocese! if there is any among you who wishes to appeal to the tribunal of peace he can do so quite aloud and without fear." The case for the plaintiff was then heard, and if the defendant put in an appearance, the matter was referred to two responsible servants of the fief to ascertain the facts and to make a report to the tribunal thereupon. The only persons exempted from the jurisdiction of the court were priests and the princes who had taken part in its creation. If the defendant or accused did not put in an appearance, he was summoned seven days by name, and if he did not reply he was publicly declared, to the accompaniment of the bell of the Church of Notre Dame at Liége, " infamous, excommunicated, and banished." The defendant was, however, left one avenue of escape. He might demand the judgment of God, or, in other words, the duel, and if he succeeded in unhorsing his opponent in the lists he escaped scot free and his character was fully rehabilitated. As the Liége convention was concluded under the auspices of a Bishop, it naturally differed from the Grammont Charter in respecting the Church's claims, and while it admitted the civic authorities to a share in the dispensation of justice, it also left ecclesiastical privilege practically untouched. The Bishop of Liége was also a secular prince, as well as a magnate of the Church, and in his former capacity he had to conciliate the good opinion of his subjects.*

Among the signatories to the juridical arrangements at Liége appears the name of Godefroid de Bouillon or Godfrey of Bouillon—perhaps the most imposing figure of the feudal ages. The similarity of the names has led some French writers, more patriotic than discriminating, to claim Boulogne as his birthplace, but it has been established, beyond the shadow of doubt, that he was born in the Castle of Baisy, near Genappe and the fields of Quatre Bras and Ligny, and that he derived the name by which he is best known from his successful defence, when a mere youth, of the Castle of Bouillon on the Semois. His father, however, was Eustace, Count of Boulogne, who had married the reigning Duke's sister, Ida d' Ardenne, of the famous family which had clung to its rights as Dukes of Lower Lorraine, in face of all the efforts of the Emperors to oust them. Godfrey the Hunchback, son and successor of the Duke known as the Courageous who had helped Baldwin of Flanders against his enemies, stood as godfather to his nephew, and in default of issue to himself had adopted him as his heir. On his death, in 1076, the Emperor Henry IV. set this arrangement aside and conferred on his own son Conrad the title of Duke of Lorraine. The action of the Emperor stirred up local enemies in the Count of Namur and the Bishop of Verdun. Ida d' Ardenne and her young son, then 17 years of age, fled to Bouillon in which their enemies besieged them. But the natural strength of the place enabled Godfrey, who displayed equal courage and coolness, to hold out sufficiently long to weary his assailants. He thus retained possession of

* The authority of the Tribunal of Peace continued to have effect at Liége and throughout Walloon Belgium for the greater part of three centuries. The first blow against its jurisdiction was struck by the Golden Bull of 25th July, 1349, when Brabant and Limburg were exempted from its control, and given the right of being tried only by their fellow countrymen, and not by "any foreigner, whether Bishop or layman." At Liége itself the tribunal continued to exercise its rights until Charles the Bold, in 1468, put an end to its existence.

Bouillon, and the Emperor, not wishing to press him further, conferred on him the Marquisate of Antwerp, one of the many titles held by the ancestors of his mother. As will be seen in the sequel, the indulgence shown by the Emperor was not thrown away.

Godfrey of Bouillon was, in several respects, ahead of his age, for he had received an education such as was then only given to men intended for the church. He was a good Latin scholar, and had a fluent colloquial knowledge of the Walloon (Roman) and Flemish (Teutonic) languages. His literary acquirements had not, however, prevented his qualifying in all the knightly exercises of the age, and he was regarded by his contemporaries as a formidable warrior, notwithstanding that he was only of the middle height. The reputation which he gained by the defence of Bouillon was immensely increased by his exploits during the war that has now to be described.

The Emperor, Henry the Fourth, had come into collision with the Pope, Gregory the Seventh, who not merely excommunicated and deposed him, but assigned the Imperial title to Rudolph, Duke of Suabia. The Emperor did not bend his back to the rod, but summoning his vassals to his support, proclaimed that he would maintain his rights against peer or prelate. Among the vassals summoned was Godfrey, who, propitiated by the Marquisate of Antwerp, and realising that he might obtain higher rewards from the same quarter, hastened to obey. When Henry invaded Saxony, and encountered Rudolph's army at Volksheim, he called upon his vassals to choose the one among them who seemed the most worthy to carry the standard of the Empire in the following action. The choice fell unanimously on Godfrey of Bouillon, and it was justified in the battle when he killed Rudolph in the centre of his army with a blow from its staff. Having overthrown his rival, the Emperor turned his arms against the Pontiff. The victorious army marched across Italy, and laid siege to the Eternal City. Here again Godfrey was to the front, being the first to scale the walls of Rome. The Emperor proved grateful, and was not sparing in his rewards to the foremost of his warriors. He recalled his son Conrad from Lorraine and recognised Godfrey as its Duke in accordance with the terms of the will of his uncle. The further career of Godfrey belongs to the period of the Crusades.

The two hundred years between the Oath of Verdun and the battle of Cassel in Flanders and the Pact of Liége in Walloon Belgium, were a period of transition from the semi-savage Merovingian and Carlovingian ages to the highly prosperous and cultured days of the Arteveldes and early Burgundian princes. Under the Baldwins of Flanders, the Regniers of Hainaut, and the great Ardenne family of Brabant, was sown the seed which produced the harvest of Flemish prosperity and Lorraine chivalry and magnificence. The details are absent, or fragmentary. The chroniclers ignore the people and burden their folios with genealogical tables of the chief families. A marriage or a tournament claims more space than the steady growth of the towns, and of that civic stateliness and individual independence among burghers which had their earliest home in the cities that dotted the flat and seemingly defenceless plains of Flanders. Yet the teaching of the Charter of Grammont, the fight on Cassel Hill, and, in only a less degree, of the Pact of Liége is clear. They show that in one country of Europe, the least favoured in position, the people were able at the moment of highest power for Feudalism and for the influence of the Church, to assert for themselves a position of independence that made them a power in the land, and, at the same time, secured for them the opportunity to become wealthy, intelligent, and progressive. A large share of the credit for these satisfactory results must no doubt be accorded to the ruling family in Flanders, which placed itself in the van of progress from the time of the first Baldwin in the 9th century. The rise of the Flemings to the height of their fortune was due, however, to their own natural qualities, and to a sturdiness, as well as steadiness, of conduct, in which their English kinsmen across the Channel soon emulated and, with greater opportunities, eventually surpassed them.

The progress made in Flanders during the tenth and eleventh centuries was slower in Hainaut and Brabant. The barons there were more firmly established, and less dependent on the popular voice. The Church possessed sees and abbeys, and was the principal landed proprietor. It exercised secular authority, and, guided by a single purpose and a continuous policy, it stretched forth its hands to grasp on every occasion the authority relaxed by divided or expiring fiefs of the Empire. The Bishop of Liége was a sovereign prelate who vied with Emperor and Duke. The townsmen in the Walloon provinces, therefore, had less chances in their favour and more obstacles to overcome in acquiring for themselves not so much an equal, as a sure position against the representatives of military power and ecclesiastical privilege. Their chief, if not their only triumph during this period was the Pact of Liége, and that left the superiority of clerical jurisdiction and law untouched, although it gave the laymen of the city a voice, and possibly a share, in its dispensation. But as a general description it may be said that there was no industrial or commercial progress, no accumulation of wealth, in the Walloon-speaking part of the state similar to that in Flanders. There were, no doubt, many causes at the root of this difference, but we must not overlook the fact of geographical position. The Walloons were cut off from the sea, and had no natural outlet for their produce which was derived to a great extent from forests and agriculture. They could only hope to benefit by the growth of prosperity among their neighbours which would react on them. The chivalry of Brabant and Hainaut was in no whit or way behind that of Flanders, and as they, especially Brabant, were more closely connected with the Empire, it is natural to assume that their courts were the more splendid of the two. But the real sources of power rested with the Flemings, and the cause of this was, no doubt, their proximity to the sea, and the fact that they had known how to make the best use of their natural advantages.

The occupants of the flat and uninviting shore, which extends southwards from the Scheldt, had from an early period been mariners and adventurers on the sea. They, like the Phœnicians, had traded with the white isle of Albion, but they had carried their wares and their search for treasure in raw materials or mineral products still further to the neglected emerald island of the Western Sea. Their Ultima Thule was the true home of Celtic lore and loyalty which gazes on the illimitable expanse of the Atlantic from Connemara or Achil. What the Menapians and Morinians had done in the days before Cæsar, the Flemings accomplished on a larger and more successful scale ten centuries later. It may be truly said of them that they had no alternative between extinction and trade. They had no pretensions to vie in arms with either their Gallic or their German neighbours. They were a small people, limited in numbers, and circumscribed in space, but the sea gave them an opening. They could not possibly be masters on land, but they might conquer a new element, or at least make it an ally for the maintenance of their independence. Therefore, they continued to trade with Saxon England and with Celtic Ireland, while later Romans and Merovingians passed to their eclipse, and when the Normans came in their swift serpent vessels, the only coast from which they retired baffled and discomfited was that of Flanders. The early Counts, after the decline of the Carlovingians, knowing the needs of their people, encouraged the wool trade with England. On Sussex downs, in the Eastern counties, multiplied the flocks whose fleeces fed the looms of Flanders, and the first Baldwin traced a broad line of policy for his successors when he said and ordered that the import of wool from England should be free, and that the labour of the weavers in Courtrai, Ypres, and the other industrial centres of his state should be unshackled by impost or by man. So it came to pass that even at the time of the Norman invasion of England, when Flanders was still but a small state, and its subjects were only at the bottom of the ladder of fame, the Flemish ships were the most efficient part of the continental flotilla which repeated the Roman conquest of this island. It seems even probable that the efficiency of these vessels was the determining factor in the success of William's enterprise. But no one must suppose that this result was attained easily or by a sudden effort. The Flemings rose to fame and commercial greatness because the inhabitants of that part of the European shores had long devoted themselves to maritime enterprise and made it almost the only free outlet and inlet from and to the mainland. It was the work of

F

centuries, a slow but sure growth, well built up, remarkable at the time to which we are referring, although it was still far short of the splendour and dimensions of its prime.

Before the end of the eleventh century, the main features of the Belgium which exists to-day had been created. It was not merely that there were the two races with the two languages, but the characteristics of each, allowing for the influences that time and the changed conditions of human existence would exercise on them, were very much what they are to-day, or, to put the point more accurately, they bore the same relation to each other. The Fleming was a man of commercial enterprise and energy, solid in his physical strength and by reason of his convictions, yet with far more vivacity and versatility than the Dutch, with whom he is very erroneously confounded. The Walloon who, whatever his ethnic origin, had certainly been more largely influenced by the Roman connection than the other Teutons, was less of a man of affairs, and represented a race or community which was more disposed to let events mould his fate than to shape them to his ends. As a warrior, however, he possesses and possessed the best qualities. The Fleming enjoyed and enjoys life because he is prosperous, because he had and has large means, and the only mode of benefiting by them was by indulging in festivities which the national painters have made famous and typical. But the Walloon has the same proclivities as his neighbour and confederate, only with him they are on a more modest and cautious scale. The great feasts with their gallons of costly wine possible at Bruges and Courtrai were not possible at Namur or Rochefort, or even at Louvain, while Brussels had still to wait for its position of pre-eminence. But while the Walloon is more simple than the Fleming he is also the more sceptical. It is the reaction, as it were, against the simplicity which kept him, for so many centuries, sunk in superstition and the servile tool of the Church. The Fleming, more fixed in his opinions, has ended by becoming the most constant and least questioning son of the Church, of which it seemed in the 16th century that he might be the subverter. In politics the Fleming, with the convictions of true liberalism and a resolute determination to maintain individual independence, has become the champion of order, and the main supporter of clericalism, while the Walloons are beginning to emerge from an innocent or infantile stage of society to assert advanced opinions, and to enter upon the dangerous path of experimental socialism. It must not be supposed that this description can be applied comprehensively to the whole race. All that is put forward is that it represents a general tendency among the two chief communities of the country.

However uncertain may be the light reflected from these early periods on the situation now existing, there must not be excluded from this brief survey the fact that the wise heads of the provinces saw, even in the tenth century, the necessity of union. Lorraine or Brabant helped Flanders out of its worst difficulties. Baldwin the Fifth would have been crushed but for Godfrey the Courageous. Baldwin himself spared no pains to, and did, unite Hainaut to Flanders, and the plan of Richilde to undo that work might be regarded as an expiring Walloon effort to bring Flanders to its knees. But at the same time the wisest and most far-seeing persons in the ruling classes of all the provinces realised that there was identity of interest among the inhabitants of the Netherlands. It was not to their interest to be the servants or the subjects of either France or Germany. Their interests pointed to a *via media*, a national and self-preserving independence to be maintained by good conduct and good faith, by inspiring respect in more powerful neighbours, as well as by showing respect for the written bond.

CHAPTER IV.

The Crusades.

DURING the stormy and semi-legendary period that we have now traversed, while certain families were making good hereditary rights in Flanders and the adjacent provinces, there had grown up in Western Europe a sentiment or custom that compelled men of the higher classes of society to conform with certain rules and to act, as it were, in harmony on the principal points of human intercourse. In one of the happiest passages of his great work the historian Hallam has depicted the growth of chivalry. The two salient duties of the members of this order, which, not possessing a charter, was still international, and included all with the least pretensions to gentle birth, were to resort to no unfair or foul means in warfare against one another, and to protect the weak and defenceless. On these terms the knightly and noble classes hoped to, and did justify the position and privileges they claimed over their serfs and villains. The masses, unarmed, untrained, and ill fed, remained passive while the chivalry of the country kept out invaders, punished robbers, and sometimes even assigned a portion of the spoil acquired in foreign wars to the benefit of their dependents. On the other hand, the adoption of chivalrous customs softened the savage character of the age, placed before the members of this indefinite but comprehensive guild a high ideal, and promoted the chances of common action against a great danger or for an object of general interest. If chivalry had not existed and had the time to mature, the Crusades would probably never have been undertaken. They furnish the conclusive historical evidence that chivalry was an impulse exciting the emotions and urging men to undertake noble deeds in defiance of the difficulties attending them. Chivalry attained the height of its power and spontaneity at the end of the 11th century. The period described in the lines:

> "Kings
> Half-legend, half-historic, Counts and Knights,
> Who laid about them at their wills and died."

was passing away, and the evolution of European politics in their present existent condition had almost commenced. Yet enthusiasm had not given place to calculation, and it was possible for the first and, perhaps, the only time in history to band the races and the princes of Europe together for the attainment of a common object from which not one of them could hope to derive much material benefit. The readiness of the response made, from all the chief states of Europe, to the appeal of Pope Urban was the proof of how far the principles and the practice of chivalry had extended, and how deeply its teaching had been absorbed by nations hostile to each other, and whose banners had never before flown together on the same side. Germans and French, Italians and Flemings, Walloons and Frisians, Normans and Scotch, all hastened to answer the summons of chivalry and the appeal of the Church, and even the Saxons, in the person of Edgar Atheling and his band, laid aside their grief and their resentment to accompany their Norman conquerors to the Holy Land. No such potent spell exists to-day. The cause is unknown, the occasion invisible which would combine the civilised peoples of the World in an undertaking for which they would have to give their blood and their treasure without prospect of return or recompense. The critics sneer at the days of chivalry, but they cannot strip them of the glory of the first Crusades.

During the 10th century the practice had sprung up among zealous Christians, hyper-sensitive as to the offences they, like the other children of Adam, had committed during their earthly career, of expiating them by a pilgrimage to the holy places associated with the origin of Christendom. The Church and the authorities of Rome encouraged that tendency because it increased the means at their disposal for retaining the hold on the superstition of the age necessary for the maintenance of their position and privileges. Every pilgrim who, with staff and scallop shell, wended his way to Gethsemane, Calvary, or Bethlehem was a living witness to the power of the Pope, and by testifying increased it. Of such pilgrims, Robert of Flanders, known as the Frisian, was the most illustrious and the ablest. All the pilgrims brought back accounts of the harshness with which Christians were treated in the East, and of the cruelty with which the Mahomedans compelled them to save their lives by sacrificing their creed. The envoys of the Eastern Emperor, Alexius Comnenus, dwelt on the dangers threatened by the fanatical followers of the Prophet, first to Constantinople and then to Europe itself. The pilgrim, Robert the Frisian, was so persuaded of the imminence of the danger that he laid aside his pilgrim's garb to lead the Imperial armies in Asia Minor with the same address as had turned the day at Cassel. Before his death in the East the danger had grown greater, yet at the same time his efforts had at least retarded the advance of the Moslem.

The origin of the movement which has now to be described, and which in no state received a nobler or more generous response than in Belgium, is generally attributed, not to Pontiffs or Sovereigns, but to a simple pilgrim priest known to all time as Peter the Hermit. This enthusiast was a Walloon of the province of Liége, a pure Belgian of the same race as Charlemagne, and the Mayors of the Palace who preceded him. He had accomplished the pilgrimage to Jerusalem shortly after the visit of Robert of Flanders, and he returned to Europe full of indignation at the wrongs inflicted on his co-religionists, and perhaps a sufferer from them in his own person. Bestriding an ass, and holding in his hand a crucifix, he rode through the towns and villages of Germany, France, and the Netherlands, recounting the common wrongs of pilgrims and Christendom, and calling on his audiences to take up arms for the rescue of the Holy Places from the infidel. Two years were passed by the itinerant priest in spreading his views and in stimulating public interest and enthusiasm. The popular excitement at last became so great that the movements of Peter the Hermit engrossed public attention, and ambitious potentates had to lay aside their projects of aggrandisement in order to range themselves on the side of a popular movement which knew no national or territorial limits but was as wide as Christendom itself. It must be noted that the priest was aided by the troubadour. The latter's appeal struck the true chord of chivalry. It was a summons to an unknown and mysterious adventure, as well as a demand for protection by the weak against the strong. The martial, as well as the religious, spirit of the age was enlisted in support of the movement, and the troubadours of Provence, by their poetic effusions on behalf of this deed of "high emprise," seconded and confirmed the religious exhortations of the enthusiastic monk. The success of the movement with the chivalrous and militant classes is not surprising, but the fervour with which the masses supported it is not to be explained by religious or chivalric exaltation alone. A more potent lever was supplied by the tales of the wealth to be found in the gorgeous East, and of the spoil that the victorious warriors would bring back after the expulsion of the unbelievers.

After two years' irregular and individual agitation, the Church, in the person of Pope Urban the Second, determined to take up the movement and to give it solemn sanction and encouragement. Accordingly the supreme Pontiff announced at Clermont in Auvergne, in November, 1095, his approbation of the movement originated by Peter the Hermit. In the presence of four hundred bishops and mitred abbots he exclaimed : "What human voice could ever describe the persecution and the cruelties which the Christians have suffered? How unhappy are we, my brothers and my children! to have lived in these days of calamity! Are we then called upon to live in this century only to see the desolation of Christianity, and to remain in peace whilst our religion is given into the hands of its oppressors? Warriors who hear me, you who seek without ceasing idle pretexts for war, Rejoice! for here is a lawful war. You, who were so often the terror of your fellow citizens, and who sold for vile lucre your arms for the terror of others, armed with the sword of the Maccabees, go and defend the House of Israel!" This harangue was received with tremendous shouts of "Deus Vult" or, more probably, with the Romance words of "Diex li volt," and to this cry of "God wills it" the audience, with frenzied haste, proceeded to attach to their shoulders the emblem of the cross in token that they would participate in the first Crusade. Garments of every kind were torn in pieces to fashion the insignia, but red was the favourite and predominant colour. Some harder dispositions, unable to procure silk or cloth, imprinted the chosen mark on their own shoulders with hot irons. Such was the fervour of the zealous participants in the First Crusade, but it must be recorded that the later Crusaders never attained the same height of earnestness and self-sacrifice.

The Pope followed up the Proclamation of Clermont by a tour through France and Belgium, during which he emulated the example of Peter the Hermit, and besought those who had their religion at heart to don the Cross and proceed to the Holy Land. But in order to demonstrate how thoroughly popular was the movement, Peter the Hermit continued his efforts and his exhortations with such success that, while princes and prelates were discussing what should be done, he was ready to take the field at the head of a gathering formidable in numbers that, with better leading and organisation, might have solved the question before a single knight had a chance of laying his lance in rest. But if the major credit for originating the crusades may be given to Peter the Hermit, the signal and speedy failure of the operations he conducted in person might have brought the whole enterprise to an untimely end. The reputation and claim to fame of the Belgian monk have been somewhat compromised by the fiasco of his march, but there is no one to dispute with him the credit for the inception of the work.

In the spring of 1096, the rude levies of Peter, composed of serfs and labourers to the number of 100,000 men, unaccustomed to war, ill-armed, and without the semblance of discipline, began their march eastwards from Belgium and France. That march, precipitate and ill-regulated, was rendered necessary by two considerations. The participants had quitted the fields of their daily labour, and were consequently deprived of their own natural resources, while the collection of thousands of men in a few localities drained the resources of the district, and threatened famine. To remain inactive under these conditions would have been to cause the disbandment of the Christian army, and to allow enthusiasm to be altogether displaced by despondency and discontent. The only chance was to set out, and Peter, still mounted on his ass, led his numerous following eastwards. The confusion surpassed description. To maintain order in that vast body it is said that the priest had only eight trained knights or men-at-arms, the chief of whom bore the expressive name of Walter the Landless. But to make matters worse it was joined, on crossing the Rhine, by a German contingent, also led by a priest, named Gotschalk, and a few adventurers. Without order or direction the force still swept, by sheer weight of numbers, across Germany and down the Valley of the Danube. It is uncertain whether absolute starvation, or the predatory instinct aroused by the promise of plunder, which had been a principal cause in originating the movement, or the religious zeal that turned the hatred of the Mahomedan possessors of the Holy Land into animosity towards the Jew disbelievers in Christ although they were equal sufferers with Christians at the hands of the Infidel, was the cause of the disorders and brutalities that attended the march of the first Crusaders towards their goal. But it is certain that the march of this horde resembled the track of a devastating invader, and not the passage of a friendly force engaged on a noble and sacred mission. When the body entered the Greek Empire it was received like an hostile army. No supplies were forthcoming, its movements were obstructed, and all stragglers were cut off. Long before the force reached the Bosphorus the disorganisation and discouragement were complete. The Greek authorities hurried the survivors across the straits into Asia, where they fell an easy prey to the enemy. Of the comparatively few survivors of this ill-fated and tumultuous force, the enthusiastic originator was one. Tarnished as was his reputation as a leader of men, it remained undimmed as the originator of the Crusades and this sufficed to obtain for him large subscriptions when he devoted himself, with his characteristic energy, during the closing years of his life, to the construction of the magnificent abbey of Neumoustier*at Huy on the Meuse.

But if the originator of the Crusades was a Belgian, it is still more remarkable that the hero of the undertaking, the man whose lofty character sustained the high ideal of its inception and the leader whose skill and fortitude alone brought the difficult campaign to a successful conclusion, should have been a member of the same race. We saw in the last chapter how Godfrey of Bouillon won his Duchy and helped the Emperor in his struggle with the Pope. The monkish chroniclers tell us that he felt remorse for having scaled the walls of the Eternal City in the guise of an enemy, and that he vowed to expiate the offence, when he could, by undertaking the pilgrimage to the Holy Land. It was the practice of the age, and the example of Robert of Flanders was recent. The preaching of Peter the Hermit, and the proclamation of Pope Urban, brought the realisation of this project before him in a new and more attractive form. It was not as an unarmed pilgrim, with "shoon and scallop shell," but as a warrior leading an army that it accorded most with the character and achievements of the hero of Volksheim for him to make his appearance in Palestine. The announcement of the First Crusade gave him, unexpectedly, this opportunity. In no country of Europe did the invocation of Peter the Hermit elicit a wider and more genuine response than in his own, in no bosom of that country did it arouse a warmer throb of noble emulation and legitimate ambition than in that of the Duke of Bouillon. Yet heavy sacrifices had to be made even to obtain the chance of gratifying these wishes. At that time the greatest chiefs possessed little money. The bishops and abbots controlled the power of the purse, and the great commercial centres of Flanders had not yet begun to contest this supremacy with them. But money was essential to buy arms for his retainers and to equip them for their

* Peter the Hermit died here in 1115. There is a statue to him in the grounds of the old Abbey. Neumoustier was only one of the 17 abbeys and monasteries that existed in the small town of Huy during the centuries of its dependency on the bishopric of Liége.

GODFREY OF BOUILLON.

dangerous expedition. So Godfrey of Bouillon sold his famous castle to the Bishop of Liége, he hypothecated his lands in Brabant to the monks of St. Hubert, and thus obtained, at the price of his own beggary, the means of undertaking the great work for which the Church promised immunity from debt as well as the forgiveness of sins. But the Church never relaxed its hold on his possessions and Bouillon remained the appendage of the Bishopric of Liége* until six centuries later the link was severed by Louis the Fourteenth.

In the summer of 1096, the forces raised in Belgium and the Rhine Valley are stated to have numbered 80,000 footmen, and 10,000 horsemen. Of these Godfrey of Bouillon was the natural chief, and he began his march from the Rhine on the 10th August. Crossing Hungary and Bulgaria, without any of the discreditable incidents that attended the movements of Peter the Hermit, this regular army reached the Bosphorus and the capital of the Eastern Empire without loss. In September the French and Flemish contingents followed in its track. The former included the Norman contingent with Robert Courthose, son of the Conqueror, and was under the nominal command of Hugh the Great, brother of the King of France. The latter was led by Robert II., Count of Flanders, the heir of that first Robert whose example inspired many who embarked on the Crusade. Here two interesting facts deserve notice. The Anglo-Saxon contingent, under Prince Edgar Atheling, was attached, not to the Norman-French, but to the Flemish, with which it fought throughout the campaign. The second fact is that while, by unanimous testimony, Godfrey of Bouillon was the hero and chief leader of the war, the verdict was not less decisive in favour of Count Robert of Flanders coming next after him in all the qualities of a noble knight and great leader. For Belgium,† both Flanders and Brabant,

---

* The sum paid by the Bishop is stated by a contemporary to have been 1,500 pounds of silver, which was obtained by forced requisition on the abbeys of the diocese. The Bishop's men are stated to have seized a gold table and three gold crosses from the Abbey of St. Hubert alone for the purpose.

† Among the Belgian knights are named, first, Eustace of Boulogne and Baldwin, brothers of Godfrey. Another relation was his cousin Baldwin

the First Crusade was a glorious epoch, and a natural subject for national pride.

The total combined forces of Christian Europe are said to have amounted to 100,000 horsemen (that is, knights, squires, and men-at-arms) and 600,000 footmen, but in the latter total seem to have been included women and children. When this immense force was concentrated at, and in the neighbourhood of, Constantinople, the Greek Emperor, Alexius Comnenus, began to tremble for his own security. All his diplomacy was exerted to get rid of the troublesome guests that he had invited into his own territory, and he might have failed if the influence of Godfrey had not been exerted in his favour. Attracted by the beauty of Constantinople and the wealth of its dependent provinces, offended by the ritual of the Greek Church which, to the Romans, bordered on infidelity, many of the Christian knights wished to begin their enterprise with the overthrow of the schismatic Eastern Empire. It was Godfrey alone who turned them from this purpose, and reminding them of the sacred mission which they had sworn to accomplish in the names of St. George and St. Demetrius,[*] he succeeded in inducing them to cross the Bosphorus into Asia. Here it is only necessary to give a brief summary of the war that began in the spring of 1097 and concluded two years later with the capture of Jerusalem. Nicæa with its 370 towers, the capital of Bithynia, which the Greeks had lost only twenty years before to the Sultan of Roum, was their first objective. The Christians drove off the covering force of Turkish cavalry, and laid close siege to the town, but the garrison held out valiantly. Several assaults were repulsed, and the assailants seemed baffled in their very first undertaking. But, unknown to the Crusaders, the garrison was in equally desperate straits, and negotiated, secretly, the surrender of the place to the officers

du Bourg. Baldwin II. of Hainaut, John Count of Namur, Philip Viscount of Ypres, Warner Count of Grez, Arnold of Oudenarde, Theodore of Dixmude, Frenbault and Theomer of Bruges, Rudolph of Alost, Walter of Nivelles, Gontran of Brussels, Siger, Steppo and Gislebert, all of Ghent, Ludolph, Everard and William, all of Tournai, were some of the leaders, while Henry and Godfrey represented the still verdant House of D'Assche.

[*] The First Crusade had been placed under their special protection as the Warrior Saints of the Christian hagiology.

of the Emperor Alexius. On 24th June, 1097, the Imperial flag was hoisted on the walls and the Crusaders were curtly informed that they must respect an Imperial city. The march was then resumed, but under incredible difficulties. Provisions were scanty, water was often entirely wanting, the heavy armed men sometimes sank on the bad roads beneath the weight of their armour. Still the force pressed on scattering in all directions the light-armed Turk cavalry that sought to harass and hinder them. On the field of Dorylæum, on July 4th, the superiority of the European force over the Asiatic was clearly established. The army of Sultan Soliman (Kilij-Arslan, sword of the lion) was annihilated by Godfrey in person, whose feats of strength excited quite as much admiration among the Crusaders as his prudence and conciliation at the Council Board. At the battle of Dorylæum he fought in the thick of the fight, and it was recorded of him that with one blow of his sword he split a man in two from the crown of his head to the saddle.

The great victory of Dorylæum raised the courage and relieved the necessities of the Christian army. But dissensions soon arose in its own ranks. The natural antipathies of race and country asserted themselves over the bonds of a common religion, and the rival pretensions of proud and fierce warriors found a frequent field of conflict in the distribution of spoil and of fame. At the capture of Tarsus, for instance, the Walloons under Baldwin, brother of Godfrey, and the Italians under Tancred came to blows in the streets as to which deserved the credit of its capture. On this occasion Tancred, who alone had refused to recognise and promise fealty to the authority of the Emperor of Constantinople, showed himself amenable to reason, but Baldwin would not be pacified and drawing off his special force marched into Mesopotamia, where he established the kingdom of Edessa until he, in turn, assumed the higher title of King of Jerusalem. The capture of Antioch marked the end of 1097. The incredible sufferings of the Crusaders during the following winter, and their desperate sortie in June, 1098, when the Mahomedan army, which seemed to hold the place in its grasp, was routed with the loss of 100,000 men, completed one of the most striking incidents in the whole war. The way was thus cleared to Jerusalem, and in the summer of 1099 the Crusaders appeared before the Holy city. On the first sight of the goal they were seeking from the heights of Emmaus they raised shouts of Jerusalem! Jerusalem! and as they took up their positions they chanted the hymn of Isaiah "Jerusalem, raise thy eyes and see the liberator who will break your chains." But of the 700,000 men who had placed the cross on their shoulders for the First Crusade only 50,000 survived. The remainder had either perished on the field of battle, of disease or of deprivation on the desert marches.

But although the Crusaders had reached Jerusalem it did not follow that they would capture it. The city presented the same imposing appearance that it did to Titus or that it does to the latter-day tourist. It was garrisoned by a force almost as numerous as that about to besiege it. If the Crusaders were animated by religious exaltation and by a higher motive than ever sent any other combatants to battle, the Mussulmans, on their side, were inspired by fanaticism and by the despair that told them to hold their last stronghold to the bitter end. The mollahs assured them that victory was certain and that the recompense of death lay in Paradise. As the result showed these incentives were inferior to the resolution of the Christians who, having much suffered and greatly dared, saw the prize before them and would not be baulked of their reward. Still it was not to be lightly won. A preliminary assault, delivered before the train had arrived, and without ladders, was rudely repulsed. Provisions and water were both wanting, and it was by no means certain that the Crusaders would have been able to deliver a second if the opportune arrival of an Italian fleet at Jaffa had not brought them succour, and the means of conducting the siege in regular form. Among these means for conducting the attack in proper form were three moving towers which overtopped the walls of the besieged town. Each of these was equipped with a drop-bridge for the purpose of giving access to the ramparts. Encouraged by these timely and useful auxiliaries, the Crusaders determined on making a second assault without any unnecessary delay.

The 14th July—a day famous long afterwards in the world's

annals for another celebrated assault—was chosen for the commencement of this final attack. The Crusaders began their operations with a solemn procession round the walls of the place, and then the three towers, commanded by the three selected champions of Christendom, Godfrey himself, Tancred and Raimond of Toulouse, moved towards as many different parts of the ramparts, while the mass of the Christian army fought in the intervals between. The first day's battle was indecisive, but at three in the morning of the 15th July the assault was delivered. The drop-bridges were let down, and

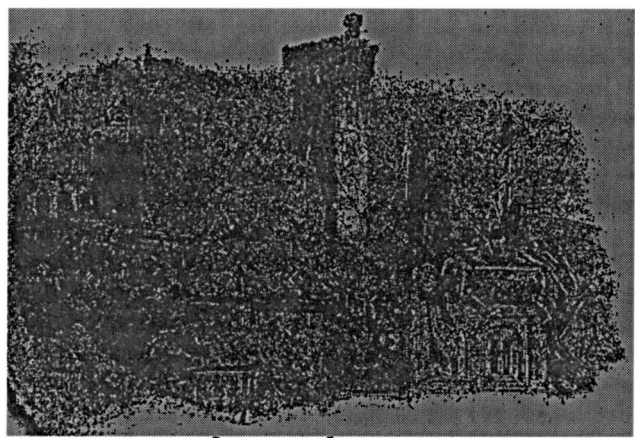
CAPTURE OF JERUSALEM.

over them poured a continuous stream of men-at-arms. From Godfrey's tower Ludolph of Tournai was the first to gain the wall, and Godfrey himself was the third. Prominent among the warriors from the other towers were the two Roberts of Flanders and Normandy. Nothing in that age could have resisted their onset, yet a week rolled by before the last Mussulman had ceased to fight, or the Christian to slaughter. After seventy thousand infidels could be counted among the slain, the Crusaders changed their guise as fighting men for that of pilgrims, and proceeded in humble attire to pay their devotions at the Holy Sepulchre.

The triumph won, the next thought of the Crusaders was

to consolidate it at the same time that the majority of them desired to return to their homes in Europe. The speedy attainment of this wish was rendered possible by the signal defeat, on 12th August at Ascalon, of the Mussulman army coming from Egypt, under the Caliph of that state, to the relief of the besieged city. It was proposed, and speedily decided, to form the new conquest into the kingdom of Jerusalem, and the chiefs of the Crusade met to decide who should be its first King. Only five names were seriously proposed, and of these two were Belgian, representing the two races composing the nationality. Godfrey of Bouillon and Robert of Flanders were the two serious candidates, for both Robert of Normandy and Tancred were merely fighting knights, and Raimond of Toulouse, the fifth leader proposed, had disgusted every one by his obstinacy. The selection between the Walloon and Flemish candidates was rendered easier by the retirement of the latter. Robert of Flanders was, scarcely in a less degree than Godfrey, a hero of the First Crusade. At Artesium and Antioch he had been in the front of the assailants. At the assault of the latter place, his Flemish squire, Foulcher the orphan, had insisted on mounting the ladder first because his master was always thrusting himself into the post of greatest peril, but at the capture of Jerusalem the tower on which Robert fought touched the walls as soon as that of Godfrey. He would, therefore, have been a formidable rival for the Lorraine Duke, but all chance of rivalry was averted by his spontaneous declaration that he would not be the first king of Jerusalem, although he did not mind accepting the honourable titles of "Son of St. George," and "Sword of the Christians." He was described by all witnesses as conciliatory and disinterested, but he gave his own reasons for declining the crown in the following characteristic language—

"I promised the Countess, my wife, to return to her on fulfilling my vow. It is very long since I could take a hot or a cold bath, or sleep between white sheets, and it is well known how accustomed are the Flemings to a good regime, to comfortable beds and well warmed houses." Robert of Flanders re-appears in the Belgian story, but his disappearance from Palestine smoothed the way for Godfrey's election. Even if he had remained, the claims of Godfrey must have prevailed, for he had shown a wisdom and a tact in leading the heterogeneous mass of crusaders that had prevented their breaking into detached and even hostile fragments, and in all the important encounters he had laid down the tactics that should be followed. As knights and combatants there were others who might vie with Godfrey, but as the discreet and vigilant leader he stood alone. Therefore it was not surprising that he should be chosen unanimously as first Christian King of Jerusalem—a lofty title, fairly earned in his case by unimpeachable merit, but one which his modesty led him to translate into the less exalted style of " Guardian and Baron of the Holy Sepulchre."

The reign of Godfrey was all too brief for the work he had to accomplish. Twelve months after his proclamation he died of fever, aggravated by the deprivations of the campaign, and by the strain of his many occupations. He found time in that short period to compile the celebrated Book of the Laws and Good Customs of the Kingdom of Jerusalem, which was the code of law in the newly founded state. With the small garrison left of 300 knights and their retainers he more than held his own, enforcing the tribute from those who had engaged to pay it, and driving off the raiding Arab cavalry that attempted to maintain the war, in an irregular fashion it is true, but still indefinitely. One striking incident during this period merits notice. The town of Arsuf, on the sea coast, not far from Jaffa, refused to pay the tribute it had promised and Godfrey marched to besiege it. The Mahomedan governor had no reasonable chance of holding out against the leader of the Christians in person, but he held, in the person of Gerard D'Avesnes, one of the best knights and most faithful companions of Godfrey, a hostage through whose person he counted on securing good terms, if not complete escape. These hopes were not destined to be realised, for when the Mussulman captain exposed his captive on the walls in the expectation that Godfrey would relent before imperilling the life of his best friend he found that public interest was superior to private sentiment with the great Crusading chief. Gerard D'Avesnes, attached to a cross on the ramparts, perished beneath the shafts of his comrades who, in turn, wreaked a terrible vengeance on the defenders of the place. Godfrey of Bouillon was buried in the Church of the Resurrection, at the foot of Calvary. It has been said of him that he was the only figure to redeem the first Crusade from the charge of being a selfish filibustering expedition, but this is going too far. There were many noble figures among the leaders of the Crusade, and whatever other sentiments may have contributed to the undertaking, a chivalrous fervour and a sincere desire to execute what seemed an imperative religious call must not be denied their place. The true distinction of Godfrey is that he possessed the qualities of a born leader of men. He was not the initiator of the movement, like Peter the Hermit, and some at least of the Princes entered upon the campaign in a more pronounced spirit of adventure and knight-errantry. But on the other hand it was his patience, fortitude and capacity for organisation that brought the war to its successful conclusion after failure seemed almost inevitable. The magnitude of his services explains the immediate selection of his brother, Baldwin of Edessa, to fill the vacant throne of Jerusalem.

Although it entails a breach of the chronological order, the part taken by Belgians in the later Crusades may appropriately fall within the limits of this chapter. When the second Crusade was preached in 1146, the throne of Jerusalem was still occupied by the descendants of Baldwin. The heads of this Crusade were the Emperor Conrad of Germany, and the King Louis VII. of France. The Count of Flanders took a prominent part in this disastrous expedition. One body of Flemish Crusaders, under the command of the Monk Arnould and the soldier Count of Arschoet, sailed from Antwerp in a hundred ships. On their way they halted off the coast of Portugal where the Moors had just obtained possession of Lisbon. At the same time another squadron of English crusaders arrived, and Alphonso, the first king of Portugal, succeeded in inducing both to join hands with him, and assist in expelling the Moors from Lisbon. Complete success attended their operations and the members of the Second

Crusade, who never reached the Holy Land, rendered a more practical service to Christendom than those who did. Many Belgians remained in Portugal enjoying special privileges, which were the more appreciated by the Flemings as Henry the Second had just ordered their expulsion from England, and founding towns, among others Villa Verde, called after the distinctive colour of their crosses. In the meantime the main expedition, under the Emperor and the King, had ignominiously failed before Damascus. But the Count of Flanders—Thierry of Alsace, son of Gertrude sister of the Robert of Flanders of the First Crusade—redeemed in some degree the members of the Second Crusade from the personal reproach of being inferior to their predecessors. After a number of romantic adventures he reached Jerusalem, and assisted Baldwin III.,

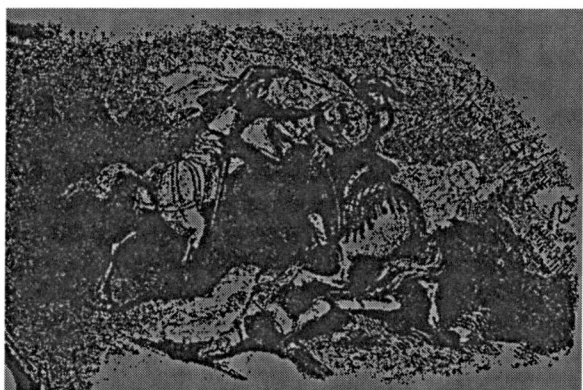

THE ORIGIN OF THE ARMS OF FLANDERS.

whose sister he had married, in the increasingly difficult task of holding Jerusalem against the Infidel. He returned to Flanders at a critical moment in its history, but only for a brief space, and then he retook the road to Jerusalem, finally returning twenty years later to die in the monastery of Waten, " dying as a hermit, after having lived the life of a hero."

The son of this Count, Philip of Alsace and also Count of Flanders, undertook a personal expedition to the Holy Land which merits notice for one fact. He was accompanied by a small but select body of Flemish knights and soldiers who took the Cross in the Church of St. Peter at Ghent. The jealousy of the ruling barons at Jerusalem, who did not give new crusaders the cordial welcome of old, prevented his obtaining, on reaching his destination, any chance of great distinction, but he at least sought or made an opportunity for displaying his personal courage in a single-handed encounter with a Mussulman chief renowned for his strength. Having vanquished this opponent, Philip carried off his shield as a trophy, and the device on it, a black lion on a golden field, became henceforth the seal and crest of Flanders. After a long interval, Philip of Alsace took part in the Third Crusade, and died of fever in the camp before Acre. Some other Flemish knights accompanied their Count to the East, and it is noteworthy that, when Philip Augustus left Richard the Lion-Hearted alone in the Holy Land, the Flemish contingent remained with the latter and took a prominent part in the great battle of Arsur. Their chief knight, James D'Avesnes, was killed, and his last words were "Richard, avenge my death!"

It was not, however, till the fifth Crusade that the Belgians can be said to have again played as prominent a rôle as they had done in the first. With a view to composing the troubles of Europe which was specially disturbed, owing to the ambitious policy of Philip Augustus bent on consolidating the kingdom of France, Pope Innocent III. endeavoured to turn men's minds in a different channel, and issued his sanction to the preaching of a fifth Crusade. The Kings of both France and England were too much occupied in their own quarrels to take any part in it, but the Emperor of Germany assumed the cross, although not the actual command of the Christian army. While the nominal lead was given to the Marquis of Montferrat, the real conduct of the enterprise rested with Baldwin of Hainaut and Flanders, which states, by a series of events still to be described, had become united in the person of his father. Baldwin was the ninth of his name to rule over Flanders, and the sixth over Hainaut. Soon after succeeding to the government he had formed an alliance with Richard of

England which the death of the "lion-hearted" brought to an abortive end, but, notwithstanding the loss of his ally, he succeeded in obtaining honourable terms from Philip Augustus, under the treaty of Peronne. He then turned his attention to the development of the resources of his states, but the summons to the Holy War, rendered more promising by the death of Saladin, proved irresistible and drew him away to a larger scene.

On Ash Wednesday, in the year 1200, Baldwin took the Cross in the Cathedral Church of St. Donat at Bruges, together with his brothers, Henry and Eustace, and a large number of knights, among whom figured members of the Beaufort, Vilain, and Bethune families, all of which still possess lineal descendants among the Belgian nobility. Leaving his states in charge of his brother Philip, Marquis of Namur, Baldwin set out at the head of his force. The route selected for this crusade was that through Venice, where the Doge and senate, by a formal treaty, had engaged to provide the necessary flotilla to convey the whole expedition to Palestine. The terms of this treaty were to the following effect. Venice agreed to allow the passage across her territory of 4,500 men-at-arms, and 20,000 foot soldiers, and to provide them with provisions for nine months as well as with some of the necessary transport. For these services the Crusaders engaged to pay the enormous sum, for that age, of 85,000 silver marks. The Venetians hoped to derive some larger measure of profit from this well-equipped force, for they offered to furnish fifty armed galleys in return for a half share in the conquests effected. The Doge of the day was the great Henry Dandolo who, although 90 years of age, assumed the cross himself and took an active part in directing the expedition towards its destination. This co-operation became the more necessary when the Flemish fleet, sent round the coast, missed its way or misunderstood its instructions in such manner as to appear at Marseilles instead of Venice.

Very soon after the arrival of the Crusaders at Venice, it became clear that they could not pay the 85,000 marks stipulated, and but for the policy and efforts of Dandolo, the enterprise would have been wrecked on the threshold. He represented to the Venetians, however, that it would not be chivalrous to press the Crusaders for payment while it might be to the advantage of the Republic to utilise their military skill and power for an undertaking which greatly interested the Venetians. Gold or silver the Crusaders had none, but they represented the flower of European chivalry. Dandolo, therefore, proposed that their debt should be cancelled on the condition that they would lend their services for the recovery of Zara in Dalmatia. Baldwin and his companions made no difficulty about undertaking so congenial a task, and, in a short time, not only Zara, but Trieste, and the whole of Istria were in the hands of the Venetians. The path being thus cleared of difficulties, the Crusaders would have set out for the Holy Land when an unforeseen occurrence altered their destination and gave a fresh turn to history. There arrived in Venice from Constantinople a young Greek prince, Alexius Comnenus, with the news that his father, Isaac Angelus had been deposed from his throne by an ambitious brother. Alexius implored the conquerors of Zara to take up his father's cause, promising them 200,000 silver marks at the same time that he propitiated their religious sentiments by declaring that the Greek Church should admit the supremacy of that of Rome. Although the Papal Nuncio, supported by some of the Crusaders, among whom Simon de Montfort was the most conspicuous, opposed the change of plans, and the Pope himself threatened to excommunicate the warriors whom he had so lately blessed, the counter attractions of Constantinople and the reward of Alexius prevailed. For an unprofitable march across the arid plains of Syria was thus substituted a pleasant trip to the groves of Byzantium, coupled with the hope of a rich reward at its close. The prospect was pleasing enough to the Crusaders, but it was still more attractive to the Venetians who had weighty political motives to serve by the establishment of their influence on the Bosphorus, and by freeing the route through the Dardanelles from existing obstructions, and rival pretensions. The fifth Crusade, undertaken for the recovery of the Holy Sepulchre, was thus converted, partly by Dandolo's wisdom and partly by accident, into a campaign for the advantage of the Queen of the Adriatic.

At the end of May, 1203, the force sailed for the Dardanelles, and on the 23rd June the fleet anchored off San Stephano point in front of Constantinople.* The headquarters of the army were fixed at Scutari, and there an envoy arrived from the usurper to demand the cause of their invasion. The answer he received was to the following effect: "The ground we tread on belongs to the Emperor Isaac, unjustly despoiled of his rights, it belongs to this young prince seated in our midst. If your master wishes to redress the wrongs he has done we will ask for his life, but if not be careful not to return." The Crusaders then proceeded to lay siege to the town by land, while the Venetian flotilla, forcing the barrier of the Golden Horn, seconded their efforts. After six days several of the towers were captured, and, on the eve of a general assault, the usurper thought it prudent to save himself by timely flight. Without further resistance the force under Baldwin's supreme command made its way into the city, the deposed Isaac was taken out of prison and reinstated in the royal palace of Buccoleon where he welcomed his deliverers. In the first flush of joy at recovered freedom he promised his deliverers all, and more than all, that his son had engaged to do. He seems to have acted with something more than the usually limited amount of Eastern sincerity, for he undoubtedly caused to be broken many of the offending icons and he induced an accommodating Greek Patriarch to get up in the pulpit of St. Sophia, and proclaim that "Innocent III. was the true successor of St. Peter, and the only Vicar of Jesus Christ on earth." But the schism between the Western and Eastern churches was far too deep to

* The following passage from the late M. Theodore Juste's *Histoire de la Belgique* gives a good picture of the scene. "Constantinople appeared to them in all its magnificence. In place of the thatched roofs, mud walls, narrow streets and miserable buildings of the West, they have before their eyes the superb Byzantium which proudly rears itself on the summits of seven hills and covers with its vast wall both banks of the Bosphorus, Byzantium with its lofty walls, its 386 towers, its marble buildings, its palaces gilded in the oriental fashion, and its masterpieces of ancient art, with its myriads of men who crowd along the ramparts, for the city contained over a million inhabitants. At the sight of these marvels not one of the fierce warriors of the West was unmoved, and each felt his hand pass involuntarily to his sword."

be healed by such proceedings, and they even tended to aggravate the position by leading the Byzantian populace to believe that they were being betrayed. The attitude of the Christian warriors further embittered the situation, and things reached their worst when, through the plundering and burning of a Jew's house by some Christian marauders, half the town was destroyed by fire. A popular insurrection followed, during which Isaac and his son were again banished and another Alexius of the Comnenus family placed on the throne. If the newcomer had attempted to establish a *modus vivendi* with Baldwin he might have succeeded in gaining his support, and in the end in inducing him to take his departure. But he posed as a national champion, inciting the people to attack the Crusaders whenever they had the chance, and attempting himself, on two occasions, to destroy their fleet by fire. There consequently remained no alternative but the usual appeal to arms.

As the Greeks were in possession of the city and the Crusaders outside, a fresh siege of Constantinople had to be undertaken, and this time the attack was made exclusively by the fleet. There was something original about the mode of attack, for the galleys sailed close up to the walls and bridges were thrown from the topmasts on to the ramparts. It was only on the second day that this attempt met with success, when one of Baldwin's vassals, André of Jurbise, effected an entrance, and planted the Flemish banner on the walls. After this the place soon fell, and thereupon commenced one of the most complete, inexcusable and unnecessary pillages of a conquered city to be found in the world's history. Both the rich and the poor suffered alike. The Crusaders spared neither patrician palace, nor plebeian cottage. The acts of vandalism committed on public monuments, works of antiquity and edifices devoted to religious purposes surpassed description, and even enumeration. St. Sophia lost its plate, and the famous marble tables of the Apostles were fractured by the mallets and maces of the knights. Many a marble masterpiece of Greek genius suffered defacement, still more numerous were the brass or other metal statues melted down into money. Almost alone amid the prevailing destruction the four horses of Lysippus were carried off by the Venetians to decorate their city where they still attract the admiring attention of the traveller. The Flemings only preserved the gold dragon of the Palace of Buccoleon which they placed over the Belfry of Ghent.

The sack of Constantinople by the Crusaders entailed the fall of the house of Comnenus, and it became necessary to elect a new Emperor. As the Crusaders themselves formed the only electorate their choice naturally fell on their leader, Baldwin of Flanders and Hainaut, who was without even a rival. First

BALDWIN'S CORONATION.

proclaimed by the Bishop of Soissons and then by his soldiers, who raised him on their shields in the old German fashion, Baldwin was solemnly crowned in St. Sophia amid loud shouts of "He is worthy to reign! He is worthy!" The Greek Empire was, however, divided, and in the distribution Venice obtained nearly one half, while Baldwin only retained a quarter. Still he possessed Constantinople, and his dynasty held its own for nearly fifty years. During that period Belgian trade found a fresh expansion in the East, and the commercial galleys from Bruges competed, on favourable terms, with those from the Italian republics. Baldwin, however, did not long enjoy his triumph. In 1205, the year after his coronation, he was drawn into a war with the Wallachians and Bulgarians, and owing to the foolhardiness of his comrade, the Count of Blois, he was taken prisoner in an engagement outside Adrianople. His subsequent fate was never accurately known, but he either died or was murdered in the prison to which his conquerors consigned him. His brother Henry acted as Regent while his fate remained uncertain, and in 1206 he was crowned Emperor. He in turn was succeeded in 1216 by his brother-in-law, Peter de Courtenay who had married their sister Yolande. The family of Courtenay* gave two more representatives to the throne of Constantinople —Robert, and Baldwin II.—and then the Greek dynasty was restored in the person of Michael Palæologus.

With the fall of the Flanders-Courtenay dynasty the Crusades ended so far as they had any influence, direct or indirect, upon the fortunes of Belgium. While those remarkable expeditions, which were partly Quixotic and partly predatory in their execution, but which in their origin were noble, formed an epoch in European history, they also exercised a distinct influence on the development of the Belgian nationality. No race in Europe took a more prominent or glorious part in their inception and realisation than the Belgians. The three greatest military leaders revealed during their progress, as distinguished from knight-errants like Robert of Normandy and Tancred, were Godfrey of Bouillon, Robert of Flanders and Baldwin of Flanders. If Cœur de Lion and St. Louis were the typical heroes of romantic achievement, Godfrey was the one sage leader equal to every emergency and the composer of the bitterest feuds. The incontestable claims of the Belgians to what might fairly be termed pre-eminence among the Crusading nations might be considered proved by the facts that

* The distinction of the Courtenay family, which in Belgium held among many other titles those of Marquis of Namur and Count of Rochefort, and in England the earldom of Devon, has been much dilated on by Gibbon in his Roman Empire. The Flemish Emperors of the East were crowned in the following style: "Balduinus Dei gratiâ fidelissimus in Christo imperator a Deo coronatus, Romanorum imperator et semper Augustus, Flandriæ et Hannoniæ comes."

the first king and dynasty of Jerusalem were Walloons, and that the first Western Emperor of Constantinople was a Fleming. France can boast of the wily Philip Augustus and the saintly Louis, Italy of Bohemond and Tancred, Germany of her Montferrats, Alberts and Othos, and England of her Cœur de Lion, Robert Courthose and Prince Edward, but none of them could boast of producing a King of Jerusalem and an Emperor of the East.

If the Crusades were a period of greatness for Belgium in the field of war, they also exercised a moulding influence on its history and proved a determining cause of much that followed in the next few centuries. They were the highest expression of chivalry, and the most strenuous effort of the feudal system. But in the result they largely contributed to the fall of both. It may be said that the great majority of the noble classes responded to the appeal to assume the Cross, and as a consequence many families were exterminated, and all diminished in numbers during campaigns of exceptional length, severity and danger. Nor were the dangers of field and flood the only enfeebling causes at work. The counts and barons hypothecated their lands and castles to equip their forces and defray the initial cost of conveying their troops to what they hoped would be the scene of a profitable enterprise. But very little spoil fell to the lot of the Crusaders, and the hypothecated lands and palaces passed out of their hands. Both in numbers and in wealth the representatives of feudalism were enfeebled by the exceptional efforts and sacrifices of the Crusades, and in no form did they receive any equivalent or compensation. This was more or less true in every participating country, but in none was the lesson more true or obvious than in Belgium, which, in comparison with its size and population, had taken a larger share than any other in the Crusades. In another respect the crusades were especially injurious to the ruling classes in Flanders and Brabant. The Belgians have always had a hard fight of it to preserve their independence between their great powerful neighbours of France and Germany. In the early middle ages their chiefs were vassals of both states, and the ambitious King of France, Philip Augustus, took advantage of the absence of the Counts of Flanders to encroach on their territory, and enlarge his own at their expense. This belongs to another chapter, but in summing up the consequences of the Crusades to Belgium, a reference to this fact is necessary, because it shows that the leaders of the Crusades were not entitled to the praise of being statesmen. They allowed their strength to be sapped, their attention to be diverted from their own interests, and their enemies to profit by their absence while they pursued a phantom. From every point of view the First Crusade escapes censure and even criticism. The object was noble, and the participation of all the states prevented any single one from attempting to take an unfair advantage over its neighbours. But it resulted in a great disillusion. The losses incurred were immense and produced a general feebleness, especially amongst the smaller states. With the fullest allowance for sentiment it may be doubted whether the capture of Jerusalem was an adequate return for the lives of the half million men sacrificed to effect it. But while much may be said in favour of the First Crusade and its participants, it was also a warning. Expeditions to the Holy Land could not be free from danger and loss, and they certainly could not prove profitable. The spoil of the Saracen camp at Tours was not to be rediscovered on the deserts of Syria. Those who took part in the later Crusades may have obeyed the dictates of chivalry, but they cannot lay claim to clear-sightedness or common-sense.

If the Crusades were the beginning of the causes which determined the fall of feudalism, they were also one of the principal means of bringing into prominence the commercial and citizen classes in Flanders. The manner in which this was brought about is neither obscure nor surprising. Distant enterprises could not be conducted without money. The knights, who had only to unfurl their banner and blow their horn for a foray or even for a war on the frontier, had to think of ways and means when it became a question of marching across foreign states, and transporting a force over the sea. For a time the Church was their only banker, and the territorial acquisitions of bishops and abbots in that capacity added much to the power and influence of their order. But while the warlike classes continued for two hundred years to be infected by the mania of crusading enthusiasm, the industrial classes and the mass of the common people held aloof from the whole enterprise, after the first rush at the bidding of Peter the Hermit. They thus entirely escaped the enfeebling causes which decimated the numbers and undermined the power of the gentle or militant division of the community. But the gain was not merely negative. While the representatives of feudalism were absent on an undertaking that could not by any possibility prove advantageous, the representatives of commerce and pacific toil were left to pursue their own business, and that business gradually took the form of making money. The Crusades may, without stretching the argument too far, be regarded as furnishing the first demonstration, in mediæval Europe, of the necessity and indispensability of money in military operations. Before them wars were conducted without money, and not only wars but such trade as there was knew only barter as a means of exchange. The knowledge disseminated by the Crusades also tended in the same direction, for the trading towns of Italy were far more advanced than those of Northern Europe in their business and exchange systems. Among the Arabs and Saracens the value and convenience of a current coin were fully known and appreciated. This knowledge, and the spread of it to the West were distinctly favourable to the commercial and industrial classes, who soon learnt the power of money which made them independent of, and eventually superior to, the classes whose sole strength and ability lay in their armour and their arms. Thus the Crusades produced far more important and durable consequences than their authors and participants ever thought of. Their historical importance is not to be measured by the hundred years' Christian rule at Jerusalem, or the Latin sway for half that period at Constantinople. Their influence in reality on human progress in Western Europe defies calculation. They gave a new turn to the development of society, introducing fresh elements, complicating the problem by the addition of unknown factors and rendering its solution the more interesting as it became more difficult, and the more necessary as it affected the growth of peoples and the life of states.

CHAPTER V.

The Decline of Feudalism.

To enable him to participate in the First Crusade Godfrey of Bouillon had, as stated in the last chapter, hypothecated his castle and his lands to the Bishop of Liége and other prelates. This step entailed a diminution of power on the part of the chief of Lower Lorraine or Brabant, the duchy which Godfrey himself held in fief from the Emperor. On the death of Godfrey, the Emperor, Henry IV., raised Henry, Count of Limburg, to the dignity of Duke, a title which was important because it signified that the holder was the lieutenant and chief representative of the Emperor among the Belgians. It would serve no useful purpose to describe at length the struggle between this great feudatory and his vassals, which formed part of, and reacted on, the greater struggle between Emperor and Pope. In the course of that contest, Henry of Limburg lost his duchy, which was placed by the next Emperor, Henry V., in the hands of Godfrey, Count of Louvain and Brussels. This prince, who gained the name of the Bearded because he had declared that he would never shave until he had recovered the ancient dominions of his family, is considered the real founder of the House of Brabant, as distinct from that of Lower Lorraine. A descendant of the Carlovingians, he received from his parents only the Countship of Louvain and an embarrassed position, but, thanks to his own energy, he completed the discomfiture of Henry of Limburg. The struggle was continued in the persons of their children, and when the Imperial Crown itself was in dispute between the Houses of Suabia and Saxony the contest for superiority in Brabant became more bitter and a faithful reflection of that in Germany itself. At the battle of Trois Fontaines, in 1143, the barons who upheld his cause placed the young Godfrey III., grandson of Godfrey the

Bearded, in his cot, and hung it up in a tree while they fought his battle and won it for him. This war ended in a not unusual manner for the period. Both Brabant and Limburg retained the style of Dukes, while a more durable peace was established through a marriage effected between the representatives of the two families.

But when this long strife ended, about the year 1155, it had been made clear that the old supremacy of the Dukes of Brabant, or Lower Lorraine, in Walloon Belgium was a thing of the past. When Godfrey the third attempted to force his authority over the Counts of Luxembourg and Hainaut he was opposed by all their forces, and, in a battle at Carnières, suffered a serious defeat. Without wearying the reader with details, which would possess no interest, it will suffice to say that, before the close of the 12th century, Brabant was divided among the Counts of Louvain, Namur, Hainaut, and Luxembourg, and that the Count of Louvain alone bore the higher style of Duke, while beyond the Meuse was the Duchy of Limburg. The part of Belgium which began with the greater lustre thus passed under an eclipse, while the national history centred more and more round the sturdy and industrious Flemings, who not merely preserved the independence of the common land, but raised it to a higher point of prosperity.

While the French-speaking people of Lorraine and Brabant were attached to the German or, rather, the Holy Roman Empire, the Flemish population of Flanders was linked with the fortunes of France. The Count of Flanders was the vassal, for the greater part of his estates, of the King of France, and he was also the richest and most powerful of the Twelve Peers of France, as the principal vassals were called. But the position of the Count of Flanders was anomalous, for, at the same time that he was vassal to the King of France for the greater part of his dominions, he was also vassal to the Emperor for the portion known as Imperial Flanders, extending from Alost to the islands of Zealand. Until the end of the twelfth century the obligations of a vassal were not onerous and implied no loss of dignity or independence. But the policy of

Philip Augustus was to change this system, and to convert the vassals into the less independent grade of liegemen. One practical instance will suffice to show the great difference between the two relationships. A vassal was bound to render his superior help in time of war, but only for forty days, at the end of which he could call off his levies and return home. But as liegeman he had to serve for the full period of the war at the bidding of his suzerain. Baldwin of Constantinople, before his departure for the fifth Crusade, was the first to take the new form of oath, but he did so with this reservation, that he would bear arms against all the King of France's enemies excepting the Emperor, to whom he was also vassal. The astute Philip Augustus, whose views were turned in the direction of Normandy and England, was fully satisfied with this first step towards realising his policy in the case of the most detached and alien of the tributaries he desired to weld into a single French monarchy.

For the correct appreciation of the events which marked the intervention of Philip Augustus in Flemish affairs, a glance must be taken at the fortunes of the House of Flanders in the hundred years between the first Crusade and the event just referred to. When Robert of Jerusalem returned in the year 1100 from the Crusade, he found his states imperilled by the ambitious schemes of his neighbours the Count of Hainaut and the Emperor. Between the years 1102 and 1108 he more than held his own against his powerful opponents, and captured the important town of Tournai from the first named. In 1111 he helped the French king, Louis the Fat, against the English, but was drowned during the campaign through the breaking of a bridge. His son, Baldwin VII., better known in his day as Baldwin with the Axe, was remarkable for the severity and even cruelty with which he sought to restore the administration of justice, or at least to repress the tyranny of the barons. He also took part, on the French side, in a war in 1119 with Henry I. of England, and it is recorded that he not only challenged that Monarch to personal combat but nailed his defiance against the gate of Rouen. On his way back to Flanders he was wounded in the head by an arrow. The wound inflamed and he died in 1119 at the early age of twenty-seven, without leaving an heir.

Baldwin was succeeded by his cousin Charles, the son of Knut IV. of Denmark and his aunt, Adela, the sister of Robert of Jerusalem. Knut had been murdered by his own subjects, and his widow and son took shelter in Flanders. There Charles became the close friend and comrade-in-arms of Baldwin who nominated him his successor, and, in the face of several formidable competitors, he succeeded in making good his inheritance. He received from his subjects the complimentary title of the Good, and his reputation abroad was so high that he was offered, on one hand, the kingdom of Jerusalem, and on the other, the Empire of Germany. He declined both titular honours in order to devote himself the more to the welfare of his own people. In the endeavour to uphold the right among his subjects and to prevent one class from preying on another he made many enemies. Some of these conspired to get rid of him, and on Ash Wednesday, in the year 1126, he was murdered in the Church of St. Donat at Bruges. This tragic incident led to what may be called the first French intervention in Flanders. Louis the Sixth marched at the head of an army against Bruges, and the Flemings rose to a man to avenge their Count. All the murderers and conspirators were in their turn slain or executed. There still remained the difficult task of choosing a new Count, for Charles, like his predecessor, had no heir. Many candidates presented themselves, among others, Henry I. of England, in right of his mother, Matilda of Flanders. Only two serious competitors remained. One was William Clito, grandson of the Conqueror and Matilda, and the other was Thierry of Alsace, whose claims were derived from his mother Gertrude, another sister of Robert of Jerusalem. The latter was the popular candidate, being called "the natural lord and inheritor of the land" by the Flemish chroniclers, but on the other hand the French King favoured the former as being more likely to assist his own projects. He, therefore, proclaimed William Clito the new Count of Flanders, and at an assembly at Arras he gained over the nobles of Flanders to his views. But the people of Flanders, and more particularly of Bruges, its capital, were not of the same way of thinking. They held several meetings, summoned the other towns and especially Ghent to co-operate with them, and appointed a deputation to discuss the matter with the King, because they wished to have as Count the man who would best defend their rights and privileges and, at the same time, preserve the peace essential for the success of their trade. Louis, however, stood firm in his plan and the Bruges citizens found themselves compelled, to "their very great regret," to accept the French nominee. William Clito, at the instigation of Louis, began his rule with various concessions to the citizens, and several of the smaller towns, such as Thielt and St. Omer, received their first charters at his hands. But this policy of conciliating the representatives of trade by concessions was far from being congenial to the rough Norman warrior. He soon cast aside his pretensions to rank as a reformer, and he deeply offended the local aristocracy by placing Normans in positions of authority. But of all his measures none so deeply offended the people as his sudden determination to recall the Jews, who had been expelled not long before his nomination. At this, one town rose after another, expelling his representatives and closing their gates in the face of his forces. The leaders of the movement at Ghent attempted to arrange a settlement by proposing a peaceful and unarmed conference at Ypres. William feigned acquiescence but filled the town with his troops. A contest being clearly inevitable, Thierry of Alsace was invited to take the lead of the national party, while, for the first time, a request was sent to England for aid against the King of France.

The preparations for the war began with set formalities. The Flemings repudiated William, and denied the right of Louis to nominate their Count. The King summoned Thierry to leave Flanders, and his ally, the Bishop of Tournai, placed the recalcitrant Flemings under the ban of excommunication. In the campaign that followed, Thierry was besieged in Lille, which he successfully defended until Louis and his forces were called off to oppose an English army that was operating on their rear, and threatening France herself with invasion. Thierry and William were thus left face to face, and the former assumed the offensive only, however, to suffer defeat in two engagements. He was pursued by William to Alost, and, as the Norman had received a strong reinforcement from the Duke of Brabant, things looked black for the popular side. The lucky or well-directed shaft of a Flemish cross-bowman ended the contest. William, riding round the walls of Alost to offer terms to all the garrison and citizens, on the condition of Thierry's surrender, presented an easy mark to a bowman who wounded him in the shoulder. The wound proved mortal, and immediately after his death the bitter struggle, which seemed likely to prove endless, ceased. Thierry became, *de facto*, Count of Flanders, and was recognised as such by the King of France. The part he took in the second Crusade has been already described, but it needs to be added that he proved himself a wise and pacific prince in his own land, showing that he thoroughly understood its necessities and the peculiar views of a people seeking to carry on industrial labours in an age and society that thought only of war, and recognised no law save that of the stronger.

In the year 1157, Thierry took his final departure for the Holy Land, resigning his rights to his eldest son Philip. The new Count justified his selection by a series of successes in the field of diplomacy as well as of arms. He began by putting an end to the undue pretensions of the Counts of Holland, who had shaken off their vassalage to the house of Flanders, and who imposed prohibitive duties on the traffic down the Meuse and the Scheldt. He freed those rivers by carrying off the Count of Holland, and retaining him as a prisoner until he expressed contrition and swore to obey the legitimate orders of his suzerain. Another important event of his rule, as much from the political as the social point of view, was the marriage of his sister Margaret with Baldwin, Count of Hainaut. By the marriage agreement the two states concluded, for the first time, an offensive and defensive alliance, with a reservation in the cases only of the King of France and the Bishop of Liége. But still, even with this qualification, the step may be termed a first move in the direction of unity. About this time, Henry the Second of England, having expelled all Flemings from the island, found himself embroiled with his eldest son, and also with the Pope. This seemed to offer his hereditary enemy of France a good opportunity for interference, and as the Count of Flanders wished to avenge the wrongs of his countrymen, and also to maintain the profitable intercourse with England, he cordially joined his suzerain in so promising an adventure. But the result was disappointing, for Henry the Second, at the head of a mercenary army, largely composed of Brabanters, baffled his enemies, and Philip of Flanders was fain to seek more easily gained laurels as a Crusader in the manner described in the last chapter.

The influence of Flanders at this period in the councils of France may be judged from the fact that Philip was godfather of the young king, Philip Augustus, who was engaged while yet an infant to Isabella of Hainaut, niece of this Count of Flanders. But this French marriage was a great loss to the Flemings, for the dowry given with Isabella consisted of the Countdom of Artois, including St. Omer and other important places. A civil, or rather family, war soon followed between Flanders and Hainaut, further enfeebling their position and strengthening that of their ambitious neighbour. Baldwin the Fifth of Hainaut, although inferior in men and resources to Philip of Flanders, made a stubborn resistance, and when the latter finally broke with the French king, he effected an alliance with Philip Augustus, and thus recovered all he had lost in the earlier stages of a struggle which was quite bewildering in the changes of parties, and in the transference of allegiance from one side to the other. The third Crusade in which the two Philips, as well as Richard of England, took part, put an end to these contests, while the early return of Philip Augustus from the Holy Land facilitated the realisation of the schemes to which attention has been called. The death of Philip of Flanders in the breach of Acre opened the door for those diplomatic intrigues in which Philip Augustus showed himself as adept as Richelieu and Mazarin long afterwards.

The death of Philip without direct heirs made his sister Margaret, Countess of Hainaut, the successor to the title and estates of Flanders, and her husband Baldwin took prompt action to enforce her rights. At the same time Ghent declared for Matilda of Portugal, the second wife and widow of Philip. The dispute between the Flemish chiefs and the King of France was not allowed to proceed to a head, as both sides agreed to accept arbitration. The question at issue was submitted to two Bishops and two Abbots, who decided that Artois went to France, and that the rest of Flanders should belong to Baldwin, excepting those towns which Matilda retained in guarantee of her dowry. The treaty union between Hainaut and Flanders, after an interval of hostility and dissension, was thus given a firmer and more consistent form by the uniting of the two countships into one under the Hainaut family. Baldwin's good fortune did not end here for his maternal uncle, the third Henry of Luxembourg made him his heir, and left him the Marquisate of Namur and the large possessions of Luxembourg and Ardenne. It is true that Henry, on marrying a second time and having a daughter, wished to go back on his promise, but the firmness of the Emperor in supporting the Count of Hainaut, and in declaring that he would never tolerate the presence of a French chief in Luxembourg prevented any deviation from the terms of his original will. The question long continued, however, to agitate the minds of the people of Flanders, and it even caused several wars which were rendered the more serious by the intervention of Brabant. The Duke of that state, jealous and apprehensive of the growing power of Flanders, arrayed his forces on the side of Luxembourg. But Baldwin anticipated the danger by routing the army of Luxembourg at Neuville on the river Mehaigne in July, 1194. In consequence of this success, Brabant came to terms with Flanders. On the death of his wife, the Countdom of Flanders passed to his eldest son, Baldwin VI., and on his own death in the following year he left the Marquisate of Namur to his youngest son, Philip, who was known as the Noble.

The fortunes of Baldwin VI., in their larger aspect as Baldwin of Constantinople, have already been described, but before he went to the East he had taken a prominent part in certain events which exercised an important influence on the national history. He was the vassal of all his neighbours in different capacities; of the Bishop of Liége for Hainaut, of the Emperor for Namur and Imperial Flanders, and of the King of France for Flanders. At the same time he was a potentate of great power and resources, not afraid to compete on equal terms with any of his suzerains. He felt a special repugnance in admitting the overlordship of France, and Philip Augustus thought it politic to lighten the concession for Baldwin by promising him the castle of Mortagne in the Tournai country. He had, however, no intention of fulfilling his promise, and thus really defeated his own policy, for on Baldwin discovering that he had been duped, his oath of vassalage did not deter him for a moment from concluding an alliance with Richard of England against the common foe. In the course of this war, Richard was killed before Chaluz, but the Count of Flanders made such an obstinate defence that Philip was glad enough to make peace on honourable terms with his resolute vassal. Baldwin followed up this meritorious success by instituting several practical reforms, and by patronising education and letters, but, unfortunately for his country, he yielded to the fascination which the Crusades still exercised and left Flanders to take part in the Fifth Crusade after the death of Saladin. It has already been seen how he became Emperor of the East and ruler of Constantinople.

Baldwin's departure for the East was the signal for the outbreak of troubles in his own country. They began with the tyrannical proceedings of Matilda of Portugal, the widow of Philip of Alsace. She had married secondly Eudes, Count of Burgundy, whose extravagance led her to commit many exactions on the people of the districts assigned to her for a dower. It was during these disturbances that news came of Baldwin's death, and Philip Augustus, ever on the watch for self-aggrandisement, at once put forward his claim to the guardianship of the two daughters that Baldwin had left under the charge of his brother, Philip of Namur, whose aid the French King gained over by giving him his own daughter in marriage. It was no doubt through his connivance that Philip Augustus succeeded in carrying off, surreptitiously from the castle of Ghent, the two young ladies themselves. Philip of Namur became in consequence the object of Flemish hatred and contempt, and dying soon afterwards his estates passed to his sister Yolande, the wife of Peter of Courtenay. Meantime Joan, the elder daughter of Baldwin, and Countess of both Flanders and Hainaut, had married a foreign prince, Ferrand of Portugal. At first the tool of Philip Augustus, his indignant subjects had obliged him to quit the side of France for that of England. Unfortunately for Flanders, the English ruler was the weak and perfidious John who, on succeeding in coming to terms with France, left his ally to bear the brunt of the French attack alone. The terrible French invasion of 1213, the first of many succeeding scourges of the same kind, found Flanders quite unready to meet the storm. One town fell into the hands of the French after another, and only Ghent successfully resisted them. The port of Damme on the Zwyn was also seized by the French fleet of 1700 ships, and Flemish greatness seemed about to pass under a long eclipse. However, some aid came from England in the person of the Earl of Salisbury whose fleet defeated the French near Damme, and Philip Augustus found himself obliged to retreat, first destroying the remainder of his fleet and then burning and pillaging the whole country along his line of march. He spared Lille because he thought it would remain loyal to him, but on the approach of Ferrand's forces it opened its gates, whereupon Philip Augustus retraced his steps and pillaged the town, afterwards setting it on fire.

The French invasion left deep resentment behind it, and Ferrand was followed by the Flemish people with enthusiasm when he organised a league of all the races of Belgium, and an alliance with the Emperor and with England for the punishment of Philip Augustus. A formidable host was thus raised for the invasion of France, which was to be divided among its conquerors. In attempting too much the confederates probably defeated their own objects, for the English army, which might have been invaluable in Normandy and Picardy, was despatched to Guienne, where its services were useless. Philip Augustus showed a bold front to the danger by which he was menaced, and advanced to defend his frontier at the head of a considerable army which was especially strong in cavalry. Up to this stage of his career, Philip Augustus had shown rather the astuteness of a statesman than the qualities of a great general. It was at Bouvines, a little south of Tournai and not far from the memorable field of Fontenoy, that the two armies came into collision on Sunday, 27 July, 1214. One of the most desperately contested battles of the Middle Ages followed, and in the result the French king won a decisive victory, thus marking an epoch which is often considered the birth or starting point of modern France. The Count Ferrand was one of the many noble prisoners taken, and passed twelve years in the Louvre before his ransom was effected. During that period his wife Joan, Countess of Flanders in her own right it will be remembered, ruled the two provinces of Flanders and Hainaut, wisely and with benefit to the people, for she was induced, either by her necessities or her inclination, to favour the inhabitants of the towns. This policy caused some resentment among the greater vassals, whose power had been much shaken by the losses at Bouvines as well as by the drain from the Crusades, and inclined them the more readily to give ear to a hermit, known as "the pilgrim with the long beard" who declared that he was Baldwin of Constantinople. The success of the movement, at the head of which he was placed, was so rapid and complete that Joan was obliged to take refuge in the strong fortress of Mons, and would probably have lost all her territory but for the intervention of Louis the Eighth, son and successor of Philip Augustus. He was able to expose the imposture, and the false Baldwin paid the penalty of his offence by being hung in chains before the market house at Lille. This movement, by throwing France and the Flemish court again into close relationship, simplified the negotiations for the release of the imprisoned Ferrand. He died not long afterwards, without leaving any heir, and his widow remarried Thomas, Count de Maurienne, by whom also she had no children. On Joan retiring into a Convent, in 1244, her sister Margaret succeeded to the government of Flanders. and Hainaut.

It will be allowed to the credit of Joan, who from her father's position was commonly known as Joan of Constantinople, that she kept the two states she inherited united, and that, despite some desperate and disastrous wars, the country increased in prosperity under her rule. But Margaret undid her sister's work, and lost as much as she retained. The principal knight at the court of Flanders during this period was Bouchard D'Avesnes, son of that James D'Avesnes who was killed in Cœur de Lion's company in Palestine. Bouchard was originally intended for the Church, but after attaining a certain rank he had abandoned the cowl for the helmet, and stood first among the chivalry of his country. When Baldwin went to the East he left Bouchard joint-guardian, with his brother Philip of Namur, of his two daughters. What was not agreed upon was that the guardian should fall in love with the ward, but Margaret had no objection and a marriage was duly celebrated and with unusual magnificence. Of this marriage two sons were born. In some manner, that the chroniclers do not condescend to explain, Bouchard's early connection with the Church had been concealed, and it was not for two years after his marriage that the secret was revealed. Then there was an outcry and Bouchard was denounced as an apostate. His wife remained steadfast to him for ten years, notwithstanding the bulls of excommunication issued against him and herself, but as she seems to have remarried the very year that she separated from him we are left in a state of doubt as to whether she left him through fear of the Church, or from her affection for his successor. Her second husband was William, Count de Dampierre, by whom she had three sons and three daughters. She abandoned the children of her first marriage, whom the Church declared bastards, to favour those of the second, whence arose one of the most serious and embittered internal strifes to be met with in the annals of the country.

On the death of her sister, Margaret, a second time a widow, went to pay homage to Louis IX. of France, but the chief object of her visit was to obtain the recognition of her son, William de Dampierre as the next Count of Flanders and Hainaut. But at the same time John D'Avesnes, the eldest of her sons, hastened to the French Court to claim his rights, and by his violence and vigour showed he was not a man to be trifled with.

King Louis, mindful of his own interests as well as the principles of abstract justice, gave judgment to the following effect:—John D'Avesnes was to inherit Hainaut and William de Dampierre was to receive Flanders. This decision satisfied nobody, and John D'Avesnes replied with equal pride and pertinency "You give me Hainaut which does not belong to you, because it is a fief of the Bishop of Liége, and through him of the Emperor. Flanders is indeed subject to you but you do not give it to me." John D'Avesnes, baffled in France, turned to the enemies of France for the attainment of his rights. The Count of Holland, the Duke of Brabant, and the Bishops of Cologne and Liége ranged themselves on his side. The brother of the French King, Charles of Anjou, took up the cause of Margaret. Again a French army harried the Low Countries, and again a Flemish national rising resulted in their complete discomfiture and retreat. Fortune, however, transferred her favours from one side to the other, and the death of the Count of Holland, who was also King of the Romans, depriving him of his chief friend, John D'Avesnes, sooner than prolong the struggle with "the Black Lady," as Margaret was called, accepted the decision of Louis IX. giving him Hainaut and William de Dampierre Flanders. In this manner Flanders and Hainaut were again severed, but the actual separation did not occur until after the deaths of the principal personages. Margaret died in the year 1280, at the age of 80, when her son Guy de Dampierre succeeded her in Flanders, his elder brother William, of whom mention has been made, having been killed in a duel in the year 1251 at Trazegnies. John D'Avesnes himself had also died soon after that incident in 1257 of the chagrin, it is said, caused by the denial of his rights, and by the doubts cast upon his birth. His son and successor, John the Second, acquired Hainaut on Margaret's death in the same manner as Guy de Dampierre inherited Flanders.

The rule of Guy de Dampierre was marked by the stormy incidents which accompanied the efforts of the French King to reduce Flanders to the same level of complete dependence as the other fiefs of France. Margaret by the treaty of Melun had made the necessary promises which her son was now called upon to fulfil. But the interests of Flanders pointed in an opposite direction. England, not France, was its natural ally by virtue of the same commercial interests and of a close and mutually advantageous trade intercourse. Guy de Dampierre moved in the popular direction, and, having tasted the hardships of a French prison, he finally threw off his dependence on the French King. He was encouraged to do this by the alliance he had formed with Edward I. of England, as that monarch had not only won Flemish sentiment over to his side by liberal commercial privileges, and by the transfer of the English wool depôt from Dordrecht to Bruges, but he had also undertaken to pay a subsidy to the Count during a period of five years for the purposes of war with France. The league against France was concluded at Grammont on 26th December, 1296, and the Emperor, the Archduke of Austria and the Duke of Brabant were all parties to it. John D'Avesnes of Hainaut was, however, not one of the allies. On the contrary he attached himself to the side of France, although his fief was distinctly German and not French, but the family antipathies of the two lines of descendants from "black Margaret" supplied the place of patriotism and even of self-interest.

The conditions of the league of Grammont were not well observed by the signatories. The movements of Edward were slow and the force he put in the field inadequate, the Emperor was attacked by Albert of Austria, one of the leaguers, and Guy de Dampierre himself was too old to take the personal command in the field. On the other hand the French King, Philip the Handsome, acted with great promptitude and vigour. He invaded Flanders at the head of 70,000 men and, defeating the inferior Flemish army at Bulscamp he captured both Lille and Bruges. Renewing the campaign after the termination of a truce of two years, and in defiance of a Papal Bull ordering him to leave Guy unmolested in his rights, Philip reduced the Count of Flanders to such straits that he agreed to surrender, and on a promise of personal safety to proceed to Paris accompanied by fifty of his principal barons. The promise given by the King's brother, Charles of Valois, was disregarded and the nobles of Flanders became the occupants of French prisons.

To complete the effect of the loss of their leaders and to consolidate the French position in Flanders, Philip, accompanied by his Queen, Joan of Navarre, came, in 1301, to Bruges where the French faction known as Leliaerts, or the friends of the lilies—the emblem of royal France—accorded them a demonstrative but deceptive welcome. On the other hand the mass of the Flemings held aloof, and the intensity of their hostility may be inferred from the name they gave their party as opposed to the Leliaerts. They called themselves Clauwaerts from the Flemish word signifying claws, and they represented the Lion of Flanders as tearing the French lilies in pieces. The fêtes held in Bruges and Ghent to celebrate the French visit were a favourable opportunity for the display of Flemish wealth and magnificence—Queen Joan is alleged to have been so much struck by the dresses of the ladies that she exclaimed "I thought I was the only Queen here but I see a thousand around me"—but the people resented deeply the French intrusion. At the same time they accepted the French King's law abolishing the tax on beer and mead, and his new system of civic government by thirteen sheriffs and thirteen councillors in lieu of the existing unwieldy Council of Thirty-nine. These measures, because they were improvements, were adopted and incorporated in the schedule of rights and privileges which remained practically unchanged till the time of Charles the Fifth.

With these exceptions the measures of the French King were not wise, and after his departure the acts of his Lieutenant-General were tyrannical. This French chief, James de Chatillon, aided by Peter Flotte, the Chancellor, aimed at reducing the free burghers of the Flemish towns to the level of French peasants, while at the same time they were set upon the profitable task of transferring their wealth to their own pockets. In this matter they showed complete ignorance of the people with whom they had to deal. The great majority of the Flemish barons were prisoners in France, but leaders were not wanting among the burghers themselves. Peter Coninc, weaver, headed a first and unsuccessful revolt. It closed with his banishment and with the loss of her privileges by Bruges.

But Coninc returned to his city, and such was the popular ferment that the French were constrained to acquiesce in his presence. John Breidel, head of the Butchers' guild, joined him in the work of freeing his country, and William of Juliers, grandson of Guy de Dampierre, consented to lead the national army in the field. The first incidents of the struggle were of an uncertain character and showed only the bitterness of feeling that had been aroused. Several detached French garrisons were massacred and their fleet and magazines destroyed at Damme. Still the French, momentarily expelled from Bruges, made good their entrance, and if they had not united the townspeople in a common fear at the reprisals they intended to make, they might have held their ground for some time longer. Seven thousand clauwaerts under Coninc and Breidel entered the town, a pass-word in Flemish, " Schilt ende Vriendt,"* was adopted, and all who could not pronounce it properly were to be put to the sword. The French garrison was driven from street to street and house to house, and when the slaughter ended 24 knights-banneret, 1500 men-at-arms and 2000 foot soldiers were counted among the slain. Chatillon, dressed as a monk, swam the ditch and escaped to France to tell the tale of the disaster.

The massacre of the Bruges garrison took place on 19th May, 1302. In the beginning of July a formidable French army under the command of the Count d'Artois crossed the frontier to exact summary vengeance from the Flemings. The French burnt and destroyed everything as they advanced, and the Flemish army, mainly composed of the burghers of the chief cities and with a very small body of cavalry took up its position on the plain of Groeninghe outside Courtrai. The Flemish army, although destitute of the knights and mailed horsemen which constituted the pride of armies in that age, did not deserve the contempt with which the French regarded it. In numbers it did not probably exceed 25,000 men, but the town contingents were well trained and well armed and knew their leaders. The infantry were armed with spears, long swords, and the formidable long-handled weapon facetiously

* Shield and Friend.

called Goedendag or Good Day.* The French army was at least 50,000 strong and included a contingent from Hainaut and Brabant. Its cavalry of knights, squires, and men-at-arms alone numbered nearly 10,000 men, and it was the unanimous opinion that a finer force had never been arrayed under the Fleur de Lys.

The Flemish position had been carefully chosen to supply the defects of its own army and to diminish the advantages of its opponents. The river Lys flowed behind the Flemish army and deterred the burghers from contemplating a premature flight, while the fortifications of Courtrai effectually protected their right flank. The army was drawn up on a plain sloping towards the French with the ditch or stream called the Groeninghe or Guinegate and the adjacent marshy ground in the dip. At several points the position had been strengthened by the addition of wooden ramparts and fences. With regard to the temper of the men it was calculated to make them a formidable adversary, for they were enjoined, under penalty of death, to think neither of making prisoners nor of booty. They were to free their soil from the invaders by slaying everyone who came within reach of their weapons, and when these orders had been issued by the chiefs a Priest mounted an altar and blessed the kneeling army, and as he did so each soldier raised a morsel of clay to his lips and swore to die for his fatherland. Then the flag of St. George was given to the breeze, and amid loud shouts of "Let the enemy come on, we are ready for them," the chiefs descended from their horses and took their places on foot at the head of their respective corps.

The battle began at seven in the morning of 11th July, 1302, with an attack of the French cavalry which, finding it impos-

* The Goedendag was held with both hands and used as a mace. The Flemish fighter struck with all his force, either the armed frontlet of the chargers, or the neck and shoulders of the horseman himself, he broke the hostile ranks with his weapon, levelling men just as the mower clears the meadow. If a knight, suffocating in his armour, or held down by his dead horse opened his vizor to make his surrender, the only reply he received was a thrust from the iron point at the end of the formidable goedendag. Belgian archæologists are far from agreed as to what this weapon was really like. One set of authorities call it "a strong iron boar spear," another "simply the coulter of a plough provided with a handle." It first established its reputation as a formidable weapon at the battle of Courtrai.

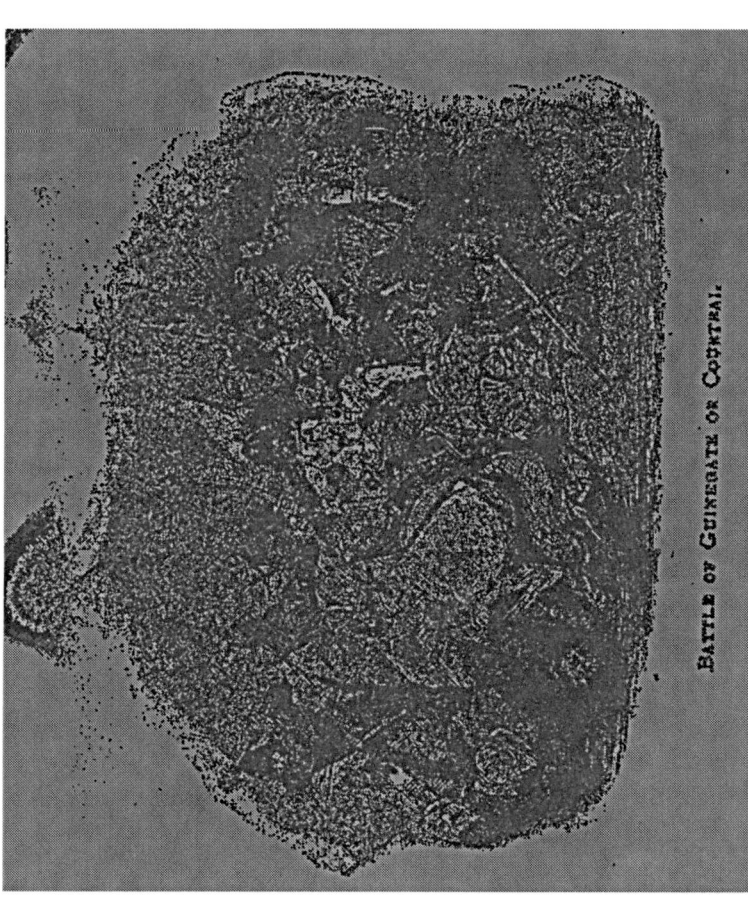

BATTLE OF GUIKEGATE OR COURTRAI.

THE BATTLE OF THE SPURS.

sible to act in the marshy ground, was compelled to retreat with some loss. The battle was then carried on by the French archers who succeeded in crossing the stream and in driving back the Flemish outposts. Their success seemed so great to the impetuous French knights, who thought they would get none of the credit or plunder of the day, that they clamoured to be allowed to charge. One of them even cried out "These villains will do so much that they will carry off the honours of the day, and if they thus end the war what has the noblesse come here to do?" To so pointed a remark there could only be one reply, and the French trumpets sounded the charge. The immediate consequence of the reckless attack of the French cavalry was the complete discomfiture of the French archers who were ridden over by their own countrymen. The ditch and marshy ground were traversed not without serious loss and much confusion, but still leaving a formidable mass of mailed horsemen fit to bear down on the Flemish ranks. At first the Flemings gave way before the shock, their leaders, William of Juliers and Guy de Richebourg, were wounded, and for a moment the day seemed lost. Part of the army turned in flight, and if the Lys had not opposed an obstacle it is possible that the whole body would have broken into a hopeless *sauve qui peut.* It was easier to advance than to retire, and the firmness of the red-coated Ypres contingent of 800 men gave time for William of Juliers to make one charge with his small body of knights and men-at-arms. And then the tide turned. Instead of the Flemish force being driven back to the Lys, the French cavalry were pressed into the marshy stream of the Guinegate, where they were massacred by hundreds. Robert of Artois endeavoured to cover the retreat by making a fresh attack with his reserve cavalry, but although he reached the Flemish standard he was struck down by a lay brother of an abbey which the French had burnt, and when he called out his name and asked for some noble to whom he could surrender he was told in Flemish, "We do not understand French and we do not make prisoners." Then a butchery of the French army began from which only the rear guard escaped by precipitate flight. Seventy-five great nobles—the proudest names in France, Robert d'Artois, James de Chatillon, Raoul de Nesle, the Counts of Tankerville, Eu, etc., etc.—1,000 knights, 3,000 squires of gentle birth, and 20,000 soldiers were counted on the plain. The body of one civilian, the tyrannical Chancellor, Peter Flotte, gave the Flemings perhaps as much satisfaction as those of all the soldiers. In the church of Notre Dame at Courtrai seven hundred gold spurs, torn from the heels of French warriors, were hung up in honour of a victory which had liberated the people and country of Flanders. The battle of Courtrai, Groeninghe, or Guinegate, is often called from this fact the battle of the Spurs, and, by a curious historical coincidence a second battle was fought on the same spot two hundred years later which obtained the same popular designation. There was one material difference. When the Flemings crushed the French, few escaped to tell the tale; when our Henry the Eighth defeated them it was to the use of their spurs that they owed their safety.

The victory at Courtrai confirmed and condoned the Matins of Bruges. Flanders had been liberated by the action of its own people. The French King made some attempts to retrieve his defeat, but success did not attend his arms. He resorted to diplomacy. Commissioners were named on both sides for the purpose of drafting terms of peace. Louis bribed the Flemish representatives to make concessions and he at the same time worked upon the desire of Guy de Dampierre, his son Robert de Bethune, and the Flemish nobles in his power to recover their liberty, so that a treaty was signed in 1305 at Athies-sur-Orge, placing Flanders in complete dependence under France. But neither the French King nor the ruling family of Flanders had the power required to give it effect. Both Philip and Guy de Dampierre died. The latter's son, Robert de Bethune, swore to observe the treaty and did his best to force it on his people, but the Flemings were stubborn. They would not waive the rights they had gained on the battle-field, and whenever French troops crossed the frontier to make good French pretensions they took up arms to assert their independence. When Robert de Bethune died, in 1322, at a great age he was succeeded by his grandson, Louis de Nevers, who had been brought up at the French Court, and was altogether French in his sympathies. Under him the struggle between the Flemings and the French was converted into one between the Count and the Communes. Louis de Nevers was besieged in Courtrai by the citizens of Bruges, the townspeople turned on him, and while the greater number of his followers were massacred, he was himself carried off as a prisoner to Bruges. Released by the intercession of France, but still more through the disappointment caused the people of Bruges by the holding back of those of Ghent, Louis de Nevers regained, for a time, his authority. He possessed no real hold on either the fears or the affections of his countrymen, and was a second time obliged to appeal to France for support. On this occasion, but for the last time, the intervention of France proved effectual. Philip of Valois and his Grand Marshal, Walter de Chatillon, led an immense army into Flanders, and, although the Flemish forces took up a strong position on the famous hill of Cassel, where they had first shown what infantry could do, their leader, Nicholas Zannekin, was induced to leave his camp and risk an attack on the French. The result was disastrous. Zannekin and several thousand Flemings were slain, the French troops plundered the country, and Louis de Nevers resumed possession of the state which he seemed only anxious to turn into a French province. Unconsciously, perhaps, but still none the less clearly he had contributed most of all his race to the downfall of the feudal system in Flanders.

In the more easterly provinces of the country, in Brabant and the Bishopric of Liége, feudalism, in its secular and sacerdotal forms, fared better. There it had taken deeper root, the people did not possess the wealth of the Flemings, and there were no communes of the stubborn metal of Bruges and Courtrai. The history of the 12th and 13th centuries there is made up of the vicissitudes of the ruling families, their descents, disputes, and disappearances. The rulers of Brabant, the Belgian province detached from the ancient Lorraine, were also more involved in the internal troubles of Germany, the endless disputes as to who should be Cæsar where none had sufficient power to wear the Imperial Crown, the sanguinary and senseless strife of Guelph and Ghibelline which only served the purpose of France. At the same time, it cannot be denied that the chivalrous court of Brabant furnishes a brilliant picture to the history of mediæval Belgium. The figure of Duke John the First is one of the most imposing and attractive to be met with anywhere during the feudal age. He combined, in a rare degree, the qualities of a skilful war captain and a chivalrous knight-errant, and when he occupied the stage the powerful Kings and Emperors who were his neighbours and titular superiors seemed to sink into figures of secondary importance. His grandfather, Henry the Warrior, after taking a certain part in the battle of Bouvines about which the chroniclers differ, devoted the last years of his long rule of 50 years to the improvement of his possessions. He took the chief cities, Louvain, Brussels, and Vilvorde, under his protection by either granting them fresh charters or extending those they possessed. He established colonies on the barren plains of Campine, and he adopted the Belgian Lion—a gold lion on a sable ground—as the arms of Brabant. He died in 1235, at a great age, at Cologne where he founded, in the celebrated Cathedral, the chapel of the Three Kings. His son, Henry the Magnanimous, followed in his steps, not forgetting to enlarge his territories at the expense of those of the Archbishop of Cologne. The third Duke Henry reigned from 1248 to 1261. He purchased Malines from the Bishop of Liége, and he asserted his authority over all the territory to the Rhine in the capacity of Lieutenant of Alphonso of Castille, whom he had mainly contributed to raise to the position of King of the Romans. In his last will he ordered that all the subjects of Brabant should be tried by the laws of the country, and exempted from extraordinary impositions except in the case of an invasion. The period of these three Dukes was therefore one of great prosperity in Brabant. Louvain, the ducal capital, became a city of importance, Brussels laid the foundation of that splendour which soon enabled it to supplant its rival. The collegial churches of St. Pierre in the former and St. Gudule in the latter testified to the architectural merit and magnificence of the age.

JOHN OF BRABANT.

The eldest son of the third Henry, also named Henry, was set aside because he was deformed in body and feeble of constitution. In 1267 the duchy was formally placed under his next brother, John the First, who soon devoted himself to those chivalrous pursuits which made his name equally famous in Christendom as knight-errant and troubadour. He and his sister Mary were distinguished, not only as the patrons of minstrelsy, but as composers themselves. But Mary left Brabant to become Queen of France as the wife of Philip the Bold. She had the misfortune to incur the dislike of the king's favourite, Peter de la Brosse, who accused her of attempting to poison the King's son and heir by his first wife. The unfortunate Mary was thrown into prison, and was on the eve of being burnt to death by the slow process when her heroic brother appeared on the scene, having ridden the whole way from Louvain with a single squire. Disguising himself as a friar, he succeeded in obtaining an interview with his sister in prison, and having convinced himself of her innocence he hastened to the Court of Philip, and demanded the judgment of God by arms on behalf of his sister. The request could not be refused, and Peter de la Brosse, afraid to enter the lists himself, paid a mercenary to fight his battle. John killed him, thus establishing his sister's innocence, and assigning Peter de la Brosse to the gibbet as a calumniator. The ordeal by combat never rendered a greater service to justice.

Fresh from this personal adventure John turned his attention to the ambitious project of recovering Limburg which, as already described, had been detached from Lorraine. The family of the Walerans died out, and two heirs in the female line of succession advanced rival claims. These were Adolphe de Berg and Henry of Gueldres, but the former, not feeling strong enough to contest the prize, sold his rights to John of Brabant. Henry of Gueldres, finding himself unequal to a war with Brabant, sold his claims to Henry, Count of Luxembourg, who in turn obtained the alliance of the Archbishop of Cologne against Brabant. While this league was being formed for the destruction of Brabant, John was absent in Spain assisting his brother-in-law of France in a war with the King of Aragon, but on his return he hastily raised all the forces of which he could dispose. The people of Brabant, menaced in their liberties, rose to a man from Antwerp to Aix-la-Chapelle, and at the head of an army, formidable by its unity as much as by its numbers, John marched to meet the confederates on the Rhine. It was while he was engaged in the siege of the castle of Woeringen, or Worringen, the stronghold of some robber chiefs, that the confederate army advanced to attack him. The encounter took place on an open heath, near the castle and close to the Rhine, on 5th June, 1288. In the neighbouring abbey church of Brauveiler the Archbishop of Cologne cursed and excommunicated the Brabanter and his allies, while on the field of battle John incited his army to fresh efforts by the following heroic address—" To-day you must be mindful of the valour of your ancestors. They never fled or abandoned their prince. Soldiers, imitate them, and glory will be your recompense. I have much to praise you for. I appreciate the services of so many lords as well as of you, the people, but a terrible danger threatens us to-day. We must triumph over it or die. Fear nothing, however. God knows I have wished for peace, and he will aid us. I will advance before you all, because I am the best mounted. You will, however, see that I am not attacked on the side or in the rear. For those who attack me in front, that is my affair. I shall know how to defend myself to our honour. If you see me flee or surrender, kill me. I order you to do so."

The Archbishop's army numbered 40,000 fighting men, while that of Brabant, reinforced by a contingent of Cologne citizens under the Count de Berg, did not exceed 15,000. The Belgian army advanced to the attack their leader exclaiming, "Forward, and shame on him who lags behind." The centre, under John's personal command, bore the brunt of the battle, and for a time it bore the combined attack of the whole of the Archbishop's army, which seemed by an irresistible impulse drawn to the spot where John rode in refulgent armour, under the great banner* of Brabant. John was unhorsed and his

* This banner, in time of peace, was preserved in the Abbey of Afflighem. The hereditary standard bearer was the Baron D'Assche—a family now represented by the Marquis D'Assche—but at Woeringen it was carried by Rase de Grez as the Baron D'Assche was ill.

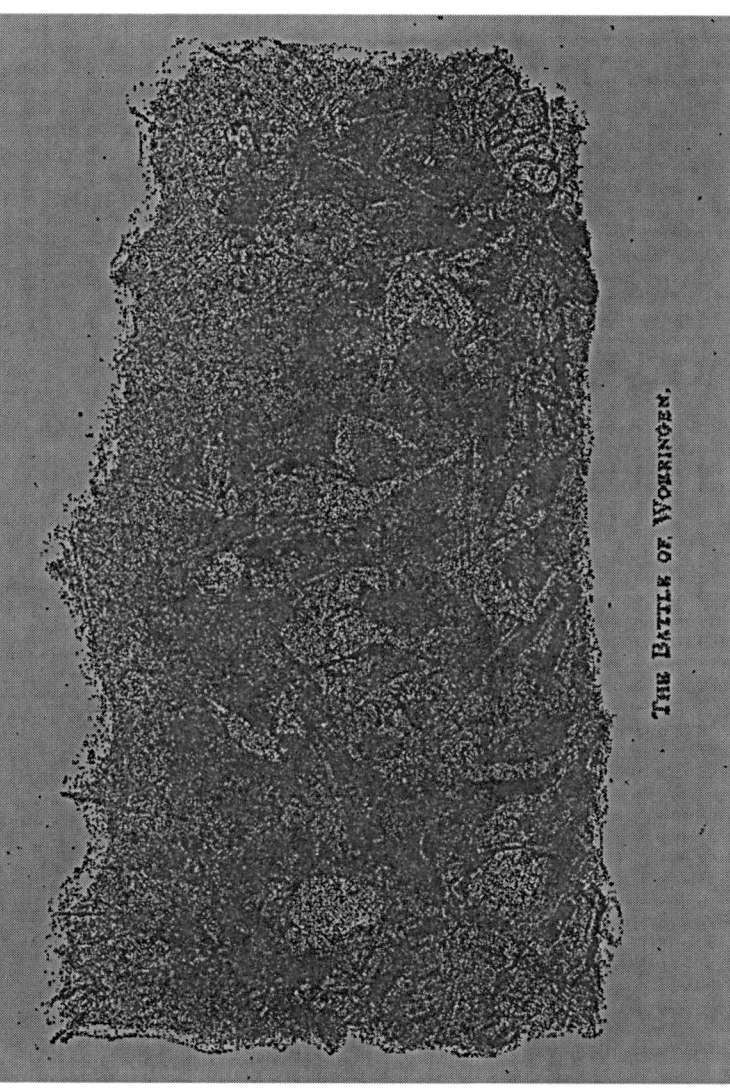

THE BATTLE OF WOERINGEN.

banner thrown to the ground. One of his knights mounted him on his own horse, and the struggle was renewed. He and Henry of Luxembourg engaged in single combat, and the latter, a gigantic warrior, throwing his weapons to the ground, caught the Duke of Brabant in his arms and was on the point of hurling him from his horse when Walter de Bisdomm, a Brabant knight, passed his sword through an opening in the Count of Luxembourg's armour. After this incident, the contest went against the Archbishop, who, with many of his knights, as well as Henry of Gueldres himself, remained a prisoner in the hands of the victor. The Archbishop did not easily recover his liberty. He had changed his robes for armour and fought like any man-at-arms. John insisted that his prisoner should continue to wear his armour even while in bed. Some time afterwards the Pope wrote to John demanding how he dared to keep a magnate of the church in prison. To which John made the following reply: "Do you think me so mad as to cause the least harm to a servant of the Church? I have never done so, and God forbid I ever should! It is true that I made some prisoners in the last battle, and that I now hold one armed *cap-à-pied* like a knight; but I ask you is that he whom you call a priest? I see no resemblance." Nor was this the only noteworthy incident of this battle, which is popularly regarded as one of the most memorable in Belgian annals. Among the prisoners was Adolphe, Count of Nassau, who greatly distinguished himself by his courage. Before being taken prisoner, he killed five Brabant knights, and on being brought before Duke John he was asked his name. After replying, he in turn demanded that of his interrogator, and when he heard he replied: "This sword which has killed five of your knights would not have failed you, too, if we had only met in the fray." At which the Duke was so struck with admiration that he granted him his liberty—an act which was well returned when Adolphe of Nassau became Emperor of Germany, and formally recognised the Duke's claims over Limburg. A general peace followed the battle of Woeringen, and in gratitude for the aid he had rendered them, John of Brabant was made "a citizen of Cologne."

The conquest of Limburg was the final military achievement of John's life, but unlike most conquerors he signalised it by making important concessions to his people. He increased the liberties of the towns, and by a series of laws called landkeures, passed in 1292, he gave them the right of electing their own sub-mayors, and other officials to govern the cities under his own Amman in Brussels, and under the mayors he had the right to nominate in other cities. He also drew up a strict code of laws which the civic authorities had power to enforce, but the Duke reserved to himself jurisdiction over "monks, nuns, priests, Lombards, and Jews." Unfortunately for his people, the Duke could not curb his love of adventure, and in 1294 he hastened to Champagne to take part in a great tournament given by the Count de Bar on the occasion of his marriage with the daughter of Edward the First of England. During the melée he received a wound in the right arm which, festering, carried him off to the great loss and grief of his people.

To complete the view given of the component states of Belgium down to the end of the thirteenth century it is necessary to include a brief summary of the affairs of Liége. A passing reference has already been made to the fact that the Bishop of that city, who was also a Prince of the Empire, had acquired possession of the district of Bouillon by providing Duke Godfrey with the sinews of war for the First Crusade. The founder of the secular importance of Liége was Notger, Archbishop during the latter portion of the 10th and the opening years of the 11th centuries. A saying was current "Liége owes Notger to Christ, and everything else to Notger." His success was certainly not diminished by the fact that his life happened to be contemporaneous with the period of the greatest power ever exercised by the Church, when kings and warriors unhesitatingly bowed down before the decrees of Rome. It may be said of him that he established at Liége that sacerdotal form of feudalism which there, and in the neighbouring archdiocese of Cologne, maintained for several centuries a power and position that enabled it to vie in political influence with Emperors and Kings. Commencing with the abbeys that depended on the bishopric, it gradually acquired a hold on the towns along the Meuse from Maestricht to Dinant. One Bishop added Malines, another bought Godfrey's property, a third placed the Bishopric in the proud position of being nothing less than the suzerain of the great Countdom of Hainaut about whose rivalry with Flanders something has been said. The German Emperors helped the Bishops, because they were their useful and subservient allies against the Pope. When the former were excommunicated for acts, not merely encroaching on the prerogatives of, but even threatening to supersede the Holy See, the latter refused to put the bulls in effect, and resorted to all the arguments suggested by casuistry in combating the Popes' decrees and depriving their anathemas of half their force and all their terror. Nor was their aid solely of a pacific character. One bishop at least put on armour, and rode beside the Emperor on two occasions when he invaded Italy as the enemy of Rome.

But while the Prince Bishops of Liége were thus able to acquire an extensive secular authority over the region intervening between Brabant and the Rhine, and to show in their sacerdotal capacity complete indifference to, and independence of Rome, they had to take their own subjects into serious account. The citizens of Liége were already known for their skill in making weapons, and in weaving cloth, and also not less, it must be added, for their turbulence. The Bishops had to display more restraint in humouring their subjects than they did in obeying their superiors. They had to concede them rights and privileges, recorded in formal Charters of which that of the year 1198 was the most important and best known. During the first quarter of the 13th century the Bishopric was drawn into a fierce and sanguinary struggle with the Duke of Brabant. The cause was the possession of the small lordships of Moha and Waleffe which, situated on the common frontier were claimed by both in virtue of the engagements of the last lord. Henry the First of Brabant, already referred to, resolved to make good his claims by force of arms, and placing 20,000 men in the field so completely surprised the Bishop's army that he entered Liége almost without resistance. There he stained his success by the excesses he committed, massacring the citizens, plundering the houses and burning the churches. The result of this raid was to provoke all his neighbours, who at once formed a league against him, but the invasion of Flanders by Philip Augustus called off the most powerful of them to attend to their own affairs, and Henry of Brabant made a second attempt to capture Liége by a sudden attack. The Bishop, Hugh de Pierrepont—a great family still represented in the English peerage and among the Belgian noblesse—had, however, repaired its defences, and the Duke of Brabant, afraid to tempt fortune a second time, drew off his forces to Montenacken. Here he was attacked by the Liége army on 13th October, 1213, and suffered a severe defeat. The victors followed up their success by invading Brabant, and Henry was besieged in Brussels itself. So completely had the fortune of war changed that Henry of Brabant was induced to make the humblest submission, going in person to Liége and asking the Bishop's pardon on his knees. The power of the bishopric being thus confirmed, it enjoyed tranquillity for the remainder of the century. The citizens, who had taken a prominent part in the war, showed increasing tenacity in upholding their rights, and an inclination to increase them by drawing more closely together in the form of "associations" or "communities," the members of which were bound by oath to remain "loyally united as good brothers."

The career of Henry of Gueldres was made stormy by his excesses, by his deposition from his throne, and by the dramatic incidents that preceded and accompanied his death. His excesses caused a popular rising under a great Tribune of the People, Henry of Dinant, who emulated the deeds of Breidel and Coninc in Flanders, and although nominally suppressed, the popular indignation was at the root of the Bishop's own deposition by Pope Gregory the Tenth. Unabashed, he resumed his position as a baron of the Empire, and lived by plunder. But he was also animated by instincts of revenge against his successor in the bishopric. This was John of Enghien, Bishop of Tournai. Pretending that he had a pecuniary claim against Liége, Henry of Gueldres invited his successor to meet him and discuss the matter. The unsuspecting Bishop accepted the interview and was at once made a prisoner. Strapping him to a horse he was carried off at a gallop to a place of security, but being very fat he died of exhaustion on the way. Three years later Henry of Gueldres was killed by a knight, Radus of the Ardenne, whose honour he had injured. John of Flanders, son of Guy de Dampierre, was the next Bishop, and under his intelligent rule the affairs of Liége assumed an aspect of tranquillity, or at least it can be said that there was peace between it and its neighbours.

By the beginning of the 14th century, to which point we have brought the record of events in the different states and principalities of Belgium, feudalism showed symptoms of decay throughout that portion of Europe which were not manifest in any other. This was due to several causes, but of these the most important, because it struck at the foundations on which the feudal system rested, was the evidence afforded as to the ability of the people to defend their rights on the field of battle, and to hold their own with the champions of chivalry. The inhabitants of the Flemish and Brabant cities did not want the protection afforded by the feudal system to the people who dwelt in the open country or, at the best, in defenceless villages. They could defend themselves very well without it. They possessed an organisation every whit as perfect and complete, from the military point of view, as that represented by knights, squires, and men-at-arms. If the field of combat favoured the movements of cavalry they were at a disadvantage and possessed fewer chances of success, but when the local conditions were more suitable for infantry their train bands or communal levies represented a force, formidable by reason of its cohesion, discipline, and weapons, to which no other state had at that time an equivalent. For these reasons, and others of a similar or dependent nature, the peoples of Belgium manifested a precocious growth of independence, and by the assertion of their rights they had sapped the position of feudalism two centuries before the Wars of the Roses and the policy of Louis the Eleventh did the same work in England and France.

CHAPTER VI.

The Growth of the Communes.

THE stirring period of the Arteveldes, and King Edward the Third's French wars, may well be preceded by a more detailed examination of the growth of the communes than has yet been attempted, for it was the people and not the nobles of Flanders who joined the English in the league against France. The origin of the Flemish communes is attributed by the majority of historical investigators rather to the assertion of the old spirit of German independence and to the influence of the Scandinavian gildes, the institution from which our own guilds were derived, than to the Roman municipalities which never extended beyond the southern or Mediterranean provinces of Gaul. Be their origin what it may, they formed a rampart in the path of that feudalism which had so completely absorbed France that the French people were silent and invisible, lost in a condition of hopeless impotence. The policy of France in broad lines was to overthrow that rampart, to crush down Flemish independence under the hoofs of her knights and men-at-arms, and to reduce the Flemings to the same dead and hopeless level of insignificance as the peasants of France. The struggle of the Flemish people with their powerful and aggressive neighbour, which went on more or less acutely and with varying conditions from the 12th to the 14th century, was a national struggle. Not merely the independence, but the very existence of the Flemish nation was at stake, and when we think how well it has been maintained down to this 20th century, over 500 years since the death of the second Artevelde, we cannot but admire the fortitude and sustained hope which kept alight, under the darkest circumstances, the lamp of freedom. The struggle between England and France, which reached its acutest stage in the 14th century, was, on the contrary, not national but dynastic. It arose from the accidental fact that the King of England was the possessor by inheritance of French territories, and it was intensified by the personal ambition of the Plantagenets to add the higher style of King of France to that their ancestors had won on the field of Hastings. But between the inhabitants and governments of England and France there were no radical causes of hatred and rivalry such as existed between France and Flanders. It was the accidental possession of Normandy which drew English warriors across the Channel. That possession was for England valueless, costly, and inevitably temporary and ephemeral. Its consequences were far more serious than any historian has yet cared to state. If the strength of England had not been strained, and for a time exhausted, by the French Wars she would have been able to lay a firmer hold on Ireland and Scotland in the 13th and 14th centuries, and to have hastened, by several centuries, the assimilation of those nations who, by their position and comprehensive interests against the rest of the World, from whom Nature has detached them, are destined to be one But if the dynastic ambitions of the Edwards and the Henries were injurious to the permanent interests of England herself, they were the means of saving Flanders from the French cauldron in which communes, guilds, and brotherhoods would have been boiled down to the same thin mixture as the French peasantry represented under corvée, tax, and toll.

Freedom has generally chosen for her home a mountainous and inaccessible region where the few and feeble may resist the many and the strong. But Flanders possessed no natural defences. A country less adapted for defence cannot be imagined. Its extensive plains from Antwerp to Tournai, from the Dender to the sea, present no acclivities. Excellent roads connected the principal towns. Canals there were for the convenience of trade, but no means of flooding the country existed as at a later period in Holland. The country lay defenceless except for its men. And when we think of those vast French armies, from the time of Philip Augustus to Charles of Valois, carrying, with the aid of Flemish nobles on some occasions, and of those of Hainaut or Brabant on most, fire and sword across this open region to the walls of Courtrai and Ypres, Bruges and Ghent, we shall not demur to the assertion that this was "the heroic epoch for the Flemings."

If Flanders, from a military point of view, possessed no natural advantages, it is also certain that it did not from a commercial or industrial. The resources of the country were few, and only adequate for the needs of a sparse population. Such mineral wealth as lay beneath the soil was undiscovered. It did not possess a great river like the cities of the Rhine, nor was it near the Mediterranean, the basin of trade in the Western hemisphere, like the republics of Italy. Yet the people rose superior to their local deficiencies, for as has been well said by one of their historians "the men were great if the country was not rich." They realised at least one grand truth, and they made it the basis of their own prosperity and power. The inhabitants of northern climes, the representatives of any society above the savage, must be clothed. The Flemings might have remained a dull and uninteresting peasantry if they had not become weavers. Yet the name of the first weaver, the truest patriot of his state, has passed into oblivion. The weavers only attracted attention when they had become numerous, and when they were powerful enough to demand, as a right, their first charter from Count Baldwin in the tenth century. But for the success of their craft they needed a sure and sufficient supply of the raw material on which they worked. On English moors and meadows browsed the flocks that supplied the looms of Flanders with all the wool they needed, and out of that trade intercourse rose a community of interest and a friendship, based on practical considerations, which was reflected in the marriages of Flemish counts and Saxon princesses, which at the period of the Arteveldes provided perhaps the most striking instance of a genuine alliance to be met with in history, and which, after forming ever since the main thread of British policy on the Continent down to Waterloo and the formation of the Belgian Kingdom, cannot be regarded as extinct to-day.

The necessities of their position compelled them to build

walled cities, and behind these artificial defences laboured and multiplied the communities. At an early period they gained the right to be ruled by their own echevins or sheriffs, although the forms of selection and investiture remained with the Count. Still the person selected was one of the burghers, a citizen and not a soldier. This meant that the community obtained some civil guarantees, and prepared the way for the acquisition of a number of privileges which gradually delivered it from all forms of feudal control. Among the principal of these, in the earlier stages of the question, was the exemption of the communes from the ordeal by combat or by fire. These concessions represented one of the earliest triumphs of civic over military justice, and when they were followed, in the 12th and 13th centuries, by the right to be tried by their own duly-elected juries (jurés or consaux), the emancipation of the citizens from feudal control might be pronounced complete. The growth of civic power and independence in Flanders passed through two distinct phases. During the first the whole community, from the mere fact of a considerable number of persons being settled together in a certain place, obtained the privilege of the Sheriff system. In the 12th century in some towns, and during the 13th in all, there was tacked on to the Sheriff system that gained by the powerful corporate bodies forming part of the community. This may be called the Jury system. The Crafts or metiers obtained the right to elect a certain number of their members to represent their interests, and, in combination with the Sheriffs, to try all cases affecting the members of their guilds. The number of these sworn representatives varied. In Bruges and Brussels there were thirteen, while in Liége, which followed closely in the track of the Flemish cities, the number was as high as forty. Among the juries one and sometimes two men were specially selected to act as burger-meisters, that is, master of the citizens. One feature in the civic life had become permanent before this, and deserves to be noted. The sheriffs, originally selected by the Counts of their own free will, had gradually asserted their independence so far as to secure the right of inheritance to the office in their families. In that way there arose in the cities a patrician civic class which looked down on the mere burghers, and the institution of the juries was a triumph over them quite as much as over the Counts. The Sheriffs by lineage were noticeably less patriotic than the juries and their burger-meisters, because they thought more of preserving their privileges than of maintaining the independence of the state. The French faction, the Leliaerts of Bruges for instance, were drawn almost exclusively from the class which boasted that the functions of the sheriffs had become hereditary in their family.

The acquisition of one privilege led to the demand and concession of another. Those mentioned secured individual and communal rights, and the establishment of a civil law based neither on military arrogance nor clerical intolerance, but adapted to the special conditions of a community devoted to industry and needing internal and external security for its pacific development. The right of confederacy among the members of a guild, and the privilege of taking the oath of fidelity to that Guild, as well as to the reigning prince, paved the way for the very definite concessions made by Philip of Alsace towards the close of the 12th century. Prominent among these was the abolition of the privileges of "mainmorte" and "half-have" retained by the Count, and weighing with special hardship on a community of traders and merchants. The privilege of mainmorte gave the Count the reversion to the property of a family dying out without direct heirs, for by it the trader or merchant could no more sell his property than the peasant his glebe. Intimately connected with this system was the minor privilege of "le meilleur cathel," that is to say the best chattel, which secured for the Count the best piece of furniture, plate, or other object on the occasion of the death of any of his vassals. But the privilege of Half-have, Flemish words indicating the affinity of the languages and their own meaning, was still more odious and quite incompatible with the free development of any industrial community. By this law the Count acquired, or rather took, the half of all the property left by his vassals whenever they died. Philip of Alsace resigned these untenable privileges. By his *lex amicitiæ* he also withdrew the privileges possessed by the nobles in litigation with simple citizens, ordering that the judges chosen in the cities should decide cases without fear or favour, and in complete disregard of the fact of the litigants being rich or poor. But a simpler measure than any of those enumerated revealed perhaps more clearly the progress of the age. It was the unwritten law throughout Christendom that when a man conceived that another had wronged him he might take it upon himself to administer summary justice, not merely in hot blood, but at the first convenient opportunity. The Church had so far asserted its influence that it had succeeded in exempting certain days, Sundays and the festivals of Easter and the Assumption, from the prosecution of what might be called the blood quest, but it was Philip of Alsace who, at the request of the burghers, absolutely prohibited, for the first time, the indulgence of what was called a natural right, and ordered that all disputes should henceforth be settled by the law tribunals alone. In obtaining these rights the other provinces were about a century behind Flanders. In Brabant, for instance, mainmorte was abolished in 1247, nearly 60 years after its western neighbour. The Charter of Cortenberg granted by Duke John II. in 1312 is considered the first of its kind in Brabant.

Looking more closely into the distribution of the commercial community of Flanders, we find that at Bruges alone there were recognised fifty-two distinct crafts in addition to the four great bodies of free merchants, viz., the cloth merchants, the linen merchants, the mercers, and the brewers, for in the 13th century beer superseded wine as the beverage of the Flemings.[*] The weavers and fullers were, however, numerically far superior to the brewers and mercers. At Courtrai, Ypres, and Bruges, the dead cities of the Flanders of to-day, as well as at Ghent, which of late years has entered on a period of exceptional prosperity, they were counted by their tens of thousands. At Ghent alone, 50,000 handicraftsmen were inscribed on the registers. It is difficult to speak with certitude of the population

---

[*] M. Vanderkindere in his very suggestive volume on *Le Siècle des Arteveldes* puts forward the theory that a change of character ensued from the change of beverage.

of these cities in their prime, but in the case of Ypres the evidence is positive that the inhabitants numbered 200,000. Bruges and Courtrai are said to have contained 100,000 each and Ghent 250,000. The total population of Flanders was, therefore, probably 1,200,000. To give an idea of the relative importance of the Flemish cities it may be mentioned that London had only 35,000 inhabitants in 1377, the year of Edward the Third's death. The prosperity of the Flemish cities was largely increased by their relations with the Hansa league, which, although it had then existed for over a century, acquired its first definite form in 1241. In 1252 the Flemish cities entered into treaty relations with it, and Bruges became, almost at the same time as London, Novgorod and Bergen, one of its four foreign factories. The port of Bruges, named Damme, on the then navigable stream of the Zwyn, owing to its direct communications with England on the one side and the Baltic on the other, became the busiest harbour in Europe, outstripping Venice and Genoa. As a consequence the neighbouring commercial city of Bruges, from which it is only three miles distant, flourished not merely on its own industries but through being the central and most convenient point of exchange. Its exchange regulated the value of money in Western Europe. But while the Flemings prospered on the strength of the monopolies they secured in conjunction with the Hansa league, the true secret of their success was the excellence of the articles they manufactured. They possessed the trade secrets, as it were, of the woollen and linen industries, and they were equally noted for the beauty, variety, and durability of their dyes. Only their own divisions and the tyranny of their governors lost them that supremacy at a later date by breaking up their associations, and consigning a considerable part of the population to an exile which benefited England, the new home of their adoption.

The industrial energy of the Flemish people secured them in the first instance a larger measure of civil and political liberty than was known elsewhere, and it also brought them much wealth and material prosperity. This was, however, the result of honest labour, for by laws repeatedly renewed the lending of money on usury was restricted to Lombards and Jews, who were never admitted to civic rights or justice, but always left amenable to the Count alone. The prosperity of the community influenced the national character and was reflected in their customs. The artisans earned good wages; it is on record that the weavers of Courtrai earned three francs a day for the lowest grade. The merchants made large fortunes. The nobles lived in a state of comfort, if not luxury, far superior to that enjoyed by their equals in either France or England. But while the prosperity of the nation was thus undoubtedly great, it must be noted also that the character of the people made them exceptionally lavish and extravagant. They made money freely, but they all spent it royally. The merchants donned silks and sables, their wives and daughters were so attired that they excited the envy of Queens, and down to the lowest grade of society the sums earned went in generous eating and gay apparel. Nor has the character of the race greatly altered despite the dark and depressing centuries of national existence that intervene. Prosperity has again come back to the Flemings and to all that constitute the Belgian people, and the love of bright clothes, good living, and much pleasure is as evident to-day as when Bruges was in its prime, and the Germans used the word flämisch to denote what was prosperous and civilised. Their prosperity and their lavish domestic style of living moulded the national character, which was distinguished from that of their neighbours by a marked voluptuousness which was quite distinct from, and never became merged in immorality. Good and plenteous feeding, deep carousals, a boisterous mirth, the love of silks and satins, the display of bright and varied colours, these have always represented for the Flemish race the acme of happiness, and have found faithful reproduction in the works of the most famous national painters.

The confederacy among the members of each craft partook of a military as well as a civil character. They were civilians in the first place bent on obtaining recognition of their rights, exemption from the interference of the military or noble class, and a form of justice compatible with their views, interests, and habits; but in the second place they could not so far ignore the character of the age, the state of the society in which they lived, as to omit all military training and organisation. Each craft or metier had its own distinct system, but all were divided into companies commanded by the local citizen who happened to be the most popular man of his day and district. In the large cities the companies of a single craft expanded to the size of a regiment, and even of an army. In Ghent the weavers more than once put 40,000 men in the field. These men were exceedingly well armed for infantry. The quality of their weapons was as superior to those of the footmen, for instance, of the French army as their greater wealth would have led one to suppose. Their discipline was by no means contemptible, being based on the recognition of a common interest, and on the fact that all being known to one another the shame of disgrace in their neighbours' eyes kept them from lightly abandoning a field of battle. Their cross-bowmen were extremely skilful, and for the defence of towns they represented the most formidable force in Europe prior to the introduction of gunpowder. The Flemish cross-bowman held the same superiority for the defence of towns that the English archers possessed on the field of battle. Every man in the different corps, moreover, knew his place and could be summoned at very short notice. It was for this reason that so much importance was attached to the acquisition of a belfry in the principal towns, and the ringing of the bell was sufficient to bring the whole community armed together within a very short space of time. The belfries of Bruges, Tournai, and Ghent were famous, and at the last the sound of "mighty Roland" reverberated beyond the city walls over a great tract of country. Where the town was not important enough to possess, or had failed to include among its privileges, a belfry, the summons was given by bell and town crier. For defensive purposes these local armies of citizens were effective and even formidable. The King of France and even the Count of Flanders who ventured into the cities without making sure of the people's good will soon found himself in a hornet's nest. The man-at-arms was there at a manifest disadvantage against the citizen in his leathern jerkin, and the theories of war provided no rules for gaining victories under such conditions.

But admirable as was the system of the Flemings up to a certain point it was not free from defects in both its civil and its military aspect. The merits of the system in its military character were essentially limited. They were great for purposes of defence and of defence under certain conditions. The examples of Cassel Hill and Courtrai notwithstanding, the Flemish army was no match for a French force of the same numerical strength that committed no blunders in the field from over-confidence in itself or contempt for its opponent. The Flemish citizens never produced a great military leader, or one whose knowledge of tactics attracted notice. On the field of battle the companies were arranged according to their civic qualifications in a solid body. Some natural or artificial objects might be utilised to cover the force which waited in solid formation the enemy's onset. The form of battle adopted by the national leaders never varied except when Zannekin, with all the chances in his favour, resorted to a night attack on the French army at Cassel and suffered a crushing defeat. It may be argued that the organisation of the Flemings sufficed for their needs which were the maintenance of their civic independence, but this representation of the situation cannot be endorsed. The question of civic independence could not be permanently or long separated from that of national or state independence, and that could only be maintained by military power and efficiency.

The defects of the system in its civil aspect, although not so obvious because not so much on the surface, were greater and more far reaching than those of a military nature. It represented in its essence the desire to exalt as perfection, and to perpetuate, the state of living, occupation and opinion attained by small sections of a community devoted to a special class of work. The interests of a citizen were concentrated in his craft, his life was passed in the commune to which he belonged, his political horizon was bounded by the walls of his city. As the State of Flanders may be said to have owed its origin to the formation of towns at the expense of the country there was nothing surprising in the towns remaining at strife with the country, but what was remarkable was that the same conflict existed between the great towns and the little. There resulted from these causes a narrowness of view, a certain local prejudice, which, during long periods of its history, exalted the commune at the expense of the country. Patriotism in its full and complete sense was unknown to the citizen of Ghent and Bruges. That ennobling instinct took a different form. The craft, the commune, the city, in all of which he formed a unit, absorbed his devotion and enthusiasm. Touch his privileges, disparage the merit of his class, assail his town, and he became a warrior capable of devotion and heroism with whom the most powerful enemy had to reckon. But he saw no further than the sound of his belfry could be heard. Just as the Flemish army never produced a great military leader, so did the Flemish community never produce a man possessing the qualifications of a statesman with the exception of the elder Artevelde. They seemed to think that each city was strong enough in itself to repel whatever storms might strike against its walls, and they were very much inclined to ignore those that assailed their neighbours. They had little or no sense of the importance of union, because the local interest overshadowed the national or patriotic, and the strong desire for individual liberty and for liberation from the yokes of feudalism and priestcraft did not suffice in their case to create a sentiment of national solidarity that would have served as a bulwark against external aggression. The Flemings might have been a nation, they never emerged even in their days of prosperity from the condition of a community.*

But in the time of the elder Artevelde the alliance of the Flemings was well worth having. They were the wealthiest race of northern Europe, and their prosperity was based on the possession of staple industries. It might seem going too far to say, as has been said, that money ruled the world as much in the 14th century as in the 19th, but certainly Edward the Third

* On this point M. Vanderkindere says in two sentences that it would be a pity to translate: "Mais l'individualisme à outrance s'il enfante des heros ne peut fonder une societé durable. Car ce n'est qu'en respectant les droits de tous qu'on impose à autrui le respect de soi-meme."

could not have carried on his wars in France without it. They were also an energetic race in the full possession of the power derived from the success of their efforts to end feudal tyranny so far as their associations were concerned. They also enjoyed at that moment, all the reputation derived from success. France had tried to conquer them and had received her answer at Courtrai. The Flemings could thus command consideration and respect. They had won their right to speak on terms of equality with Emperors and Kings, and in the solution of the question of military superiority between England and France the side to which they inclined must needs possess a marked advantage over the other. When it is borne in mind, however, what the Flemings were, their local prejudices, their disinclination for any protracted war that took them from their occupations, and their aversion to act in conjunction with their neighbours, it will not be surprising to find that in reality their alliance was not so valuable as it seemed at first, and that it was liable to much uncertainty and to prove intermittent in its operation. They could not be expected to show more devotion and obedience to a foreign king, such as Edward of England, than they did towards their own Counts, and as the latter could only rely on their military support for a few weeks even to repel invasion, the former could not complain when the alliance formed for a dynastic end, snapped under the strain of years. The subject will naturally recur later on, it is only introduced here because it serves the purpose of illustrating the state of society among the Flemings.

But if the patriotism of the Flemings was circumscribed by their intense localism or even individualism, there was no limitation to their anti-French feeling, which was based on material considerations and inflamed by differences in language, customs, and character. The French king was the champion of the feudalism from which the Flemings were shaking themselves free, and he was the more dreaded by them, not only because their Counts were his vassals, but because the ruling House after the imprisonment of Guy de Dampierre became infected with the desire to be subservient to his decrees. The defeat of the popular leader Zannekin at the second battle of

Cassel, 23rd August, 1328, paved the way for the important events that have now to be described.

The family of Capet became extinct in the direct male line in 1328 with the death of Charles the Fair. Philip, the eldest son of Charles de Valois, brother of Philip the Fair, succeeded his cousin as sixth of the name. The Salic Law excluded from the succession the two princesses in the direct line, daughters respectively of Louis the Headstrong and Charles the Fair. Edward the Second of England had married the daughter of Philip the Fair, and his son and successor Edward the Third was induced to put forward a claim to the throne of France on the ground that the Salic Law, while it disqualified females, did not invalidate the claims of their sons. He advanced his claims before the Twelve Peers of France, among whom was the Count of Flanders, and they were rejected. But Edward the Third was by instinct a leader of men, and a great captain. He was not to be turned from his course by the adverse decision of a body of French nobles dependent on the House of Valois. He resolved to appeal to the arbitrament of arms, but for so considerable an undertaking allies were necessary and the only possible allies were the Flemings. At that moment the circumstances seemed adverse to the formation of any alliance, for the Flemings were despondent, and their Count Louis de Nevers succeeded in coercing them so far as to induce the chief citizens of Ghent and other cities to proceed to Avignon to take an oath of fealty to France before the Pope. This was in the year 1335. But Edward was not without the means of action. He suspended the export of wool from England, with the result that the staple industry of Flanders was seriously affected, and the people of that country received a practical lesson as to the value of the English alliance which weighed heavier with them than the Pope's exhortations or threats.

Nor was King Edward without the means of exercising some influence in the country, for he had married Philippa, the daughter of the Count of Hainaut, who took up the claims of his son-in-law, and rallied several of the nobles of the Netherlands to his cause. The whole of the year 1336 was spent in negotiations carried on by Robert Bishop of Lincoln on the part of Edward, but if these had only led to an alliance with the Count of Hainaut and his friends, the English ruler would not thereby have been made much the stronger. The course of events favoured his policy quite as much as the efforts of his diplomatists. The distress in Flanders had now become deep and general. Murmurs of discontent were heard on all sides, and Ghent took the lead in agitating for a renewal of friendly relations with England. But the restoration of commercial intercourse could only be had at the price of a political alliance. Such were the terms of the English prince, and for the conclusion of such an alliance Ghent required a leader and spokesman. The Count of Flanders was at the Court of the Valois and French in his sympathies beyond reclaim. The Count of Hainaut had no influence or authority in Flanders. At that moment there appeared on the scene the greatest popular leader and statesman whom the countries of the Netherlands, in all their tumultuous history, have produced.

Jacques, Jacobus, or James van Artevelde was a member of a family which ranked high in the civic aristocracy of Ghent. His father, John, a prominent cloth merchant, had been echevin or sheriff of the city on several occasions, and held office at the time of his death in 1328. During his life he was distinguished by his patriotic opposition to Count Louis de Nevers. He married a lady of the well-known family of De Groote, which in a subsequent century produced the learned Grotius, and one of the sons of this marriage was James, born about the year 1285.* There is some good ground for thinking that John Van Artevelde was one of the hostages carried off to France with Guy de Dampierre, and that his son passed the early years of his life in that country. It is at least certain that James accompanied Charles de Valois on his expedition to Rhodes, and that he thus obtained some military knowledge which he turned to account later on as captain of the ward of St. John. On his return to Flanders he married Christine, the daughter

---

* Much new light has been thrown on the career of Van Artevelde by the researches of Mm. Kervyn van Lettenhove and Lentz among the records of Bruges and Ghent.

of Sohier de Courtrai, considered as the foremost knight of Flanders and a model of chivalry. This brief statement as to his origin and family will suffice to show that James Van Artevelde was no "simple brewer," and no positive evidence has yet been found to show that he was even a member of The Brewers' (brasseurs) Guild. It was far more probable that, like his father, he was a cloth merchant, while his status in society was that of the families in which the office of échevin had become hereditary.

He shared his father's opinions in opposing the French pretensions, and he could not but be very much struck by the sad state of the country and the great depression of trade which affected his class. He was strongly opposed to Count Louis de Nevers, who tried to overcome his opposition first by promises and then by threats. The bold stand made by this tribune to the pretensions of the Count attracted attention, and as Van Artevelde was naturally a great speaker he did not hide his views on the situation. He might have declaimed, however, to deaf ears on the iniquities of the Count in allowing France to draw from the country six millions of our modern money in less than 30 years, and in making Flanders a mere appendage of the French Crown, if he had not gone on and declared that he knew of a remedy for existing evils. That gave him quite a new position in the eyes of his fellow townsmen who came to him in a deputation to ask his counsel in their difficulties. They saluted him as "the wise man" who knew of some means of removing their trouble. Froissart gives the following graphic account of their interview. The spokesman of the delegation said "Dear Lord, we come to you to take counsel, for we are told that you can cause plenty to return again to Flanders. Teach us how this may be, and you will be giving us alms." "My lords and comrades! I am a citizen of this city, that is to say your cause is mine. Know that I would help you with all my power in what concerns the good of the country. If there is one among you who would take the lead I would expose for him my body and my goods." As all were silent he continued "Very well, then! Will you swear to aid me like brothers? Although I recognise my insufficiency yet I will willingly undertake what you ask." To which they all cried out, "We promise to aid you loyally in all things, for we know that in the whole county there is no one but you who can save us."

It is difficult if not impossible to fix the precise date of this declaration but it was probably towards the end of the year 1336 when the pressure from King Edward's measures was being most acutely felt. In his first public utterance he defined the political task before him in the following words, "It is necessary for us to be friends with England for without her we cannot live." He went on to add "I do not mean that we should go to war with France. Our course is to remain neutral." That was the policy dear to every true Fleming's heart. He wanted peace all round so that he might carry on his trade. The raw supplies of England were essential to his existence, but that did not mean that he would willingly lose the French market. Other states were impelled by dynastic projects and national hatreds, but the cities of Flanders, despite the warlike conditions of society, thought mainly of the figures in their ledgers and the freights of their ships.

The Flemings were at the same time extremely sensitive to tyranny, and Louis de Nevers left them in no sort of doubt that he was a tyrant. He employed foreign mercenaries, chiefly Italians, and a fleet mainly composed of their vessels was drawn up off the island of Cadzand and controlled the navigation of the Scheldt and the Zwyn. But of the many injuries he inflicted on his suffering subjects not one caused a greater outcry or more injury to his reputation than the murder of Sohier de Courtrai, the aged knight who had been the comrade-in-arms and in prison of Guy de Dampierre and Robert de Bethune. The circumstances under which the crime was perpetrated added to the popular indignation. Sohier lay ill in bed when the Count's emissaries burst into his chamber, and stabbed him despite his supplications to be left to die in peace. The murder of his father-in-law increased the personal resentment of Van Artevelde towards Louis de Nevers, and no doubt was the chief reason of his policy becoming more marked in favour of the English alliance, and less tinged with the inclination to preserve a middle and neutral course between the two combatants. It was at this point that England took the first active step in the matter.

Edward the Third had for some time been pondering over his French adventure, but even the inducements offered by the adventurous Robert D'Artois failed to make him rush into so serious a business. Robert D'Artois claimed to be the Count D'Artois with the right to rule one of the chief provinces of France, but even his services in the French service, seconded by plausible if false pedigrees, failed to convert Philip of Valois to his views. Robert therefore fled to England with his grievances and his talents. He accompanied Edward on one of his Scotch expeditions, and he used all his powers of persuasion to induce him to undertake a campaign in the sunny fields of France rather than on the barren moors of Scotland. He incited his barons and knights with tales of what might be done from chivalrous motives and what from motives of plunder, and he so worked on the feelings of the ladies that many of them declared that they would regard with no favour any knight who had not broken a lance in their name against the French. At that moment came the news of the troubles in Flanders, and of the hostile fleet guarding the avenues of trade. Perhaps Edward also received some direct communication from Artevelde to the effect that the Flemings had at last formed a national party of which he was the leader. Be that as it may, an English fleet was fitted out in the Thames in the autumn of 1337, and sailed under the command of the Earl of Derby, to attack that of Louis de Nevers in the Scheldt. King Edward did not accompany this expedition of which the Earl of Salisbury, Sir Walter de Manny, Sir John Chandos and many other famous English knights besides Robert D'Artois, whose incitements to the war had produced a great effect, formed part. The fleet of the Count of Flanders was found at anchor off the shore of the island of Cadzand and was at once attacked. In this battle, fought on 10th November, 1337, the fleet of the Count of Flanders was destroyed with that of his Italian allies. Five hundred Flemings of the Leliaert or French party were among the slain, and the island remained in the possession of the

English. The battle of Cadzand is specially remarkable as the first naval victory of England subsequent to the Norman conquest, having preceded the more famous battle of Sluys by nearly three years.

This battle was followed by more active negotiations between Edward and Van Artevelde. The former appointed, as his representative, the Count of Gueldres, and Van Artevelde visited him several times at Louvain where the basis of an arrangement was agreed upon at a formal meeting held in the Convent on 1st February, 1338. In consequence of these proceedings, which attracted all the more notice because Van Artevelde then stood publicly forward for the first time as the leader of the Flemish race and defined what their policy should be in a speech of much power and eloquence, Philip of Valois advanced at the head of an army from Tournai to Ghent. The strength of the town deterred him from risking an attack, whilst Artevelde advanced to attack the Leliaert faction at Biervliet. At this critical moment the citizens of Bruges rose and declared in favour of an alliance with their rival city. Ypres followed suit, and a delegation from the three cities proceeded to the Castle of Mâle to dictate terms to Louis de Nevers. The French King had for the moment reached the end of his patience and resources, and the Count had no alternative save to take over again the oath of fidelity to the constitution of his country. This occurred on 29th April, 1338, and about the same time Philip of Valois announced that he would raise no objection to the Flemings carrying on a trade with the loyal English. The exact significance of the word loyal does not appear, but the concession possessed no practical meaning seeing that the English fleet had opened the rivers and that the Flemings were resolved to trade with England. Still the question had taken a peaceful turn when a treaty was signed at Antwerp on 10th June, 1338, between the cities and communes of Flanders and England opening the English market to the Flemings without binding them to fight the French. One week later a similar treaty was signed at Paris with France, so that for the moment all the objects of the Flemish people had been attained. They had open doors for trade without any obliga-

K

tion to interfere in the quarrels of their neighbours. However brief was the period during which it lasted, this happy and prosperous condition of neutrality was what Van Artevelde had promised them in 1336, and as a consequence of its attainment his reputation reached a great height.

But if this arrangement satisfied the Flemings it was not sufficiently good for either the King of England or his neighbour of France. The former by his sharp measures in 1336 had made the Flemings realise the importance of the English market which he re-opened to them in 1338. But he wanted his equivalent and some time after the signature of the treaty he proceeded to Antwerp at the head of a considerable fleet. Here he took council with the Counts of Hainaut, Gueldres and others who had promised him their aid in a war with France. But he found them possessed with doubts and fears lest by joining him they should give offence to their suzerain the Emperor of Germany, for it must be remembered that all these provinces of modern Belgium, with the single exception of Flanders, held their fiefs from Germany and not from France. To obtain their support it was necessary for Edward to open negotiations with the Emperor, at that time Louis of Bavaria. He accordingly proceeded to Germany, and succeeded so well in his task that the Emperor proclaimed him his Vicar west of the Rhine, with full powers to decide the law and the right among his vassals. This proclamation was made with all due and proper form in the Imperial City of Frankfort, and the feudal chiefs of Belgium, including the most powerful of them all the Duke of Brabant, were made amenable to the orders of the King of England.

But useful as was the aid these German vassals could render in war it was not precisely that which Edward sought or of which he had the greatest need. The alliance of the Flemish communes was what he sought and what he was determined to obtain. Of knights and men-at-arms he had enough, his archers were unsurpassed, but the sinews of war were as necessary in the 14th as the 20th century and they lay in the coffers of the merchants of Flanders. But his first efforts to win over the Flemings to a more active part were not successful.

They had established their neutrality by two treaties, and had no wish or thought of breaking it. Even Van Artevelde, whatever he may have thought of the likelihood of the arrangement with France proving durable, was bound by the wishes of the Flemings. He and sixty of the chief citizens of Flanders went in deputation to Antwerp to represent that they wished only to preserve their rights of neutrality which Edward himself had promised to respect. Edward might have returned to England empty-handed, if Louis de Nevers had not reappeared on the scene. The Count of Flanders returned to show that the oath he had taken in the Castle of Mâle under compulsion had no terrors or force for him, and that he was resolved to assert all his privileges with the aid of the King of France. As proof of his intentions he fled from Mâle to Paris, and the presence of a large French army on the frontier left the Flemings in no kind of doubt as to what treatment they might expect from Philip of Valois. King Edward marched with his army to meet the French near St. Quentin, but no battle was fought, and when the English force retired the French proceeded to ravage the territory of the Flemings, who had stood carefully aloof from the hostilities and taken no part in them. Under these changed circumstances Flemish opinion became modified, and Edward proceeded to Brussels, where he was visited by Van Artevelde. The negotiations between them and the Duke of Brabant—John the Third—resulted in the conclusion of a Tripartite Treaty signed on 3rd December, 1339. England, Brabant, and the Flemish cities of Ghent, Bruges, Ypres, Courtrai, Alost, Audenarde, and Grammont bound themselves by a defensive and offensive alliance. The negotiations at Brussels were completed at Ghent, whither the English monarch proceeded as the guest of Van Artevelde. It was there that the most striking episode of these three years' preliminary discussions took place.

Edward, on his own initiative, and perhaps at the instigation of Robert d' Artois, had advanced his claims through his mother to the throne of France and had seen them summarily rejected by the peers of that kingdom. It was known that he intended to establish his rights by force of arms, and that all his policy pointed in that direction. But he had not been recognised as French King by any foreign power. The Flemings were in the person of their Count and by the usage of centuries the vassals of France, and many among them had scruples of conscience or interest on the point of defying its king. Van Artevelde proposed to Edward that he should declare himself King of France, as in that capacity the Flemings would be more willing to obey him. To give greater effect to this declaration the Flemish statesman proposed that Edward should claim the throne of France, not as the grandson of Philip the Fair, whose memory was execrated in Flanders, but as the descendant of St. Louis the patron of the Communes, whose name was revered throughout Christendom. Van Artevelde's advice was taken, the proclamation* was issued and the cities and communes of Flanders paid homage to Edward as King of France. While Edward hastened back to England to obtain the ratification by the Barons and Commons of this momentous step, his Queen Philippa remained as a hostage at Ghent, and there in the winter of 1339-40 her son, John of Ghent, the "time-honoured Lancaster" of Shakespeare, was born. About the same time also Van Artevelde had a son for whom the Queen stood as godmother and who received from her the name of Philip. In these acts may be seen the closeness of the alliance between the countries, and Edward, before his departure, succeeded in obtaining a loan from the Bardi family, bankers at Bruges but of Italian origin with branches in the chief cities of Lombardy. It is curious to note that among the securities deposited by Edward were the sceptre of Edward the Confessor and the sword of Richard Cœur de Lion. It is glancing far ahead, but a favourable moment may not recur to state that the loan was never repaid, that the Bardis were ruined in consequence, and that their descendants still cherish a legendary claim against England.

The terms of the arrangements concluded at Brussels and Ghent were duly submitted to the Parliament summoned at

---

* On this occasion also, Edward quartered the French arms with those of England. By the proclamation he was "King of France and of England." He also annulled in it all treaties adverse to the Flemings, recognised their independence, and promised to restore them Lille and other frontier towns whose loss they regretted.

EDWARD III. AND JAMES VAN ARTEVELDE.

Westminster on February 7th, 1340. The barons and the burgesses of the five great cities, London, Warwick, Norwich, Lincoln, and Bristol, and the Cinque Ports formally ratified the convention, approved the assumption of the style of King of France by Edward, and declared in favour of the war with France. They were perhaps the more eager to take these steps because a French fleet had appeared in the Channel, and, aided by Italian corsairs, had not merely plundered several places on the English coast but threatened to sever communications with Flanders. Fresh force was given to this apprehension by the tidings that the French fleet had seized the island of Cadzand and destroyed the garrison left there. The communes of Flanders had also failed to gain any advantage on the French borders although Van Artevelde placed 60,000 men in the field during April and May, 1340. The French army evaded a regular engagement, and after a few weeks the citizens wished to return to their occupations. Such was the situation when Edward fitted out his fleet at the mouth of the Orwell to strike his first real blow against the power of France. On board his vessels were the chivalry of England and the archers who were to become famous in the Hundred Years' War which began with that departure. But numerically the English fleet was not more than half the strength of its opponents, and there is no reason to suppose that the ships composing it were in any way superior. If there was marked superiority anywhere it rested with the Italian Squadron under the Genoese admiral Barbavara. The French fleet with its Italian allies was drawn up anchored along the coast, from Blankenberghe to Sluys or Ecluse, at the mouth of the Zwyn, the stream which carried commerce and wealth to the doors of Bruges.

When the English fleet came in sight Barbavara advised the French admirals to quit their anchorage and fight their enemy at sea. It was well for England that these ignorant warriors rejected the advice of the skilful sailor, but Barbavara refusing himself to be caught in a trap put to sea, and after a severe engagement, in which he suffered not more loss than he inflicted himself, escaped with the greater portion of his squadron. After this preliminary engagement the English fleet, with King Edward's vessel in the van, bore down on the French in their false position. Some of the French galleys seem to have advanced to the attack, but they were either destroyed or driven back on the stationary line. The English attached their boats by grappling irons to the French, and soon the combat was raging on this wooden platform almost as if it were being fought on land. Long and furiously was the contest kept up on that memorable 24th June, 1340. The issue was still in doubt when towards five o'clock troops and ships from Bruges began to arrive. While the former, marching direct across the dunes to Blankenberghe, assailed the French from the land, the boats sailed down the Zwyn and attacked their right flank. After this the battle became a slaughter. The French galleys were destroyed, the two admirals Nicholas Behuchet and Hugh Quieret were killed, the former being hung to the mast of his own ship by the Flemings for some injury he had done them, and thirty thousand French soldiers and sailors were slain. There is no more sanguinary battle in the naval annals of England, but it is right to remember that the Flemings of Bruges took a prominent part in making it the decisive victory that it was. The battle of Sluys secured the coasts of England and Flanders, and rendered possible the passage of large English armies to the Continent.

This great naval victory was not followed, however, by similar successes on land, and the successive campaigns from the year 1340 to 1345 were uninteresting in their course and undecided in their result. There is no necessity to dwell on the details of the 80 days' abortive siege of Tournai, or on the heroic episode, so often described, of the defence of Hennebon in Brittany by Jeanne de Montfort, sister of the Count of Flanders. With those exceptions the war with France did not partake of any interesting feature. There were marches and counter-marches, offers of battle leading to no engagement, and even truces involving a suspension of arms during the greater part of the year. No certain evidence was furnished during that period as to the relative strength and superiority of the English and French armies, and Edward himself was brought no nearer to the possession of the Crown of France.

But if the military events of these years were few and unimportant the political incidents and the internal affairs of Flanders proved to be of much interest and importance. They were determined by two different chains of circumstances. There were first the position and policy of King Edward. There were secondly the internal affairs and the political views of the Flemings. The English King wished to obtain a much more vigorous and sustained support from the Flemings than they had rendered. The Flemings had only so far enlarged their neutrality as to be willing to help the English troops in defending their frontier and their shores against the aggression of the French. Van Artevelde, with the larger views of a statesman, would have gone much farther in his measures, knowing well that a merely defensive policy would never avail to keep the French out of Flanders. He therefore devised fresh schemes for consolidating the alliance with England, and among these was the marriage of the young Count, Louis de Mâle, son and heir of Louis de Nevers, to the Princess Isabella of England. This marriage was first projected at the time of the negotiations in 1339-40, but it acquired more force as events showed how necessary it was to act upon the feelings of sentiment and self-interest of the Flemings. But there is no evidence on which one can suppose that at any time Van Artevelde proposed to elect the Black Prince or any of King Edward's sons as Count of Flanders. During these years Van Artevelde was the life of the cause, advising King Edward, and stimulating his own countrymen at the same time. The English King became the more dependent on his counsels, as in 1342 the Emperor of Germany revoked his authority to act as Vicar of the Empire. The defection of Brabant foreshadowed in that incident rendered a close accord with the Flemings all the more necessary. Van Artevelde was led by patriotism and no other motive to support the English alliance, but his energy and fertility of resource necessarily laid him open to the charge of being a partisan. His success and prominence made him an object of jealousy to many, but the only accusation formally made against him, as shown on the records[*] of the time, was

[*] Kervyn van Lettenhove.

that of aspiring for himself to the military dictatorship of his country. In 1343 Jean de Steenbeke formally accused him of this ambition. The matter was placed before the civic council of Ghent, and after much discussion Van Artevelde was acquitted and his traducer exiled. Still the incident revealed the hostile element in Flemish society. Van Artevelde was too great a man for a community which, after all that can be advanced in its favour, did regulate its policy by the price of linen and the cost of wool. He sought to establish a people's liberty on the only durable basis in associating himself with those whose interests coincided with his country's in the world's movement, and in opposing those who aimed at its humiliation and destruction.

One effect of de Steenbeke's charges may be seen in the decision adopted in the following year to appoint a Regent or Ruvaert to act for the young Count Louis de Mâle whose father, Louis de Nevers, had taken up his residence permanently at the French Court. To this post, not Van Artevelde but his brother-in-law the second Sohier de Courtrai was elected; still it probably had the effect of strengthening his position throughout Flanders. But notwithstanding his popularity, and the influence he was able to exert through his wife's family, there were undoubtedly many Flemings who thought that Van Artevelde aspired to too much authority, and also that he was too much the servant of the English king. But these personal considerations were as nothing compared with the complications created by the trade strife between the different cities and even guilds. The prosperity and greatness of Ghent, Bruges, Courtrai, and Ypres were the result of monopoly. They would not tolerate any competition, even that of the smaller towns of their own kith and kin. The inhabitants of the small towns where life was cheaper and where there were fewer opportunities of extravagance or display could undersell the larger in the staple products on which the prosperity of the whole state equally depended. But the proud and powerful communes would not tolerate this competition, and to give an instance of their measures it may be stated that the citizens of Ypres attacked the small neighbouring town of Poperinghe, whose rivalry was beginning to embarrass them, and destroyed its citizens and plundered their possessions with as much energy and thoroughness as if they were the barbarous invaders of a foreign country.

But this internal strife assumed its most dangerous and sinister form when the different guilds of a city commenced to fight with each other. In no city did these feuds take a bitterer form than in Ghent, the birthplace and abode of Van Artevelde. We may call them merely trade riots or a strike, but the fact remains that the struggle partook of all the dimensions and bitterness of a civil war. The weavers represented the aristocratic class among the citizens, and whether he was a weaver or not Van Artevelde was the representative of that class, and depended on its support for power. The fullers who claimed an increase of wages were on the other hand the artisans, and represented the mass of the people. There is no reason to think that Van Artevelde had any influence over the artisans who would naturally regard him as identified with their trade enemies and tyrants. In the market place of Ghent the feud between the two industries was fought out as if it were a pitched battle, and on one of these occasions as many as 1,500 corpses were counted on the ground. The disorders in their own city did not, however, prevent the citizens of Ghent from attacking and destroying the neighbouring and rival town of Termonde.

It was amid these internal disorders and civil strife that Van Artevelde had to labour for the preservation of the political power and independence of his countrymen. He had also to keep his engagements with King Edward who, after a long cessation of active operations, was at last on the point of renewing them. A formal conference was held between them at Sluys in July, 1345. The marriage of the young Count and the Princess Isabella was practically arranged, and the terms of a convention for joint military action against France were drafted. Fresh from this conference Van Artevelde arrived in Ghent on Sunday, 17th July, 1345. The faction feeling seems to have been at its height, and emissaries from Louis de Nevers were in the town trying to make the most of the strife between weavers and fullers, but above all things bent on effecting the downfall of Van Artevelde. Hostile sentiments found open expression in the streets as Van Artevelde, after his brief absence, returned to his house in the Calanderberg. The Ghentois, of whom he had been for nine years the hero, now contained among them as many enemies as friends, and unfortunately his friends were inactive while the enemy was up and doing.

What happened is told very much as follows in the pages of Froissart and the contemporary chronicles.* As Van Artevelde passed through the streets to his house he noticed a marked change in the attitude of his fellow-citizens. Many who had been in the habit of saluting him turned their backs on him, and others, bolder in their opposition, called out "Here is one who thinks himself the master of Flanders." Soon a crowd began to collect, and then to assume a menacing attitude. Van Artevelde hastened his steps, and on entering his house ordered his servants to barricade the doors and windows. A great crowd collected outside the house and proceeded to attack it. The servants offered a stout resistance, but the outer doors were soon forced and the crowd rushed through into the courtyard. Then Van Artevelde appeared at a turret window of the house bare-headed and proceeded to address the mob as follows: "Good People! what do you want? In what way have I incensed you? Tell me that." To which came back the angry shout "What have you done with the treasures of Flanders?"

"Certainly, Sirs, I have never taken anything out of the treasury. Withdraw quietly, I beg of you, and return to-morrow morning when I will satisfy you as to this." "No!" shouted the people, "We will not withdraw. We know for certain that you have long sent, unknown to us, the treasure to England, and for that reason you must die." Loud cries were then raised of "Death to him." On hearing these shouts Van Artevelde seems to have been very much affected, for he exclaimed with much emotion "Sirs, I am what you have made me. You swore to me formerly that you would defend me against every one, and now you wish to kill me without any reason. You can do this

* John of Dixmude, and the researches among the Ghent and Bruges records of M. Kervyn van Lettenhove.

if you wish, for I am only one man against you all. But recall the past. Think of my services. Have you forgotten how low commerce had sunk in this country and how I have raised it? During the nine years I have governed you you have had everything you could wish, corn, oats, and money. You give me little thanks for all I have done for you." But these words and reproaches had no effect on the excited mob, and were greeted with coarse shouts of "Come down," and "Stop preaching," and "Account to us for the treasure of Flanders." Then Van Artevelde closed the window and thought of flight—at least so far as to take sanctuary in the nearest church. But it was too late. Four hundred infuriated men held the courtyard and all the means of exit. When Van Artevelde appeared before them he was at once struck by some unknown hand, and the mob soon completed the work upon which it was bent. Ten of his chief supporters were killed at the same time, and his house was burnt to the ground.

Thus perished, at the hands of a section of his fellow citizens whose political interests and whose social welfare he had done much to promote, Jacques or James Van Artevelde. The King of England on learning of this outrage threatened to exact a summary vengeance for the murder of his great friend and dear fellow (*grand amy et cher compère*), but there were no means available to carry out this threat. Moreover the Flemings of Ghent disclaimed all intention of offending the English, or of breaking off the alliance. Their cry they said should still be "The commune and the King of England," and political schemes could not be arrested or laid aside for the sake of any individual, however deeply his death might be deplored. The murder of Van Artevelde had, therefore, no immediate or apparent consequence, but after his disappearance the alliance with England was maintained in a less effective and vigorous fashion. While he lived the King of England made Flanders the base of his operations against France, but on his death this policy was changed. The English war-fleet no longer came to Sluys, there was an end to the intimate conferences of Antwerp and Ghent, and Edward diverted his operations to Normandy and Guienne with the result that the great victories of Crecy and

Poitiers were won without the aid of the Flemish people. The death of Van Artevelde signified the end of that skilful policy by which he had made the personal ambition of the English King a means of defending the frontiers of Flanders against the incursions and pretensions of France which, since the time of Guy de Dampierre, had increased to such a degree as to threaten its independence.

Van Artevelde has been called the greatest statesman of the 14th century, and his claim cannot be seriously disputed. Kings like Edward fought for personal objects gratifying to their pride or military spirit. Their wars were not intended to benefit their peoples except by adding to their military reputation. They were undertaken in a moment of caprice, on a sudden impulse, under the incentive of a challenge which partook more of the spirit of knight-errantry than of the settled purposes of men who were charged with a heavy responsibility. The splendid royal figure of the third Edward, with all his undoubted military genius and personal courage, furnishes the contrast to the Flemish leader. The motives which inspired Van Artevelde's conduct were very different from those of the English ruler. He was not animated by any love of reckless or unprofitable adventures. He could fight and well if need be, but his views, like his profession, favoured peace. Circumstances compelled him to resort to warlike measures to attain his ends, but those ends were the independence of his people, their right to carry on trade with whom they chose, and their exemption from the tyrannical interference of the Count of Flanders and the King of France. Van Artevelde placed before himself these definite and necessary objects, and then he sought the best means for attaining them. It is true that his choice was limited to the practical alternative of the English alliance, but his merit lay in knowing how to derive from it the maximum of benefit. But while Van Artevelde realised the advantage, he knew well that he could not hope to gain and to retain it without giving something himself in return. He therefore gave Flemish policy a vigour, sincerity, and energy which it never knew before or since. The fanciful and unprofitable schemes of the Plantagenet to acquire the throne of France were turned under his influence into serious projects to weaken French military power for the security of Flanders.

But Van Artevelde's schemes were too great for his fellow-citizens. Their horizon was bounded by the city walls, their policy was controlled by the spirit and the feeling of the commune. The lavishness with which Van Artevelde dispensed the public treasure signified in their eyes its unauthorised abstraction, the whole-heartedness with which he threw himself into Edward's plans seemed nothing but subservience to England. Sooner than gain patriotic laurels on the fields of Picardy they prepared to engage in faction struggles among themselves and to crush with weight of numbers the opposition and trade competition of minorities. Van Artevelde showed them a brighter and a broader road, but they would not take it. The consequence will be clearly traced in their later history. The Flemish cities, it will be seen, gradually lost the political power which Van Artevelde wished them to possess, and which they could only gain by being closely united among themselves, and by merging local interests in the common weal. They retained much of the commercial prosperity gained by their industry and skill, but political power gradually passed out of their hands into those of the inheritors of feudalism. Each individual city continued to show in the defence of its rights, privileges and charters, the tenacity of purpose and self-sacrifice that, employed by them all for a single purpose, would have saved the state. But after the elder Van Artevelde no master mind arose to indicate the way, or to simplify the task which under far greater difficulties was attempted two centuries later by William the Silent, and so far as Flanders was concerned attempted in vain.

CHAPTER VII.

The Communes Lose Political Power.

THE murder of Van Artevelde, which at one moment threatened to cause a breach between the Flemings and England, was only productive, as has been said, of a change in King Edward's military plans. The year following that event was marked by the English descent on the Norman coast, the advance towards Paris, and the subsequent retreat before the army of Philip of Valois, culminating in the glorious English victory at Crécy— 26th August, 1346. The Flemings took no part in that battle, but their Count, Louis de Nevers, not more hostile to the English than to his own subjects, fought in Philip's cause. Another Belgian chief, John of Luxembourg, King of Bohemia, was also present on the French side. Both these princes fighting bravely, and the blind King of Bohemia in such a manner as to suggest to a well-known painter his ideal of courage, were slain. The death of Louis de Nevers, or de Crécy as he was called after his death, transferred the Countdom of Flanders to his son, Louis de Mâle, then a youth of sixteen years of age, who also fought at Crécy and is said to have been knighted on the field. The memorable siege of Calais began in the following year, and a Flemish Contingent took an honourable part in it. While the siege was in progress the people of Ghent, hearing that Edward had suffered a reverse, offered him a levy of 100,000 men. The report was not true, but Edward went to Ghent to thank them in person. Their successful defence of Cassel by embarrassing the French relieving army also contributed to the result. After the capture of Calais (4th August 1347), a truce of one year, extended into a peace of eight years, followed. The cause of that long cessation of hostilities was not merely the temporary exhaustion of the combatants, but the appearance of the Plague, or Black Death, which decimated the population of Europe, and nowhere laid its hand more heavily on the people than in the cities of Flanders.

Immediately after the death of Louis de Nevers the project of marrying Louis de Mâle to an English princess was revived, but the young count, who had fought for the French with his father at Crécy, had formed a repugnance to the marriage, and declared that nothing would induce him to marry the daughter of the man who had killed his father. This sentiment was expressed with more or less discretion because the Flemings had recognised him as Count, and sanctioned his taking up his residence in "the Counts' Castle" at Ghent. But if the Flemings were anxious to keep the old ruling family on the throne of Flanders, they were none the less determined that it should follow their policy, and, as a means of breaking off the subservience to France, they saw no better course than to force on the old scheme, which had been first projected in 1339, of a marriage between Louis de Mâle and the Princess Isabella of England. When they discovered the young Count's opposition they set a watch on his movements, and he became virtually a prisoner in his own castle. Louis de Mâle, if young in years, showed himself old in astuteness. He changed his attitude of opposition for one of seeming assent, and he even visited King Edward in his camp at Bergues-St.-Winnox where he saw the Princess Isabella and was formally betrothed to her. The English monarch, with that large-hearted chivalry which was so eminently characteristic of him, assured the young Count that he had in no way been privy to his father's death, and a date having been fixed for the marriage, Louis de Mâle returned to Ghent. The vigilance with which he had been watched up to this was relaxed, and ten days before the marriage-day he rode out under the pretence of hawking along the Scheldt. Fresh horses were in waiting for him, and he escaped over the French frontier to Lille, whence he made his way to Paris and paid his fealty to the French King.

Another marriage project had been made on his behalf. This was with Margaret, the daughter of John the Third, Duke

L

of Brabant, and during his visit to France this scheme was revived. It had a double recommendation, for France because it might detach that Duchy from the English alliance, for the Count because it would secure for him a base in the operations to bring his troublesome people to subjection. Louis de Mâle accordingly hastened to Brabant, and on the 1st July, 1347— that is to say, a few weeks before the siege of Calais terminated —he was married to Margaret of Brabant in the Abbey Church of Tervueren, half-way between Brussels and Louvain. The marriage was brought about under French auspices, and was a triumph for the House of Valois. But although Louis de Mâle had gone over as completely to the French Court as his father, he only brought his personal aid with him. He had flouted King Edward, but his subjects remained staunch to the English alliance. There were different degrees of staunchness, however. Ghent and Ypres would have carried theirs to the point of deposing the Count, but Bruges and the other cities favoured his being allowed to return to Flanders. In all these cities the old Leliaert or French faction began to reappear, and even at Ghent there was a Count's party, however much it might be in a minority. On the whole, however, Ghent was firm for the English alliance, and Ghent was in a relative sense the most important of all the cities, as the prosperity of Bruges had begun to decline.

Although Louis had evaded the English marriage, his prospects of recovering the possessions of his family did not seem particularly rosy. The aid which his father-in-law of Brabant could give him was not great, and that of France had been much diminished by the reverses of the war. When he attempted, with such forces as he could raise and with the aid of the Leliaerts, to advance his cause by an appeal to the sword, he was worsted in the field by the levies of Ghent. Discouraged by these reverses, and apprehensive of the loss of the Brabant alliance, Louis de Mâle determined on a new policy. He caused it to be made known that he was willing to adopt the English policy of his subjects, who at that point were especially anxious for a cessation of their internal disputes on account of the terrible ravages of the Black Death. The Leliaerts made the most of this declaration and supported him to a man, and the stubborn Ghentois, deprived of a leader, modified their opposition so far as to consent to receive the Count on his coming to terms with England. King Edward, either because he was tired of the war or because he wished to have some definite person to deal with in Flanders, raised no objections, and received the overtures of Louis de Mâle in a friendly spirit. By-gones were to be by-gones. The breach of his betrothed word was to be forgiven, and the young Count was to be again taken into English favour and at the same time preserve for the Flemings their much-prized neutrality. Louis de Mâle visited the English court at Dunkirk, where on 1st December, 1348, a formal ratification was given to the new arrangement. Nor did the friendly protestations of Louis de Mâle towards England end there. Very soon after the birth of his daughter, the Lady Margaret of Flanders in 1349, it was proposed that she should marry in due course the Earl of Cambridge, one of the sons of the English monarch, and Louis de Mâle encouraged the scheme which was to bury all the bitter memories left by his own conduct.

In this manner Louis de Mâle returned from exile and recovered his possessions. But he soon made it very clear that he was again only playing a part, and that his policy was the policy of Louis de Nevers, played, however, with more astuteness and fewer scruples. The proposals for the future marriage of his infant daughter were quite fresh when suddenly, and without warning, in October, 1351, Louis de Mâle banished 380 of the principal citizens of Ghent on the charge of having negotiated with England, and followed up the step by proceeding in person to Paris and paying homage to King John. There were no grave consequences of this act, because the truce following the capture of Calais remained in force, and also because the ravages of the plague had exhausted the nations. But its consequences in Flanders were more important for it encouraged the Leliaert party, and weakened those who opposed the unfettered feudal authority claimed by the Count. The exact details of Louis de Mâle's procedure during the years intervening between his Paris visit and the war with Brabant have escaped record, but there is no doubt that he strengthened his position and, that so far as he dared, he tyrannised over the representatives of the English faction. During this period, too, the intervention of England in Flemish affairs became less and less active. King Edward was wise enough to leave the Count and the citizens to fight out their own battles, confining his action to the practical course of giving hospitality to Flemish exiles and inviting all those Flemings who suffered from tyranny at home to come to England, where in graphic phrase he promised them "good beef, good beer, good beds, and companions better still, the English girls being the most renowned in the world for beauty." The proceedings of Louis de Mâle in imitation of those taken by his suzerain, the King of France, against Etienne Marcel, the Mayor of Paris who sought to found the liberties of French cities on the model of those of Flanders, contributed to the material prosperity and strength of England, for undoubtedly many Flemings came to England and established there the wool manufacture which had formed the true basis of the wealth of their own country.

The marriage of Louis de Mâle with one of the daughters of the Duke of Brabant had given him an interest, and some right to have a voice, in the affairs of that State. Before describing his intervention in it, it will be well to cast a glance over Brabant history in the first half of the 14th century.

As has been said the industrial prosperity and civic life of Brabant followed that of Flanders at an interval of a century without ever quite attaining the same height, for which there was a natural explanation in its greater remoteness from the sea. The cloth industry formed, however, the basis of its prosperity, and the weavers of Brabant were no less interested in the continuance of the wool supply from England than those of Flanders, and, as a consequence, the citizens of Louvain and Brussels were in favour of the English alliance. The two cities named were prosperous communities, each of approximately 50,000 inhabitants, and in them arose, as elsewhere, the question of disputed rights and privileges between the noble or gentle class and the mass of the citizens. Although the patricians were in greater force than in Flanders, and formed considerable minorities, the guilds gradually won from their Dukes rights and privileges which gave freedom and security to the community. The communes did not obtain these concessions without some severe fighting for them, and at the battle of Vilvorde, in 1306, they experienced a rude defeat at the hands of Duke John the Second. The vitality of their cause, as well as the stubbornness of their disposition was shown in the fact that six years later the same Duke, on his deathbed, drew up and signed the Charter of Cortenberg, which was the first regular charter conferring free justice on the citizens and abolishing their military obligations throughout the Duchy of Brabant. Dated September, 1312, this concession was amplified by the well-known Flemish and Walloon charters of 1314, granted by his son and successor, John the Third, or, as he was called by the populace, John of Caudenberg, the ducal castle at Brussels.

John the Third was a successful warrior. He conquered Malines, but was obliged, by external intervention, to admit that Louis de Nevers, as Count of Flanders, had equal rights there with himself. This occurred in 1337, but in 1346, when pressed for money to make the campaign that led to Crécy, Louis had sold his rights to the Duke of Brabant who thus acquired sole control of Malines. There is considerable doubt as to whether Louis de Nevers ever received the whole of the sum stipulated, and Louis de Mâle at least made this one of the excuses for his invasion of Brabant in 1356.

The premature deaths of John's three sons made the question of the succession in Brabant one of pressing importance. Of his three daughters, Joan, the eldest, had married Wenceslas of Luxembourg,* younger son of the blind King of Bohemia slain at Crécy. The elder son had become the Emperor of Germany under the style of Charles the Fourth. This family connection influenced the proclamation, in 1349, of the famous Golden Bull of Brabant by the Emperor Charles, which gave an Imperial sanction to the Charters issued some years before. The second daughter, Margaret, had married Louis de Mâle, as described, but the union had not proved altogether happy

* The circumstances attending the birth of Wenceslas seem to have suggested to Shakespeare those of Macduff.

in all probability, because the only issue had been the Lady Margaret during whose infancy so many matrimonial schemes were formed on her behalf.

Under these circumstances it became necessary for the Duke to name his heir, and the people of Brabant were unanimous in deciding that there should be no divided inheritance. John accordingly made a will leaving his Duchy to his eldest daughter Joan, and the nobility and citizens of Brabant held a meeting at Louvain to formally ratify the arrangement. This happened in the year 1354, and on the 5th December, 1355, Duke John died. On the 3rd January, 1356, Wenceslas and his wife Joan, in right of whom he took the style of Duke of Brabant, entered Louvain, and swore to observe the constitution of the Duchy as set forth in the Charters and the Golden Bull. This was called the Joyous Entry (Joyeuse Entrée) of the Duke Wenceslas. It constituted a formal confirmation and acceptance of the rights won by the citizens of Brabant, and the Joyous Entry figures prominently for all time among the most treasured constitutional deeds of the State, although it was no more than the ratification of concessions previously obtained.

It was at that moment of internal rejoicing that Louis de Mâle intervened in Brabant. Several reasons were put forward to justify the step. It was said that his father-in-law, the late Duke, had never paid him the dowry he promised with his daughter. A second reason was that the money to be paid for Malines had never been received. A third ground of quarrel was created by Louis' treatment of his wife, Margaret of Brabant, whom he had imprisoned, and by his resentment at being called to account by her sister Joan. In these facts or assertions there was enough material for a serious quarrel, and in 1356 Louis de Mâle led his army out of Flanders. He encountered the Brabant army at Scheut, defeated it, and occupied Brussels without further opposition. A Flemish garrison was left there, but after a few weeks' apathy a Brabant knight named Everard T'Serclaes, at the head of a small band, escaladed the walls and, being joined by the townspeople, turned out the Flemings. Louis de Mâle, however, succeeded in retaining possession of Malines. Before describing his later fortunes it will be well to describe some of the principal events that happened in Brabant during the long life of the Duke Wenceslas, more especially as they formed the counterpart of very similar incidents in Flanders.

Notwithstanding the charters and their confirmation by the Duke, the old question of the rivalry between the patrician and plebeian classes in the cities remained acute and a cause of feud and danger. It was in Louvain, however, that the matter attained its most formidable development. There the artizans, or to use a more comprehensive phrase the mass of the people, had found a skilful and energetic leader in Peter Couterel, a member of a patrician family. It is not very clear what were the grievances that induced the people of Louvain to begin, in 1360, the serious rebellions which, after continuing for twenty years, left them in a state of comparative helplessness. The first rising occurred in 1360 when the Joyous Entry was an event of recent occurrence, and from this outbreak it may be inferred that its promises had not been fulfilled. In that year Peter Couterel, who as Mayor of Louvain specially represented the Duke from whom he held the appointment,* took up the popular cause in a very pronounced manner by imprisoning 26 knights and 149 squires from among the patricians of Louvain. At that time the Duke was supposed to be better disposed towards the people's party than towards the patricians, and his intervention in 1361 in the dispute aimed at obtaining equal rights for the two parties in the community. A new civic constitution was framed at Louvain. The Jury before which all disputed matters were to be decided was to be composed of eleven patricians and eleven plebeians. There were also to be four patrician sheriffs (echevins) and three plebeian. As Couterel had too prominently identified himself with the latter he ceased to be Mayor, and became one of the duly elected Sheriffs. In the very next year, however, Couterel was banished from Louvain, and when the people were thus deprived of their leader the patricians gradually reasserted their authority.

* Mayor and Burgomaster which are so often treated as convertible terms really meant something quite different—the Mayor being the appointed nominee and representative of the Duke or Count, and the Burgomaster the elected head of the people.

In 1372 Wenceslas was compelled by his own necessities, arising from an unsuccessful war on the Rhine during which he had been taken prisoner by the Robber Knights under William of Juliers, and only released by the direct intervention of his brother, the Emperor, to make an appeal to his subjects for financial aid, and in return for a substantial grant of money he reconfirmed all existing charters. This incident goes to prove that the charters had not been very effective in ensuring liberty and civic rights, and the value set upon his own word by the Duke Wenceslas may be gathered from the fact that he followed up this ratification of the Charters by constructing the strong fortress of Vilvorde, where he felt more secure from popular attack than in the ducal palaces of Brussels and Louvain.

The questions at issue between the citizens and the noble classes, to whom the Duke had finally transferred his support and influence, reached their height at Louvain in the course of the years 1378-82. The artizans there assumed the White Hoods which at Ghent had been made the insignia of independence, and of resistance to the privileges of the oligarchs. The nobles retired to Brussels whence they threatened vengeance. The Duke made some attempts to compose the difficulty between the contending parties in his state, and he agreed to receive a deputation from the citizens of Louvain. They accordingly sent some representatives to Brussels, and one at least of them, named Walter Van der Leyen, was a person of some importance, having filled the office of burgomaster. He seems to have been received by the Duke, and on his way back to have been assassinated by two knights of Louvain. Other representatives of the commune were killed or maltreated. When news of these outrages reached Louvain the people rose in fury and demanded a summary vengeance. Seventeen nobles took refuge in the Town Hall. The White Hoods gathered in the square, the doors were forced, and this handful of unfortunate men were overwhelmed by the crowd and thrown out of the windows on the pikes of the men in the square below. The massacre of the nobles in 1379 was the signal for a war which lasted over three years. It resulted in the triumph of the nobles, aided by the

Duke. On 27th January, 1383, the commune of Louvain made an abject surrender, and Wenceslas entered the city through a breach in the walls as a conqueror. The popular defeat at Louvain was no doubt the counterpart and consequence of the more disastrous overthrow of the Flemish communes at Roosebeke six weeks earlier.*

After the battle of Scheut Louis de Mâle devoted his attention to the strengthening of his personal authority in the communes, and above all things to the humbling of the pride of the burghers of Ghent. Perhaps this latter object, quite as much as the desire to preserve feudal privileges intact, explains the bent of his policy towards the side of France. At Dunkirk, in 1348, Louis de Mâle had accepted the English alliance, and in 1350, after the birth of the Lady Margaret, he had trifled with the English ruler on the subject of her future marriage, but notwithstanding the great victory of Poitiers every subsequent year carried his policy further in the direction of France. Clear evidence of this was given when in July, 1361, the young Lady Margaret, heiress of "the county of Flanders, the noblest, richest and greatest which is in Christendom," was betrothed to the young Duke of Burgundy at Audenarde. Although the death of the young prince a few months later ended this alliance, the fates had decreed that the heiress of Flanders should bear the title of Duchess of Burgundy.

The Dukedom of Burgundy was to pass through several distinct phases after its first creation by Charles the Bald of the Carlovingian family. Almost on his death bed in 877 he had bestowed the title on his son-in-law, Richard the Justicer, and a descendant of his had exchanged the duchy for the throne of France in the declining days of the Carlovingian dynasty during the 10th century. The younger branch that remained in Burgundy fared better than the elder on the throne of France. Its Dukes, Hugh the Great, Otto, and Henry the Great, were the allies of France and negotiated on equal terms with the

* Wenceslas died in the same year—7th December, 1383—and his widow Joan ruled Brabant until her death in 1406. As she had no children she was succeeded by her great-nephew Antony, the grandson of her sister Margaret and Louis de Mâle, and the son of Philip the Bold, Duke of Burgundy, and the Lady Margaret of Flanders. (See next chapter).

Capetian family. The Kings of France by marriage became Dukes of Burgundy in the 11th century and then, in revenge as is said, a Duke of Burgundy became once more by survival King of France. In 1032 that Duke, King Henry II., made his brother Robert Duke of Burgundy, and for more than three hundred years this family continued. The youth to whom the Lady Margaret was betrothed was the last of his line. Both he and his father died a few months after the betrothal at Audenarde and with them the first two creations of the Burgundy title ended. In 1364, King John of France, the prisoner of the Black Prince at Poitiers, revived the title by conferring it on his favourite younger son Philip, already known as the Bold. This prince had fought at Poitiers with conspicuous gallantry, and accompanied his father during his imprisonment in England. A few months after this creation King John died, and was succeeded on the throne of France by his eldest son Charles the Fifth, or the Wise.

After the death of the young prince to whom she was betrothed in 1361, the proposal to find an English husband for the Lady Margaret was revived with greater prospects of success, for Louis de Mâle cherished some grievance against the Dauphin Charles who, during the negotiations, became King. In 1364 English and Flemish representatives met at Dover, and Lady Margaret was formally betrothed there to King Edward's son Edmund, Earl of Cambridge. As the former was then approaching a suitable age her marriage might be expected to soon follow her betrothal, and the excitement at the French Court was proportionally great. It was openly admitted there that if England and Flanders became thus closely united they would be too powerful for France, and consequently Charles devoted all his intelligence and influence to the prevention of a marriage that seemed almost inevitable.

The chroniclers declare that little success attended the efforts of French policy until Charles invoked the aid and intervention of the widow of Louis de Nevers. This lady, who had been the Princess Margaret of France, went to her son and entreated him to break off the English marriage because they had made her a widow. She is alleged to have made but little impression on her son, "until, baring her bosom, she declared that she would cut it off and give it to the dogs for food unless the only child it had nourished obeyed her wishes." We are told that on this threat Louis de Mâle allowed himself to be persuaded, but the true explanation of his change of policy seems to have been the promise of the French King to pay a large sum of money and to restore Lille, Douai, and other towns which had been ceded to France by Robert de Bethune under the Treaty of Athies-sur-Orge. In this way the arranged English marriage fell through. The vows of Dover on behalf of the daughter were no more binding than those of the father at Bergues-St.-Winnox. Edmund of Cambridge was supplanted by Philip of Burgundy. On the 19th June, 1369, the heiress of Flanders was married to the young French prince, who was to give a new dynasty to her country, in the Abbey Church of St. Bavon at Ghent. That it almost caused a rupture between England and Flanders is not to be wondered at. A bad feeling was certainly engendered, and with or without adequate justification the English destroyed a Flemish squadron in Torbay harbour. In 1372, however, a fresh arrangement was made binding both nations to observe the peace.

Having given his daughter to a French prince Louis de Mâle resorted more and more to the French system of policy, not merely towards England, but towards his own subjects. He regarded the latter solely from the point of view that they had to provide him with the means of enjoying the state and pastimes to which he felt inclined, and as his tastes were extravagant the claims he made on his subjects were proportionately large. The frequency of his requests for a subsidy roused much discontent and many open protests. But of all his measures the most unpopular was his selling many new privileges to the Lombard bankers who, with the Jews, were by the Statute laws of the country alone allowed to lend money. As the merchants and citizens of Ghent had to provide the greater part of his subsidies, the discontent there was more deeply rooted and more freely expressed. At Bruges the spirit of independence and nationality had declined, but at Ghent it continued to assert itself with unabated vigour. Moreover, the commercial prosperity of Bruges had declined owing to the silting up of the Zwyn, which gave it the means of communication with the sea, and it could only be restored by some exceptional effort or new departure. Unfortunately Bruges could only prosper at the expense of Ghent, and when it proposed to construct a canal to the Lys the people of Ghent protested because it would have the effect of diverting much of their trade, particularly that in corn from northern France. This was another instance of commercial rivalry interfering with and arresting the political development of the Flemish communes. Louis de Mâle thought only of his own personal needs, and when the people of Bruges offered him a large sum he at once granted them the necessary charter in complete indifference to the opinion at Ghent.

But in this disregard for Ghent opinion he went too far. The White Hoods were reorganised. A popular leader was found in John Yoens, the head of the corporation of the Boatmen, who were especially affected by the projected canal, and for a moment his eloquence and energy made men believe that a new Van Artevelde had appeared. He was also successful, for he led out the White Hoods, defeated and scattered the Bruges forces covering the works at Deynze, and when Louis de Mâle sent 200 men-at arms to Ghent with a sheriff to make him a prisoner he slew the sheriff, took the men-at-arms prisoners and tore up the Count's banner on the public place. Not content with this, he and the White Hoods sallied forth and burnt the Count's new chateau at Wondelghem on which he had spent a large sum of money. The popular party at Bruges and Ypres encouraged by these successes agreed to join those of Ghent, and again was raised the national cry "We shall all be one, they with us and we with them." But at this critical moment John Yoens died suddenly, poisoned it was said by an emissary of Louis de Mâle, although the joy expressed by the latter at the death of his powerful enemy is not conclusive evidence of his guilt. A war then followed with varying fortunes and confusing changes of rôle, the only two constant features in the struggle being the determination of Louis de Mâle to exercise supreme power, and the equal resolution of the city of Ghent to retain its liberties and commercial pre-eminence.

Louis de Mâle and the members of his party took up their abode in Audenarde which they strongly fortified. Here they were closely besieged by sixty thousand White Hoods. The Duke of Burgundy hastened to his father-in-law's aid, and by his efforts a truce was arranged and Audenarde was saved from the unpleasant necessity of surrendering. This was in December 1379, and by the terms of the agreement Louis de Mâle was to take up his residence at Ghent. He entered that city, but his very first utterance revealed his temper. He demanded the suppression of the White Hoods, and as this step was naturally not taken he fled secretly to Paris thus showing that no reconciliation was possible between him and his subjects. In France he obtained some aid and the promise of more. He established his headquarters at Lille, and thence succeeded in reorganising the Leliaert party at Bruges. With the view of clearly distinguishing them he ordered them to adopt Red Hoods, and with their co-operation he gradually obtained possession of every town throughout Flanders with the exception of Ghent. Even Ypres, the staunchest of all its allies, succumbed to the combined attack of the French and Leliaerts. Under these circumstances (1380) the people of Ghent, without a leader, for none had yet been found to take the place of Yoens, sent representatives to Louis de Mâle with the view of coming to terms. His reply was to blind and cut off the hands of the envoys and to send them back, in this maimed condition, to Ghent. He followed them at a brief interval with a large force hoping to end the war by the capture of Ghent. In this he was disappointed, nor had he better fortune when he renewed the attempt the next year (1381) although his arms were crowned with one signal success at the battle of Nevele when two of the principal Ghent leaders, Rasse de Herzeele and John de Lannoy, were killed.

Louis de Mâle's victory at Nevele caused a profound discouragement throughout Flanders and even in Ghent itself. The want of a leader was greatly felt, and people began to cry out "If James Van Artevelde were only alive then our affairs would be prosperous, and we should have peace." It was only in their greatest extremity that they remembered the great popular leader whose services had been so ill appreciated and requited in his life-time. On the death of John Yoens, four leaders had been elected, and of these Peter Van den Bosche was the best known, but their combined efforts had not brought any success to the national cause. The public references to the first Van Artevelde seem to have suggested to Van den Bosche the idea of using the popular name as a rallying cry in Ghent, for a second Van Artevelde was available. The reader will remember that in 1340 Queen Philippa had stood as godmother to the young Philip Van Artevelde at Ghent. Nothing is known of his career up to his coming into prominence beyond the fact that in the campaign of 1381 he had commanded a division of the national army. In this charge he had shown considerable courage and capacity. We are told by contemporary writers that on 24th January, 1382, Peter Van den Bosche paid him a visit and that the following conversation took place between them.

Van den Bosche broached the subject in the following words—"Philip Van Artevelde, will you follow my advice, and I will make you the greatest man in all Flanders?" "And how can that be?" said Philip, to which Van den Bosche replied, "We have need of a chief captain of great renown. You shall have the government and administration of the city. You will revive in this country your father. It is easy for me to put you in his place." "Peter," said Van Artevelde, "you offer me a big thing. I trust you and promise you that if you secure this authority for me, I will do nothing without your counsel." "But there is one thing necessary before all," concluded Van den Bosche, "Will you show yourself inflexible, for the times and the people demand severity?" "I will do all that is necessary."

On the following day Van den Bosche proposed that Philip Van Artevelde should be elected to the chief command, and the people raised loud shouts of approval. The heads of the different guilds then proceeded to his abode to invite him to take over the charge of their military and political affairs. After some hesitation and observing that their treatment of his father had not been just or encouraging Philip consented, and proceeding to

Philip Van Artevelde Haranguing the People.

the Friday market-place he was sworn in as First Captain of the city of Ghent and Regent of Flanders.*

The difficulties of the moment were great and many. Ghent was without a single ally, and the policy of Louis de Mâle had closed the frontiers of Brabant and Hainaut for the despatch of supplies to the last city struggling for political power. In these circumstances Ghent was soon threatened with famine and Louis de Mâle counted on its making an abject and complete surrender. Some of the citizens wished to come to terms, but Philip Van Artevelde, hearing of the proposal, arrested and executed them forthwith. This did not prevent his going in person to Tournai to ascertain from the representatives of Louis de Mâle what were the terms on which peace could be concluded. So confident was the Count of success that he demanded that all the citizens of Ghent from the age of 15 to 60 should come out in their shirts and with cords round their necks meet him at a place half way on the road to Bruges. On 30th April, 1382, Philip informed his fellow citizens at the public meeting place of the Friday-market of the result of his mission, and how Louis de Mâle would accept nothing save an unconditional surrender. He then continued—" You know, Good people, that we have no more provisions, and that there are in this city 30,000 persons who, during the last fortnight, have not tasted a morsel of bread. There remain only three courses for us to take—the first is to shut ourselves up in the town, to go and confess our sins, throw ourselves on our knees in the churches and await then the death of martyrs; the second is for all of us, men, women and children, to go with naked feet and cords round our necks to meet and entreat pardon of His Lordship the Count of Flanders; and the third course is to

* The following edict will show that the condition of the internal affairs of Ghent demanded treatment as well as its external. "Who commits homicide shall lose his head; all personal enmities shall be suspended until the fourteenth day after the conclusion of peace with the Count; whoever fights his enemy but without wounding him shall be condemned to forty days' imprisonment on bread and water; blasphemers and disturbers of the peace shall suffer the same penalty; the complaints of the poor shall receive the same attention as those of the rich; the account of the city revenues shall be rendered once a month, and every citizen shall wear a white gauntlet bearing these words, 'God help my,' the Flemish for 'God help me.'"

M

choose five or six thousand of our best armed and most valiant men and to send them out at once to attack the Count's armies. If we die, at least it will be with honour. God will pity us and the world will say that we loyally upheld our cause. Now then Citizens, which of these three courses will you choose?" The citizens cried out "We have full confidence in you, decide for us." Then Philip said "In good faith my advice is that we sally forth armed to encounter the Prince."

A force of between five and six thousand men was consequently equipped for the desperate enterprise, and we are told that all the available provisions were collected and sent with it —viz., five waggon loads of bread and two barrels of wine. Philip had acted with such celerity that two days after he returned from Tournai he marched out of Ghent at the head of this corps, and on the following day he pitched his camp on the heath of Beverhoutsweld not far from Bruges. He fortified his position and placed behind entrenchments the small swivel guns of which he is said to have possessed three hundred. In this position he awaited the attack of Louis de Mâle's army, which numbered about 40,000, and in anticipation of the contest he divided the bread and the wine among his soldiers. When the repast was over Philip Van Artevelde exclaimed "If you want more you must win it at the sword's point." The Count's army marched out of Bruges to attack the small Ghent force in full confidence of an easy victory. The tactics adopted by Philip were extremely simple. He allowed the enemy to come very close to his line of entrenchments and then he fired one volley from his three hundred guns. Having done this he ordered a general charge before the enemy had time to recover. The Bruges militia, which composed a large part of the Count's army, were thrown into confusion, the knights and men-at-arms were unable to get open ground and Louis de Mâle himself was unhorsed and reached Bruges with difficulty. The victors had, however, entered the city with the vanquished and the fight was continued in the public square and the streets. Louis de Mâle had to take off his armour and put on the clothes of his servant. Even thus he could scarcely hope to escape capture, and he took refuge in a miserable hovel. Fortunately for himself he had occasionally given alms to the woman who owned it, and she concealed him in a loft with her children. The next morning he was let down from the wall by a rope and escaped in the disguise of a priest.

This opportune victory, followed by the occupation of Bruges and the destruction of its walls so that it became useless as a base of hostilities, raised the reputation of Philip Van Artevelde to a high point. At Ghent he was publicly proclaimed " Philip the good judge! worthy of being Captain of Flanders!" The cities of Ypres and Courtrai threw in their lot with Ghent, and a large portion of the citizens of Bruges rallied to the cause of their fathers. But Louis de Mâle was a formidable opponent, and his necessities compelled him to seek and obtain, at all cost, the suport of France, while the Flemings had no hope of support from any one, for England was ruled by the weak and incapable Richard the Second, while Brabant was in the throes of the struggle between the Duke and his people. All hope of an accommodation with Louis de Mâle was also ended when he executed the envoys sent from Courtrai with the object of bringing it about.

The partisans of the Count, known under the comprehensive name of Leliaerts or friends of France, threw themselves into Audenarde where they made a stout and successful defence against all the attacks of Van Artevelde. In the meanwhile Louis de Mâle, with the active co-operation of his son-in-law, the Duke of Burgundy, had obtained a cordial promise of support from Charles VI., the young king of France. The question at issue was represented as the large one of chivalry against the communes, of the nobility against the jacquerie, and consequently it appealed with exceptional force to the king and nobles of France who constituted the bulwark of feudalism. Even in England, where the King and the commons had been drawn into conflict, some doubts had arisen as to the wisdom of supporting the Flemings, and this current of opinion sufficed to delay the negotiations opened by Philip Van Artevelde for an alliance until the moment for helpful action had passed by.

Charles the Sixth, declaring with youthful fervour that he was delighted to have the opportunity of first bearing arms in the field, raised an army of 80,000 men and advanced towards the Flemish frontier accompanied by Louis de Mâle, the Duke of Burgundy, and Oliver de Clisson, Constable of France, who held the chief command. One remarkable feature in the composition of this army was that all communal levies were carefully excluded from it. It was essentially a feudal army composed of the nobles, knights, and squires of France with their armed retainers. The French communes were in sympathy with the cause of the Flemings, and remained ready to take advantage of the discomfiture of the royal army to the extent of acquiring the rights and privileges of civic government. The forces of the commune of Paris, for instance, were drawn up under the order of John Desmarets and Nicholas the Fleming as the chivalry of southern France passed its walls en route for the northern frontier.

In face of this impending storm, Philip Van Artevelde seems to have lost neither courage nor confidence. He had broken all the bridges across the Lys, and he greatly relied on the difficulties the French would experience in crossing that river. But by a remarkable effort Oliver de Clisson succeeded in sufficiently repairing the bridge above Commines, while the attention of the Flemish army posted in the neighbourhood was distracted by the attack of a few knights who had crossed the stream partly by swimming and partly in their boats. Oliver de Clisson then succeeded in overwhelming the force commanded at this point by Peter Van den Bosche. Nine thousand Flemings are said to have perished in the fight, and as the consequence of this reverse Commines was sacked and Van Artevelde obliged to raise the siege of Audenarde. With the exception of Courtrai all the towns of West Flanders surrendered, and Van Artevelde instead of remaining on the defensive advanced to encounter the French army. It was at Roosebeke that the two armies drew near to each other on 26th November, 1382. Van Artevelde had 40,000 men under his command and the French numbered probably 70,000, but the Flemings were so confident of victory that on the Duke of Burgundy sending a herald to ask them to surrender on good terms they replied " The right is on our side, and we entrust our cause to God." In the evening of the 26th November, Van Artevelde gave a banquet and his men feasted, and early in the morning of the 27th they left their camp under the cover of a fog to attack the French position.

News of the coming onset was brought in by several French knights who had ridden out to examine the Flemish position, and Oliver de Clisson made some skilful arrangements to take the advancing enemy in flank. Van Artevelde relying too confidently on success had formed his men into a solid body and given it orders to march onward and thus crush the centre of the French force. But he had omitted to provide for the defence of its sides, and at the moment of attack the fog lifted. For a time the onset of the Flemish phalanx proved irresistible, but the success was brief, for the French horsemen coming down on each flank threw them into confusion, and the whole Flemish force was seized with one of those unreasoning panics which sometimes suddenly affect an army. Philip Van Artevelde is said to have been trampled under foot and killed by his own men in their flight while endeavouring to restore order. Twenty-five thousand Flemings are stated to have fallen on the field, and the victors, on making a careful search, found the body of Philip Van Artevelde among the slain in a wood at a little distance from the battle field. A wounded Flemish soldier near at hand acknowledged that it was "the Regent of Flanders," but on being offered his life if he would become French he proudly replied "I was, am, and always shall be Flemish." He was then slain and his body denied burial while that of Philip Van Artevelde was hung up for the kites and crows of the country he had tried to save.

The public career of Philip Van Artevelde covered less than a year. His name was first publicly mentioned on 24th January, 1382, and on the 27th of the following November he was slain at Roosebeke. Any comparison between him and his father would be out of place and of little practical value, but it may be said that the circumstances of the day made him less of a statesman and more of a soldier than his predecessor. Beyond saying that he was a sturdy fighter there is no reason to credit him with military capacity. None the less, he was the last upholder of the liberties of Ghent so far as they related to the exercise of political power.

After their great victory the French sacked Courtrai and returned to their own country where they proceeded to punish the communes and to nip the growth of civic liberty in the bud. At Paris John Desmarets and Nicholas the Fleming were summarily executed. Encouraged by the retreat of the French army the people of Ghent refused to acknowledge Louis de Mâle, and under Francis Ackermann, one of Van Artevelde's lieutenants, they kept the field during the summer of 1383. An English contingent of 3,000 men under Henry Spencer, Bishop of Norwich, came to their assistance, and together they laid siege to Ypres which was, however, defended with such obstinacy that the French king had time to come to its aid. A truce was concluded at Calais and some months later Louis de Mâle died at St. Omer (30th January, 1384). According to another account he was murdered there by the Duke de Berri.

The deaths of Wenceslas and Louis de Mâle within a few weeks of each other marked the end, in Brabant and Flanders respectively, of the attempts of the communes to gain and retain political power. Both these representatives of the feudal system succeeded in more or less crushing the communal power in its attempt to vie with kings. Civic privileges, rights, and immunities continued to exist and to pass through successive stages of lapse and revival, but the political power for which the communes had struggled under the two Arteveldes eluded their grasp. Neither Wenceslas nor Louis de Mâle benefited personally by their successful efforts to maintain intact their own rights, and although they revoked charters and tore up treaties they were unable to bring their subjects into harmony with, or submission to their plans. Louis de Mâle died on foreign soil, slighted by his French patrons to whom he owed the success of his arms. His allies left him in no doubt that in helping him they had only been thinking of themselves, and that on his death the rich county of Flanders would pass into the hands of a French Prince, and become, as it were, the appanage of the Crown of France. Such were at least their expectations. How far they were disappointed will be seen in the history of the House of Burgundy. But in one particular at least French policy was successful. It aimed at preventing the communes of Flanders from becoming a political power, and it attained its object, for all the efforts of the citizens of Ghent failed to establish a stable independent government whether as a republic or under the name of their dynasty of Counts. The failure of the Flemish communes, with many advantages in their favour, entailed that of the French cities which had less wealth and power and consequently fewer chances in their struggle with the King and his peers.

One of the chief causes of the failure of the Flemings was that, with all their natural courage, and combative character, they never produced a great military leader. They formed an essentially citizen army with all its defects and elements of weakness. Despite the excellence of their arms, due to their possession of money as well as to the skill of their handicraftsmen, they never seemed able to derive much advantage on the field of battle from this superiority, and the record of their French wars is one of almost unbroken defeat with the exception of the battle of the Spurs. Nor is there much obscurity as to the cause of these reverses, which were almost exclusively due to the tactical errors of the citizen acting as general in command. The communes were also without cavalry, and cavalry was still the most formidable force on the battle-field. When the Counts and their citizens pursued the same policy the former brought with them a certain number of horsemen in the nobles and knights of their fiefs with their retainers, but in the struggle with Louis de Nevers and Louis de Mâle all the feudalism and chivalry of the country was on the other side. The English alliance energetically sought and loyally maintained would have supplied this defect, but while the Flemings were in the main for the English alliance they were heartily and emphatically only for one thing, and that was neutrality. In times of great peril those who make neutrality their ideal generally go away empty-handed. The policy of Edward the Third had been based on a close connection and understanding with Flanders, but during the thirty years following the death of James Van Artevelde it became less and less cordial, and in the critical years of Louis de Mâle's rule the helping hand that would have saved the Flemings was never offered. The sympathies of Richard the Second, engaged in a struggle with his own cities, were probably on the side of Louis de Mâle.

The military defects of the Flemish position will not alone explain the loss of the political power for which they struggled so hard and, up to a certain point, fought so well. It was caused also by internal divisions, the rivalry of towns and the contentions of classes, and by a decline in commercial prosperity produced by natural and clearly traceable causes. The essentially communal and narrow view on which the Belgian races worked was fatal to the success of any broad scheme of national development. The State might have found safety and durability in the triumph of Ghent as the one supreme city, but the strength of Ghent was sapped by the civic discord and strife prevailing in its midst. Nor were the towns at harmony with each other. The open schemes of Louis de Mâle for the suppression of the liberties of his subjects could not make the people of Ghent manifest any forbearance towards those of Bruges when they learnt that the construction of a canal might lead to a slight diversion of their trade. In the action of John Yoens, for instance, one is inclined to see rather the injured interests and angry sentiments of the barge contractor menaced in his business than the zeal of the patriot thinking and grieving for his country's wrongs. Nor when victory attended their arms did they forget to place their rival in such a position of inferiority and helplessness by the destruction of a great part of its defences that Bruges remained for some years at the mercy of any assailant. That was evidently not the way to bind the various sections of a race together and to form a nation, but throughout the whole of the Flemish struggle for political independence local jealousies stifled the common weal and prevented the cohesion without which durable success was impossible.

But it has also to be recorded that a considerable decline had taken place in the commercial prosperity of Flanders during the fifty years after the murder of the elder Van Artevelde. The Plague or Black Death was one cause, the closing up of the

Zwyn channel connecting Damme, the port of Bruges, with the sea was another, but perhaps the most important of all was, that by the transfer of many Flemings to England, that country had become a manufacturing country as well. The loss of population from two of the causes named affected Ghent less than the other places, but towns like Courtrai and Ypres sank to one-tenth of the population and importance they had possessed in the year made memorable by Crécy. The ravages of the French armies which came to assist the Counts were also mainly felt in south-west Flanders, which has never recovered the prosperity it enjoyed at the beginning of the 14th century. These changes, disasters and dislocations of trade injured the general commerce of the country which had possessed a monopoly in north-west Europe. They might have produced a fatal result if the industry of the Flemings and their mechanical skill had not been so great. Thus their commercial prosperity and wealth continued, different in its causes, less comprehensive in its action, but still real and remarkable. It enabled the communities to maintain their more immediate privileges, their social splendour, and the civic dignity which formed their ideal in life. They no longer possessed the monopoly of business north of the Alps, Bruges ceased to be the exchange of the Western States, but in a narrower sphere, on a less comprehensive scale, they remained a prosperous community, richer than any of their neighbours and more exclusively devoted to the pursuit and acquisition of wealth. But the prospects of political power and independence receded and disappeared with the death of Philip Van Artevelde and the humiliation of Louvain. The greatness of Flanders never attained the zenith which the feudal glory of the Crusades and the civic glory of James Van Artevelde had promised.

CHAPTER VIII.

The House of Burgundy.

IF the history of Flanders in the fourteenth century was largely coloured by the struggle between the communes and the native line of Counts who had adopted French views and policy, it was characterised in the fifteenth century by the contest, openly maintained, between the representatives of nationalism and the French princes who by marriage had added the Low Countries* to their patrimony in Burgundy. The struggle would have ended in the triumph of the latter, and the sure if gradual incorporation of the Belgian states with the French monarchy if the House of Burgundy had been content to play a subsidiary part to that of Valois. But during the century of its existence it was engaged during the first half in an unsuccessful effort to secure the control of the destinies of France, and during the second in founding a separate Burgundian kingdom which should be able to hold its own between the Empire and France. The Burgundian strength was not equal to its ambition, and circumstances compelled Philip the Bold and his successors to lean on outside support, with the inevitable result that the French provinces fell away from their system and the Belgian rallied, by the natural law of self-preservation, to the side of Germany. The history of the House of Burgundy forms the most interesting attempt to found that third state in north-west Europe which should be able to maintain its existence against France and Germany that was first attempted in the break-up of the Empire of Charlemagne, and the idea of which was revived on the part of William of the Netherlands at the Vienna

---

* A few years after the establishment of the House of Burgundy this name was used for the first time.

Congress in 1814-5. The project never had any real chance of success except in the hands of Philip the Good and Charles the Bold.

Philip, Duke of Burgundy, who had gained the title of the Bold* by his conduct at Poitiers, was in the prime of life when the death of his father-in-law, Louis de Mâle, made him Count of Flanders. The observant Froissart credits him with qualities not often combined. The Duke was "wise, cold, and imaginative, and in his undertakings saw far." He had also acquired some knowledge of Flemish affairs, having taken a prominent part in several negotiations between Louis de Mâle and the representatives of Ghent. But the uppermost thought in his mind was how to detach Flanders from the English alliance and to obtain control of its resources for the benefit of France, injured and humiliated by the military successes of King Edward. For above every other consideration he placed the interests of his native land. The first of his name and fief, he thought and worked not as Duke of Burgundy but as Regent of France, acting for his young nephew, Charles the Sixth. There were facts in connection with the situation in Flanders itself which strengthened this tendency, for the citizens of Ghent not only looked to England for support, but had actually admitted a small English garrison under Sir John Bourchier, to whom Richard the Second had given, in a rare moment of decision, the title of Regent of Flanders. Moreover, the national party under Ackermann was still evincing much activity. In the eyes of Philip the Bold, therefore, the English were not only the enemies of France, but they were the abettors of sedition in Flanders. These views very largely coloured the policy of his life and reign.

In April, 1384, Philip entered Bruges and was acknowledged

* The titles or epithets applied to the names of all the Dukes of Burgundy were given by the Court chroniclers of those princes, without any regard for their appropriateness or for their being deserved. An exception can be made in favour of Philip the Bold, who showed much courage at Poitiers as a youth of 16, even if we do not accept without some reservation Montalembert's anecdote as to Edward the Third having exclaimed "You are indeed Philip the Bold!" when Philip protested at a banquet in London because Edward was served at table before King John of France—"the vassal before the suzerain."

there as Count. A few weeks later Audenarde was captured from Ackermann by one of Philip's knights named D'Escornay. The capture of this place was effected by a stratagem. A number of carts with provisions were sent towards the city, and a gate was opened for their admission. Once in the narrow passage the pin bolt of a waggon was drawn, and the gate thus prevented from being closed, whereupon D'Escornay, at the head of a party in ambush, suddenly made his apearance and forced his way into the town. The capture of Audenarde, considerable as a military success, did not bring the Duke any nearer to the subjugation of Ghent. It was counterbalanced by the rude defeat of the Leliaert faction there, and by the open hoisting of the English flag. Very soon after this incident Sir John Bourchier arrived with a few men-at-arms and a thousand archers. It seemed as if the English king had at last shaken off his irresolution, and that the Flemings might count on his support. The year 1384 closed, therefore, without any recognition by the larger half of the Flemish people of the Duke of Burgundy as their Count.

The year 1385 opened with events which further embittered the struggle. The Ghentois made an attempt to recapture Audenarde, but were repulsed and lost some prisoners. These were deprived of their sight and sent back to Ghent where the proposal to exact a terrible revenge by treating the Burgundian prisoners in the same fashion was only abandoned through the humane intervention of Bourchier, who induced Ackermann to give the proposition only a future application. The second event was the plan formed by Philip the Bold for the invasion of England. As a Frenchman he hoped thus to obliterate the memory of his country's reverses and his own imprisonment. He seems to have had no doubt also of the success of his plans to bring the greater portion of the Flemish nation round to his way of thinking for he selected Sluys as the base of his expedition. This hope was no doubt largely caused by the intervention of his aunt, the Duchess of Brabant, on his behalf, and by the marriages concluded at Cambrai in April, 1385, which united the three great states of Brabant, Flanders, and Hainaut in a family league. Philip's eldest son, John, was married to Margaret of Bavaria, daughter of the Regent of Hainaut, and William, the latter's eldest son, married Margaret, daughter of the Duke of Burgundy. At the same time the Duchess of Brabant formally recognised her grand nephew Antony, second son of Philip the Bold, as heir to the Duchy. The marriages of Cambrai formed a very important step in the breaking up of the old feudal fiefs into which Belgium had been divided, and in the gradual attainment of political unity.

Before passing on to consider Philip's anti-English project, a few lines may be given to the history of Hainaut, which had sunk into comparative unimportance with regard to Flanders and Brabant. Hainaut, in a degree more marked than Brabant, was a state of feudal creation. Its only towns, Mons and Valenciennes, were, in the communal sense, as far behind Brussels and Louvain as those cities were behind Ghent and Bruges. Its temporary union with Flanders had not altered its character in any essential features, and, isolated from the rest of the state, it remained in the words of some of its representatives a poor country of proud men. Only in modern times has the discovery of its great mineral wealth altered the character of the province and placed it in the fore-front of Belgian prosperity and progress. The family of D'Avesnes* maintained its position despite the efforts of the rival Dampierre family of Flanders to dispossess it, and added to its titles those of Counts of Holland and Zealand with possession of the Frisian islands and marshes between the Scheldt and the Zuyder Zee. The marriage of Edward the Third of England with Philippa of Hainaut detached Hainaut from France, but the premature death of her brother, Count William II., put an end to the D'Avesnes dynasty in the male line. The Emperor, Louis of Bavaria, claimed Hainaut on behalf of his wife Margaret, eldest sister of Count William. The claim was valid and admitted, but in Holland and Zealand the Salic law prevailed, and after an abortive attempt to maintain the union of the provinces, Margaret ceded her rights over Holland and Zealand to her second son, William. The death of her husband the Emperor altered the position. She then took up her residence

* See ante page 108.

in Hainaut but regretted the loss of the northern provinces. She soon found an excuse for invading her son's territory, and the Dutch divided themselves into two factions, the one upholding her cause calling themselves Hooks, and the other for her son taking the name of Cods. Margaret had the worst of the struggle, and by the intervention of her brother-in-law, Edward the Third, a peace was concluded on the basis of the original agreement. A few years later (1356) William of Bavaria's rights were acknowledged over Hainaut as well as Holland. In this manner the countdom of the D'Avesnes passed to the House of Bavaria, and when William's brief career was ended by a fit of madness his brother Albert was declared Regent in his place (1358). It was the marriage of Albert's son and daughter to a princess and prince of the House of Burgundy at Cambrai in 1385 that rendered this digression necessary.

Strengthened in his position by these alliances Philip the Bold reverted to his plan for the invasion of England. It was not difficult for him to enlist the sympathy of his young nephew, the King of France, in such an undertaking, but for its success the possession of a Flemish port and Flemish ships were essential. With the view of keeping open their communications with England whither pressing messages for aid were despatched, the Ghent forces, turning Bruges, seized its port of Damme, and Philip's first enterprise was to recover it. As the French army numbered 100,000 men, and the Ghent garrison only 1,500, resistance was impossible, and Ackermann escaped with his force by making a timely retreat during the night. The French then destroyed Damme by fire (August, 1385), and the promised aid from England not arriving, through the alleged appropriation by De la Pole, Earl of Suffolk, of the sum voted by the Westminster Parliament for the war, Ackermann was unable to do anything to prevent the French force following up this success by plundering the fertile region of the Four Trades. The French laid waste these districts in a pitiless fashion, massacring man, woman, and child, and it is said that when twenty-four prisoners, all members of the same family, were brought before Charles who wished to pardon them on their recognising his authority, they rejected his terms in the following words: "The King of France may conquer brave men, but he can never make them change their views. Kill all the Flemings, our bones will rise up to fight the French."

The campaign of 1385 closed without any further progress being made towards the invasion of England, but the people of Ghent, alarmed as to their position, began to think it was time to make terms with their powerful opponent. Several of the guilds declared in favour of the recognition of the Duke, and Ackermann promised not to oppose the conclusion of a truce although he continued to declare that he reposed no faith in the promises of the French. It must also be admitted that the absence of any sufficient aid from England had rendered unpopular for the moment the English alliance. A deputation of 150 Ghent citizens was accordingly sent in December, 1385, to Tournai with the object of coming to terms with the Duke. The negotiations almost broke down at the commencement, for Philip insisted that the burghers should beg for mercy on their knees which they stoutly refused to do. The wife and the aunt of Philip, in other words the Countess of Flanders and the Duchess of Brabant, threw themselves on their knees and begged mercy on behalf of their people, and the Duke of Burgundy allowed himself to be so far appeased as to sign the Treaty of Tournai of 18th December, 1385. As the consequence of this arrangement the English garrison under Bourchier returned to England and with it went Peter Van den Bosche, the confederate of the second Van Artevelde, but Ackermann, very unwisely trusting the Duke's promises, decided to remain. The Duke and Duchess of Burgundy made their formal entry into Ghent in the spring of 1386, and took, in the Cathedral Church of St. Bavon, the oath to "uphold the laws, privileges and liberties of the city of Ghent." On the other hand the citizens of Ghent recognised their vassalage to France under the Duke of Burgundy, and promised to have nothing more to do with the King of England.

In his arrangement with Ghent, the stronghold of Flemish liberty and the centre of Flemish wealth, Philip the Bold had been mainly thinking of his suspended expedition against

England. The moment was deemed especially favourable for the enterprise as the best of the English troops had accompanied the Duke of Lancaster to Spain to win the Crown of Castille. In 1386 accordingly the French army was again summoned to the Flemish coast, and an immense flotilla of nearly 1400 vessels was collected in the port of Sluys. The necessary preparations occupied many months, and the French contingent arrived slowly. When everything was ready the year was far advanced, and although a start was made the leaders of the force seem to have lost all hope in its success, and a storm at sea resulted in the abandonment of the enterprise. A few months later (March, 1387) the Burgundian war fleet was practically destroyed by an English squadron under the Earl of Arundel and Peter Van den Bosche. The battle was fought off Blankenberghe, 126 Burgundian ships were destroyed or taken, and the Flemish exile especially distinguished himself. Even if family dissensions had not broken out among the Valois all danger of a French invasion of England was thus removed.

Having gained over the citizens of Ghent for a war which events made abortive, Philip set himself to the task of establishing his authority over them on the French model. He resorted to every means for strengthening the Count's party in the city, even stooping to the stratagem of introducing arms into the city in wine barrels for the purpose of being employed against his own subjects. But Ackermann remained, and in that experienced captain he saw a future popular leader. Ackermann had not opposed the recognition of the Duke of Burgundy, but he had never believed in the promises he had made. He was, therefore, the object of the Duke's suspicion and resentment. As a precaution he always went about the streets of Ghent armed and accompanied by some of his relations and servants also armed. This natural precaution was represented in the light of an incitement to a breach of the peace, and it was also said that it reflected on the justice of the Duke. The matter was accordingly brought before the city Council, and Ackermann was forbidden to carry arms or to employ an escort. A prudent man would have applied the moral of this prohibition to defend himself, and withdrawn to a place of safety. But the incautious or over-confident Ackermann remained, with the result that a few weeks later he was murdered. As if to show beyond all need of evidence the authorship of the crime, the Duke banished the nephews of Ackermann as the sole bearers of his name, and took his murderers under his special protection so that they escaped scot free. But while he thus prosecuted to its natural end his hatred of the commune Philip soon realised that for the prosperity of his Flemish subjects an open trade with England was necessary, and that unless they were prosperous there was little chance of his receiving the subsidies that he needed for the due maintenance of his position at Paris where he passed the greater part of each year, thinking not of the interests of Flanders but of his rivalry with his brother, the Duke of Berri, for the Regency of France, and of the growing pretensions of his nephew, Louis of Orleans, brother of the mad King Charles. For these reasons Philip acquiesced in the conclusion of the truces, several times renewed, between England and Flanders.

While Philip was engaged in different operations with the view of rendering certain the reversion of the Duchy of Brabant to his second son, Antony, his eldest son, John, had been brought into notice in a prominent and tragic manner. The chroniclers tell us that this young prince, born at Dijon on 28th May, 1371, caused his parents much anxiety on account of his mental deficiencies and want of enterprise. When he was 25 years of age he had done nothing worthy of his race and station, and had allowed himself to be over-shadowed at the Court of France by his brilliant cousin, Louis of Orleans. At this juncture an appeal came from the King of Hungary begging the princes and knights of Western Christendom to aid him against the formidable Bajazet. A crusade was declared in 1396 and John, the heir of Burgundy and Flanders, was entrusted with the chief command. The leaders seem to have anticipated an easy success and formed grand schemes, but on the field of Nicopolis Bajazet established his claim to superior generalship by practically annihilating the Christian force. With very few exceptions the crusaders taken prisoners were executed after the battle, but among the more fortunate was John of Burgundy. Opinions differ as to the reason, and while some declare that it was for the sake of the heavy ransom of 200,000 ducats in gold that Bajazet was merciful, others tell the romantic tale that as John was being led off an Eastern astrologer intervened and begged Bajazet to spare this man's life because he foresaw that if he lived he would be the cause of more Christian deaths than any Mussulman. In any case there seems no doubt that John played anything but a hero's part. He certainly took no part in the battle of Nicopolis because the enemy surprised him unarmed in his camp, and it is more than probable that he begged for his life and obtained it by the promise of what was an immense ransom. Yet he came back from this disastrous crusade with the undeserved name of "the Fearless" which history has perpetuated.

The raising of so large a sum as two hundred thousand ducats in gold took several years, and when John the Fearless arrived in Belgium to thank the citizens of Ghent for the generous contribution they had made towards his ransom his father's rule was nearly over. Philip the Bold very soon after this incident went to Brussels in 1404 to make sure of his second son's succession in Brabant, and while there he was suddenly taken ill with a serious malady. He wished to return to France, but died on the way at Hal in April of this year. He was succeeded by his son, John the Fearless. His widow, Margaret de Mâle, died in a convent at Arras in March, 1405, and her sister Joan, Duchess of Brabant, also died in 1406, whereupon Antony of Burgundy became Duke of Brabant. On his death-bed Philip the Bold gathered his three sons round him, and with his dying breath urged them to be good liegemen of the King of France. There was no need for the exhortation. The princes were essentially French in blood, sentiment, and up-bringing. Two were to die for France on the field of honour in one of the most signal of national defeats, the third gave his life and blood for the retention of his father's position as Regent of her affairs.

John the Fearless had thanked the people of Ghent for the help they had rendered when he was a prisoner in the East. On assuming the control of his county he paid them a state visit, or made his "joyous entry" among them. He was still in mourning for his parents when he took the oath to the constitution and swore to observe the Charters in St. Bavon.* On the same occasion a new arrangement was drawn up and signed by the Duke of Burgundy as Count of Flanders on the one side and the Flemish representatives on the other. The latter were the delegates of the three great cities of Ghent, Bruges, and Ypres, while four special members represented the Franc† or Free country round Bruges. By this convention John bound himself to four different points. He was (1) to reside in Flanders and when absent to leave the Duchess as his representative (2) to observe and uphold the privileges of the towns (3) to sanction and secure a treaty with England and (4) to allow, among several minor points, the exclusive use of the Flemish language in all intercourse between the members of the Franc and himself. Finally he abolished the arbitrary tax known as the "taille" which existed in France for the benefit of the King or of the person to whom he might delegate his rights. But although he had promised to promote a peace with England he was none the less deeply enraged with his Flemish subjects when they refused to co-operate heartily with him on the occasion of an English descent on the Flemish coast, and to their indifference he attributed the capture and destruction of the castle of Sluys. He was neither the first nor the last of their rulers to experience the capacity of the Flemings for passive resistance to any course of which they did not approve.

The thoughts and ambition of John the Fearless, like those of his father, were not in Flanders but in France. There Louis of Orleans had gained the ascendency since the death of Philip the Bold, but his popularity, in Paris at least, was not great owing to the severity with which he levied the "taille." On

* It was then known as the Cathedral of St. John.
† This is the first occasion on which this term was employed. The Franc country round Bruges was bordered on the east by the district of the Quatre Metiers and the districts of Courtrai and Vieux Bourg, on the south by the limits of Ypres and Furnes, on the north and west by the Scheldt and the sea, The country was ruled by Free Sheriffs, whence its name. Its origin goes back to the 12th century, but it was only in the 15th that it obtained a formal place as "the fourth division of Flanders."

the other hand the Duke of Burgundy was considered quite a liberal ruler and his arrangement with the city of Ghent strengthened the conviction. When the Duke of Burgundy marched on Paris in the spring of 1406, he encountered no resistance and the city opened its gates. Orleans fled south of the Loire, and both sides prepared for war. Doubt of the result or some other circumstance that has escaped precise notice induced the two rival princes to come to a pacific understanding. They entered Paris riding side by side, and to give their protestations of friendship a more sincere and convincing appearance they passed the first night in Paris in the same bed. Not content with this demonstration they took the sacrament together. Yet all the time they were resolute in their mutual hatred and bent on each other's destruction. While the Duke of Orleans published a scurrilous song on the Duchess of Burgundy, John the Fearless nursed in his heart a more terrible revenge. On the 23rd November, 1407, Orleans was supping with the Queen, Isabel of Bavaria, when a message was brought him that the King, Charles VI., who had recurring moments of sanity, wished to see him. He at once left the Queen's hotel to proceed to the King's residence. Accompanied by two squires mounted on the same horse, and by a few foot servants carrying torches he mounted a mule himself and hastened, singing gaily on his way. When he reached the old street of the Temple opposite a house bearing the name of " The Image of our Lady," a band of twenty armed men fell upon his party. The Duke of Orleans was quickly despatched, and the leader of the band, a tall man with a red hood, supposed to have been John the Fearless himself, ordered his men to put out their lights and to ride off without delay. In this manner the actual murderers were never discovered or punished, but among them seems to have been one Raoul d' Actonville, or d' Auquetonville, who was subsequently largely rewarded by the Duke of Burgundy.

Whether John the Fearless took a personal part in the crime or not he remained to face the storm raised by the murder of the Duke of Orleans, and to boldly avow his responsibility for it. His uncle, the Duke of Berri, warned him not to present himself at the Palace, and to take good care of himself as the Orleanists suspected him of the crime. " I will take good care of myself, but let no one be accused of causing the death of the Duke of Orleans as I alone am responsible for what has been done." For a time John the Fearless left Paris, but after he had punished with severity a rising of the citizens of Liége against their Bishop, his brother-in-law John of Bavaria, he returned there and made it his headquarters. The citizens of Paris were for the time heartily on the side of the Duke of Burgundy in the hope, no doubt, that he would respect their privileges as a commune and promote their trade. Although he continued very careful in his treatment of Ghent to whose citizens he never gave cause for umbrage, the severity with which he chastised the citizens of Bruges for demanding concessions promised by Louis de Mâle, and the butchery of over 20,000* Liége inhabitants during his last campaign raised grave doubts as to the sincerity of his liberal promises and pledges. A weakening of his hold on Paris was probably the explanation of the Duke of Burgundy's readiness to conclude the Reconciliation of Chartres with the three sons of the murdered Duke of Orleans, viz., the new Duke of Orleans, the Duke of Vertus and the Duke d'Angouleme. This deed was signed in March, 1409, but so hollow was the truce that a priest ventured to preach a sermon on it the next day with the text " Peace, Peace, where there is no Peace."

After a suspension of arms during nearly two years the enemies of the House of Burgundy had become more powerful by the marriage of Charles, the young Duke of Orleans, with the daughter of the ambitious and able Count D'Armagnac, who gave his name to the anti-Burgundian faction. The Armagnacs adopted the white scarf which was the ensign of the Count's house as their badge, and the Burgundians the blue hood of Burgundy and St. Andrew's Cross. On the 18th

---

* At least this number perished at the battle of Othée—23rd September, 1408—when it was proved once more that an army of city or communal militia was no match for the heavy cavalry of the royal or feudal armies. But many more perished during the executions and drownings in Liége itself. The wives of offending citizens were tied back to back, and thrown over the Bridge of Arches into the Meuse. At the same time Liége was deprived of all its charters and privileges.

July, 1411, the three Orleans princes sent John the Fearless their message of defiance and hate in the most approved style, and on the 14th of August the Duke of Burgundy made his reply in an equally lofty strain. The Armagnacs, after ravaging the region between Paris and the Loire, advanced threatening the Duke in Paris. He placed himself at the head of an army largely composed of a Flemish contingent from Bruges and Ghent, but he failed to bring the Armagnacs to action. So skilfully did they conceal their whereabouts that the Flemish contingent declined to believe that there was a formidable enemy in the field, and, anxious to return to their homes, withdrew from John's army notwithstanding his prayers and entreaties. There is no doubt that this defection of the Flemings alone saved the Armagnacs from complete destruction in September 1411, but after this John's fortunes in France declined. By his haughtiness he alienated his allies and even his relatives, the citizens of Paris with "their proverbial fickleness," according to Brantôme, or more probably because they found that under John the Fearless they had no increased privileges, turned upon him, and finally the poor King with a return to reason assumed the Armagnac scarf and proclaimed Burgundy the enemy of France. The Duke of Burgundy bent for the moment to the storm, retiring himself to Dijon and sending his son the Count de Charolais to govern Flanders in his name. By the treaty of Senlis in October, 1414, he bound himself not to return to Paris except at the King's own summons.

At this juncture new and more important characters enter on the scene. Henry the Fifth of England was about to revive the pretensions of the Plantagenets to the throne of France. There were personal reasons for the House of Lancaster feeling resentment towards the Valois, because at the invitation of the Percies the French King had promised his support to dispossess it of the throne that it had seized from Richard. One of the replies of the fourth Henry to these intrigues had been to strengthen his relations with Flanders, to enter into correspondence with his "very dear and especial friends" of Ghent and Bruges, and to promise them the trade advantages which were the basis of their prosperity. In this way both Henry the Fourth and his successor made sure of the neutrality of the Flemings. With the Duke of Burgundy personally they had no relations. He was a French prince who had shown a marked hostility towards England, but without the Flemings he was no very formidable opponent. His own personal quarrel with the Armagnacs, and the arrangement which forbade his appearance at Paris, alone prevented his joining the French army as became a Peer of France when Henry the Fifth landed in Normandy. But the same reasons did not operate against his brothers Antony, Duke of Brabant, and Philip, Count of Nevers. They took their places in the French army, fought at Agincourt, and contributed their names to the list of the slain. They at least had not forgotten their father's death-bed at Hal. After Agincourt, John the Fearless visited Henry the Fifth at Calais. The victor gave him a condescending reception and called upon him to recognise him as King of France. John the Fearless seems to have been able to evade compliance with this request, and returning to Paris succeeded in re-establishing his position there with the aid of the Queen Isabel of Bavaria.

The haughty demeanour of Henry the Fifth appears to have quite alienated any good feeling John the Fearless may have first entertained towards him, or perhaps the latter thought that he might acquire greater power and fame as a patriotic leader. Having recovered possession of Paris in May, 1418, John the Fearless endeavoured to come to terms with the Dauphin to whose sister he had succeeded in marrying his son Philip, Count de Charolais. On the 11th July, 1419, he took an oath to the Dauphin to aid him to the full extent of his power ".against the damnable enterprise of his ancient enemies the English." With the view of concluding definite arrangements for the realisation of the new alliance, an interview was agreed upon between John the Fearless and the Dauphin. Montereau on the Seine was selected for this memorable meeting, and both sides resorted to every precaution against treachery. The Duke of Burgundy held the castle on one side of the river, and the Dauphin the town on the other.

The bridge was fixed upon for the actual interview, and solid barriers were erected at each end, while in the centre a wooden hut or room was constructed for the actual interview to which each was to bring only ten followers. Here the Duke of Burgundy was to take the oath to the Dauphin as representing the Crown of France. As what followed took place under cover it is not surprising that the accounts were meagre, and that the Burgundian and the Armagnac versions varied in the determining cause of the tragedy. The Burgundians alleged that the Dauphin's party, composed of friends and servants of the murdered Duke of Orleans, came to the interview with the express object of slaying John the Fearless. According to them the moment the Duke bent on his knee to take the oath, cries of "Kill! Kill!" were raised, and the Dauphin's followers fell upon the Duke and killed him and nine of his companions, one escaping by jumping into the river. The Armagnacs represent that the treachery was on the side of the Duke of Burgundy, or that his murder was due to an unfortunate or accidental movement which led to the belief that he was about to draw his sword against the Dauphin. One's faith in this plausible story is shaken, however, by the admission that one of the Duke of Orleans' old servants, William le Bouteiller, was present and struck one of the first blows at the same time exclaiming "Here's for my master!" The one certain fact is that at Montereau on 10th, September, 1419, John the Fearless expiated his crime at Paris of 23rd November, 1407, with his own life. The priest who delivered the obituary sermon, at loss for a better explanation, styled it the Judgment of God.

John the Fearless, although Count of Flanders, was essentially a French Prince in his views, ambitions, and experience. The greater part of his life was passed in France; Paris was his favourite place of residence and when expelled from it he preferred Dijon to Ghent. He was by tradition and instinct the enemy of England, whereas his Flemish subjects were by tradition and interest her friends. He followed towards Ghent a reasonably liberal policy because it gave him in return large subsidies, but his real sentiments on the subject of communal liberty were those of the despot, and were faithfully revealed in his harsh treatment of the Liége citizens from whose purses he had no expectations. But the main feature in the career of John the Fearless was the evidence it supplied of the incompatibility of the position of a French Prince with that of a Flemish Count. He and his father were essentially and before all things French princes, who only valued Flanders for the revenues and resources they derived from it. The rule of the third Duke, known as Philip the Good, marked the transition period in the decline of French proclivities and the creation of what might almost be called a national and certainly a separatist sentiment throughout the dominions of the House of Burgundy.

The young Duke Philip was resident in Ghent when news was brought him of his father's murder. It is said that his grief and anger almost deprived him of reason, and that everything French became so hateful to him that he imprisoned his wife, the Princess Michelle of France. She was the daughter of Charles the Sixth and the sister of the Dauphin, and Philip conveyed the news of the terrible event to her in these words: "Michelle! Your brother has killed my father!" The unhappy princess died two years later. When John the Fearless was murdered he had practically concluded an alliance with France against England, which was rendered all the more necessary for the safety of the former country by the military genius of Henry the Fifth. But the immediate consequence of the murder was to throw Philip into the arms of England. He summoned the representatives of Flanders and notified to them his intentions. They, only too glad that their prince should be impelled to follow their national policy of an alliance with England, promised to assist him "with their money and their goods, and to the full extent of their power." The vassals of Burgundy were no less forward in promising their support, and it was agreed that the Dauphin should under no circumstances be regarded as the heir to the throne of France. But to invest this decision with the necessary weight and the desired prospects of success, an understanding with the English King was above all things necessary. This was effected by the famous treaty of

Troyes of 21st May, 1420. England and Burgundy agreed to wage a common war on the Armagnac faction and to make no separate peace. Henry the Fifth was to wed the Princess Catherine, sister of the Dauphin and the Duchess of Burgundy, and to receive as her dowry the crown of France, the empty title of King being left to Charles the Sixth. At the same time Philip's sister was betrothed to Henry's brother, the Duke of Bedford. The alliance effected at Troyes in 1420 remained more or less in force until broken in 1435 by the Duke of Burgundy in the treaty of Arras.

A few weeks after the signature at Troyes Charles, Henry, and Philip rode into Paris, and the last named derived such satisfaction for his father's murder as might be found in a decree of forfeiture and banishment passed by the Paris Parliament on the Dauphin, Charles of Valois. Philip then returned to his hereditary states, and it was not long before some trifling matters arose to create an unpleasant feeling between the English and Burgundians. Among these the affair of Jacqueline of Bavaria demands further consideration, but the exclusion of Burgundy from all share in the government of France by the energetic and triumphant Henry was the root cause of differences that took twenty years to reach a head. The defeat of the English at the battle of Baugé by the Dauphin was some evidence that the French national cause was still alive, and Philip himself had no better fortune against the same opponent at the fight of the ford of Blanche-Taque near Pecquigny. A common interest in face of the same danger tended to the maintenance of the alliance, when the whole situation was suddenly changed by the successive deaths in the year 1422, of Henry, Charles, and the Duchess of Burgundy. On his bed of sickness—caused it was generally supposed by the plague—the English King uttered as his last advice the words "Keep on good terms with Burgundy," and the counsel was better kept by his brother, the Duke of Bedford, even than it had been by Henry himself. At Amiens the stipulations of Troyes were renewed, and the Duke of Brittany became a third party to the arrangement. The new alliances were cemented by the double marriages of Bedford and Anne of Burgundy, and of the Count of Richemont, brother of the Duke of Brittany, with her sister Margaret of Burgundy, widow of the Duke of Guienne. This alliance remained in unabated force till the death of the Duchess of Bedford in 1432, and it was not finally dissolved until three years later.

Owing to the English possession of Paris, where Bedford acted as Regent of France as well as of England in the name of his nephew, Henry the Sixth, the Duke of Burgundy took very little direct part in the government of France. He was consequently able to devote more of his attention to the proper affairs of Flanders where, unlike his two predecessors, he preferred to fix his residence. He thus raised Ghent and Bruges to a higher position in the dukedom than the proper dynastic seat of Dijon. The greater wealth and importance of Flanders gradually asserted its natural weight by drawing the Burgundian princes from their French belongings and making them, in some sense of the word, national princes. For Ghent Philip manifested in the earlier years of his reign a special favour, defending it in the maintenance of its exclusive rights, as against Ypres, for instance, by restricting navigation on the Yperleet or canal constructed for the benefit of that town. The principal events of this earlier period were undoubtedly the incorporation of Hainaut and Brabant with the Duchy of Burgundy, and the incidents attending the former acquisition were of a romantic character. An annexation of considerable but minor importance was that of the County of Namur, where a younger branch of the Dampierre family had ruled for nearly a century and a half. This principality had got into financial difficulties through the deficiency of its revenues and the exactions of the Prince Bishop of Liége. Philip ended the matter by buying out the last Count, John the Third, for the sum of 132,000 crowns.* The agreement was concluded in 1420, but Count John who gave up several of his forts to a Burgundian garrison was left in nominal possession till his death which occurred nine years later.

* About £60,000. The arrangement was that the County of Namur should go with the county of Flanders, not the Duchy of Burgundy, in which fact may be seen evidence that the Flemish cities provided the money.

Antony of Burgundy, Duke of Brabant, the uncle of Philip, was killed at Agincourt. His two sons John and Philip succeeded him in turn as Dukes of Brabant. After a brief regency the elder of these, John the Fourth, was entrusted with the control of his State in 1418 when only 16, and at the same time he married Jacqueline of Bavaria, daughter and sole heiress of William, Count of Hainaut and Holland. Had that marriage proved a happy one the house of Burgundy would not have risen to its great height of power, and the first union of Belgium might never have been brought about. The union of Brabant, Hainaut, and Holland in the same hands was a counterpoise to the union of Burgundy and Flanders. History cannot impute the blame to the adventurous, spirited, and beautiful Jacqueline that these provinces did not maintain their independence. But her husband, frail in body and mean of spirit, was also dissipated and rendered her life unbearable at the same time that he showed absolute cowardice in defending her rights which were assailed in Holland by her uncle, John the Pitiless, Prince Bishop of Liége. This prelate succeeded in acquiring possession of Holland, Zealand and Frisia, and the Duke of Brabant ceded him all his own and his wife's rights therein for twelve years. At the same time the Duke persecuted his wife, refusing to provide for the ladies of her court who were natives of Holland, and inflicting many humiliations on her under the influence of his mistress, Laurette d' Assche. Jacqueline was not the woman to submit tamely to such treatment and she fled to Quesnoy in Hainaut, while a popular rising in Brussels imposed on John an administration at the head of which was his brother Philip, Count of St. Pol.

This popular movement in Brussels was rendered remarkable and formed a landmark (1420-1) in its history by the fact that the citizens then obtained the right to divide their crafts into the Nine Nations which still exist. The event was signalised by the public execution of the Duke's favourites, among whom was Everard T'Serclaes, the compliant husband of Laurette d' Assche.

While these events were occurring at Brussels Jacqueline had fled to England where she contracted, during the life of her husband, a second marriage with Humphry, Duke of Gloucester, Henry the Fifth's brother, on the strength of a dissolution of her first marriage by the Avignon anti-Pope, Gregory XII. The object of this marriage was political, as Jacqueline needed some one to fight her battles. She induced her new husband to raise a force of 5,000 troops with the view of recovering her patrimony in Hainaut, and she enjoyed the momentary triumph of entering Mons, the old capital of her family. But this success was but brief. Philip of Burgundy declared in favour of his cousin of Brabant and marched at the head of his forces into Hainaut. It was agreed that the question should be decided by a duel between the Dukes of Gloucester and Burgundy, but Bedford, alarmed for the Burgundian alliance, intervened and Gloucester returned to England leaving Jacqueline to fight her own battles. She was besieged in Mons by the Burgundians and compelled, in June, 1425, to surrender. She was confined in the castle of Ghent for some time, but through the fidelity of two of her followers in Holland she succeeded in escaping in man's clothes to Breda. The old Hook party rallied to her side and some aid was received from England, but the Duke of Burgundy was the more resolute in attacking her because the death of John the Pitiless gave him a guarantee that the spoils of victory would be his. Jacqueline had no adequate means of opposing her powerful adversary, and she was further discouraged by the news that her second husband had repudiated her to marry his mistress Eleanor Cobham. By the treaty of Delft on 3rd July, 1428, she surrendered Holland, Hainaut, and her other possessions to Philip, promising moreover not to marry again without his assent, for her husband John of Brabant had died twelve months before that treaty. Jacqueline broke the terms of this arrangement, in 1432, by falling in love with and marrying Philip's own governor or stadtholder, Frank Van Borselen, who subsequently received the title of Count d' Ostrevant. Philip thereupon again invaded Holland, and as Jacqueline had no forces she could offer no real resistance. She succeeded, however, in saving her husband's life by making an abject and complete surrender, formally renouncing all her rights at

Mons in 1433. Her last marriage was no more fortunate than its predecessors, for in 1435 she made representations* with the view of recovering her jewels and private property from her husband, the Count of Ostrevant. Her death in October, 1436, without heirs ended her stormy and unfortunate career, and Hainaut, Holland, and her other dependencies finally passed into the hands of the House of Burgundy.

The acquisition of Brabant had been effected at an earlier date and in a more peaceful manner. The death of Duke John IV. on 14th April, 1427, had awakened no regret, and his brother Philip, the Count de St. Pol, who had already acted as Regent and who was popular in the Duchy, became Duke. His reign was of very brief duration as he died suddenly in August, 1430, without having been married. Philip of Burgundy at once put forward his claims to the succession, and although they were contested by his aunt, Margaret of Burgundy, Countess of Hainaut and mother of Jacqueline, they were recognised by the Estates of Brabant. In October he made his "joyous entry" into Louvain and a few days later into Brussels.

While Philip of Burgundy was thus engaged in extending his authority over the extensive region to the north of France and in adding numerous titles to those of Duke of Burgundy and Count of Flanders, with which he had begun his rule, a series of events was steadily alienating him from the English alliance. The rage arising from the murder of Montereau had subsided and left room for more politic considerations. The exclusion of Burgundy from France, first by Henry the Fifth and then by the Regent Bedford, however skilfully disguised, was not rendered the more palatable by the interference of the Duke of Gloucester in the affairs of Hainaut. To that step Philip had promptly put a check and the extension and consolidation of his power throughout the provinces increased the

* M. Gachard's note to De Barante's *Histoire des Ducs de Bourgogne*. Contrast with this Motley's erroneous statement in his *Rise of the Dutch Republic* (p. 22 of the one vol. edition of 1897), "consoled for the cowardice and brutality of three (two) husbands by the gentle and knightly spirit of the fourth (third)." With regard to Baraate's history it may be well to recall its description as possessing "the charm of romance and the substance of history."

risk for those who sought to interfere with him. But the good sense of Bedford, the restraining influence of his Duchess, and curiously enough, the appearance of Joan of Arc all tended to defer the breach which was sooner or later inevitable.

It was in harmony with the age that all these political problems should have reached their culminating point round a marriage. Philip of Burgundy, left a widower in 1422 by the death of Michelle of France, had married in the second place Bonne d'Artois, Countess of Eu and Nevers, but this childless marriage had no political importance. In 1430 his third marriage, one of a very different character for several reasons, was celebrated with exceptional pomp at Bruges. The bride on this occasion was the Princess Isabel of Portugal, the great granddaughter, on the mother's side, of John, Duke of Lancaster. For the celebration of this marriage the Duke and Duchess of Bedford came to Bruges, and the auspicious occurrence was signalised by two events of historical importance. One was the transfer of the Regency of France from the hands of Bedford to Burgundy and the other was the founding of the order of the Golden Fleece.

The circumstance which dictated the former event was the dubious fortune of the war in France after the appearance of Joan of Arc. It is true that the defeat of Clarence at Baugé had been amply atoned for in Bedford's victory at Verneuil over Alençon and Douglas, but the loss of Orleans and the defeat at Patay, in 1429, had marked the turn of the tide in favour of French patriotism The Burgundian alliance, always valuable, had become essential to the maintenance of any position in France outside of Calais, and the dying advice of Henry the Fifth was now re-echoed in the accents of self-preservation. The step taken by the Duke of Bedford at Bruges was, therefore, one of necessity, although it was skilfully concealed under the cloak of friendship and even affection. The Duke of Burgundy showed his appreciation of it a few months later when, on capturing Joan of Arc at Compiègne (May, 1430), he handed her over as a sorceress to the tender mercies of the Church in the person of the Bishop of Beauvais. That step may be termed the last act of complaisance shown by Philip of Burgundy to England in the person of his brother-in-law, the Duke of Bedford. The death of Anne, Duchess of Bedford, in November, 1432, led to an estrangement between them, and Bedford's own death soon afterwards broke the personal link in twain.

But a more interesting event in connection with the Bruges fêtes was the proclamation of the Order of the Golden Fleece* which, in age and lustre, is the only order of the Continent that can vie with the Garter of England, established three parts of a century earlier. The idea of an order especially associated with the Low Countries did not originate with Philip of Burgundy, for in 1290 an order, dedicated to St. James, had been granted by Florent, Count of Holland, and in 1382, Albert of Bavaria, Count of Hainaut, had associated the name of St. Antony with another. But those orders had proved as brief lived as their founders while Philip, happily thinking that the House of Burgundy might become extinct, ensured the perpetuation of the order by passing on its sovereignty to the husband of the last heiress of his family.

The order, dedicated to the Virgin and St. Andrew, was appropriately enough named the Golden Fleece, in consideration of Bruges being the centre of the Wool Trade, while the quest of Perseus suggested the idea at the root of all chivalry. The first motto selected by Philip had special reference to the circumstances of the hour—the words "Aultre n'aray" being completed by the line "Dame Isabeau tant que vivray," but after some years' use this motto was entirely superseded by that of the House of Burgundy itself "Je l'ay emprins," "I have undertaken it." In addition to the sovereign prince there were to be 24 knights, and among the first list the names of Croy,† Villers, Lannoy, and Commines are still represented in the Golden Book of the Belgian nobility. But, perhaps, the most remarkable points in connection with the new order were the privileges it bestowed on its members. They enjoyed a

* Consult *Histoire de l' Ordre de la Toison d'Or* par le Baron de Reiffenberg, Bruxelles, 1830.

† Pronounced Cro-ee. The name of Lalaing, the doyen of the Hainaut nobility, was added a few years later in the person of Simon de Lalaing, the uncle of the famous James.

personal security against the laws of the land and the tyranny of princes by being amenable only to their brethren and comrades of the order. This privilege was deemed inviolable until Philip the Second broke it in the case of Egmont and Horn. The division of the order, in 1725, into two branches, those of Austria and Spain, has slightly diminished its splendour, but the care with which the Hapsburgs have dispensed it has preserved its lustre and reputation.*

The first sixteen years of Philip the Good's reign pointed to two main conclusions. On the one hand all the feudal states and territories, which had been not only independent but often hostile towards each other, were united under a single sway, and one of the direct consequences of that union was to greatly increase the feudal or personal power of the ruler who became less dependent on the support of the communes, or, to express the point differently, better able to coerce them. The precise significance of this change will be seen in the later portion of Philip's reign and in that of Charles the Bold. The second conclusion lay more on the surface. The Burgundian alliance with England had reached the natural term of its existence. It was quite distinct from the old Flemish alliance with the country on the opposite side of the Channel which was based on mutual interest and on some racial fellow-feeling. The three first Burgundian princes had as little regard for England as any other Frenchmen. But their personal enmities and ambition in France led the second and third of them to espouse the English side for their own ends. The value of that alliance in their eyes was to enable them to overcome the Armagnacs, and to control the destinies of France. When Philip discovered that the practical result was to establish an English ascendency it lost its charm. When he perceived through English pretensions in Hainaut and in Flanders that their ambition could not be excluded from a region within his power the alliance assumed an absolutely sinister aspect. The more secure and powerful he felt at home the more willing was he

* The archives and treasury of the Golden Fleece originally preserved at Bruges were transferred at an early date to Brussels where they remained till the French Revolution when they were removed to Vienna.

O

to break off from the conventions of Troyes and Amiens. Time had blunted the rage and grief he had experienced after Montereau, and the triumph of his schemes within the natural boundaries of the Provinces rendered him sufficiently powerful to dispense with a foreign, distasteful, and exacting alliance.

The direct cause of the Duke of Burgundy's defection from the English alliance, in 1435, is stated by the Court chroniclers to have been pity for the distresses of France. They were undoubtedly great enough to arouse pity in the breast of any one brought in contact with them. The whole country north of the Loire had been depopulated and ravaged by war and rapine. From Laon to the German frontier it was said that not a house was left standing outside a few fortified positions. The fields were untilled, and the starving peasantry were reduced to the worst horrors in their search for sustenance. A sentiment of horror and compassion may not have been foreign to Philip's mind, when for weighty political reasons he entered into negotiations with the king of France for the conclusion of a peace. Arras was fixed upon as the scene of the negotiations in which England was at first represented because their ostensible object was the conclusion of a general peace. But the English representatives soon discovered that the only real object of the conference was to establish an accord between the French and Burgundians against them, and they promptly withdrew with dignity from any further part in the proceedings. A few weeks after their departure the following treaty was signed, on 22nd September, 1435, between Philip the Good and Charles the Seventh.

> Art. 1.—Charles VII. affirmed by the medium of his Ambassador, and in writing, that he had had no part in the assassination of John the Fearless, which he regarded as the blackest crime produced by the foulest treachery.
>
> Art. 2.—He engaged to order, as reparation, and furnish the endowment for a mass to be said every day of the week in perpetuity in the chapel of Montereau in memory of those killed on the occasion.
>
> Art. 3.—He would also cause a service to be held daily for the repose of the Duke's soul in the Carthusian Church of Dijon where his body was buried.
>
> Art. 4.—He gave Philip the counties of Macon, Auxerre, etc., etc., until the repayment of the sum of 400,000 crowns in gold which Charles recognised as a debt of France.
>
> Art. 5.—He also ceded the property of the counties of Boulogne and Guines.

Art. 6.—He released for his life the lordships and domains of the Duke of Burgundy from all service, homage, etc., with which they might be burdened towards the Crown.

It will thus be seen that the Treaty of Arras was not only personally gratifying to Philip, but that it conferred many material advantages on him, and made him, for his life at least, an independent prince. On his side he not merely made peace with France, but he gave her his protection against the English who by this time had again lost all their French conquests excepting Calais and its neighbourhood. In this manner Philip established the truth of his own statement that he had been "an English ally," but that he "had never an English heart." The reception of his notification about the Arras treaty in London was not, however, what he expected. His letter was torn in fragments, his herald was slighted and sent back without any written reply, and a certain number of the Flemish merchants always resident in London were plundered and perhaps even murdered. On the latter point the evidence is not clear, but early in 1436 Henry the Sixth found it necessary to accord a formal Act of Protection to Flemings resident in his country. The defiance of the English to the Burgundians was not limited to words. They scoured the Channel and North Sea in pursuit of Burgundian vessels, and the garrison of Calais made frequent raids into the Burgundian possessions of Artois and West Flanders. The arrangement of Arras, however gratifying to the personal sentiments of Philip as Duke of Burgundy, was not conducive to the establishment of that peace which was its ostensible object. France certainly derived direct benefit from it, for the scene of hostility was transferred to Flanders, which was now to feel the heavy hand of its despotic ruler. But the policy of Philip, who aimed at independence, would have been more fruitful of beneficial result if it had been based on preserving the friendly understanding with England, which would have harmonised with the views of his Flemish subjects, without entailing any aggression at the expense of France.

The conclusion of the first period of Burgundian history is therefore clearly marked by the breach with England, which entailed, as will be seen, a further breach with the Flemish communes. A dark page of Flemish history has been reached, yet Philip, notwithstanding, has retained in the most national histories his epithet of the Good. He proudly declared at Arras that his "heart was not English," and now in a very little space of time he was going to show more clearly, and in crimson characters, that it was not Flemish. The miasma of French sentiment and sympathy which has hung over Belgian history for centuries, and which is still epidemic in spite of the clearest wrongs and the most unprovoked aggressions traced along the pages of history, attained, under the influence of Duke Philip, its most virulent strength.

CHAPTER IX.

The First Union of Belgium.

HAVING successfully negotiated the treaty of Arras, Philip wished to celebrate the change in his policy by some striking deed, and the insults of the English seemed calculated to gain for him the support of the Flemish communes in a war with that nation. He showed a close acquaintance with the character of his subjects when he asked for their support not on the grounds of sentiment but of material advantage. The enterprise he invited them to embark upon was nothing less than the capture of Calais which "commanded the Channel," and the Flemings had had reason to accept the accuracy of the statement in the recent loss of many of their vessels. But the arguments with which he supported the project were of a material character and based on the representation that the English trade had become far less valuable in itself and far less needful to the Flemish people. In a public address to the people of Ghent, delivered by the mouth of his bailiff, he set forth—" My very redoubted lord has remarked that the prosperity of Flanders is based on the cloth trade, and that the wool of England has been raised to such a high price that our merchants are deprived of all chance of profit. Moreover, by a measure which entails the ruin of our money, they pay only two florins for one noble. Finally it is worthy of notice that the wool of Spain and Scotland begins to equal that of England, and to be as much sought for. Enlightened as to the culpable designs of the English, and taking into consideration the increase of our population and the decay of our commerce and public prosperity menaced with fresh disasters, he desires, therefore, both as good prince and as good shepherd, to drive the wolf far from the flocks. Remember, also, that the town of Calais touches your country and in ancient times belonged to it."

At the time of that address Philip was a popular prince, who had not laid a finger on any of the privileges of the communes, and the Flemings were also for the moment irritated against England. The expedition against Calais was consequently approved by the popular vote, and Ghent promised a contingent of 17,000 men. Bruges and the rest of Flanders were to bring up the total to 30,000. In this manner, and for the first and only time in their history, were the Flemings induced to take up arms against their "natural ally" across the Channel. Ghent was carried away by its belief in the good Duke, and the rest of Flanders followed in its wake, but as will be seen the mood was of far too fleeting a character to satisfy their prince or enable him to realise his ambitious scheme. Thirty thousand Flemings with the feudal forces of Burgundy and its dependencies sat down before Calais in June, 1436. The English garrison was weak but it made a stout resistance and aid was promised from England. After a month's duration the besiegers had made no progress, and when the Holland fleet under De Hornes made its appearance off the port for the purpose of co-operating with them the hopes raised by the sight were soon dispelled by the arrival of an English squadron which obliged De Hornes to make a precipitate retreat. Experience had shown that the communal armies of Flanders generally wearied of a campaign, away from their homes, in three weeks, and they had now prosecuted the siege of Calais for ten, or from the 11th June to the 26th August. Dissatisfaction at the meagre results of the siege, a returning sense of the value of the English connection, and of the folly of having broken off from it, soon produced open sedition in the Flemish camp, and all Philip's arguments and entreaties failed to restore a sense of discipline. Rumours of treachery were also in the air, and without taking into consideration military necessities or the safety of their Duke, the Flemish levies set fire to their camp, and shouting "Go, Go!

we are all betrayed!" marched back to their own country. The Duke felt this desertion the more acutely because his knightly honour was involved in a personal challenge that had passed between himself and Humphry of Gloucester. His helplessness increased his resentment, yet necessity compelled him to bend to the storm when he found that the Flemings, on their return from this expedition, reasserted their communal rights and privileges with increased ardour against himself as their Count.

Philip returned from his discomfiture before Calais with the fixed determination to curb the pride of the communes and to compel them to yield to his autocratic power the obedience necessary for the success of military operations. The

FLEMINGS ABANDONING SIEGE OF CALAIS.

arrogance with which the cities clamoured for their rights, and the indifference with which they treated all questions affecting the country at large, amounted to a tyranny in itself, and provoked the conflict for which the Duke was himself only too ready.

The citizens of Bruges precipitated a collision by asserting the rights of government over the Franc, which had been formally recognised as the fourth state of the country on several occasions, the last having been by Philip himself during the siege of Calais. They are said to have added personal outrage to political opposition by insulting the Duchess of Burgundy and imprisoning the Duke's officers. In May, 1437, Philip accordingly proceeded to Bruges at the head of a considerable force nominally taking the place on his way to Holland, but really coming there with the intention of punishing his enemies. His force of men-at-arms and archers, not large enough as the result showed to overcome the inhabitants of a town fighting in the streets, was still sufficiently numerous to cause alarm, and the delegates of Bruges met him outside the walls with a request that he should only enter with his knights and a few servants. Philip refused to comply, and after two hours' discussion ordered some of his men to seize one of the gates. He then forced his way in, accompanied by a small part of his force under the command of the aged Marshal de l' Isle Adam. But the citizens were not to be coerced so easily. They swarmed down the streets to the market place whither Philip had made his way, and on two respectable citizens greeting him with marks of respect the mob promptly tore them to pieces. On this outrage the Burgundian archers fired on the crowd and in a few minutes the fight became general. Philip's small force had to beat a retreat, while no aid could come because the drawbridge had been raised and the gate closed. The Marshal de l' Isle Adam was killed, and Duke Philip would no doubt have shared his fate if some of the citizens, unwilling to shed the blood of their Count, had not contributed to his escape by forcing the bolts of the gate and lowering the portcullis. Philip promptly made his escape with a few of his personal followers, but two hundred of his soldiers were slain to celebrate what was known as the Bruges Vespers* of Whit Wednesday, 1437.

The citizens of Bruges were intoxicated by their success and did not dream of danger. Unfortunately they sullied their victory by numerous excesses, and they thus incurred the general opposition of the country. Ghent, in particular,

* In contrast with the Bruges matins of 19th May, 1302, see ante p. 111.

declared against them, and lent its powerful assistance to the Duke. Before long it was to have cause to regret this deviation from the policy of union among the communes. Bruges was placed under a strict blockade. Its trade was stopped, its supply of provisions cut off, and soon its proud citizens were compelled by starvation to submit themselves to "the pity, command, and will" of their Count. It is said that the people of Bruges did not surrender their pretensions until 24,000 had died of pestilence and famine,* and until their courage had been undermined by a continuous frost of three months' duration. The terms granted by Philip were exceptionally hard, and were contained in his Sentence on Bruges of March 4th, 1438. They were divided into five chapters. (1) When the Duke of Burgundy should first visit Bruges after this sentence, the citizens should meet him three miles out with bare heads and naked feet, and receive him in a kneeling posture. The sheriffs should then hand over all the keys of the city. Finally, a stone Cross was to be erected where this ceremony took place. (2) An annual mass was to be celebrated on the 22nd of May. (3) An indemnity of 200,000 gold Philips was to be paid (this sum was reduced to 30,000). (4) The loss of their civic privileges and the reassertion of the Duke's rights and supremacy. (5) The execution of 42 leading citizens and of at least one woman, the wife of the chief leader of the Bruges faction, Louis Van de Walle. In addition to these very tangible penalties, Bruges finally abandoned all claim to control the affairs of the Franc. The Duke sent John of Cleves at once to receive the submission of Bruges, but he did not visit it himself till December,† 1440, when he was received in the manner prescribed and graciously took Bruges again into his favour.

* The famine of the winter of 1437-8 was long remembered. Monstrelet cites the case of the woman of Abbeville murdering her children, salting their flesh, and selling it as food.

† Curiously enough Bruges was on this occasion, as in 1430, the scene of marriage festivities. The poet Duke of Orleans, released from his English prison, married the Duke's niece, and at once Philip began to intrigue in the hope of securing for him the Crown of France at the expense of Charles the Seventh. Orleans was received into the order of the Golden Fleece, and tournaments were held in which James de Lalaing, nephew of Simon de Lalaing, began his chivalrous career. A truce with England for five years added to the popular rejoicings.

He was the more disposed to show indulgence because at that moment he was contemplating the task of humbling Ghent as he had treated Bruges.

Soon after these events the Duke obtained possession of the whole of the Duchy of Luxembourg which had been governed for many years by Elizabeth of Gorlitz, widow of Antony of Burgundy, Duke of Brabant. By an arbitrary measure the Emperor of Germany, Albert of Austria, bestowed it on his son-in-law the Duke of Saxony, whose representative, Count Gleichen, occupied the chief towns. Philip, making an arrangement with his aunt, invaded the province, and his favourite son, Cornelius the Bastard of Burgundy, succeeded in taking the reputedly impregnable fortress of Luxembourg by a *coup de main* whereupon the Saxons were expelled from the province. These events happened in 1443, but it was not till the death of Elizabeth, in 1451, that Philip formally assumed the title and quarterings of Luxembourg.

As has been stated the motive of Philip's exceptional condescension to Bruges lay in his intention to humble and exact obedience from the more powerful and populous city of Ghent. The struggle covered a period of thirteen years and at first it seemed as if Philip would fail in his designs, for having ostentatiously removed, in 1440, the seat of the Council of Flanders from Ghent to Courtrai, he found himself constrained to restore it. With his usual persistence he returned to his purpose five years later, transferring the Council first to Ypres and then to Termonde. The citizens of Ghent, however much they might have felt the slight, would probably not have openly resented any act of the Duke's which left their pockets unaffected, but Philip was not long in furnishing them with evidence as to his intentions and a sufficient motive for rebellion. In 1448 he ordered the levying of a gabelle or salt tax in Ghent The tax itself had a bad name in the ears of all citizens, both in France and the Low Countries. Its institution in Paris by the Orleanists had been one of the chief reasons for the popular support accorded to the Burgundians in the French capital, and now the son of John the Fearless ordered it to be enforced without regard for the past or for the sentiment of his own subjects. With the same firmness that it was ordered was it refused. Ghent would not pay the tax, or take any orders from the Duke in infringement of its privileges. The toczin was sounded for the popular council in the market place. Twelve captains were elected, the White Hoods were revived, the supporters of the Duke were driven beyond the city walls. But Ghent was to find in Philip the Good a more formidable opponent, and a severer judge than it had yet encountered. While the citizens were protesting their intention and resolution to uphold their privileges Philip formally accused them of " defying their prince, assailing his privileges and those of his other subjects of Flanders, and of assuming themselves the rights and authority of the ruler of the land." There was a great deal more truth in Philip's representation of the case than is allowed by the blind admirers of civic liberty and the communal system of government. At the same time it is certain that Philip was the more hurt because he had made a personal and direct effort to establish the justice and necessity of the salt tax by setting forth the objects and bent of his policy for the welfare of the whole country. Ghent did not care one jot for the country, but for Ghent alone, and replied to his eloquence and candour with an absolute and unequivocal " No."

The gabelle dispute was followed by another as to the nomination of magistrates, both sides claiming the right to appoint them. But it is probable that nothing would have been heard of this matter if the acceptance of the Duke's nominees had not been regarded as the preliminary to the enforcement of the tax. The magistrates proposed by Philip, Philip de Longpré and Peter Baudins, were creatures of his own, and the citizens, ignoring them, elected others, of whom Daniel Sersanders was the most important, and not only elected them, but called on Philip to ratify their choice. The Duke's reply was to invite Sersanders and the other magistrates to visit him at Termonde, and then to banish them for a long period. The reply of Ghent was to massacre Tincke and other members of the Duke's party on the market place. Throughout the whole of this struggle the popular leaders evinced a cruelty and brutality which would have made any individual ruler infamous, but being perpetrated by the blind and intangible *demos* has passed into oblivion. Yet it should not be forgotten as furnishing some excuse or palliation for the repressive measures of Philip.

While the citizens were engaged in strenuous efforts for the maintenance of their assumed rights and the successful refusal of those of their prince, Philip was not inactive. He collected such forces as were available, and in his archers of Picardy may be seen perhaps the first nucleus of a regular army in Europe. He warned his vassals to get ready for a war with his defiant city. He cut off the communications of Ghent with the outside world, and he placed a garrison under Simon de Lalaing, his best commander, in Audenarde. The pressure thus caused was so severely felt in Ghent that a large force was sent in April, 1452, to besiege Audenarde. Lalaing made a gallant and skilful defence, and despite the formidable Ghent artillery succeeded in holding the place until relief was brought him by his nephew, the heroic knight, James de Lalaing. The Ghent forces were defeated with heavy loss outside the town and many of the fugitives were cut off before reaching Ghent by Duke Philip in person. The citizens, alarmed and indignant at the unexpected reverse, executed the unfortunate commanders, and on both sides the prisoners were massacred in a barbarous manner. The struggle continued throughout the month of May and actions were fought at Gavre, Termonde, and Nevele with results favourable to the Duke. It was on the open plain between Rupelmonde and Basele that the battle was fought which decided this part of the struggle. The young Count de Charolais, afterwards known as Charles the Bold, was sent by his father to Brussels so that whatever the result of the battle the dynasty should not be imperilled, but Isabel of Portugal insisted that he should return so as to be beside his father in the hour of peril. He arrived at Rupelmonde in time to take part in the battle of the 16th June, 1452. It is said that this was Charles's first battle, and the stubbornness with which it was fought must have given him an early taste of the obstinacy and courage of those citizen armies with which he had to contend throughout his career. The result was a signal victory for the Duke, saddened, however, by the death of his favourite son, Cornelius* the Bastard of Burgundy. In vengeance for this loss Philip executed all his prisoners.

The battle of Rupelmonde was far, indeed, from ending the struggle, and it seemed as if the pride of Ghent and the irritation of the Duke might lead to its indefinite extension, for external sympathy was not wholly lacking to the Flemish city. Charles the Seventh of France sent his Herald with promises of aid and a demand for information. England, where the Wars of the Roses were looming on the horizon, promised 7,000 archers and sent a few, for certainly fifty of them fought in a skirmish at Moerbeke. It was evident to the Duke that some special effort was necessary, and with the object of hastening the end of the war he sent for De Blanmont, the Marshal of Burgundy, a man who, despite his limping in his walk and being misshapen in his body, was reputed the best general of the age. Charles the Seventh finding that the people of Ghent still clung to the English alliance endeavoured to patch up an agreement on terms which were favourable to the Duke, but the citizens angrily rejected them. In June, 1453, they were so encouraged by the arrival of a body of Engish archers from Calais that they decided on again assuming the offensive, proclaiming according to the contemporary city records "War! War! They shall see what the loyal citizens of Ghent, fighting for their liberty, can do." It is probable, however, that this decision was not taken in a hasty mood, but as the only means of thwarting Marshal De Blanmont's plan of reducing them to submission by devastating the whole of the surrounding country. The Ghentois obtained some slight successes, perhaps the killing of James de Lalaing, the Burgundian Hector as he was called, at Eenhaem was the most remarkable.

In the meantime the Duke's agents had been at work inside

---

* The funeral of this warrior was celebrated with extraordinary pomp in the Cathedral of St. Gudule at Brussels which, under the Burgundians, took the place of the Abbey Church of Tervueren as the place of sepulture in Brabant. Philip the Good had many bastards—at least seven sons and six daughters are known by name.

Ghent itself, and had bribed Arnold Van der Speeten, chief of the Guild of Masons, and at least two Englishmen named John Fox and John Hunt. The Burgundian army took up a position outside Gavre, held by a small garrison. The Burgundian spies inside Ghent represented that it would be easy to surprise the camp and relieve Gavre. The advice was adopted, and the Ghent army moved out to surprise a force which knew only too well of its coming. When the citizen army reached the neighbourhood of the Duke's camp the traitors galloped over to it, exclaiming, "We have put the Ghent army in your hands." Although the conditions of the ground were entirely in favour of the Burgundian army, which was composed of the flower of the chivalry of the Low Countries, the resistance of the Ghent citizens was such that no onset availed to shake the solid phalanx of pikemen protected on one flank by their artillery and on the other by the English archers. Philip who had incited his troops by saying "You will all be rich this evening" began to despair of the result when the explosion of a powder waggon threw the Flemings into confusion, of which the Burgundian heavy cavalry at once took advantage. The battle then became a slaughter, but the best of the Ghent foot troops with the English archers, anxious to show that they were no parties to the treachery of a few of their number, fought stubbornly to the last. Philip himself had a narrow escape as, pursuing the enemy too eagerly, he was in turn assailed on marshy ground by several hundred spearmen. His horse was killed under him, his son Charles was wounded in the foot, and only the arrival of his main force saved the house of Burgundy from extinction thirty years before the appointed date. The battle—23rd July, 1453—was sometimes spoken of as "the red sea of Gavre." Twenty thousand of the Ghent army were slain, and only three hundred prisoners were taken. These latter were all hung, the English archers among them being hung from the loftier trees because they had not followed the traitors Fox and Hunt.

The memorable battle of Gavre closed with an instance of heroism on the part of a peasant not unworthy to rank with the feats of arms of any of the warriors on either side. Duke

Philip, having won the battle, wished to complete the result by intercepting the fugitives before they could re-enter Ghent, and perhaps even to enter the city with them. He accordingly called for a guide, and a peasant of the locality offered himself, or was appointed for the task. He led the Burgundian army across fields and by-paths, but after a march of several hours the victor found himself not at the gates of Ghent, but back in his own camp. It was but a poor equivalent for a lost opportunity to hang up this unnamed but devoted peasant to the nearest tree.

Having failed to capture Ghent by the *coup de main* with which he proposed to follow up the victory of Gavre, Philip, remembering all the possibilities of resistance to the bitter end that might exist behind the walls of Ghent in the bosoms of a stubbornly defiant race, was disposed to offer and accept an arrangement which would establish his privileges but leave the citizens some of theirs. The sight of the piles of slain on the battle field is said also to have touched Philip's heart, for in reply to someone's congratulations he replied with tears in his eyes—" I do not know who is the gainer by this victory, as for me you see what I have lost, for these were my subjects." Two days after the battle a treaty was accordingly signed in Philip's camp at Gavre. Among the disqualifications inflicted on the city were the suppression of the White Hoods, and the confiscation of the banners of the several guilds. The city privileges were curtailed in respect of the number of magistrates, and their rank in comparison with those who were nominated by the Duke. Finally, a heavy fine of 200,000 gold ridders for the Duke, and 50,000 more for the Church, was imposed on the city. On the other hand the Duke withdrew the objectionable gabelle, the cause of the whole war, and he promised that the personal liberties of all the citizens should be respected. In conveying that intimation Philip spoke in French although he knew Flemish well, and he concluded with these words " Be to us henceforth good subjects, and we shall be to you a good and loyal Lord." In that sentence was contained the assertion of the prerogative for which Philip the Bold had contended in vain, and emphasis was given to the change by Philip's Herald of the Golden Fleece throwing the guild banners as they were handed him into a sack. A few days later they were deposited in equal portions in the Churches of Notre Dame at Hal and at Boulogne of which latter place Philip was the Count.*

Having established his authority in the principal and most turbulent of his cities, Philip's next care was to marry his only son Charles to some princess of whom he approved. He selected his niece Isabel, daughter of the Duke of Bourbon. Unfortunately this choice did not accord with the wishes of either Charles or his mother who, mindful of her own semi-English origin, wished her son to have an English bride. For two years the struggle continued to disturb the harmony of the prince's family, and on one occasion Philip became so enraged that he banished Charles to Termonde, and treated his wife, Isabel of Portugal, so harshly that she retired to the Convent of the Grey Sisters. During this period the Dauphin of France, afterwards Louis the Eleventh, having been involved in his uncle Alençon's plot against Charles the Seventh, fled to Philip's court, and was treated with marked generosity. He ostentatiously allied himself with Charles while he secretly intrigued with the De Croys, who were in such high favour with the Duke that his son did not count, but as it was not to his interest that Charles should marry an English princess he took a prominent part in inducing him to marry their cousin of Bourbon. When the infant princess, subsequently known as Mary of Burgundy, was born in 1457 it was the Dauphin who acted as her godfather. Even then he had, in his own mind, constituted himself the heir of much of her dominions. Soon after this auspicious event Philip paid a formal visit to Ghent where he was received with exceptional rejoicings and feastings, such as had never characterised any previous visit. Curiously enough this same year (1458) was marked by the receipt of a formal summons from the King of France to the Duke to meet him like the rest of his vassals at Montaigu. The order, which was a clear breach of the treaty of Arras, was ignored.

* It is a little curious that Chastelain, who was Golden Fleece, and who may have been the very herald on this occasion, speaks of the Flemish nation as "a very grave people possessing towns of great policy which should be ruled by justice and by right."

Charles the Seventh intended it as an insult to Philip for continuing to harbour the Dauphin after the revelations of the Alençon trial.

In the same year as the battle of Gavre was fought Constantinople was captured by the Moslem, and an attempt was made to revive the Crusades for the expulsion of the Infidel from Europe. Philip, who was known throughout the east as "the Great Duke of the West," took up the idea with special energy and single-mindedness, and to the end of his life cherished the hope that he might follow in the footsteps of Godfrey of Bouillon and Robert of Flanders. He was quite willing to lead the crusade in person, and with that object requested the Emperor of Germany to create him King of Lorraine, or at least Vicar of the Emperor. This request was not granted, but probably Albert of Austria only withheld his sanction until the preparations of the Crusade had reached a more definite stage, for in 1464[*] Philip said to the Chancellor of France, while on a mission at his Court, "I wish all to know that if I wished I could have been king."

In July, 1461, Charles the Seventh of France died, and Louis the Eleventh became king in his place. In return for the hospitality accorded him at the Burgundian Court he showed marked deference to the Duke, invited him to take the most prominent part in his coronation and to visit Paris. On this occasion Philip was accompanied by his principal nobles and an escort which assumed the proportions of an army. In brilliance the Burgundian cortege quite surpassed that of the king himself, and the Parisians, attracted by the glitter of this pomp or stirred by old memories, greeted the Duke with a boisterous welcome—"Right glad are we to see you after so long an absence." Twenty-six years had elapsed since he visited it after signing the Treaty of Arras. Having entered Paris Philip did not show much desire to leave it, and Louis, somewhat alarmed at the length of his stay, felt obliged to give his powerful guest a hint by taking his own departure, carrying

---

[*] In this year an advance guard under the command of the new Bastard of Burgundy, brother of Cornelius, did sail from Sluys for the East. Its chief exploit was to relieve Ceuta, then hard pressed by the Moors.

off with him the Count of Charolais as a hostage, although nominally for that young prince's own security against the intrigues of the Croys.* Duke Philip took the hint and departed in his turn, but when he became seriously ill shortly afterwards, Louis allowed the Count de Charolais to return home in the belief that his father was on the point of death. Thanks it is said to his son's good nursing Philip recovered, but the antipathy between them continued and Charles found it prudent to retire to Holland.

The intrigues of the Croys with Louis the Eleventh, who wished to recover through them the towns on the Somme of which he promised to make one of them, the Count de Chimay, governor, increased the animosity of Charles towards that House, and at the same time made them unpopular in the country. Philip continued to protect them and to refuse naming his heir, saying that he would leave his states *à Dieu et à bonne garde*, which meant practically their sub-division among rival claimants. But even the infatuated and enfeebled Philip seems occasionally to have had some doubts as to the proceedings of his favourites for on at least one occasion he said "Croy! Croy! it is difficult to serve two masters well!" The popular feeling under these circumstances gradually rallied to the side of Charles, who publicly proclaimed the Croys enemies of the State, and called on all men to oppose them. A general petition was signed throughout the country on behalf of Charles, who went to the length of inviting the delegates of the States to meet him at Antwerp, while his father had summoned them to a similar meeting at Bruges. This was in January, 1464. If Philip had not been enfeebled by age and illness this step would have brought matters to a climax between father and son, but physically unequal to the struggle, Philip yielded to the pressure brought to bear on him, and a reconciliation was effected at Bruges in the following February. It was not, however, until April 1465, that the

---

* Louis bestowed on Charles the government of Normandy, but merely in an honorary sense. He also assigned him an annual pension of 36,000 livres, the same sum that Duke Philip had allowed him while resident in the chateau of Genappe.

reconciliation was made complete by the Duke proclaiming Charles his sole heir at Brussels.

Charles at the same time took over the government, joined "the league of the public weal" against Louis, and led a Burgundian army into France to assist the discontented nobles of that country against their sovereign. The battle of Montlheri, fought and won by Charles on 16th July, 1465, closed the brief war which Louis was far too astute to continue when he found that he was getting the worst of the struggle. By a treaty signed at Conflans Louis recognised the Burgundian claim to the towns on the Somme for the term of Charles's life. But while Louis was unable to prolong the open struggle with Charles he was just as implacable in his resentment, and what he could not gain by direct means he sought by indirect intrigues and circuitous devices. Louis was well aware of the latent discontent in all the cities of the Low Countries arising from the vigour and success with which Philip had asserted his authority. This hostility existed with greatest intensity at Liége which had suffered heavily at the hands of Burgundy in the time of Louis of Bavaria. The loss of its privileges had been keenly felt, and a popular party had been formed there which looked mainly to France for support and success. The anti-Burgundian sentiment there had been increased by the success of Philip's policy in procuring the nomination, as Prince-Bishop, of his nephew, Louis of Bourbon, whose sister was the first wife of Charles the Bold. A crowning touch was given to this sentiment when the Pope, ignoring all secular and civic rights, bestowed upon Louis supreme authority over his subjects. The citizens of Liége then rose in open revolt, repudiated Louis, and proclaimed the Marquis of Baden as their Prince. At that moment Louis was constrained to sign the treaty of Conflans, and Charles was thus left free to turn his arms in the direction of Liége. The battle of Mortenaeken —15th October, 1465—resulted in the defeat of the Liége troops with a loss of 2,000 men, and it was followed by the signature of the convention of St. Trond (22nd December) which not only restored Louis of Bourbon, but constituted Duke Philip perpetual and hereditary Mambour of Liége.

But the extreme party in Liége resented the convention of St. Trond, and withdrew to Dinant, then an important and flourishing city boasting a population of 60,000 people. Owing, no doubt, to the continued intrigues of Louis, the inhabitants of Dinant defied the power of Burgundy, and embittered the struggle to, as it proved, their own destruction by insults to the persons of Philip and his son which would not be tolerated in more modern times. The position of Dinant on the Meuse with its castle on the lofty cliff above the right bank seemed so strong, and the promise of aid both from France and Liége was so sure that the inhabitants resorted to insolence, and ridiculed the well-meant suggestions of some of their friends to gain lenient terms by a prompt surrender. Their confidence in the receipt of succour from their neighbours was so great that after the arrival of Charles, accompanied by his father with 30,000 troops, they refused to make the apologies some of the more respectable citizens had volunteered on their behalf for the personal outrage to the family of Burgundy.*
In face of these outrages the Duke and his son swore a great oath to capture the town and to raze it to the ground. The siege was prosecuted with extraordinary vigour, and the heavy bombardment soon effected a breach. The garrison had also lost 700 men, and no aid appeared from either the side of France or of Liége. Then the townspeople wished to surrender, but their emissaries were turned back, and the bombardment continued. Orders were given to deliver the assault when, on 27th August, the besieged opened their gates and surrendered at discretion. The town was then given over to pillage, Charles, however, allowed the women, children, and priests to retire in the direction of Liége. After four days' pillage the town was set on fire and to complete the destruction Charles paid several hundreds of labourers a daily wage to destroy

---

* They declared that Charles, or Charlotteau, was not Philip's son. They hung an envoy from the neighbouring town of Bouvignes, and they sent a message or hung up a notice in the following words: "What has your old mummy of a Duke taken into his head? Has he then lived so long as to wish to end his days here by a vile death? And your Count Charlotteau, what is he doing here? Let him rather go to Montlheri to fight the noble King of France, who will not fail to come to our succour, because he has so promised! Your Count has too yellow a beak to take us, and the people of Liége are coming very soon to drive him ignominiously away."

the walls and more substantial buildings, so that his vow might be fulfilled of not leaving one stone standing on another. The prisoners were either hung or thrown into the Meuse from the projecting cliff at Bouvignes. A few escaped to lead a life of exile in France or England, and some succeeded in founding a small colony at Middelburg. The sack of Dinant* has been described as a dark stain on Charles's memory, but it must be allowed that he received great provocation.

In the summer of 1467 Philip was attacked with apoplexy while residing at Bruges. His illness lasted two or three days, terminating fatally on 15th June. Charles who was absent had just enough time to reach his father's death-bed. The funeral in the Cathedral of St. Donat at Bruges was carried out on such a scale of splendour as made it one of the most imposing pageants of the Middle Ages. Thirty thousand persons passed by the bier of the Duke whose final resting place was not, however, the Bruges Cathedral, but the Carthusian Church at Dijon.

The hesitation shown in endorsing Philip's claims to the description of the Good need not be felt in describing him as a great prince. The union of provinces and states which had never been united, and which were divided in language and by the past from each other was in itself no small achievement even when simplified by the natural working out of the law of inheritance. His long and bitter struggle with the powerful communes which aimed at reducing the prince's authority to a shadow by the elevation of their own, resulted in the disciplining of the people of the towns which, at least, wiped off the slate the political pretensions they had advanced and at one moment seemed likely to establish. His policy towards his own subjects reached its climax on the field of Gavre and in the successive humiliations of Liége, outside his direct administration it is true, but directly subject to his influence in the person of his nephew and by his acquired rights of Mambour. In his

* A relieving force had set out from Liége, but retraced its steps on hearing of the fall of Dinant. Humbercourt, the Burgundian Chancellor, was sent to arrange terms with the city of Liége which craved peace. Louis of Bourbon was reinstated as Prince Bishop, a contribution was paid towards the expenses of the war and 300 hostages were sent to Brussels.

dealings with the majority of his subjects he figures, therefore, more as a severe ruler than as a beneficent leader in the paths of peace. It might be said of him that he corrected his subjects with rods, while it was reserved for a later Philip to chastise them with scorpions.

But if the means employed arouse stricture the results achieved claim praise. There is no doubt that under Philip the prosperity of the Flemish nation largely increased, and reached a point little inferior to its prime. Bruges, as the favourite residence of the Duke, as the seat of his Order of the Golden Fleece, had recovered much of its original prosperity. It was no longer, it is true, the banking centre of north-west Europe. A monopoly of commerce was no more possible, as other countries had not stood still. But the Flemings waxed rich and prosperous. There was more wealth in Burgundy, and especially in Flanders, than in France or England. The people lived and dressed more luxuriously, the Duke's treasure, stored in the strong castle of Hesbin on the Somme until fear of Louis' designs led to its transfer to Bruges, was valued at several millions of our money, and even the terrible loss of human life at Gavre seems to have been repaired in a few years. Dinant, indeed, disappeared from the list of prosperous cities, but Ghent certainly did not decline, and Bruges made considerable progress. Nor was the prosperity confined to Flanders. The cities of Brabant made still greater strides. Brussels began to assume the appearance of a capital. The fortress-palace of the Caudenberg threatened to displace the Count's Castle at Ghent. Antwerp vied as a port with Sluys, and, as evidence of its growing importance, the local records show that the Place de Meir was first paved in the reign of Philip the Good. This general prosperity extended to places of minor importance like Namur. A people, in estimating the character of their rulers, forget their methods but remember the results. For this reason the reign of Philip the Good is remembered by the Belgians with special feelings of gratitude as a period of national union, considerable power and undoubted material prosperity.

There were other and special reasons to mark out the reign

of Philip as a glorious epoch. It was under his patronage
that the Van Eycks laid the basis of Flemish art, and in the
introduction of printing, which revolutionised the conditions of
life and thought throughout the world, the Flemings of Bruges
had no inconsiderable share. Some of the magnificent
cathedrals and town halls, which constitute the architectural
glory of Belgium, were begun and completed during his lifetime, others dating, in their origin, from a period before the
House of Burgundy itself were finished, many more, such as
the Cathedral at Antwerp, were in turn begun, to be handed
down to a later generation for the realisation of the original
design. The town halls of Brussels, Louvain and Mons in
their entirety remain to testify to the splendour of Philip's con-
ceptions as a builder. His patronage of the artist brothers
Van Eyck was shown by the fact that he sent John Van Eyck
to Lisbon to paint the portrait of his intended bride, Isabel of
Portugal. In the credit for the introduction of printing into
general practice his direct participation was limited by the prejudice and narrowness of the Bruges citizens whose envy of
Wiliam Caxton as a foreigner led to their banishing him from
their city. But it was in the house of Colard Manson at
Bruges that Caxton learnt his trade and made the type with
which after his banishment he printed his first work at Cologne
in 1469. This work curiously enough had direct reference to
Philip, for it was the speech delivered by the Bishop of Lincoln
on presenting the Duke with the Order of the Garter.

The fifty years during which Philip directed the destinies
of the State which arrested the expansion of France on the one
side and of the German Empire on the other were consequently
remarkable from the social point of view as much as from the
military and political. The accumulation of wealth led to the
indulgence of luxury, and luxury entailed the patronage of art
in all its forms. For these reasons, as well as for the fact that
he established a political union between all the provinces, the
figure of Philip the Good stands out, large and commanding,
across the unhappy, stormy and disunited epochs of national
history to the last three generations of Belgians who have seen
the works he accomplished again happily realised.

His son and successor Charles, to whom had already been given the name of the Bold or the reckless, was of a more extreme and impatient character than Philip. What he wished he wished quickly, and the least opposition aroused his anger which soon passed beyond control. It is also probable that in the first days of power he presumed on his assumed popularity with the Flemings, forgetting his father's saying "I have known the Flemings love the heir of their Count, but their Count, never." Charles was destined to have very early proof of the truth of this statement. On the 28th June, 1467, after attending his father's funeral at Bruges, he made his "joyous entry" into Ghent. He performed the ceremonies of the occasion, ringing himself the mighty Roland to announce his succession, and receiving at the hands of the citizens a respectful and sufficiently cordial greeting. But on the next day the whole scene changed and the details furnished by different witnesses, conflicting with each other, leave the mind uncertain as to the cause. Probably the true explanation was the sudden and violent coming into direct collision of the fierce temper of Charles and the not less fierce disposition of the artizans of Ghent.

When Charles entered Ghent many of the citizens were on pilgrimage to the neighbouring shrine of Houtem St. Liéven. They returned the next day, and it is affirmed that many of them were intoxicated. On entering the city they resorted to noisy demonstrations, one of which was to destroy a toll house for the levy on corn. They then proceeded to the market place, when they were joined by others, all of course being armed. Another element of discord and danger arose from the presence of a large party of men—784 it was said—who had been banished in the time of Duke Philip, and who availed themselves of Charles's entry to return, partly with and partly without his sanction, to their native city. A vague clamour was then raised for their privileges, but apparently without any definite purpose, or clear design. While calling for the summary punishment of their enemies they continued to protest their affection and obedience to the Duke. Charles sent them word that if they would go home he would listen to anything that

CHARLES THE BOLD AT GHENT.

their representatives might put before him. This suggestion did not chime in with their mood. They refused to move, and the clamour increased. Then Charles imprudently rode on to the market place with a very few attendants, and demanded imperiously what they wanted. Having listened to their clamorous cries for a few moments he said he would think over what they asked for and again invited them to break up their meeting and go home. They might have done so if Charles had not impetuously seized one of them and ordered him with a push to make haste. Then the people broke into open mutiny, and their threats of personal violence to the Duke would certainly have been carried out if the Baron de la Gruthuse, whose influence in Ghent was great, had not thrown himself before the Duke, restraining his wrath with the observation "Do you not see all our lives hang by a thread," and with words of moderation and promises of complete compliance with their wishes gradually restored calm among the people. At his suggestion the Duke returned to his hotel, promising to listen to what they had to say from an open window and to make them a suitable reply. When Charles reached the window the crowd renewed its clamour and seemed unable to give coherent expression to what were supposed to be the popular demands. A dramatic turn was given to the situation by a man in black armour forcing his way up the staircase, and formulating for the mob the conditions they expected at the hands of the Duke from the very window where he stood, and which was regarded as reserved for the Count of Flanders. This man's name was Bruneel and as he formulated each condition in the guise of a question the popular answer came back to him in thunders of applause.

These conditions were the removal of bad magistrates, the abolition of the gabelle, the restoration to the Guilds of the right to have Banners, the re-opening of the three gates closed by the Treaty of Gavre, and the confirmation of their ancient privileges and usages. Having thus made known what they wanted the citizens of Ghent consented to disperse on the Duke's promising compliance. In yielding Charles was actuated mainly by apprehension for his only daughter and child Mary whom he had brought with him, but he gave expression to the threat " If I live ten years they will see with whom they have to deal." He left Ghent for Malines on 1st July, and from Brussels he wrote, on 28th July, the letter conferring on Ghent all it had demanded, which document is still in existence. The privileges conceded at Ghent had also to be bestowed in their several degrees of importance on Brussels, Louvain, and Malines. Within a few weeks Charles, therefore, saw himself compelled to restore to the communes all the privileges his father had wrested from them during his long reign. These concessions went very much against the grain of the imperious Charles, and in his heart he vowed as complete and speedy a revenge as circumstances would permit of. The character of Charles would not admit of his tamely accepting these affronts to his person as much as his authority. Reckless in courage and intolerant of opposition, he was far less likely than his father to put up with the opposition and self-assertion of the towns. With the instincts of a soldier more than those of a statesman it was said of him that he preferred the tent to his castle, the company of soldiers to that of his nobles, and the association of condottieri and military adventurers to that of his Flemish and Burgundian chiefs. How then was it that the citizens could have persuaded themselves that such a Duke would long keep his covenant with them?

A very few weeks after these concessions Charles gave clear proof of what his real views were. The people of Malines rose in insurrection and plundered the houses of several of the wealthier citizens. Some blood was spilt and more than one rich merchant was murdered, for it should be noted that much of the discontent in the cities arose from the jealousy and ill-will between the poor and the wealthy. Charles decided to strike the first blow and hastened to Malines at the head of a small but select Burgundian force. Neither in numbers nor in organisation had the citizens of Malines any means of resistance, and the Duke entered the city with the determination of reading them a severe lesson. Charles always tempered his severity with a rough elementary form of justice which on several occasions saved him from committing a crime. Even at Malines he began by instituting a sort of inquiry into the grievances of the insurgents, and although he punished many by fine and banishment his wrath had so far cooled down that, by the time the scaffold was erected on the market place opposite his residence for the excution of the more guilty or less fortunate, severity gave place to clemency. The sword of the executioner was raised to decapitate the first victim when Charles gave the signal for pardon, and so great were the manifestations of popular approval and joy that the Duke, relieved of personal apprehensions, could not forego the exercise of the privilege so rarely used in those days of a general forgiveness to his political enemies. None the less his personal authority was fully established at Malines, and he would probably have been encouraged to proceed to equal extremities with Brussels and Ghent if his attention had not been called off by serious matters elsewhere.

While occupied at Malines news arrived that the people of Liége, regardless of the fact that the Duke held three hundred of their fellow-citizens as hostages, had not only risen in revolt, but had captured Huy on the Meuse. The Bishop, Louis of Bourbon, had fled to Namur, whence he wrote imploring the aid of his cousin Charles. The Duke received the news with his accustomed rage,, and vowed that he would die or bring the people of Liége to a sense of their duty "by whip and stick." He summoned his vassals from far and near, and they came freely because a war with the rich city promised much plunder. But before the campaign began the question of the fate of the three hundred hostages had to be decided, and many of Charles's advisers were in favour of their execution. Contay, for instance, insisted on the exaction of a summary and complete vengeance, but fortunately for the reputation of Charles the more humane and wiser counsels of Humbercourt carried the day. That statesman, whose tact and skill often served as a foil to the impetuous militarism of Charles, succeeded not only in saving their lives but in inducing Charles to restore their liberty, for on returning to Liége he rightly argued they would not only testify to his magnanimity but use their influence against the party supported by France. For there is no doubt that the rising at Liége, in 1467, was directly fomented by King Louis and his agents, and that its citizens would never have assumed the offensive if they had not had reason to believe that a French army would come down the Meuse to their aid. In October, 1467, Charles was ready to march at the head of an army of 100,000 men on Liége. Envoys arrived at the moment of his departure from Louis XI. with the insidious proposal that he would abandon the Liége leaguers if Charles would abandon the Duke of Brittany, to which Charles gave the following frank reply. "I mean to march against the Liégeois, and see whether I am Seigneur or valet. I expect to fight them in three days. If I lose the day you will do what you like, but if I win you will leave Brittany in peace."

The Burgundian army marched to attack St. Trond in which there was a garrison from Liége, and on their side the Liégeois marched with 30,000 men to its relief. The two armies arrived, within a day or so of each other, in front of that place, and while Charles left a portion of his force, among which 500 English archers from Calais were specified, to keep the garrison of St. Trond in check he marched with the bulk of his army to attack the enemy in their position on Brusten heath. The battle, fought on 28th October, resulted in a decisive victory for Charles who is said to have never displayed greater skill in the arrangement of his forces. The Liége citizens left 4,000 killed on the field, and St. Trond surrendered a few days later. Charles compelled the citizens of that place to level their walls, to pay a heavy fine, and to surrender a certain number of citizens whom he promptly executed. He then advanced on Liége arriving before it on 11th November. The citizens decided to surrender without fighting, the more hostile or courageous withdrawing from the city, and on the 12th of the month three hundred of the principal citizens in their shirts, with bare feet and heads, proceeded to the Burgundian camp bearing with them the keys of the city gates. Charles at once sent Humbercourt in to take military possession, but he refused to enter himself by any of the gates. He required a sufficient breadth of the wall to be levelled to admit himself and an imposing cavalcade so that there might be no uncertainty as to who was the conqueror, and to give the occasion increased importance he was accompanied by the French Ambassador, whose mission was to warn him not to attack Liége, and by Louis of Bourbon, its dispossessed Bishop. The terms imposed on the defeated city were naturally severe and set forth in a treaty of 47 articles. Several thousand citizens were banished, a few of the chief leaders were executed, and a heavy fine of 120,000 florins was imposed. As a final indignity the celebrated perron of Liége, which was identified with the origin and greatness of the city, was carried off, and set up in Bruges with the addition of the following offensive inscription, that "this venerable token of the noble origin of Liége, hitherto the glory of an unconquered people, would now serve as the object of the populace's ridicule." Having thus effectually humbled Liége, as he thought, Charles returned in triumph to Brussels leaving the prudent Humbercourt to act in his absence as Lieutenant-General.

Having thus vanquished Liége the next care of Charles was to provide against the machinations of its abettor, Louis of France, who was plotting against him in every direction. Not content with inciting the citizens of Liége, Louis had encouraged John, Count de Nevers, to claim the Duchy of Brabant against his cousin Charles, and had even recognised him by that title. It was perfectly clear that the most powerful aid to Burgundy could come from England alone, and in February, 1468, an offensive and defensive alliance was concluded between them. The military power of England had been much enfeebled by the insane Wars of the Roses, but at that moment the Yorkists seemed to have established their position under Edward the Fourth. Charles, who sometimes called himself a Portuguese and sometimes an Englishman on account of his mother's descent, had long been well disposed to the English alliance and in his youth had wished to marry an English princess before his father compelled him to marry his cousin Isabel of Bourbon. The project was now revived, and one of the first conditions of the treaty was that Charles should marry Margaret of York, sister of King Edward. The marriage was celebrated with exceptional splendour at Damme, the port of Bruges, on 2nd July, and was followed by a triumphant entry and eight days' feasting and jousting in Bruges itself. A chapter of the Golden Fleece was held for the principal purpose of admitting King Edward among the Knights of the Order, and at the same time Charles's old enemies, the Croys, were banished from the duchy. After the marriage Charles, believing in the validity of a truce which he had signed with Louis after the capture of Liége, went to Holland where he passed several weeks in receiving the congratulations of his subjects in those provinces on his marriage, and on the alliance with England. Louis promptly seized the opportunity afforded by Charles's absence to attack the Duke of Brittany with an overwhelming force, to crush him in the field and compel him to abandon the Burgundian cause and recognise his duty as a vassal and peer of France. When Charles heard of Louis's proceedings he hastened to Peronne where his army was ordered to assemble, but it was too late to prevent the detachment of Brittany from his side.

It was at this moment that Louis came to his extraordinary decision to visit Charles, and to negotiate in person with him. His knowledge of Charles's character led him to think that the scheme would be unattended with any personal peril after the Duke had signed a Safe-Conduct, which is still preserved in the Paris Library and which bears the signature of "your very humble and very obedient subject, Charles." He entered Peronne accompanied by only sixty knights and eighty of his personal guard of Scottish archers, but although he was entertained with all respect and hospitality his hazardous diplomacy did not make much progress, when an unexpected event placed him in extreme personal danger. Louis entered Peronne on 9th October, 1468; two days later the news arrived that the citizens of Liége had risen in revolt, captured the Bishop and Humbercourt at Tongres, and it was rumoured put them to death. The Duke went into one of his habitual fits of rage declaring that the King had only come to Peronne to deceive him and throw him off his guard, and vowing that

CAPTURE OF LIÉGE.

Louis should dearly suffer for it. Fortunately for Louis the improbability of his having anything to do with the fresh rising at Liége, at a moment when he had trusted himself into the power of Charles, was evident to all the Burgundian Councillors, who restrained the Duke, and further news coming to the effect that the Bishop had not been killed and that Humbercourt had been released, the personal danger to Louis passed off. But he had to buy his safety by signing, on 14th October, a treaty yielding to his rival all the points and advantages he had promised to gain himself by his superior address. He had to do still more, for in order to establish his good faith in the matter he had to disown Liége and to promise Charles that he would combine with him in punishing it for its gross breach of faith.*

The two princes marched in company on Liége, the Duke accompanied by a large army, the King by only three hundred Scottish archers, and, in token of the alliance, Louis and his men wore the Burgundian Cross of St. Andrew. The people of Liége had made all possible preparations for defence, but their hopes of success were very faint when they saw that the sovereign on whose aid they so greatly relied was fighting against them. Their only chance was in a successful sortie, and the first made was so easily repulsed that they thought it wise to mollify the wrath of their enemy by the voluntary surrender of Bishop Louis of Bourbon. A second sortie carried out by the men of Franchimont was nearly successful, and its failure was due more to the calmness of Louis and the steadiness of his archers than to the easily excited courage of Charles. The moment of surprise having passed the assailants were cut down to the last man, and the next day the besiegers marched into the city prepared to carry it by storm, but no resistance was attempted, the bulk of the inhabitants having fled into the Ardennes while those who remained took shelter in the churches. After thanking God for the victory in the Cathedral of St. Lambert, Charles asked Louis what should be done with the rebellious city, and he is reported to have replied

---

* The details of the interview of Peronne live in the memoirs of Philip de Commines. Scott in his great romance, *Quentin Durward*, has brought the whole scene vividly before the English reader.

Q

oracularly "Who wishes to drive off the birds should first burn their nest." Liége was accordingly given over to the army to sack, and apparently only the Cathedral of St. Lambert escaped pillage. After this act Louis, humiliated in his person and thwarted in his policy, was allowed to depart for France while Charles remained to destroy by fire the captured city where the churches and convents were alone left standing. The same fate was meted out to Franchimont. The prisoners were either executed or drowned in the Meuse. Forty thousand persons in all are said to have perished during the sack of Liége. The destruction wrought in this city of the Church elicited the Pope's protest, and Charles bought absolution by various concessions, and the present of a gold figure of St. George to the treasury of St. Lambert. The impression produced throughout the whole country by the sack of Liége was deep and lasting. The rumour was spread that Charles intended to treat Ghent in a similar fashion, and the citizens of the bulwark of Flanders determined to avert the peril by a voluntary and abject surrender. On the 8th of January, 1469, the delegates of Ghent arrived at Brussels making, on bended knees before the Duke in his palace on the Caudenberg, a complete "renunciation of all its liberties."* At that moment the Duke, and with him the House of Burgundy, reached the apogee of its power.

Louis returned from Liége with the full determination to exact revenge for his defeat and humiliation, but it was not until the revival of the Lancastrian party in England, under Warwick the King Maker, that he felt strong enough to show his intentions, as that event, and the subsequent flight of Edward the Fourth† to Belgium, relieved him from all appre-

---

* The citizens read out their charter, the Duke declared it null and void, and his secretary cut it in pieces with a penknife. The guild banners were placed at the feet of the Grand Chamberlain. The Duke then recited his grievances against his rebellious citizens, adding his pardon in these words: "If you keep your promises, if you will be our good people and children, you will obtain our pardon, and we shall be to you good prince and archimandrite."

† Edward's exile was not of long duration. In October, 1470, he arrived in Holland and thence proceeded to Bruges. In May, 1471, after recovering his crown he wrote to his good friends, the citizens of Bruges, thanking them for "their hospitality, courtesy, and affection" during his stay among them.

hension of an Anglo-Burgundian invasion. Then it was that Louis convened a Parliament at Tours which relieved him from his oath to Charles, as having been made under compulsion, and at the same time summoned the Duke to come to Paris to explain his treatment of his suzerain. The King's messenger who brought this summons to Ghent was publicly whipped and narrowly escaped with his life. At the same time Louis allied himself with the Swiss cities which, previously more friendly to Burgundy than to France, had become frightened by the occurrences at Liége and Charles's avowed policy of humbling all the communes. What that policy was may be gathered from the following speech in reply to the inquiries made by Ghent delegates eighteen months after the surrender at the Caudenberg as to how the levies he proposed to make for the maintenance of a standing army were to be distributed. "It seems to me that you ask this question through malice and subtlety, and that neither you nor those who sent you have any wish or intention to please me. Heavy and hard Flemish heads that you are, you always remain fixed in your bad opinions, but know that others are as wise as you. I am half French, half Portuguese, I will know how to provide for your heads. You Flemings with your hard heads have always either despised or hated your princes. I prefer to be hated to being despised. Take care to attempt nothing against my highness and lordship for I am powerful enough to resist you. It would be the story of the iron and the earthen pots."

There must in justice be allowed this much of merit to Charles's policy in favour of the maintenance of a standing army, that it had become necessary in consequence of the French king having adopted the same system. The possession of a force on whose services the ruler could count at any moment signified a very considerable military advantage over the rival who could summon only feudal or communal levies. Charles fully realised the fact and urged the Flemish cities, somewhat too imperiously it is true, to provide him with the means of maintaining a regular force of 5,000 cavalry. His representations were strengthened by the offensive policy of the French King who, suddenly invading the Somme valley, succeeded in capturing several towns of which Amiens was the most important. Deprived of other allies by the astute policy of Louis and the internal troubles of England, Charles was obliged to appeal to his Flemish subjects for loyal support in defending his dignity. They could see for themselves that the danger was real, and they at once responded to their prince's request with a grant of 120,000 crowns and a levy of the communal forces. With a large army Charles proceeded to besiege Amiens, and his presence in the field sufficed to revive the project of a league of the Princes against Louis. Promising as its chances seemed at one moment, the stubborn defence of Amiens and the poisoning of the Duke de Guienne by his brother Louis led to the collapse of the scheme, and the Flemings wishing to return to their homes, Charles was constrained to sign a three months' truce. When he resumed the contest on its expiration, by the invasion of Normandy, he was again repulsed before the walls of Beauvais, the garrison of which place was incited to make a resolute defence by the heroism of a woman, Jeanne Hachette. A further truce was then concluded, and although the policy and proceedings of the two princes remained hostile to the end of Charles's brief reign, the seige of Beauvais was the real termination of his military operations against France. The Treaty of nine years signed at Soleuvre in September, 1475, was the formal ratification of the truces concluded after the repulses before Amiens and Beauvais, although a fresh chain of events on a different field conduced to the occurrence.

Philip the Good declared that he might have been a king if he had wished; Charles the Bold determined to seek a crown for himself. In order to rival Louis, and to figure on the same plane he began negotiations with the Emperor of Germany, Frederick the Third, for his elevation to the rank and style of king, and Frederick was by no means unwilling to comply with his neighbour's wishes, especially as he desired to bring about the marriage of his son Maximilian with the daughter and heiress of the Duke, Mary of Burgundy. Accordingly Frederick invited Charles to visit him in the old Imperial city of Treves, and all the preliminaries were arranged for the proclamation of Charles as King of Burgundy, and the consequent betrothal of Maximilian and Mary. The day before the event was to be consummated the Emperor suddenly left Treves at night for Cologne, without assigning any reason for his departure, thus evading the necessity of explaining his reversal of policy. Its causes are by no means clearly ascertained as the intrigues of King Louis to which everything was attributed in that age could scarcely have produced this result. It is more probable that Frederick was swayed by the representations of the other princes of the Empire whose jealousy was aroused by the ostentatious display of wealth made by Charles, and who easily persuaded Frederick that once he was king the Duke of Burgundy would outshine the representative of the Cæsars.

Charles returned from Treves not only disappointed in his principal wishes, but also incensed against Germany, which led him into enterprises on the Rhine that diverted his attention from France and thus resulted in the breach of the understanding with England, for Edward, on reaching Calais in accordance with the treaty of July, 1474, for a joint invasion of France, threw up the project in disgust on finding that Charles had no available army. The result was that Edward concluded a treaty of peace with Louis at Pecquigny in August, 1475, and Charles found himself obliged to follow suit one month later by the Treaty of Soleuvre already referred to. This would not have happened but for the unfortunate visit to Treves and its consequences. The desire to figure as a King had led Charles from his true policy into distant adventures which sapped his power and offered no adequate benefit. Louis the Eleventh is affirmed to have said in reference to his rival's actions about this period "When Pride rides in front, shame and loss follow close behind."*

Before the treaty of Soleuvre gave him a sense of security on the side of France Charles had been committed to hostilities on the Rhine which embroiled him with the Emperor, the Prince Bishop of Cologne, and the Swiss. His arms were not fortunate, and in the fruitless siege of Neuss he lost many of his troops and much valuable time. In Lorraine Duke René

* "Pride goes before a fall."

revived the question of his rights. In Alsace Charles's governor, Peter de Hagenbach, was seized by the people he had oppressed, and executed on the square of Brisach. The Marshal of Burgundy was routed by the Swiss near Hericourt, thus giving his master a warning of what might follow from which he did not profit at either Granson or Morat. Relieved on the side of France Charles hastened with fresh forces to retrieve these reverses and punish his enemies. The reconquest of Lorraine was not accompanied by any serious difficulty and he re-entered Nancy in triumph. The successes of the Swiss in Burgundy and Savoy touched him the more nearly because they had been gained over some of his oldest and most loyal vassals. The Swiss wished for peace and to be left in undisturbed possession of their mountain homes. They sent a deputation to Nancy to assure the Duke of this desire, and to say that there was more gold in the spurs and bridles of his horsemen than he would find throughout the whole extent of Switzerland. But Charles was implacable, and with a blind confidence in the army of 30,000 men under his banner he ordered the invasion of their country. The first passage of arms was fortunate, for the small fortress of Granson, overawed by the size of the Burgundian army, surrendered on terms which Charles violated in the most dishonourable manner, and the unfortunate garrison was destroyed. Some were drowned in the neighbouring lake, the greater number were hung. A summary vengeance was at hand. The forces of the Cantons aided by a certain number of German knights and their followers advanced to attack the Duke, who took up his position on a hill not far distant from Granson. There on the 2nd of March, 1476, he was attacked and completely defeated by the Swiss who, advancing in a solid phalanx pierced the Burgundian army through and through. There is every reason for accepting the accuracy of the most recent inquirers in stating that the actual loss of men on Charles's side was not very great. The serious blow was to his reputation and the confidence of his troops.

In his difficulty also Charles was compelled to turn for aid to the Flemish people, and to call upon them to come to his succour partly by threats and partly by entreaties. Despite his reiterated promises that no further imposts should be raised, he was compelled, by his resolution to prosecute the war with the Swiss to the bitter end, to make fresh levies and to call upon the Flemings to render military service under pain of confiscation of such fiefs and under fiefs as they might hold. Notwithstanding the threats of his Chancellor Hugonet, the communes rejected their Duke's proposal to order a *leveé en masse*, and they only voted a certain sum of money on the condition that no further subsidies should be asked for under six years. The open country could not be as obstinate as Ghent, and reinforcements reached Charles from it to the extent of ten thousand men. With these, the Burgundian levies, a corps of English mercenaries, and an increased body of Italian condottieri, Charles, three months after Granson, again took the field. On reviewing his new army he is reported to have said " By St. George, we shall now have vengeance."

Charles was delayed ten days by the small fort of Morat, the garrison of which, warned by the fate of Granson, offered a heroic resistance. This gave the Swiss levies time to assemble, and both of Charles's German enemies, Sigismond of Austria and René of Lorraine, hastened to aid them with their counsel and a considerable force of knights and men-at-arms. The battle of Morat—22nd June, 1476—was fought under every disadvantage for the Burgundian army. The Swiss concealed themselves in a forest until they saw that the Burgundians, exhausted by a long and vain search to discover their position, could be taken at a disadvantage, when they made their attack to the cry of Granson! Granson! The Burgundian-Flemish army was speedily thrown into confusion. The Swiss showed no mercy and no prisoners were taken. Eighteen thousand, Burgundians, Flemish, and English, were killed in all, but Charles escaped at an early stage of the battle with 3,000 cavalry. The star of victory that had so long shone over the House of Burgundy began to wane at Granson, and within the short space of sixteen weeks suffered its complete eclipse at Morat.

Still Charles, injured in his pride to such an extent by this defeat at the hands of people whom he described as "mere tailors and cobblers" that fears were entertained for his sanity, did not abandon the hope of vanquishing the Swiss. His appeals to the people of Flanders and Brabant for further help in his extremity were rejected in silence or repulsed with the statement that he was the aggressor and had only himself to thank for his defeats. Some of his Burgundian vassals showed greater devotion or, being nearer the Swiss frontier, felt more bound to take measures against Swiss incursions, and provided a contingent of three thousand fresh troops. With these and the fugitives of Morat he hoped to make head against his enemies, but he was surrounded by foes on all sides, and his own followers had lost faith in him. His old implacable enemy, Louis, detached from his side all who were amenable to a bribe, and Campo-Basso, the chief of the Italian condottieri, agreed to betray his master at the first opportunity. Under these circumstances began the last campaign of the last reigning Duke of Burgundy.

René of Lorraine had profited by the victory of Morat to the extent that he recovered the greater part of that province including Nancy. When Charles had gathered together the last army in his service he laid siege to that town and René hastened to Switzerland to obtain assistance. Nancy made a stout defence and all Charles's efforts to take it failed. A severe winter caused further ravages in the Burgundian army, and before Charles could make up his mind to retreat the Swiss arrived and cut off his communications with Luxembourg. The treachery of Campo-Basso paved the way for Charles's easy discomfiture. Still it was he who offered battle to his more numerous opponents. Sallying forth from his camp with a force of less than four thousand men, he strove to cut his way through the circle of his enemies. He failed in the attempt, and perished himself with the greater part of his last army. The battle of Nancy (5th January, 1477) completed the ruin of the military power of Burgundy which was begun at Granson and Morat.

The death of the great Duke of Burgundy produced an immense impression throughout Europe and remains one of the tragedies of all history. In ten years he lost the power which Philip the Good had taken fifty years to accumulate. Yet the early incidents of his reign seemed to promise an addition to rather than a diminution of that power. His triumph over Liége had been so complete and so terrible that all the other cities had made humble deposition of their rights at his feet. No Duke or Count ever obtained larger or more frequent subsidies at the hands of the Communes. Against their traditions they even gave him the right to maintain a standing army. Nor did his reign begin with less brilliance in the department of foreign affairs than in that of his home relations. He more than held his own with the King of France, and he revived the relations with Germany which promised to serve as an equivalent for the decline of the offensive power of England through its own internal troubles. But in his foreign policy, as in his domestic, he carried his arbitrary inclinations too far. He humbled the French King at Peronne and Liége, dangerous in the case of any Monarch, but especially perilous and imprudent in that of one so vindictive, dexterous, and patient as Louis. He offended the poor but proud German Emperor and kinglets at Treves by a lavish and unreasoning ostentation. He created in the breasts of his subjects of Flanders and Brabant—the states forming the real base of his power—such resentment that it only needed an occasion to burst forth for the humiliation of his helpless daughter and successor, Mary. His pride and arrogance led him finally into unnecessary and unprofitable military enterprises which brought him into collision with the Swiss and the Germans. His headstrong career ended at Nancy by the side of the frozen lake, where his defaced and mangled body was discovered two days after the battle,* at which fortune, that first deserted him at Granson, finally turned her back on him.

When her father died the young princess Mary, who inherited his titles and states as the only child of his three

---

* "Bearing two wounds, half-frozen and the visage partially devoured by dogs and wolves."—Barante. The remains of Charles were removed from Nancy in the 16th century, to the magnificent tomb prepared for them and those of his daughter Mary in the Bruges Cathedral, by their descendant, the Emperor Charles the Fifth.

marriages, was 19 years of age. She began her reign by summoning the States to meet at Ghent, and she was soon confronted with the stern realities of her position. The States met not to condole with her on the loss of a parent, nor to provide the means of exacting, if not reparation, at least an honourable peace, but to assert their own rights and proclaim their grievances. Their uppermost thought was to recover the privileges of which Charles and his father Philip had deprived them. They knew well that they were masters of the situation. The military power of the House of Burgundy had fallen with Charles, and in his place stood a young, inexperienced, and helpless girl. In every detail the situation was favourable for a people to recover its liberty.

The States began by demanding the appointment of a Superior Council of twenty-two members, half to be elected by the cities, half to be named by the Duchess and the Church. There were to be two secretaries, one speaking French, the other Flemish. Having thus provided for the suitable government of the country with a due regard for their own interests, the States proceeded to dictate terms to their young ruler. All the taxes imposed by Charles, and his objectionable law confiscating private property for disobeying his orders, especially those relating to military service, were to be abolished. The treaty of Gavre, the surrender at Brussels in January, 1469, were to be cancelled. A new Charter, dated 11th February, 1477, embodying all the old privileges was to be drafted, and only when Mary agreed to sign it was it made known that she could carry out the accustomed "joyous entry" into Ghent. Thus, in a few days, all the privileges gained and usurpations effected by three Dukes of Burgundy were lost or surrendered by the inheritress of their name. On the 16th of the same month Mary took the oath in the Ghent Cathedral, and rang the bell announcing the fact to the assembled citizens in the prescribed form. It was noticed at the time that her efforts, controlled by either agitation or weakness, only gave forth five feeble sounds, which the superstitious, looking back after the event in the habit of prophets, interpreted as signifying that her reign would not exceed five years.

But the communes wanted more than their rights. They wanted compensation for the personal insults and affronts they had received at the hands of Charles whose words had cut deeper into their self-esteem than his deeds had into their privileges. For the sweetness of revenge, which was in that age perhaps the most vital force among the sentiments of nations or princes, some more direct retribution had to be obtained from those who represented the House of Burgundy than the imprisonment of the sheriffs and magistrates who had signed the arrangements with the last two Dukes. An appropriate occasion soon presented itself for the gratification of these sentiments.

Louis the Eleventh, who had rejoiced at the downfall of Charles to which he had so materially contributed, hastened to turn the event to account by a double invasion of Burgundy and Artois, and it was given out that in the latter undertaking he aimed not only at recovering the towns on the Somme, but also at reviving in a practical form the pretensions to authority over the Flemish people claimed by the French Crown. At the same time Louis was willing enough to attain the latter object in a pacific manner by bringing about a marriage between his eldest son, the Dauphin Charles, and the young Princess of Burgundy, and when the latter made a personal and affecting appeal to him for protection as his god-daughter, it was to this project that he reverted although it did not prevent his prosecuting his military enterprise with energy. Mary herself was not averse to the French marriage at first, declaring that she would wed whomever the States liked, and several of the Burgundian ministers, Humbercourt and Hugonet at their head, were in favour of it. The sentiment of the Flemish people was more uncertain, but Louis, who had all his life coquetted with the communes, felt so sure of success that he sent his confidant, Olivier le Dain, as ambassador to Ghent. The selection of this barber-surgeon as envoy was in every way unfortunate, for he was himself a Fleming of low origin of Courtrai, and the citizens of Ghent were as touchy on the score of dignity as any prince in Christendom. While the young Duchess herself was amused, saying "My cousin the

King must think I am ill since he sends me his doctor," the citizens treated the envoy with haughty indifference, and when he demanded a personal interview with Mary, he received the curt reply that it would not be proper as she was still young and unmarried. The people hearing of this smashed the windows of his hotel and threatened to throw him into the Scheldt, whereupon Olivier hastened to leave.

In the meantime Louis in his camp before Arras had been negotiating on his own account. Margaret of York, widow of Charles and Mary's stepmother, intervened in the marriage question to support the claims of an English prince who would not have been unpopular with the Flemings, but unfortunately she combined with it an intrigue for the setting aside of their authority by nominating a secret inner Council composed of herself and the Burgundian leaders. Louis would have had no objection to treat with this Council on the basis of a marriage with the Dauphin, but as soon as he realised the Dowager's scheme he took a signal and summary means of retaliation. The formation of the secret Council had been indiscreetly notified to him in a letter partly written in Mary's own hand, stating that no one else was accredited by her, and in order the more to conciliate the King secret orders were given to the governor to surrender the town—not the citadel—of Arras. In due course arrived the Ghent deputies, whereupon Louis informed them that they had no power to negotiate, and produced the incriminating document. The deputies could not dispute the handwriting and taking the letter with them hurried back to Ghent. The Duchess, confiding in her belief that Louis would not be so mean as to betray her, denied any correspondence with him until the production of her own letter left her no course save to excuse herself on the ground of "her youth and inexperience." The citizens of Ghent were not so hard of heart as to resist the appeal of their young princess, and on the 23rd or 24th of March, 1477, they passed a formal vote of reconciliation with the Duchess. But they had no mind to let the others escape. Hugonet, Humbercourt and others were arrested, and on 27th March, Mary was forced to sign the nominations to a Tribunal of Eight for their trial. They were speedily condemned and to the death of traitors, but Mary hoped to save at least their lives by making a personal appeal on the ground that these men were servants of the House of Burgundy and not Flemish ministers. She hastened, on the 31st of the month, to the Hooghuys overlooking the market place, and addressing them from the Count's window implored the people to have compassion on her and spare her old faithful servants. But Hugonet and Humbercourt had in the days of their master not spared the people of Ghent, and had used bitter and scornful words which had rankled. The few who were moved by the tears of a girl were overwhelmed by the many who remembered the gibes and jeers of Charles's chief ministers. The efforts of Mary were unavailing and she returned disconsolate to her hotel, but it was not until three days later that the condemned ministers, after undergoing torture,* were executed. Mary does not seem to have known of the execution on that Good Friday morning until after it had happened, so that the story of her intervention having been made at the foot of the scaffold instead of three days earlier from the window of the Hooghuys belongs to the realm of romance.† At Brussels, Antwerp, and other towns, the chief representatives of the Duke Charles were either imprisoned or executed.

In betraying his tools to the Flemish leaders Louis thought he was advancing his policy, while as a matter of fact he was ruining his chances. The French marriage scheme became most unpopular,‡ and the English was discredited by the anti-communal intrigues of Margaret of York. Under these circumstances the project of a German marriage was revived.

* Torture was applied with the object of enforcing confession of guilt before execution. This cruel practice was abolished by the Emperor Charles V. in 1532, but it was revived by Alva in the reign of Philip II.

† M. Kervyn van Lettenhove in his *Histoire de Flandre* makes this quite clear, and moreover, it is the more in accordance with probability. In Mary's pathetic speech she introduced these words "Good people! Remember that I have forgiven you all your faults towards me, and you ought equally to forgive those who have committed faults towards you."

‡ The Duchess' lady of honour, the Dame d' Halewin, said of this proposal —the Dauphin being only eight years old—"The Duchess is of an age to have children, not to marry a child."

Mary had been more or less formally betrothed to the Archduke Maximilian at Treves, and disgusted with her godfather's treatment, she declared her willingness to marry her father's choice. She was at Bruges engaged in signing its new charter and in restoring the ancient organisation of Flanders when an Embassy arrived in April, 1477, from the Emperor of Germany to execute the marriage between his son and the heiress of Burgundy and Flanders. A few days after its arrival the formal betrothal was celebrated, the Duke of Bavaria acting as proxy for Maximilian, and, in accordance with the etiquette of the Imperial Court, passing the night in the same chamber on the bed of state with the naked sword between, and the attendant guard of archers. The marriage was popular because it removed the fear among the communes as to France restoring another line of Burgundian Dukes and tyrants, while Mary signalised it by the gracious act of restoring the Banners surrendered at Brussels and ignominiously deposited in the churches of Hal and Boulogne. Four months later Maximilian, described then as a slow and sluggish youth of 18, arrived at Ghent when the marriage was celebrated in a quiet and unostentatious manner. In this way was introduced into the national life of Belgium the influence of Germany which soon acquired the ascendency that it retained for three centuries.

The astute ruler of France had not anticipated this turn of events, nor could he be expected to foresee that the unscrupulousness with which he sought to turn to account the youth and inexperience of his god-daughter would recoil on him and destroy for centuries the French sympathies that he thought he had planted in Flemish bosoms. Baffled in his policy he turned to arms and with the more confidence because Burgundy had made complete submission and accepted its destiny as part of France. The campaign of the autumn of 1477 did not, however, realise his expectations, the vigorous defences of the citadel of Arras and the town of St. Omer greatly retarding the advance of the French army. The former surrendered on terms which the King observed in the letter but broke in the spirit. He left the camp and closed his eyes while his troops pillaged it. Some weeks later he gave orders for the town to be destroyed and a new free town constructed in its place. The latter of these places was defended by the Sire de Beveren, son of the Bastard Antony of Burgundy, then a prisoner in the hands of Louis. Unable to take the place by force Louis threatened to execute his captive, but Beveren replied that "much as he loved his father he loved his honour more." The truce of Lens—18th September, 1477—ended this brief and inconclusive campaign. The next year's campaign was also marked by several sieges such as the gallant defence of Condé by its lady, of Ypres and of Arras. A contingent of English archers under Sir Thomas Erpingham rendered useful service, and especially distinguished itself in the repulse of a sortie by the garrison of Tournai. But on the whole the campaign was uninteresting and purposeless, closing with a fresh truce on 11th July, 1478.

The campaign of 1479 was more decisive. The English contingent was raised from 1,500 to 5,000 men, and a considerable force of German knights and heavy horsemen, ritters and lanzknechts, arrived under the Landgrave of Hesse. Maximilian also took the field in person. The French army was commanded by Philip de Crèvecœur, a Burgundian chief who had deserted Charles the Bold and, as his reward, been appointed Governor of Picardy by Louis. A special bitterness had been imparted into the struggle by the systematic plundering of defenceless villages by French bands and the Flemings were anxious to put an end to these incursions by defeating the main French army. The operations of the war centred round the siege of Therouanne by the Flemish army. Crèvecœur marched to the relief of the place and Maximilian drew up his army to oppose him on the field of Guinegate. The battle which was to decide the war was fought on 7th August, 1479, and its alternating fortunes faithfully illustrated the bitterness of the struggle and the equality of the combatants. After some severe fighting Crèvecœur succeeded in driving back the Flemish forces opposed to him, but carried away by his impetuosity, or misled as to the extent of his success, he continued the pursuit while his archers proceeded to plunder the camp. In the meantime Maximilian had maintained his ground with the English archers, his German contingent and some of the Flemish troops, and after a desperate struggle succeeded in driving back the remainder of the French army and in capturing the French camp. When Crèvecœur returned from his rash pursuit he found, like Prince Rupert at Naseby, that the day was lost. The victory, although not as signal as it might have been made, closed the long struggle with Louis in a manner favourable to the security of Flanders.

During these years the princess Mary had been growing in popularity with her subjects who were satisfied with her foreign policy because it was controlled by themselves, and not alienated by her wars with France when waged for defensive purposes. Being thus content in matters of state they had the leisure to watch and consider her in a personal sense, and such were the grace and charm that distinguished her that she became the most popular of all Flemish rulers. Her excellence as a skater formed the theme of popular observation, and of favourable comparison with the clumsy movements of her husband. Her love of hunting was carried to the verge of excess seeing that when she met her death she was far advanced towards confinement. The people admired her for her comeliness and activity, and if she had been spared the power and prosperity of Flanders might have been established on a surer basis than ever before. Knowing the leaning of the people towards England she began to negotiate for a marriage between her infant son Philip, born 22nd June, 1478, and the Princess Anne, daughter of Edward the Fourth. A summary conclusion was put to these projects and to a life of so much promise by the accident that occurred to the young Duchess at the beginning of March, 1482. She was hawking in the neighbourhood of Bruges when her horse threw her and she was found stunned by her attendants lying against the trunk of a tree. The accounts vary as to the gravity of her injury, which was certainly neglected although it appears doubtful that the neglect arose from the bashful refusal of the princess to show the doctor the injury. Her death ensued on 25th March,

1482,* and her rights passed to the infant Philip, for the states were too jealous of their recently acquired rights to entrust more than the limited authority of "bail and mainbourg" to Maximilian.

The death of Mary of Burgundy forms a convenient point for the conclusion of this survey of the rule of the House of Burgundy. The contraction of its dominions after the death of Charles had resulted in the solidification of its power in the Provinces, and as Mary was the more exclusively dependent on them so did she make it the more her object to study their wishes and to abide by the charters she had acknowledged. The Flemings were easily governed if left undisturbed in the possession of their privileges, and if not called upon to take part in military undertakings of an offensive character. They wished to attend to their own affairs, and to wax rich and prosperous. Only under the compulsion of an invasion were they willing to fight beyond their city walls. The brief reign of Mary, alone among all the members of her family, complied with these conditions and humoured the views of her Flemish subjects. As a consequence she was popular and regretted. There is no doubt that even in these few years of internal peace the prosperity of the community made marked progress, and much of the loss caused by the heavy exactions of Charles was recouped. The world was on the eve of great discoveries, and although the sword was still the universal arbiter, men's minds had turned to the view that commerce was as necessary to the health of a nation as prowess in arms. The Flemish artisans still retained their old industrial pre-eminence and at every lull in the international conflict around their borders they promptly reasserted it.

But while the Flemish people, and the same may be said of the peoples of Brabant and Hainaut, saw what was harsh, bad and costly in the Burgundian system, they did not

* She was the mother of two children, Philip and Margaret of Austria. Gaillard, *Histoire de Marie de Bourgogne* accepts the story which is at least more probable than that of the anonymous "*Histoire Secrete de Marie de Bourgogne*," Lyon 1694, which attributed death to a disappointment in love with the Count d' Angouleme, cousin of Louis XI. He was grandson of the Duke D'Orleans murdered by Philip the Bold, but is still better known in history as the father of Francis I.

recognise its merits. They did not see that it was endeavouring to hammer them into a nation, and to fashion out of a collection of cities, counties, and communes a state that could hold its own with either France or the Empire. They did not realise this fact and they would not have appreciated the attempt if they had done so. They could not be expected to be endowed with qualities not included in their national characteristics, and their robust, homely virtues were precisely those which have never been associated with any great gift of foresight or, in other words, of statesmanship. Perhaps it must also be admitted that the rashness or insanity of Charles placed an unfair strain on the obedience of his subjects whose common sense revolted against enterprises that were undertaken without a sound motive and prosecuted without judgment. With the Burgundian family, and for this purpose it terminated with Mary, there none the less disappeared the first favourable opportunity of welding the provinces watered by the Scheldt, the Meuse, and the Moselle, and bounded by the Rhine into a State to be respected for its power, and secure in its own strength and resources against the covetousness and greed of its neighbours.

CHAPTER X.

The Transition to Spanish Rule.

THE death of Mary of Burgundy was the prelude to fresh troubles between the political and civic powers in the country. The former, represented by Maximilian, thought mainly of perpetuating the alliance with the Empire as against France, while the latter, typified by the stubborn citizens of Ghent, strove to uphold their local rights at all hazards. Maximilian claimed the guardianship of his son and daughter, and the control of the former's estates, as Mainbourg, during his minority. The claim, reasonable in itself, was admitted by the states of Brabant, Hainaut, etc., but it was as resolutely denied by those of Flanders, who held in their possession at Ghent the persons of the two children. Ignoring the pretensions of Maximilian, four guardians were appointed to act in the name of Philip who, although less than five years of age, was solemnly inaugurated as Count of Flanders, on 10th January, 1483, at Ghent. The Flemings had combined with this measure a very clear departure in their foreign policy by negotiating, on their own account, with the King of France whose alliance they saw was necessary to enable them to hold their position against the Empire. The peace negotiations, begun with France at Ypres in July, 1482, resulted in the signature of a treaty of peace in the following December. By this treaty Philip was to pay homage to the King of France as suzerain, and Philip's sister Margaret was to marry the Dauphin; while on the other hand Louis restored to the Flemings all their ancient trading privileges in France. The young princess Margaret was sent to France to be educated, and her formal betrothal with the Dauphin was celebrated at Amboise on 23rd June,

1483, two months before the death of Louis XI., whose policy of ranging the Flemish communes on his side against the House of Burgundy thus seemed at length crowned with success.

Maximilian had no part in these negotiations, which excited a general joy throughout Flanders, but he was collecting all the forces he could for the assertion of his rights. He wrote complaining to the Ghent Council because they held his son "in despotical servitude and subjection," and they replied in a tone of defiance, denying even his right to preside over the Order of the Golden Fleece. Maximilian had on his side the natural rights of a father, and also the fact that he had led the Flemish armies to victory in repelling the invader. The Ghent Council did not strengthen its case by adding insults to its opposition, and the son of the Emperor was not a personage to be lightly flouted, even by the citizens of Ghent. The blame for this renewal of the old perennial struggle between the ruler and the communal authorities must not be altogether cast on Maximilian. His claims were not unreasonable in themselves, and the personal extravagance laid to his charge during the life of his wife was not sufficient to justify their rejection without some consideration and further trial. It is impossible to grasp, by reference to such precise and inanimate materials as mediæval documents, the sense or the drift of public opinion, but there seems some reason to believe that the intensity of Flemish feeling was not so much against Maximilian as a man but as a German, a foreigner, who had brought a new race into the country to batten on its wealth and prosperity. The Flemings were never tolerant of foreign intruders, and they planted their feet firmly in repelling the Germans who followed in the train of the Austrian Archduke. This sentiment was echoed in the other great cities beyond the limits of Flanders, and explains why the commune of Brussels declared against Maximilian in the words "nothing shall separate us from Ghent."

Maximilian resolved to appeal to the arbitrament of arms. Having collected his forces, many of whom were attracted from Germany solely by the hope of the plunder of the rich cities of Flanders, he struck the first blow by the capture of Termonde in November, 1484. He took this place, and the still more important town of Audenarde by stratagem, and other places by open force. The Ghent citizens left the shelter of the city to attack him, under the command of an aged citizen, Thierri de Schoenbrouk, who had led them at Gavre, but they suffered a sharp defeat with the loss of several of the banners that Mary had restored. They might have lost Ghent, too, if a relieving French army had not arrived in time to save it (February, 1485). The general in command was Crevecœur, the noble who had deserted Charles and been defeated at Guinegate by Maximilian. In some unknown way he offended or alarmed the people of Ghent and, after a four months' occupation, the French army was obliged to quit Ghent secretly at night, leaving its artillery behind it. During the interval Maximilian had seized Bruges, and from that place he had no doubt succeeded in bringing over to his side a certain number of the Ghent citizens. While the French army was rallying under the walls of Tournai, Maximilian completed the negotiations recognising him as Mainbourg or Regent for his son. This arrangement was concluded and announced on 21st June, 1485, ten days after the departure of the French army. Soon afterwards Maximilian, who was met by his son Philip outside the town, entered Ghent attended by 5000 troops, chiefly Germans under Martin Schwartz who, by a curious coincidence, was killed in England the very next year at the battle of Stoke. The citizens, who had just been relieved of the presence of one foreign army, did not refrain from something more than murmuring their displeasure, and shouts were even raised "Deliver us from these Germans whom you have brought with you; or else we will deliver ourselves." This provided Maximilian with the excuse he needed for inflicting punishment on the hostile city. For a moment he thought of destroying the city, but he was restrained by the Duke of Cleves, who said "Would you destroy the flower and pearl of all your States?" He imposed, however, a heavy fine on it, and punished some of the chief citizens with death and others with exile. He then crowned his revenge by compelling the magistrates of the people to appear before him bare-headed, and with naked feet, and confess their fault. The only promises Maximilian made in return were that when his son was of sufficient age he would hand over the ruling power to him, and that in the meanwhile Philip* should be educated at Ghent by Flemish tutors and in accordance with Flemish customs. Still, none the less, Maximilian had made good his chief pretensions.

Soon after this first pacification of Ghent, Maximilian went to Frankfort to be elected King of the Romans, but he was recalled to Flanders by a fresh war with France, instigated by Henry VII. The campaign proved unsatisfactory, although Maximilian had formed the military system identified with the term landsknecht or lansquenet, with which originated modern standing armies. But on this occasion it did not counterbalance the apathy of the Flemish cities, who refused to send any men to fight the French. The ill-success of Maximilian's arms in the field encouraged the communes to make a fresh effort to recover the rights they had lost. Maximilian proceeded to Bruges, where the States were ordered to meet, and arranged for a fresh army, on the march from Germany, to join him there. He intended with this force to crush all resistance, but when it arrived within striking distance he left the city to give its commander instructions as to how he should effect an entrance. Having done this he incautiously returned, because the object of his excursion could not be concealed. At once the citizens rose in revolt, seized the gates, and sent off messengers to summon aid from Ghent and Ypres. Maximilian, or his friends, aggravated the situation by attempting to set fire to the town in five places. Then the King of the Romans and his officers were seized, and placed in confinement in the house on the Market Place known as the Craenenburg. The

---

* The contemporary chronicle relates that when Philip went out to meet his father at Ghent he did not know him, and burst into tears on being caressed. Among the citizens fined and punished was Louis de Gruthuse (Earl of Winchester in the English peerage), who had saved Charles the Bold at Ghent. During this period Louis of Bourbon, Bishop of Liége, was murdered (1482) by William de la Marck, the Wild Boar of the Ardennes, who in turn was executed at Maestricht (1485). The affairs of Liége remained in great confusion for some time.

register of the payments made for barring up the windows and strengthening the doors on this occasion still exists. The principal Germans were thrown into the far gloomier prison of the town, and three of them were arrested in Maximilian's own chamber. All the leading citizens who had favoured his pretensions were brought before a popular tribunal whose only mission was to condemn. The chief of these, Peter Lanchals, long evaded capture, but when taken the city celebrated the event as if it were a fête day, and gloated over his torture by a machine of his own invention of which he was destined to be the first victim. During the eleven weeks that Maximilian remained a prisoner in the Craenenburg executions went on daily, and only one of his German knights, the Count of Zollern, escaped, in the guise of a peasant woman carrying a basket of onions, to perpetuate, in modern times, the mighty House of Hohenzollern.*

The holding in restraint of the person of the King of the Romans, the heir to the title of Cæsar, and the Emperor's Vicar west of the Rhine, by a party of lawless citizens, who stained their victory by brutal excesses, aroused the deepest indignation in all the Courts of Europe excepting France. The Emperor raised a considerable army to rescue his son, and the Pope placed Ghent and Bruges under his anathema. But meantime Maximilian, relying on himself, had entered into negotiation with the States and had promptly notified his willingness to accede to their terms. In his difficult and dangerous position, for the citizens wished to put him to death, he exhibited both courage and calmness, and on 16th May, 1488, terms were drawn up and signed to the following effect: Maximilian resigned the Regency, engaged to conduct the German and other foreign troops out of Flanders, and to make himself a party to the last treaty with France. He took the oath to observe these conditions solemnly on the Bruges market place, but the citizens would not let him depart until Philip of Cleves went bail for his faithful observance of the engagement. It is affirmed that on leaving the city Philip asked him to tell

---

* The rising must have been popular as the foreign merchants in Bruges subscribed a thousand crowns to fight the King of the Romans.

him candidly whether he meant to abide by the Treaty or not, and that Maximilian reassured him with the words that it was a binding engagement.

It is not necessary to inquire how far Maximilian was sincere at the moment of escaping from imprisonment in giving that reply, but in that age the engagements extracted by force, as at Peronne and Bruges, were not binding after the necessity controlling the signatories had passed away. The Emperor Frederick, who had come in person from the heart of Germany to rescue his son, cut the Gordian knot, if the doubts of Maximilian constituted any such obstacle, by relieving him from his promise. On the 19th May, three days after his reply to Philip of Cleves, Maximilian wrote informing the people of Bruges that he did not intend to abide by the terms of the convention they had forced upon him. At the same time he hastened to Frankfort to demand further assistance from the Diet to prosecute the war vigorously against France, for the Flemings were represented as her allies, and they did as a matter of fact make the strongest appeals to Charles VIII. for assistance. The Emperor, at the head of the first German army, established his camp outside Ghent, where Philip of Cleves, hostage for the good faith of Maximilian, had publicly declared his loyalty to the Flemish cause and been in turn elected Captain-General. The campaign of 1488-9 proved of a desultory and uninteresting character. By virtue of the alliance between Henry VII. and Maximilian, an English force, under Lord Daubeny, attacked and defeated the Flemings at Beerst, and Philip of Cleves was compelled to sanction the capitulation of Brussels to Albert of Saxony, a skilful soldier, then entrusted with the command-in-chief of the Imperial armies. But the fatal blow of all was the defection of France which, tired of the war, made peace with the Emperor at Frankfort on 22nd July, 1489. After this the Flemings could not prolong the struggle, and negotiations were commenced under the mediation of Charles VIII. at Montils which resulted in a definite treaty, dated 30th October of the same year. By this arrangement Maximilian was reinstated Mainbourg or Regent, the immense indemnity of 500,000 crowns was to be paid him by Ghent, Bruges, and Ypres, and the magistrates of these three cities were to apologise, bare-footed, to him for the wrongs and affronts they had offered. Ypres surrendered at once, and paid or promised to pay its share of the indemnity, but both at Bruges and Ghent some delay occurred before the provisions of the arrangement at Montils could be put in force.

The citizens of Bruges and Ghent did not hold out against the proposed restoration of Maximilian or the humiliation of their representatives, but they quarrelled about the division of the indemnity, and its incidence on one another. An Imperial army under the Count of Nassau was sent to besiege Bruges. Having occupied Damme, it soon reduced the city to extremities, and as Ghent was involved in the same difficulties no aid could be received from that quarter. A treaty was accordingly concluded on the 29th November, 1490, at Damme, the Brugeois paying 80,000 gold crowns and surrendering sixty citizens, many of whom were summarily executed on the market place. Maximilian thus avenged the affront its townspeople had offered him, and the massacre of his own friends and supporters. But a still more severe blow had been dealt the prosperity and strength of Bruges by the silting up of the Zwyn, which had begun to show symptoms of occurring half a century before and which about this time became complete. The port of Damme ceased to be a port, and the foreign merchant guilds, or nations as they were and are still called, removed to Antwerp, thus laying the foundation of the commercial importance of that city.

At Ghent the opposition was more protracted, partly on account of the natural obstinacy of its citizens, partly because the belief that France would not allow them to be crushed remained strong, and also, no doubt, for the simple reason that Philip of Cleves was a capable leader in whom they had confidence. When it was realised that no aid would come from France, the peace party began to prevail, and after some hot disputes at the Council Board, during one of which one councillor stabbed another, the brothers Coppenholle, who were the chief advocates of resistance to the bitter end,—a fact not surprising seeing that they were the principal instigators of the Bruges executions during Maximilian's imprisonment—were executed to propitiate the King of the Romans. A formal treaty was signed at Cadzand on 30th July, 1492, by which Ghent paid its share of the indemnity imposed, and made, in abject manner, the amende to the slighted dignity of the ruler. Here again the red blood on the scaffold testified to the reality of the concessions recorded in ink on the parchment. The treaties of Damme and Cadzand sealed the downfall of the proud Flemish cities and prepared the way for that emphatic assertion of Imperial power which took place in the reign of Maximilian's grandson. They resented their fate, and chafed at it, but the progress of the countries constituting the Empire reduced their importance as political entities, and they sank gradually from a position of equality with potentates and powers to one of local insignificance. They had failed to see the tendency of the age, which Maximilian, with all his defects, had seen. The interests and rights of the commune were only of weight in so far as they formed part of those of the State, and Maximilian had good reason on his side when, in response to remarks as to the sufferings inflicted on Flanders by the long struggle, he replied "Better that the country should be spoilt than that it should be lost."

Margaret of Flanders had been sent, at the time of the arrangement with Louis XI., to France to be educated for her marriage with the Dauphin, now become King himself under the style of Charles VIII. The desire to convert the fief of Flanders into an indirect possession, by marriage with the sister of its Count, strong in the breast of Louis XI., was less strong with his son, who aimed at the direct and immediate acquisition of Brittany by his own marriage with Anne, the heiress of that Duchy. In December, 1491, this project was duly realised by the marriage of the King and the young Duchess at Langeais, while Margaret of Flanders was sent back rejected and disdained to her native country. Maximilian, then relieved as to his worst apprehensions about Flanders, made this affront an excuse for a declaration of war, and if his ally, Henry VII. of England, had only remained true to their alliance the French King might have paid dearly for jilting the daughter of the King of the Romans and the last Duchess of Burgundy. But Henry allowed the French ruler to buy him off for 745,000 golden crowns, although it should not be overlooked that Henry had some cause for resentment and distrust of the ruling family of Flanders on account of the several times repeated attempts of the old Duchess, Margaret of Burgundy, to revive the Yorkist cause in the persons of those extraordinary impostors, Lambert Simnel and Perkin Warbeck. Henry's defection compelled Maximilian also to make peace, but the interruption of trade and good relations between England and Flanders continued for four years, and they were not restored until, in 1496, a Flemish deputation proceeded to London and arranged the outstanding differences, which related to fishing along the coasts as well as to commerce.

In August, 1493, Maximilian succeeded his father as Emperor, and in the following year he came to the Netherlands with the express purpose of handing over "the lordship and princedom" of the estates of the Duchy of Burgundy to his son, Philip the Fair. On 26th December, 1494, Philip was formally inaugurated Count of Flanders in the approved style at Ghent. But greater events were in the air. The union of the crowns of Aragon and Castille in the persons of Ferdinand and Isabella, and the expulsion of the Moors from Spain, had opened, to the imagination of Maximilian, a new and more certain alliance than that of England, at the same time that the opportunity was afforded of effecting marriages for his children that would compare in brilliance with those of France. It was accordingly arranged that Philip was to marry Joanna of Aragon, and Infanta of Castille, while his sister, Margaret, was to wed Don John, the heir of the double crown of Spain. Joanna of Spain arrived at Antwerp in September, 1496, and in the following month her marriage with Philip was celebrated at Lierre. The marriage of his sister with Don John was prevented by the sudden death of her intended husband in 1497, and in the following year the Queen of Portugal, the eldest daughter of Ferdinand and Isabella, also died, thus leaving Joanna the heiress of that great Spanish dominion which had established a first claim on the Americas. Maximilian's policy

268   THE HISTORY OF BELGIUM.

had only aimed at obtaining a good ally against France, and some suitable alliances for his children. It resulted in the concentration in the hands of his grandson of an Imperial power which in its way has never been surpassed. It was not

ARRIVAL OF JOANNA OF SPAIN.

surprising that in a moment of exaltation he should declare that Austria was destined to rule the Universe.*

The brief career of Philip presents little subject for description or comment. His handsome youthful figure occupies the stage for but a short interval between the turbulent Dukes of

* He took as his motto the five vowels, because A.ustriæ E.st I.mperare O.rbi U.niverso.

Burgundy and the great monarchs who possessed the States as an appendage of their wide-stretching domains. He inherited his mother's popularity with the Flemish people, among whom he had been brought up, and for a time he even sympathised with their views in favour of an understanding with France as against the wider ambitious projects of Maximilian. The death of his mother-in-law, Isabella of Castille, called him to Spain, where, despite the opposition of Ferdinand of Aragon, he was recognised as her heir in right of his wife, and on 14th January, 1505, they were both proclaimed as King and Queen of Castille, Leon, and Granada from the Steps of St. Gudule at Brussels. A year later Philip, accompanied by his wife and their two sons, Charles and Ferdinand, sailed for Spain, where Philip was destined to find an early grave. On 25th September, 1506, he died at Burgos in consequence, as was stated, of drinking iced water when over-heated from playing tennis. A tragic feature was added to the occurrence by the fact that his widow went mad through grief, and that she is permanently known in history by the designation of Joanna the Mad. The death of Philip was regretted throughout his dominions, where many fancied they detected in his character the qualities of his great grandfather, Philip the Good, but it tended to consolidate the power of Maximilian, who might have encountered some opposition from his son.

Philip was succeeded by his elder son, Charles, born at Ghent on 24th February, 1500, on whom Maximilian had conferred the Dukedom of Luxembourg, but who, after his maternal grandmother's death, was known as the Prince of Castille. The Emperor at once put forward his claim to act as Regent for his grandson, and this pretension was recognised by the council of the States that met at Malines. Neither Flanders nor Hainaut was represented on this Council, and it was a question how far they might acquiesce in the reassertion of the authority of Maximilian, whose name re-opened old sores and threatened unpopularity. Still Maximilian, so far as form went, was again recognised as Regent for his grandson as he had been for his son, and he notified his acceptance of the post in a very gracious speech in reply to the deputation that brought him the announcement. But at the same time the cares of an empire, and the direction of a policy not confined to the Netherlands, left him no leisure for conducting the routine work of the administration in those provinces. He very wisely decided,* therefore, to entrust the government of the States of Burgundy to his daughter, Margaret of Austria, who would have been Queen of Spain if Don John had lived, and who was now the widow of Philibert, Duke of Savoy. In her, the Belgians found a ruler who knew how to respect their privileges, and at the same time to carry them along the course desired by the requirements of her father's policy.

With the exception of the one campaign of 1513, when an English army, under the personal command of Henry VIII., co-operated with Maximilian and won the Battle of the Spurs, besides capturing the strong places of Therouanne and Tournai, the administration of Margaret was pacific, and she succeeded in establishing the authority of the States over Liége by treaty, and in Frisia by purchase of the rights ceded to Albert of Saxony. When Charles was inaugurated in the possession of the Low Countries in January, 1515, he took over the territory of the Burgundian family in a state of exceptional prosperity. His aunt had ruled so well and with such skill that there were no difficult questions or disputes left for him to solve, while the commercial condition of the country was so flourishing that it was valued at forty million gold florins.† Margaret had also devoted special care to the education of Charles, who benefited, by the instruction of the learned Erasmus among other

* How far this decision may have been affected by the implied warning in some of the phrases employed by the heads of the deputation must be judged for oneself. "The Belgian," said the Chancellor of Brabant, and the observation is remarkable as one of the first recurrences to the comprehensive generic name, "recognises that he is submitted to the Monarchical Government, but this government will only be solid and durable so long as the prince will confide the deposit of his authority to ministers who know how to merit the confidence of the nation by their talent and virtue. The Belgian, naturally generous, can despise the comforts of life; but if he is treated as a slave he is prompt to resist and to mutiny. If on the other hand he is governed according to the laws with kindness and moderation, there is no people more faithfully attached to its sovereigns."

† M. Gerard in the *Revue de Belgique* (1874-5) considers this sum more than the equivalent of 30 millions sterling to-day.

tutors, to such an extent that while he was heir to seventeen kingdoms it was credibly affirmed that he could speak the languages of all of them. It was certainly an age when linguistic attainments were highly prized and indeed necessary for the conduct of affairs between the nations, when the *lingua franca* of the priests was being set aside by the natural assertion of the right of the peoples to speak their own tongues, and Charles either said himself, or allowed some one to say for him, that " he wished to know Italian in order to speak to the Pope, Spanish to talk with his mother Joan, English to write to his Aunt Catherine, the first wife of Henry VIII., German to communicate with his grandfather, Maximilian, Flemish to converse with his fellow citizens and friends, and finally French to talk to himself." One year after his acceptance of personal authority in Belgium Charles came into actual possession of the states to which he was heir, in Spain, Italy and America, by the death of Ferdinand the Catholic. This event compelled Charles to visit Spain, and during his absence the government of the Low Countries was again entrusted to Margaret of Austria. Before his departure he organised the Privy Council, composed of knights of the Golden Fleece, and some of the principal members of the national Council of Malines. This constituted a radical change in the system of administration in force in the Low Countries. The Count de Nény, in his remarkable report prepared for the Emperor Joseph II., describes the change effected in the following passage—

"The form of government in the Low Countries had several changes until the reign of the Emperor Charles V. The affairs of state, those of justice and of the higher police, of pardons and of the finances, were sometimes separated by department, sometimes re-united under the same direction; more often there was a special minister charged with the chief administration of the finances, sometimes under the name of Governor of the Finances or Superintendent, sometimes under the title of Treasurer-General or Controller-General; but the Chancellor of Burgundy had always the right of entry and the presidency over all assemblies where the direction of the finances was discussed. The government received a new form in 1517. By letters patent of 23rd July of that year, Charles V. established a Privy Council, at the head of which was placed his aunt, Margaret of Austria. This council was a true Council of Regency; but there was also a special council composed of heads of departments, the treasurer general, and several clerks accustomed to the routine of finance. By further letters patent of 19th October, 1520, the Emperor instituted another Privy Council on the occasion of his proceeding to take possession of his hereditary states in Germany. At this period the governing councils were not permanent. They were established for a certain time only, during the period of absence of the sovereign, or for some similar cause. When the Emperor Charles V. paid his second visit to Spain, in 1522, he again established a Privy Council of Regency, and this continued to exist down to 1531."

In 1519 Maximilian died and Charles had to quit Spain for Germany. He arrived there almost at the moment that Martin Luther was burning, on the square of Wittemberg, the Papal Bull excommunicating him, and the books of the canonical law. It was the great crisis in European history when modern times really began, and the most powerful secular ruler since Charlemagne was called upon to deal with some of the gravest problems affecting the human race, many of them still unsolved. But here no attempt need be made to follow the Emperor through his career which suggested to his contemporaries comparisons with Augustus and Charlemagne. We are only concerned in tracing the details of his reign in so far as they related to Belgium. His intrigues with Cardinal Wolsey, and his cordial reception of the too showy embassy of that ambitious prelate, which was one of the chief causes of his downfall, are chiefly notable because Bruges was the scene of the interview, and the aged Erasmus hastened there to converse with Thomas More. His summoning of the Diet of Worms, his denunciation of Luther as a heretic, and his declaration that "everything must be done to arrest the progress of the new and dangerous opinions which threatened to trouble the peace of Germany" were the precursors of the policy of repression which his son Philip was to carry out so thoroughly in the Netherlands. The first war between Charles and Francis was important to Belgium because the Emperor's general, Henry of Nassau, captured Tournai, which, with the adjacent district known as Tournaisis, has remained Belgian ever since. About the same time Charles succeeded in procuring the election of one of his tutors, Adrian Boyens, Archbishop of Toledo, as Pope in succession to Leo X. He also resigned to his only brother, Ferdinand, the personal direction of the affairs of the Archduchy of Austria and its dependent states. His aunt, Margaret, remained Regent of the Netherlands, and by this wise subdivision, while retaining personal direction of the whole, Charles was able to retain his popularity and to concentrate all his attention and power on whatever question happened to be most pressing.

The second war between Charles and his rival, Francis, resulted in the battle of Pavia and the capture of Francis. That victory was so complete and crushing—Francis said describing it "of all things honour and life alone are left me"—that Charles became virtually supreme on the continent and could think of nothing else worthy to employ his time than to revive the crusades. The general who won the battle of Pavia for him was a Belgian, Count de Lannoy,* and the news was received as a national victory with great joy in the Netherlands where the populace sang songs in honour of the House of Burgundy to the refrain—

"Lion of Flanders, cease to complain!
For the King of France is a prisoner."

After one year's imprisonment Francis was released by the Treaty of Madrid—14th January, 1526—and among its terms was the cancelling of the old claim to regard Flanders as a French fief. Francis had, of course, no intention of abiding by the treaty which his necessity had compelled him to sign, even although he married Charles's sister, Eleanor, and surrendered his two sons as hostages for his good faith. A few months later he formed the League of Cognac against the Emperor, and when reproached with the breach of faith he had committed, he briefly replied that the terms of the Treaty of

* A de Lannoy appeared among the first creation of the Golden Fleece.

S

Madrid were not such as could be put into execution. It was then that Charles sent Francis, by the King-at-Arms of Burgundy, a personal challenge to combat which Francis, notwithstanding his reputation for chivalry, evaded. The fortune of the war* that he thus provoked proved adverse to Francis, and a second peace was concluded at Cambrai (3rd August, 1529) by which he again renounced his claims over Flanders. The treaty of Cambrai was popularly called the Ladies' Peace, because it was mainly negotiated by Louise d' Angouleme, the mother of Francis, and Margaret of Austria, the governess of the Netherlands, while Eleanor of Austria and Queen of France also took part in the transactions.

While the Emperor was prosecuting these wars with his rival, or endeavouring to stamp out the new sect by the votes of the Diet at Spires and Augsbourg, the Netherlands enjoyed peace and prosperity under the wise government of Margaret. The national sentiment of those states demanded peace above all things, and she gratified it in a measure beyond all precedent, thanks, however, to the good fortune that attended the Emperor's arms. The Belgians appreciated the result, but they were somewhat blind to the cause, and accepted the gratification of their wishes as the consequence of their own merit rather than their good fortune. Still it must none the less be noted that the period associated with the name of Margaret of Austria was one of great and almost unexampled prosperity in the country. She† was the patroness of arts and letters, as well as an acute politician, thoroughly understanding the narrow but fixed idiosyncrasies of the nation. Her career was suddenly cut short in November, 1530, by the result of what seemed a trifling accident. An attendant, in taking a basin of water from her, let it drop, and a fragment struck the foot of the duchess. The wound seemed slight, but soon mortified and amputation was performed. The mischief had spread too far,

---

* This campaign lies outside our subject, but it may be mentioned that three of its chief incidents were the Imperialist capture of Rome by the Constable de Bourbon, the failure of the French attack on Naples, and the defeat of the French at Landriano by Antony de Leyva.

† Margaret was herself a poetess, her albums of verse form part of the splendid collection called The Burgundy Library at Brussels.

and death followed. In the last letter dictated from her dying couch to the Emperor she described her own governorship, " I leave you your countries on this side, which during your absence I have not only guarded as you left them to me at your departure, but greatly increased, and I restore to you their government, of which I think I have loyally acquitted myself, and in such a way as to hope for Divine reward, your contentment, and the good opinion of your subjects. I recommend you to maintain peace, and especially with the Kings of France and England." The Count de Lalaing in announcing the event to Charles said—" This is a heavy loss for your Majesty and for all your states and subjects on this side."

The success of female rule in the Netherlands had been so considerable that Charles appointed his sister Mary, the widowed* Queen of Hungary, to succeed his aunt Margaret. The appointment was announced in January, 1531, and for a period of twenty-five years the Queen of Hungary acted as Regent of the Netherlands, only indeed resigning the office when her brother abdicated the Imperial Throne. At the same time she was not over eager in accepting the appointment, and only did so because the Emperor's wishes were a command. She stipulated that in return for her obedience she should not be required to marry a second time, and that as soon as possible she should be relieved of a task for which the delicate state of her health unfitted her. Although the position was never agreeable to her, and notwithstanding that she never pretended to have the same sympathy with the Flemings that her predecessor really possessed, she retained the government during a quarter of a century. If she was not as popular with the Belgian races as her aunt, she was, on the other hand, a more docile instrument in the hands of the Emperor, making her policy subservient to his, and confining the chief measures of her government to the execution of his orders.

Charles in person inaugurated his sister in the government of the States at Brussels in October, 1531, and at the same time enlarged the administration by the creation of three separate

* She was born at Brussels in 1505, and her husband, Louis II., was killed at the battle of Mohacz (1526) with the Turks.

Councils with collateral powers. These councils were designated of State, the Privy, and of Finance. The Queen was President of the Council of State, and the knights of the Golden Fleece were, *ipso facto*, members during their residence at Brussels, which had for some time become the fixed seat of the Court and the capital. Relieved on the side of the Netherlands, Charles turned with renewed energy to the prosecution of his schemes against the Infidel, rendered more necessary by the advance of the Turks in Hungary, and more attractive by the hope they afforded him of being able to reunite Christendom under the shadow of the Cross. The campaign of 1532—the year which saw the addition by Pizarro of Peru to the many states of the Emperor—was marked by the expulsion of the Turks from Hungary, although the Sultan Soliman evaded defeat by a well-timed and skilful retreat. The recovery of Hungary was the precursor of a more important and memorable enterprise, undertaken in the year 1535 against Soliman's Admiral, Khair-eddin Barbarossa, who had established at Tunis a formidable piratical power by the supersession of its legitimate ruler, Muley Hassan. The conquest of Tunis, the restoration of Muley Hassan as a vassal of Spain accompanied as it was by the deliverance of 18,000 Christian prisoners, constituted the most brilliant military achievement in the career of Charles. If it impressed Christendom, it did not, however, prevent Francis, despite his being "the eldest son of the Church," from allying himself with the Sultan and reviving his twice renounced claims over Flanders. At the moment when Francis thus reopened his long rivalry with the Emperor, his Ambassador in London, Castillon, was scheming[*] to form a league between Francis, Charles, and Scotland for the purpose of dethroning Henry the Eighth, and dividing his kingdom. The divorce of his aunt, Catherine of Aragon, and the adoption of the new religion by the titular Defender of the old, had alienated the sympathies of the Emperor from his former ally.

[*] Brantôme mentions about the same time that Charles entertained the idea of converting the Netherlands and the adjacent provinces into "a kingdom of Belgic Gaul," extending from Cologne to Ypres and from Strasburg to Antwerp.

For the purposes of the war with France, Charles instructed his sister to demand from the States a subsidy of 1,200,000 florins. One-third of this sum was to be paid by Ghent, then described as the greatest city of Europe, and the other two-thirds by Bruges,* Ypres and the Franc. The demand for this subsidy was presented to the States in June, 1536, by the Regent at Brussels. The representatives of the three last named assented, and in due time paid their quota, but those of Ghent protested and refused. They alleged various reasons against their liability, overlooking altogether the treaty of Cadzand, and offered to supply a contingent of men in the ancient fashion but no money. Their offer was rejected, and the Regent proceeded to arrest a number of Ghent citizens who happened to be residing at Brussels, Malines, and Antwerp. This step did no good. It irritated the citizens without frightening them. The French war continued, however, to demand the whole of the Emperor's attention, until in June, 1538, a truce of ten years was signed at Nice followed by an interview between the Emperor and King at Aigues Mortes. The absence of any effective measures of repression had confirmed the citizens of Ghent in their opposition, and, unmindful of the very different opponent they had to deal with in an Emperor, instead of a Duke of Burgundy, they carried themselves with an insolence and insubordination that stood not on form and that would not listen to compromise. The active directing power in the city passed into the hands of a new association, apparently composed of the artizans rather than the merchants, and known by the name of the "Creesers," a term signifying, according to some authorities, the Criers, according to others "the fighters," or, less complimentarily, the plunderers.†

The "Creesers," ignorant of the significance of the interview at Aigues Mortes, sent envoys to the Court of Francis in

* In 1538 Bruges was visited by Ignatius Loyala who founded there the order of the Jesuits.

† There is contemporary evidence to a decline in the moral status of the citizens of Ghent at this time as compared with those who had struggled for their privileges with Louis de Mâle and his Burgundian successors. Meyer in his *De Rebus Flandricis*, "The old represent that everything is changed in the customs of our citizens and they complain that instead of simple, frank, loyal, courageous, robust, and tall men a generation has succeeded corrupted by vice, idleness, ambition, and pride."

order to solicit the aid which the French King had been in the custom of rendering the citizens of Ghent against their liege lord. They returned with a snub from "the friend and ally of the Emperor." Still the "Creesers" did not take warning and would not listen to the proposal to submit their grievances to the Council of the States at Malines. Their insolence and self-confidence reached their height in the autumn of 1539 when they destroyed the Calfod of 1515, recording the confirmation, by Charles himself, of the Treaty of Cadzand. They also seized those of the magistrates who sought to uphold the Imperial authority. The chief, Lievin Pym, was executed on the market place, but before his death he delivered an address, full of warning, and told his murderers that they would repent when "too late." Mary of Hungary was herself compelled to bend to the storm, ceding the keure demanded by the "Creesers," but adding, for her after-justification, "By force, and to avoid the greatest evils, I have consented to the Commission." Even when Adrian de Croy, Count des Rœulx, arrived as Charles's representative, and called upon the citizens to return to their obedience, they refused to listen to him, and proceeded to strengthen the gates and place the city in a position to stand a siege. Their confidence arose mainly from the fact that the Emperor was in Spain, and they consequently believed that it would be impossible for him to take promptly any repressive or punitive measures against them.

The extraordinarily friendly attitude of Francis inspired Charles with an idea that under any other circumstances would not have been feasible. Francis sent the Emperor full particulars of the overtures from the Ghent citizens with many protestations of good will. Charles replied that "far from being the enemy of the Kings of France, he wished the French had twenty Kings," whereupon Francis in a letter of October, 1539, begged his Imperial brother not to risk a voyage by sea to punish his rebellious subjects of Flanders, but to journey across France. After some reasonable hesitation Charles decided to avail himself of this offer, but at the same time he prudently augmented its chances of success by putting forward a proposal to marry his eldest daughter to the Duke of Orleans, and to make them King and Queen of Flanders. Whether the Emperor had any serious intention in making this proposal cannot be known, but it was at least in harmony with his earlier plan of creating a kingdom of Belgic Gaul. It certainly served its more immediate purpose of giving distinction and promise to his French visit, which passed off in the most satisfactory manner. On New Year's day, 1540, Charles entered Paris, and three weeks later he was met at Valenciennes by his sister, the Queen of Hungary. At the same time there arrived deputies from Ghent bearing humble messages. The only ominous answer made was that the Emperor would bring his answer in person. Nearly four years had elapsed since Ghent had refused to pay its share of the war subsidy, and in the interval the offence had been aggravated by many acts of defiance and rebellion, and now the hour of expiation had arrived suddenly and without warning.

The unexpected appearance of the Emperor took the heart out of the citizens of Ghent. They at once realised the peril of their position. A few of the more desperate thought of resistance, but the majority recognised it to be impossible, for the King of the Romans had brought a large army to Brussels from Germany to aid his brother, and even in Flanders Ghent could not claim an ally or well-wisher. There was no choice but to resign themselves with the best grace to the Emperor's judgment, which, even if just, could not fail to be terrible, for in addition to the slights to his authority Ghent had to expiate the murders of Lievin Pym, and other Imperial officers. On 14th February, 1540, Charles* entered Ghent, surrounded by his courtiers, generals, and attended by a chosen army of 10,000 men. The passage of these troops occupied six hours, according to one account, and the whole day, according to another. The Emperor placed guards at the gates, and ordered the arrest of the popular leaders. At the same time he gave instructions that their trial was to be conducted in due form, and that, in

* Motley's facetious remarks at the expense of Paul Jove, the Ghent citizen from whose description of the entry he largely quotes, are quite out of place. There cannot be two opinions that on this occasion Ghent had invited her own punishment, or that the tyranny and bloodthirstiness of the Creesers were as great as those of any Emperor.

accordance with the usual formula, strict justice was to be done. Formalities require time. The indictment of Ghent was prepared by Baldwin Lecocq, the Procurator General of the Council of Malines, and then further delay was caused by the unwise decision of the citizens to justify their conduct. On 17th March the trial concluded with the execution of seven[*] of the men who had sentenced Lievin Pym, and four days later Charles pronounced the first part of his sentence to the effect that a castle should be erected on the site of the Church and Monastery of St. Bavon. April drew towards a close before Ghent learnt the full extent of its punishment, of which the precursor may be said to have been the laying of the foundation stone of the new castle on 24th of that month.

On the 28th April [†] Charles published his decision, final and irrevocable, in a decree that had been made the subject of much careful deliberation and that was to end the pretensions of Ghent for ever. It began by depriving the town, body and communalty, of all privileges in perpetuity. Ghent was deprived of municipal government, and the guilds, as well as the city, lost their charters. All sheriffs and magistrates were to be appointed by the Emperor alone. Public property, including artillery, was also to be ceded to the Emperor, and the famous Roland, which had so often given tongue to the discontent of the land and summoned its people to arms, was sentenced to eternal silence. The city was ordered to pay at once the four hundred thousand florins of the war subsidy, and also a fresh sum of one hundred and fifty thousand towards the Imperial expenses. In addition, Ghent was to provide annually 6,000 florins to the State Exchequer. Finally the city representatives, and others from the Guilds, were to appear bareheaded before the Emperor, and confess their faults, and ask forgiveness in the prescribed style, and, to give greater effect to the ceremony, fifty of the people were to be present in their shirts, bare-footed, and with halters round their necks. This crowning ceremony took place on 3rd May. In

[*] Kervyn van Lettenhove. Motley says 19.

[†] Kervyn van Lettenhove. Motley gives 29th, and T. Juste 30th as the date. It seems possible that the decree, dated 28th, was not published till 29th.

this manner Ghent finally lost its privileges so well beloved and so long preserved. If the Emperor dealt with it in an uncompromisingly severe manner, it must also be allowed that his settlement was singularly free from bloodshed.

The Netherlands played but a small part in the concluding fifteen years of Charles's reign, although they were destined to be closely associated with the closing act of his abdication. Charles again consigned the government to the hands of his sister, and then hastened to Germany to give his personal attention to the religious question which was distracting that conglomeration of independent States, and also to the renewal of his ancient rivalry with Francis. For the chivalrous French King, in giving Charles a safe passage across his country, and in averting him of the Ghent designs, had not been without hope of some tangible reward. He may not have had much faith in, or wish for, the kingdom of Flanders for his brother, but he thought that the Emperor would at least give him the Milanais. Charles had no intention of giving up anything, and the war of 1542 ensued. Of the five armies Francis placed in the field three invaded the Netherlands, but the Queen of Hungary had made timely preparations and showed a resolute front.* The French armies, repulsed at Antwerp and Valenciennes, were compelled to retreat, but Francis succeeded, by Fabian tactics, in avoiding a pitched battle and consequent overthrow. He was also fortunate in detaching Henry VIII. from the Emperor, between whom the ever fertile cause of quarrel, religious differences, caused a breach at the very moment that the road to Paris lay open to their armies. Charles, in September, 1544, signed the treaty of Crespy with Francis, thus ending his twenty-five years' rivalry with that prince.† For the last time, and finally, France withdrew her claim to regard Flanders as the fief and dependency of her Crown.

* It was said at the time that "after God, the Queen saved the Netherlands." Charles was not unpopular in the states. Despite the humiliation of Ghent more than one city declared it would make every sacrifice to help him in carrying on his wars "even to selling their own children."

† Francis died soon after, March, 1547. The Duke of Orleans who was to have been King of Flanders had been poisoned in September, 1545, by Catherine de Medicis, wife of the Dauphin.

The acts and alliances, by which the Emperor combated Protestantism from the time of the Augsburg Convention to that of Passau, did not affect the position in Belgium, although it may be noted that during this period Charles tried hard to undo the cession he had made of Austria to his brother, Ferdinand, and to reunite it with the whole of the Empire under the authority of his son. With that object in view he summoned that son from Spain to present him to his future subjects in Belgium and Germany. It was in July, 1549, that the Infante, as Philip was called, arrived in the Netherlands. He had been educated in Spain according to the severe punctilio of the Court of Castille. He had been trained in the suppression of feeling until none was left, and the haughty disdain with which he had been taught to regard the rest of the world deprived him of all sense of identity with the human race. Philip, surrounded by nobles and prelates of the same caste of mind as himself, came to the Netherlands as a stranger, and the jovial, pleasure-seeking people of that land were chilled by his austere demeanour, and the lack of interest he displayed in the public feastings and rejoicings intended to do him honour, and provided for out of the voluntary subscriptions raised by the citizens of the towns he visited. If Philip was a failure in the Netherlands, so far as popularity was concerned, he was not more of a success in Germany where the princes scrutinised and criticised him without wasting any of their limited supply of florins on his entertainment. Charles had the good sense to see that there was no likelihood of his succeeding in forcing his unattractive son on the Diet, at the expense of his brother Ferdinand, and his popular son, Maximilian. Austria, the parent stem on which had been grafted the female lines of Burgundy, Castille and Aragon, thus continued under the sway of the junior line of the Hapsburgs, in descent from the Emperors Frederick and Maximilian I. The only practical step taken in connection with Philip's tour was his proclamation as Duke of Brabant at both Louvain and Brussels.

The Belgians took a prominent and distinguished part in the terrible French war of 1552-4, culminating in the sanguinary and doubtful battle of Renty. Then were heard, for the first time, words of praise for that Walloon infantry which was long the admiration of Europe. It was to Belgium also the Emperor turned for those subsidies which were necessary to support him in his final struggle with French power. For these reasons it was not unnatural that he should select it as the scene for the final termination of his secular career. In Germany his power was nominal and the transmission of authority had been provided for, Spain was too far off, and there practically remained no other choice but the States of the Netherlands which in wealth and prosperity were at the head of the many divisions of his Imperial power. Philip, who had only the year before been married to Mary of England, thus cementing an alliance which was intended to be both religious and political, was summoned by his father to Brussels to take his part in a ceremony, the like of which the world has never seen.

For reasons of health Charles had come to the decision to abdicate, and as he could not add the dignity of Supreme Pontiff to his many titles he decided to seek the solitude and peace of a monk's cell. Disappointed ambition, for which nothing attainable was left to seek, as much as the bodily maladies that the anatomist, Andrew Vesale, predicted must terminate fatally within a brief period, may have led him to resign the cares of government. Prematurely aged by the attacks of rheumatism and gout, for which medical skill had in his age discovered no palliatives, and physically unfit for the discharge of his manifold and onerous duties Charles did not require the promptings of his friend and schoolfellow, Louis de Blois, to turn his thoughts in the direction of a religious retreat. Always of a religious cast of mind, the state of Christendom distressed him, and the application of a remedy was beyond his strength. Perhaps his decision was hastened by the evidence he received of his son's desire to grasp the crown, and by grief on learning that to attain his ends, Philip had not refrained from spreading reports of his father's incipient madness. The cession of the crowns of Sicily and Naples had whetted Philip's desire to be independent and supreme, and Charles, wearied and unfit for power, resolved to gratify him, and at the same time to terminate his earthly cares.

In the summer of the year 1555, Charles notified the States of his intention to abdicate, and he summoned to Brussels, not only his son Philip, but also his nephew Maximilian to whom the Austrian succession had been secured. The arrangement of the necessary preliminaries for so extraordinary an event as the abdication of an Emperor required several months, but at last these were completed, and the 25th October was fixed for the memorable ceremony. Brussels had now become definitively the capital, and the castle of the Caudenberg was selected as the scene for the proclamation. The hall of this palace was specially prepared for the occasion. The dais was hung with the rich tapestry of the House of Burgundy, and on the walls were displayed the banners taken at Pavia and Tunis. Besides the princes named were the Emperor's two sisters, the Queens of Hungary and France, and a conspicuous figure was William of Nassau, Prince of Orange, the youthful favourite of the old Emperor. The Knights of the Golden Fleece, the noblest order of chivalry that the world has ever known, were present in full muster, and the spacious hall was filled to overflowing with councillors and soldiers, bishops and priests, and the members of the Imperial household. On the dais were placed three chairs, that for the Emperor in the centre. On his right sat the Queen of Hungary as Governess of the Low Countries, and on his left at first Philip about to be invested with supreme power in Spain, its colonial possessions, and the dominions of the House of Burgundy. After the whole of the audience had taken their appointed places Charles entered, supporting himself with a stick in his right hand, and with his left on the shoulder of William of Orange. On his appearance everybody rose and bent towards the Emperor who, on taking his seat requested the audience to be seated, while the Councillor of State, Philibert of Brussels, read an explanation of the motives which had led the Emperor to abdicate, and to seek a place of retreat in Spain. In that memorial a detailed description was given of the Emperor's bodily ailments which had an interest

ABDICATION OF CHARLES V.

of practical significance to that audience which they could not possess in the pages of history. The humour that turns them into a subject of ridicule* is, however, forced and in bad taste. When Philibert finished the Emperor rose, again supporting himself on the shoulder of William of Orange, and addressed the audience in an oration which set forth the principal events of his long government in the forty years since he had been invested with personal authority in that same hall.

The description of that reign, the most remarkable in Christian history since that of Charlemagne, could not fail to be interesting; recited in the words of the chief actor it impressed the audience and still forms one of the most striking of human documents. Charles recalled the numerous expeditions in which he had taken part, and with the art of an orator he numbered them at forty, the same as the years of his reign. Nine journeys had he made in Germany, six to Spain, seven in Italy, ten in the Netherlands, four in France, two in England, and two in Africa, and with many of them were associated some memorable event like the battle of Pavia, or the capture of Tunis. Each reference to events in which many of those present had taken a part was received with applause or tears. In concluding he said "I confess that I have committed faults, either through want of experience in my youth, or through pride in my mature age, or from some other weakness inherent in human nature. Yet I declare that never knowingly and willingly have I done injury or violence to anyone whomsoever. If, nevertheless, such a thing has happened I deeply regret it, and I beg those, present or absent, to forgive me." Then he bestowed his blessing on his son who knelt before him, and amid the tears and grief of the whole attendance he sank back exhausted in his chair, exclaiming, "My dear children, your affliction pierces my heart. I leave you with grief."

When the Emperor had finished, his sister, the Queen of Hungary rose, and announced her resignation of the office of Governess of the Low Countries which she had held for twenty-four years. Philip thus acquired not merely the name but the

* Motley.

direct responsibility for the government of the seventeen* provinces. The ceremony in the Caudenberg referred expressly to those provinces. Three months later Charles transferred to Philip the sovereignty of Spain and it was not until September, 1556, that he sent his brother, Ferdinand, the Imperial insignia by the hands of William of Orange. During the intervening eleven months Charles resided in a small house† in the park attached to the Caudenberg, but the reasons for deferring his departure are uncertain and variously given. Some declare that his illness rendered it impossible for him to travel, others that he waited to see how the administration would progress after the withdrawal of his guiding hand. At last, on the 17th September, he took ship from a port of Zealand for Spain, accompanied by his two sisters, and a few faithful attendants who were resolved to share their master's retirement from the world. The Emperor had selected the monastery of St. Juste, in Estremadura, as the place of his retreat. During the two years prior to his death there, on 21st September, 1558, he occupied his time in reflection and the practice of the craft of watch-making. A few weeks before his death he received the gratifying intelligence of Egmont's victory at Gravelines, a success due more to the opportune arrival of some English warships than to the efforts of the hero of St. Quentin. It seemed to him as if the authority he had resigned three years earlier had passed securely and in a consolidated form to his son.

The strictures passed on Charles's government of the Netherlands by the most popular historian‡ of the period seem quite unmerited. If the reader will compare the peaceful half-century between the death of Philip the Fair and the abdication of Charles, with the disturbed and disastrous condition of the country during the greater portion of the previous half-century, there will be no difficulty in arriving at a more just conclusion. The only trouble Charles had with the stiff-necked Flemings

---

* These were Brabant, Limburg, Luxemburg, Gueldres, Flanders, Artois, Hainaut, Namur, Zutphen, Holland, Zealand, Antwerp, Malines, Utrecht, Over-Yssel, Frisia, and Groningen.

† This small house is believed to have been situated near the point on the Boulevards of the Upper Town where stood the Porte de Louvain.

‡ Motley.

was at Ghent, between the years 1536 and 1540. His solution of their differences, if it possessed a dramatic side, was remarkably free from bloodshed. The execution after a fair trial of a few men, who had themselves been guilty of sentencing some of their compatriots to death for very inadequate reasons, will contrast favourably for mildness with the proceedings of Charles the Bold or Maximilian. Charles was essentially a clement prince, and neither his aunt nor his sister, to whom he left the practical part of the administration over the States, could be termed tyrannical. It is true that the States had to pay considerable taxes and subsidies for the prosecution of the wars with France, whose avowed intention was to reduce Artois and Flanders to the condition of French provinces. Charles may, in a certain sense, have been fighting for ambition, but he was also fighting for the safety of his dominions including the Netherlands. The citizens of every State have to contribute to the maintenance of their ruler's majesty, reputation and position. The difference between Belgian citizens and those of other countries was that the former had the available wealth and resources to meet the demands made upon them, whereas the inhabitants of less favoured countries at that time, such as England and France, had not. The evidence is conclusive that the material prosperity of the Netherlands was at its height at the close of Charles's reign. On the exchange of Antwerp, for instance, as much business was done in one month as on that of Venice in two years, yet Venice was still the leading mart of the Mediterranean. In contradiction to the historian cited, the reign of Charles the Fifth in the Netherlands may be described as one of much prosperity and steady progress. The monarch retained, too, a personal popularity that recalled that of Philip the Good, and which may have had its origin in the fact that after all he was Charles of Ghent.

The following passages from a popular Belgian history* give an interesting description of the material condition of the country at this period. "The seventeen provinces then constituted the richest state of Europe. They contained 208 walled towns, 150 boroughs or open towns, and 6,300 villages with a

---

* Th. Juste's *Histoire de Belgique*, tome II., 151 et seq.

T

church tower. Their commerce in the conveyance of goods especially with Northern Europe enriched the Dutch provinces, while industry was the source of prosperity in the southern provinces. Each of the last excelled in some special fabric, and the production varied almost from town to town; here velvet, silk, or damask stuffs; there embroideries, a little further on metal wares. Brussels, Arras, and Tournai exported their carpets, Courtrai its table linen, Louvain its gloves; the cloth and linen of the Flemings were famed throughout Asia and Africa. Only one city, formerly the rival of Venice, had lost its ancient splendour. The troubles and wars of Flanders under the regency of Maximilian, the departure of the Hansa merchants, the gradual silting up of the Zwyn bay forming the port of Damme, the removal of the depôt for colonial produce, were among the chief causes of the decay of Bruges, and of the transfer of its trade to Antwerp, the situation of which was far more advantageous. The period of Antwerp's greatest splendour was between the years 1550 and 1560, when it contained the houses of not fewer than a thousand foreign merchants. These houses were divided among six nations, the Spaniards, the Danes and the Hansa together, the Italians, the English, the Portuguese and the Germans. In 1560, more business was done in one month at Antwerp than in two years at Venice, although that place was still one of the chief seats of trade in the world. Every day nearly 500 vessels entered and left the great port on the Scheldt, two thousand waggons entered the city every week from France or Germany. Between 1550 and 1577 the total of the population of Antwerp fluctuated between one hundred and fifty and two hundred and fifty thousand. Ghent and Liége each possessed over one hundred thousand and Brussels between seventy and eighty thousand."

CHAPTER XI.

The Spanish Rule.

THE description with which the previous chapter closed shows the condition of the Belgian and Dutch provinces at the time of the accession of Philip the Second. They formed the most prosperous division of an Empire that extended westwards from the Turkish frontier to the Pacific. The new ruler was little known in the Netherlands, but during the tour in 1549 already mentioned he had not known how to conciliate the good will and popularity of its inhabitants. If every statement connected with this period—the battle ground of Catholics and Protestants— has to be closely scrutinised, and only accepted with some amount of reservation, there is still no doubt that Philip appeared in the eyes of his northern subjects as a stranger, a man in whom the blood of the ancient families of Flanders and Burgundy had turned to the water of a foreigner.* The antipathy was strengthened by the preference Philip showed for Spanish courtiers and advisers, and the national spirit which had resented the influx of Germans under Maximilian now became aroused against the introduction and influence of Spaniards under his great grandson. But unpopularity is neither active hatred nor open opposition, and if Europe had not been distracted at the moment by the great religious upheaval which separates modern from mediæval history, Philip might have concluded his reign of forty-two years in peace, and left no worse reputation behind him than that he was reserved and haughty of manner, and little appreciated by his subjects of the Low Countries.

But the time in which he lived was not one that admitted of

* Suriano, a Venetian envoy, said "He was little pleasing to the Italians, very unpleasing to the Flemings, and hateful to the Germans."

compromise. It called forth the strongest passions of human nature, and the deeds that stain the records of the age were done in the name of all the virtues and from the loftiest motives. Repression failing to secure uniformity, the contest necessarily became one of extreme bitterness. It was a life and death struggle, from which mercy was banished. Men had not then the delicate regard for human life and suffering that the growth of civilisation and material comfort has created, and the butcheries and burnings that horrify the reader in the pages of Motley were but repetitions in a slightly novel form of the tale of slaughter which provided the main current in human history from the beginning of time. Round the name of Philip has collected the hatred of one side and the approbation of the other, but he was not the originator of the immortal struggle in which he formed so prominent a figure. He was a bigoted, obstinate man, endowed with uncontrolled power and unendowed with any generous sentiment, and even those who wished complete success for his cause and efforts could not work up any enthusiasm for his person. But none the less the struggle would have occurred if he had never been born, and he was not worse than many of his contemporaries whose names are allowed to pass without reproach. He may rightly be regarded as one of those mortals who should be criticised, not so much as individuals but as instruments of fate. Viewed in that light it may be affirmed that the influence of Philip on the character and fortunes of the Netherlands has been permanent and is not effaced to-day. To an unappreciated degree he has been one of the chief moulders of their history, and it is in that light chiefly that we have to regard him here.

The peace which the Emperor Charles had laboriously created for the purpose of his abdication proved short-lived. The new King of France, Henry the Second, thought the moment presented by Philip's accession and by the separation of Germany too favourable to be neglected for recovering some of the possessions lost by his predecessor. Without condescending to the formality of a declaration of war, Henry despatched one army into Italy and another into Artois. In Italy, the Duke of Alva baffled the Duke de Guise with his favourite Fabian tactics and reduced him, without the loss of a pitched battle, to such an ignominious position of helplessness that he had to listen, before his return to France, to the Pope's reproach that "he had done little for the interest of his sovereign, less for the protection of the Church, and least of all for his own reputation." But the real interest of the war centred in the Netherlands, which Philip had entrusted to the governorship of Emanuel Philibert, the banished Duke of Savoy, whose patrimony had been seized by Francis. A considerable army took the field on both sides. The French force was commanded by the Constable, Anne de Montmorency, with whom served Admiral Coligny, while the Duke of Savoy led that of Philip, who was still resident in the Netherlands. It is important to note that the army of the latter was not a Spanish force, but a Walloon and Flemish, with an English contingent of seven or eight thousand men, under Lords Pembroke and Clinton, provided by the efforts of Philip's wife, Mary of England. A considerable part was formed of the bandes d' ordonnance,* a cavalry *corps d' élite* of the Belgian national militia, commanded on this occasion by Lamoral, Count of Egmont, a scion of the House of Gueldres. The foot largely consisted of Walloons who gained, in this war, a reputation for invincibility that remained unbroken to the day of Rocroi, and for gallantry that has not yet decayed. What Spaniards were present seem to have been restricted to a small corps of cavalry, while the names of the commanders, without exception, are those of well known families in the Low Countries.

The campaign centred in the siege of St. Quentin and the famous battle that was fought in its neighbourhood. The place was held by a small force under Teligny, who was killed in an unfortunate sortie, and the only reinforcement that succeeded in entering the place was Coligny himself, whose heroic defence even now excites admiration. The French army

* General Guillaume in the *Academie Royale de Belgique* (tome XVII.) says this was "a *corps d'* *élite* of cavalry divided into fourteen companies, ensigns, cornets, or bands. Each company was generally composed of fifty men-at-arms, one hundred archers, and two trumpets. The command of the companies was given to the principal seigneur of the county. This famous militia lasted down to the year 1671."

under Montmorency approached with the view of assisting the hard-pressed garrison, but while he succeeded in throwing five hundred men into the place his own army became involved in a marshy country which placed it at a manifest disadvantage. It is affirmed that the credit of taking advantage of this opportunity was due to Count Egmont, who insisted that such a chance of destroying the flower of the French army was not likely to again present itself. His advice prevailed and his rapidity in seizing, with his cavalry, a pass which the French army would have to traverse during its retreat, mainly contributed to the day's triumph. The battle of St. Quentin (10th August, 1557) was one of the most decisive in history. The French army was practically destroyed, and all its chiefs, with the exception of the Duke de Nevers and the Prince of Condé, were killed or taken prisoners. The victory was the most decisive ever won by a Belgian national army. Philip visited the camp, and, in delight at his triumph, ordered the construction of the Escurial in honour of St. Lorenzo, on whose feast day the battle was fought. The surrender of St. Quentin, three weeks later, followed by the sack of the town, one of the most terrible that occurred during the brutal and ruthless warfare of the next hundred years, brought this year's campaign to a conclusion.

The French renewed the struggle with the commencement of 1558, and began the year with the memorable recovery of Calais by the Duke de Guise, who thus retrieved the reputation he had lost in Italy. The English contingent, which fought at St. Quentin, had returned to England, and the garrison was left in a very weak state owing to the generally accepted view that no one would carry on war in the month of January. Calais, which Edward the Third besieged for a year and which the Flemings called the key of the Channel, was recovered in a week, and Guines, the last English possession on the Continent, shared its fate a few days later. These French successes at the expense of England were not followed by any corresponding successes in the Netherlands. The decisive victory won by Egmont at Gravelines (13th July, 1558) over the French army, which was practically destroyed, ended the war and left France no alternative but to conclude the disastrous peace of Cateau

Cambresis. The death of Mary of England simplified the negotiations by allowing France to remain in possession of Calais, and among the numerous points ceded by France was the restoration of Emanuel Philibert to his patrimony of Savoy. Philip thus lost a governor while Europe gained a reigning prince. The serious negotiations ended with the festivities celebrating the marriage of Philip and the Princess Elizabeth of France, during which Henry the Second had the mishap to be mortally wounded in a tournay by Montgomery. With the French the treaty was most unpopular, because it entailed the surrender of nearly two hundred fortified towns.

On the other hand it was most popular in the Netherlands because it furnished the promise of a long peace, and peace had for four centuries been the ideal of the Flemish people. The event was greeted with public enthusiasm and rejoicings that extended over more than a week. The Belgian public were not aware of the sinister arrangements that preceded the treaty, and that were destined to produce such bitter fruit. They saw merely the termination of a long and costly war, and its termination in such a decisive manner as to promise a long and stable peace. The announcement of Philip's intention to return to Spain did not raise any cloud of dissatisfaction or expression of grief, because it was notorious that he did not share his subjects' sentiments on many matters and especially their amusements. His nomination as Governor of the Netherlands of Margaret of Parma, natural daughter of Charles the V., was by no means an unpopular measure as she had been brought up in the Netherlands under Mary of Hungary, and knew the characteristics of its people. The success of female rule had been practically proved during two regencies. There seemed no reason why Margaret of Parma should succeed less than Margaret of Austria or Mary of Hungary. Her mother was a Fleming, of the Van der Genst family of Audenarde, and a large measure of popularity was thus, in anticipation of her deserving it, assured for her.

Philip might thus have taken his departure from the Netherlands, unregretted it is true, but still amid the tokens of respect due to so exalted a potentate, if he had not presented the States with a request for three million florins to enable him to meet the expenses of the late war. Ghent was the scene of this farewell demand, and clear evidence was furnished of the prosperity of the country and of the general content of the people in the fact that this, for the age, enormous sum was voted without any serious objection. But, while acceding to the demand the Flemings sought to impose a condition which was exceedingly galling to the spirit of a despotic prince. They demanded the departure of the four thousand mercenary soldiers, Spaniards and others, garrisoned in the country, and in naming this condition they were only true to their national dislike and distrust of all foreigners.* But there were other and deeper reasons at the root of this demand. The soldiers themselves had become very unpopular and even hated on account of their conduct and excesses. But the chief reason of all for this demand was that William, Prince of Orange, had been informed though an indiscretion on the part of Henry of France of the plan concerted between him and Philip for the uprooting of the Protestant heresy. So far as the Netherlands were concerned this garrison of foreign mercenaries was to form the nucleus of the army with which Philip intended to crush the religious heresy in the Low Countries. Moved by these revelations William of Orange, who then acquired the name of the Silent or the Taciturn, inspired the delegates to demand, with one voice, the recall of the foreign troops. Philip had to bend, so far as appearances went, before this unanimous request, and to promise that as soon after his return to Spain as possible he would send for these regiments, and that at the latest they should be withdrawn within four months. On this understanding Philip took his departure from the Netherlands, but at the moment of leaving Flushing he revealed his knowledge of the fact that the request was due as much to the organisation of the Prince of Orange as to the voluntary action of the States in an outburst of wrath at that prince's expense, "Not the States, but you, you, you!" In that excited ejaculation began the struggle between them which continued for five and twenty years.

* It was on this occasion that Philip made the remarkable exclamation and admission—" I, also, am a foreigner. Would you wish to expel me?"

Philip, in addition to appointing "his sister" to the nominal head of affairs, arranged for the carrying on of the administration on the same lines as his father had done. The three councils, privy, of state, and of finance, were revived, and the great nobles were appointed stadtholders or governors in the different provinces. Of these latter we need only particularize that Egmont was assigned Flanders and Artois; Orange received Holland, Zealand, and Utrecht, while both were members of the State Council. In form, therefore, the old constitution was preserved and the Regent was held to be bound to consult men who were natives of the Netherlands, and who were more or less solicitous to maintain their interests. But in reality Philip had introduced a change which placed arbitrary power in the hands of his own nominees and rendered all constitutional guarantees valueless. The Regent was to be guided solely by an inner body or consulta composed of only three members, of whom the chief was the Bishop of Arras, afterwards Cardinal Granvelle. This prelate-politician had taken the principal part in negotiating the Treaty of Cateau Cambresis, and in coming to the secret understanding with the French king, or rather the Guise family, which had been indiscreetly revealed by Henry to the Prince of Orange.

It is now time to turn to the details of this understanding, and to review dispassionately the religious struggle that ensued. Charles the Fifth, as was very natural, had been very bitter against the new heresy, and had sanctioned various enactments for its suppression. Its spread in the Netherlands raised political as well as religious dangers, for it made most headway in great cities, like Antwerp and Ghent, where the monarch had always to apprehend opposition to the unfettered exercise of his prerogative. If Charles looked upon the question with some of the zeal of a Catholic, and more of the apprehension of a practical statesman, Philip regarded it exclusively from the stand-point of a horrified and scandalised member of a church which denied salvation outside its portals. There can be no question of the sincerity and depth of his convictions. He was persuaded that in taking upon himself the special task of crushing out the new movement in all its forms he was doing a righteous act for which he would obtain deathless fame, and perhaps he would not have been wrong in this expectation if he had only succeeded to the full extent of his intentions and desire. With this view he not only terminated the war with France, but he formed a league with the ancient enemy of his house for the extirpation of heresy. He naturally enough experienced no difficulty in winning over the Pope to approve of his measures, and to second them by enlarging the powers of the Inquisition, the tribunal that decided orthodoxy in the faith.

Of the various forms taken by this institution, the most severe was that designated the Spanish Inquisition, which is not surprising when it is borne in mind that it was devised expressly against Moors during the long struggle for their expulsion from the peninsula. It was a short and sharp mode for discovering whether an accused person was a Christian or an infidel, and it was enforced solely against Mahomedans and Jews, until the conquest of Mexico and Peru extended its operation to the Indian races of America. But the terrible feature of the Spanish Inquisition was that it had the power of passing sentence, and its uniform decree was burning at the stake garnished with preliminary tortures. Senseless and brutal as this method of proceeding was when applied to persons who had never had any opportunity of becoming Christians, it was justifiable according to the fanatical religious views of the age, and especially of Spain, on the ground that the infidels were outside the pale, and should be extirpated. But it was never contemplated that this terrible engine of human destruction should be employed for the maintenance of complete uniformity of opinion within the Church, and that Christians should have the right to burn their brother-Christians by the secret and summary decree of a few priests. Some form of inquisition by the bishops had always existed more or less in the Netherlands as in other Christian countries, and in 1550 Charles the Fifth, alarmed by symptoms of the extension of the new religion from Germany into the Provinces, had obtained the introduction of what was called the Papal Inquisition. Severe and sweeping as were its provisions, especially against recusant priests, it differed in two material points from that developed by Torquemada. The trial was conducted in accordance with the civil law in public, and the civil authorities were charged with the execution of the sentence. At least, the process was slower and more formal than that introduced by the Spanish Inquisition, whose decrees were as secret and inexorable as their sentences were swift and appalling.

When Philip left the Netherlands two schemes were in his mind and they formed part of a single policy. The concentration of a strong Spanish garrison in the Provinces was to be the preliminary of the introduction of the Spanish Inquisition, which was to uproot heresy. His promise to withdraw the few regiments he left behind him was not binding, because he had made it under compulsion and to evade a difficulty! In this task he could count on the cordial co-operation of Margaret of Parma, and of Cardinal Granvelle, who was privy to all his plans. The greater part of the then powerful aristocracy of the Netherlands shared his detestation of the new heresy, and supported his measures against it to a degree that would have satisfied any less exacting autocrat. Not one of them, at this time, had shown the least intention of quitting the fold of the Church, and there can be no doubt that William of Orange was at first moved by sentiments of national policy, and by what one would like to call, even in that dark age, the ordinary dictates of humanity, into opposition to the plans of Philip. He would probably never have gone into revolt but for the very two steps on which Philip most prided himself. William and his friends were the champions of the rights of the Provinces. Philip's measures were calculated to destroy those rights quite as much as the persons who rejected the decisions of the Council of Trent. The King of Spain knew that he must regard Orange and his friends as opponents of his scheme to cow the inhabitants of the Provinces with a Spanish garrison, but there was no reason to regard his father's favourite and the hero of St. Quentin and Gravelines as heretics in disguise.

While the new religion, or rather the reform of the old, had made no converts among the Belgian and Dutch aristocracy, there is no doubt that it had established its influence firmly among the Flemish and Dutch peoples from Tournai to Amsterdam and Utrecht. There were many other reasons, besides the extension of the theories of Luther and Calvin, to explain this result. The internal condition of the Church of Rome was scandalous, and immorality and extortion reigned to such an extent in the ranks of its clergy that successive Popes expatiated on the inevitable consequences to the Church from this disorder. In the Netherlands the reputation of the priesthood could not have been lower. On the other hand the civil population enjoyed a high state of worldly prosperity and from being in communication with different parts of the world they were more susceptible to outside influences. Many English refugees took up their abode in Flanders during the persecution under Mary; Huguenots from France, and Calvinists from Switzerland and the Rhine also arrived to shake the belief in the infallibility of Rome. But their efforts would have borne little fruit if the evidence of Catholic corruption had not been patent in every Flemish city. To complete the impression on the public mind the support of the Roman Church became identified with the introduction and maintenance of a foreign tyranny. But for that fact it is clear that Philip's measures would have encountered far less opposition in the Belgian provinces than they did, although the spreading of a sceptical sentiment in the land is not to be denied.

The opponents of Philip's extreme measures might be said to be every native, high or low, of the Netherlands, and, as it seemed to him to be necessary to crush disbelief with foreign armies, that opposition was both resolute and unanimous. But a little examination shows that it was very far from being as fixed as it seemed, and that many of those who struggled with him were in secret sympathy with some of his objects, although they disapproved of his means, and thought his punishments excessive and even cruel. As the question proceeded towards a solution these views came more and more to the front, and while Philip's policy through sheer exhaustion and failure tended to become softer and more human, the people of the southern provinces veered round to support his religious views. This result, after a long and sanguinary struggle, provides evidence that if Philip had been wiser and more moderate before it began he would have been supported by a large majority in the Provinces. He alienated this support by alarming his northern subjects in their national predilections, and he completed the breach by an excess of cruelty in an age which was not over particular about shedding human blood. But the root cause of the disaffection and opposition he encountered was that he interfered with the privileges and sentimentalities of the Belgians and their brother races. Hence arose chiefly the religious civil war in which his lieutenants stamped out, with ruthless severity, freedom of thought south of the Meuse, but only at the price of the loss of the territory north of it.

These reservations do not apply, however, to William of Orange, who was not a Belgian noble but a German. His family had supported the new religion, in which he had himself been brought up until the Emperor Charles took him into his household, first as page, and afterwards as his most intimate and trusted attendant and councillor. It was leaning on his shoulder that he appeared at the Abdication scene, and it was by his advice that he told his son to be guided in all matters affecting the Provinces. Unfortunately, Philip had not heeded his father's counsel, and, when leaving the Provinces, had passed over William's claims to be Governor in favour of Margaret of Parma, although he was well aware that he expected it, and then had offered him the public insult described at Flushing. The man who might have been the prop of his throne thus became its most serious danger. Unlike the majority of the representatives of the Low Countries, William of Orange had no sympathy whatever with any of the objects of Philip's policy. He was certainly not in sympathy with the Inquisition, and his views on all religious matters were sufficiently broad to make him appear, in the eyes of a Churchman, as a Sceptic. But he was also animated by a very keen but wholly intelligible ambition. He knew himself to be abler than any of his compeers, and he would have been more than human if he had not resented Philip's treatment, and longed to pitt himself against him as a rival. Philip seems to have known by instinct who would be his chief opponent, and there is some ground for

thinking that he proposed to carry off the Prince of Orange*
with him to Spain, when the loss of his temper furnished the
Taciturn with a decent excuse for not accompanying him on
board ship. The relative capacity of the two men may perhaps
be accurately gauged by the fact that William then evaded
captivity, and that Philip was accompanied by William's spy,
Van der Nesse, in the capacity of his private confidential
secretary. It was to that precautionary measure that William
owed his personal safety in the crisis of the struggle† that
ensued.

Philip, framing his policy on the interests of the Church,
naturally sought to carry it to a successful issue through its
instrumentality. The right to extend the operation of the
Spanish Inquisition to the Netherlands was the first step, the
increase of the number of bishops was the second. Up to this
point the Netherlands, including the whole of the seventeen
provinces, had enjoyed the privilege of possessing a very
limited episcopal hierarchy, four‡ bishops being deemed
sufficient. On the other hand the number of abbeys and
monasteries was considerable, but their inmates were men of
independent spirit, and strong national sympathies. Even in
the name of religion they would not have allowed Philip to
tyrannise over their fellow countrymen, at least to the extent
of wholesale execution and butchery. For Philip's work Philip

---

* William of Nassau—the Silent, or the Taciturn—was born at Dillenbourg, 25th April, 1533. His branch of the Nassau family was distinguished by the name of Dillenbourg, and looked to the Netherlands rather than Germany as their home. In 1544 William of Nassau succeeded his cousin René as Prince of Orange, a little principality in France between Dauphiny and Provence which had come into the Nassau family by the marriage of William's uncle Engelbert with the heiress Claudia of Chalons. The manner in which William acquired the sobriquet of the Silent, or the Taciturn, has been described. The reader will remember, or can easily refer to, Motley's description of the character, personal magnificence and the splendour of the household maintained by William of Orange.

† Van der Nesse (probably Nest) sent him word in 1567 that Alva's instructions were "to arrest him" and "not to let his trial last more than twenty-four hours."

‡ These were Arras, Tournai, Cambrai, and Utrecht. The Prince-Bishopric of Liége was a distinct political and religious entity dependent on the Archbishopric of Cologne in Church matters. During the whole of this stormy period it succeeded in keeping aloof from the troubles of Philip's rule.

then had to look for allies elsewhere, and he proposed to the Pope a large increase of bishops to which the Pontiff had no objection. The necessary Bulls were accordingly issued by two successive Popes for the creation of three Archbishoprics, Malines, Cambrai, and Utrecht, and of fifteen bishoprics under them. In the place of four prelates eighteen were created, and of these three were of a higher grade than had ever before been known in the Low Countries. Much discontent was aroused by this measure, among the nobles because each prelate being entitled to a seat among the States the increase in their numbers diminished their proportional influence, and among the abbots because they had to surrender a great part of their revenues for their support. One of the Popes declared that he had made these creations on the ground that "the harvest was plentiful, but the labourers were few." The important point of this fresh creation was that the directors of the Church in the States were new men, devoid of all sympathy with the national sentiment in the country, and bent solely on executing the orders received from Rome. At the same time they were to form part of the Inquisition. To ensure the proper working of the whole system Granvelle was appointed the first Archbishop of Malines or Primate of Belgium, and thus the new bishops moved in harmony with a previously agreed upon and combined plan. The Bishops and the Spanish garrison were to be the agents of Philip's policy and the terrible instrument termed the Inquisition was to decide how heresy was to be discovered and then stamped out. Philip would have met with more considerable success if his terrible earnestness and frigidity of disposition had not led him to run counter to all the cherished views and aspirations of the races of the Netherlands. The great majority of them wished to adhere to the religion in which they had been brought up, but they did not see why some of them should be burnt for reading the Bible, discussing theology, or for saying that some priests led immoral lives.

William of Orange had inspired the request for the recall of the garrison, and he now took the lead in opposing the creation of the new Bishops, which he denounced as " forming part of one grand scheme for establishing the cruel Inquisition of Spain." In this opposition he had the sympathy of the people, and the co-operation of the whole of the Belgian aristocracy with Egmont and Horn at their head. The outcry in the country and the opposition at the Regent's council table had curiously enough an opposite effect to what might have been expected. The bishops remained in absolute possession of their new sees, but Granvelle and the Regent had to yield, without Philip's sanction, on the subject of the Spanish troops who in January, 1561, were quietly shipped from Flushing. During this period the new religion continued to gain ground, or at least its votaries acquired greater confidence when they found that the native governors refused to take any repressive steps against them. One even replied to the Regent's exhortations to stamp out heresy with the remark, "It is no part of my functions to burn heretics." The departure of the troops deprived the Regent of the means of repression, and no aid was to be looked for from men who, at that moment, thought very little about the religious question, and everything about the manner in which their own influence and privileges were being set aside by Granvelle. The antipathy felt generally for that prelate attained its most intense form in the person of Egmont, who, on one occasion, drew his dagger at the Council Board and threatened to send him to a better world, a threat which he would have fulfilled but for the intervention of William of Orange. The progress of the struggle gradually brought face to face, as the leaders of the opposing factions, Granvelle and Orange. Both were men of exceptional capacity, but Granvelle, while recognising the "profound genius and vast ambition" of his opponent, was disposed to underrate him on the ground of inexperience, he being by sixteen years his junior.

In the summer of 1562 a decisive step towards acquainting the King of Spain with the discontent existing in the Provinces, provoked by the proceedings of Granvelle, was taken by the despatch of the Baron de Montigny, brother of Count Horn,* as envoy and representative of the Knights of the Golden Fleece. The immediate cause of this mission was the receipt of an "order" from Philip that the Provinces should send

* The correct name of this family is Hornes.

two thousand cavalry to assist the Catholics of France in their war with the Huguenots. The mere proposal by the Regent raised such a storm that she withdrew it, and on her own responsibility substituted another voting a supply of money to the King in lieu of cavalry. But even this suggestion was rejected on the ground that the French war was nearing its end, and the bitterness of this blow was rendered the greater for Philip because, never doubting that the supply promised by Margaret in her letters would be voted, he had drawn a bill for the amount on her government. The mission of Montigny had no results. Philip dissembled and gave him a friendly reception, promising to visit the Netherlands and examine, in person, into the causes of discontent. But these promises meant nothing, and in consequence William of Orange, Egmont, and Horn addressed a joint letter to Philip, directly attacking Granvelle, and demanding his removal from office. The reply of Philip to this demand was to say that he could not condemn one of his ministers on hearsay, and he invited one of the great lords making the accusation to come to Madrid and support it in person. As it was believed that the King only wished to obtain a hostage for Granvelle's safety the invitation was declined, and in a second and firmer letter they repeated their demand for Granvelle's removal, at the same time withdrawing themselves from the State Council. They also represented that the only hope of restoring order to the country lay in the summoning of the States General, the constitutional proceeding that Philip was resolved never to take because it would give expression to the general discontent in a manner beyond the possibility of being ignored.

The withdrawal of the three most prominent nobles led to an increase in the public manifestations against Granvelle, who was denounced as the real tyrant. This was heightened by lampoons published at the Cardinal's expense, and by Egmont's device of dressing his servants in a livery half monkish, half of the Court fool style, which was intended to reflect on Granvelle, and which caught the public fancy in such a degree as to become the rage. In this case ridicule seems to have had a more deadly effect than serious representations as to the mischief caused by his policy. Even the Regent became alarmed at the magnitude and varied form of the popular excitement, or she saw in it the opportunity of paying off old scores with the Cardinal, who had incurred her resentment by assuming all the powers of government, and by refusing to accept through her mediation the Cardinal's hat which she had asked and procured for him, until Philip had given his consent also. She therefore sent her secretary to Spain to represent that the recall of Granvelle provided the only means of calming the Provinces. Her representations were successful, and with the view of gaining time for the execution of his ulterior plans, Philip recalled the minister through whom he had in the first place intended to root out heresy in the Provinces. The departure of Granvelle was regarded as a triumph by what may be called the National Party, but they were soon to have reason to think that he was by comparison with his successors a mild governor after all. However, it produced for the moment a tranquillising effect, and Orange and his friends returned to the Council board, and devoted their energies to measures of necessary reform.

During the whole of this period the Inquisition had continued its labours under the direction of Titelmann, the Torquemada of the Netherlands. There had been some "burnings of heretics," especially at Valenciennes and Antwerp, but not enough to satisfy Philip, or to attain the ends of his policy in complete uniformity. He wrote to his sister enjoining and commanding her to enforce the decisions of the Council of Trent, and to publish his Decrees thereupon. This proposal when brought before the Council roused the open opposition of Orange who, while declaring himself a good Catholic, asserted that the Inquisition was tantamount to a breach of the privileges of the country. Egmont was deputed as special ambassador to Madrid in order to tell Philip the truth, but Philip knowing the object of his mission overwhelmed him with such a cordial welcome and so many honours that Egmont never delivered the messages with which he had been entrusted. Like all the nobles of the Netherlands at this period, Egmont had seriously embarrassed his estates by extravagant living and lavish entertainment. Philip made him large presents in money, and dismissed him with letters conveying his reply to the message which Egmont had never had the courage to deliver in its full form. The reply was to the effect that "no change of religion was possible." and that "some new way of executing heretics" must be discovered. The King of Spain's goal remained unchanged, and he pursued his relentless course undisturbed. He not only insisted that the Edicts should be enforced in their literal significance, but he sent lists of persons denounced by Spanish priests, or their agents, in the Netherlands, who were to be arrested forthwith and as summarily executed.

An assembly of bishops and doctors was summoned by Philip's orders to discuss the publication of the Canons of Trent, which excited much controversy, and the assembly was rendered remarkable by the fact that all the civil doctors and lords urged that no one should be executed for so-called heretical opinions. None the less, the clerics carried the day in favour of the extremity of repression and punishment. After some further efforts to delay publication, and to induce Philip to waive some part of his plan the Inquisition was published throughout the length and breath of the land. It was then that the Prince of Orange prophesied "We shall soon see the commencement of a great tragedy."

To decree the Inquisition at the Council table was not difficult, to enforce its publication proved less easy. Several stadtholders flatly refused to allow it to be made within their jurisdiction, and the four principal cities of Brabant successfully invoked their charter—the joyous entry of Wenceslas—and obtained their exemption from the Inquisition. A more pronounced step was taken by the celebrated Compromise, drafted by Philip de Marnix, Viscount de Ste. Aldegonde, and eight other nobles in the castle of Breda (1566). It bound the nobles of the Netherlands to stand by one another in opposing the religious and political domination of Spain, and may be said to have given expression to the deep national feeling that had been aroused by the introduction of the Inquisition, and still more by the want of consideration displayed for the rights and sentiments of the Provinces. But at first Orange and the leading nobles held aloof from the Compromise which could scarcely be distinguished from an act repudiating the King of Spain's sovereignty, and for this neither the country nor its more responsible leaders were ready. At the same time their refusal to accept the Inquisition was just as resolute, and the Regent could only write to her brother begging him to come in person and see the state of the Netherlands for himself. How bad that was may be judged from the fact that a steady emigration set in towards England, whither as many as thirty thousand settlers are said to have proceeded. The Compromise was followed by the preparation of a request or petition, and after some softening in the language employed the petitioners, accompanied by their servants, proceeded to Brussels for the purpose of presenting it. The cavalcade, numbering several hundred horsemen, was headed by Count Brederode and Louis of Nassau, the brother of the Prince of Orange.

The next day, 5th April, 1566, the petitioners, to the number of three hundred, proceeded on foot to the Palace to present the Request to Margaret of Parma as Governor General. Count Brederode was chosen as speaker for the occasion and after a brief address the Request was read aloud. The Duchess was very much agitated by the recital and shed tears at its conclusion, although the petition began and ended with protestations of devotion and loyalty to the King and herself. The most remarkable passages in this document were (1) that Philip's policy would provoke a general rebellion, (2) that he should be requested to withdraw the Edicts ordering the Inquisition, and (3) that pending a reply the operation of the Edicts should be suspended by the Regent. With the view of obtaining the satisfaction of their demands it was suggested that a delegate from them should be sent to Spain to induce the King to summon the States General and thus allay the growing discontent. The Regent's only answer was that she would consider the petition with the aid of the Council, and after their departure Berlaymont, with the wish to encourage the Duchess, uttered the famous phrase "They are only a body of Gueux (beggars)!"

The Regent's reply, given the next day, was to the effect that she would forward the petition to the King, and ask him to

MARGARET OF PARMA RECEIVING THE GUEUX.

consider it favourably. She could not, however, suspend the Edicts without a royal order, but she would request the Inquisition to moderate its proceedings as far as possible. The petitioners were compelled to rest satisfied with this indefinite reply, and their efforts might have failed to obtain any distinct place in history but for the memorable banquet with which they concluded. Brederode entertained his associates in the hotel* of the Count of Culembourg, situated on the Petit Sablon, and close to the hotel of the Arembergs. Here turning the phrase of Berlaymont to his purpose he imposed on his allies and co-plotters the celebrated vow of the Beggars—" They call us beggars, let us accept the name. We will fight the Inquisition, but remain loyal to the King, even till compelled to carry the beggar's wallet." The response came in loud shouts of " Vivent les gueux! "

Margaret of Parma fulfilled her promise. She forwarded the petition to Spain, and at the same time sent, as her special envoys, Montigny, Horn's brother, whose first mission has been referred to, and the Marquis Berghes, one of the stadtholders who had refused to enforce the Inquisition. Neither was destined to return from his dangerous mission, Berghes dying, as was suspected, of poison in 1567, and Montigny being secretly executed in prison three years later. With regard to the object of their mission no answer could be extracted from Philip, and with delay the state of the country became worse. The confederate beggars held a further conference at Duffel, and presented a second petition to the Regent, demanding the immediate assembling of the States General, whereupon they promised to cease from their agitation. The demand was couched in such imperative language that the Duchess told the petitioners that " it was clear they wished to be king themselves," and there is no doubt that the defiant and disrespectful language employed by these turbulent representatives of their countrymen had much to do with hurrying on Philip's pre-

* The site of the building, displaced by a prison, was shown till recently in the Rue des Petits Carmes, leading out of the Petit Sablon; but it is now incorporated in the new barracks of the Belgian Grenadiers.

parations for effectual coercion. This excess of language on the part of Brederode and his friends was soon reflected in excess of deeds on the part of the masses, who had either adopted the new religion under the influence of the Field Preachers or disapproved of its votaries being coerced. Fanaticism was soon displayed on the side of the Lutherans and Calvinists as well as by the Zealots of Rome. The churches became the mark of a blind and unreasoning rage. Image smashing was the pastime of the Protestants, the priceless treasures of Antwerp Cathedral were the spoil of the mob, and at Tournai scenes of senseless desecration continued for weeks unchecked by the helpless authorities. When tidings of these outrages reached Philip's ears he took a vow that it should cost their authors dear. But such was the extent of the popular excitement that the Regent proposed to leave Brussels for Mons, and when she was dissuaded from this step her fears so worked upon her that she signed an Accord abolishing the Inquisition. There was much joy in the country at this nominal success, but the Regent justified herself to Philip on the plea of necessity and avenged herself by denouncing Orange, Egmont, and Horn as the King's three real enemies.

By this time Philip's slow moving schemes for decisive action were nearly ready, but before they were actually carried into effect two or three matters claim notice. One of these was a new oath, to be taken by all officers and functionaries, binding them to do everything they were ordered on behalf of religion. Many nobles took it, Egmont among others, but William of Orange flatly refused, and thus began his open opposition to Philip. He is reported to have said, "What! You would have me sign an order to deliver my wife Anne of Saxony to the executioner!" The rising of the citizens of Antwerp, in consequence of an attack on one of the field meetings outside the walls, although it was allayed by the tact and energy of William, showed how the temper of the people was rising to a dangerous point. Nothing indeed could avert the inevitable struggle, neither Orange's moderation at Antwerp nor Egmont's gallantry in assaulting the Protestant garrison of Valenciennes. News reached William of Orange that Philip was at last ready to strike a mortal blow at the liberties of the Provinces, and that Alva had been appointed Captain General with orders to at once arrest Orange, Egmont, and Horn, and not to let their heads remain twenty-four hours on their shoulders. Orange, duly apprised of this kind intention, warned his two friends, and left the Netherlands for his estates in Germany. Egmont, in particular, was confident of his own safety. He was a good Catholic, his measures at Valenciennes afforded recent abundant evidence of that, and after all he was still the hero of St. Quentin. It was absurd to think that the King would lay a hand on him. His confidence was so great that he even sought to induce Orange himself to remain with some gentle raillery to the effect that if he left the country he would be a "landless Prince," to which Orange replied prophetically "Farewell, headless Count."

For some time before he appointed him Captain General of the Provinces Philip had consulted the Duke of Alva on the policy to be pursued in that part of his dominions, and this general, as might have been expected from his record as the most severe commander of the age, was in favour of very sharp and summary measures. If Philip had adopted his advice the pacification of the Netherlands by military force would have begun some years earlier than it did, but even Alva could not succeed without an army, and this had to be collected and conveyed to its destination. Genoa was appointed the place of meeting for the troops who were to take part in this expedition, and who were to be specially chosen from the veterans in Italy as well as Spain. Great honour was conferred on those chosen to take part in it, and the promise of much spoil was held forth in the rich cities of the north. In this manner ten thousand men, the élite of the King's army, were assembled in Lombardy and as the French King refused to allow it to cross France, for fear of offending the Huguenots, Alva led it by way of Savoy and Lorraine, the two duchies intervening between the Provinces and Italy, towards its destination. After halting at Thionville and Luxembourg Alva reached Brussels on 22nd August, 1567, but, before appearing in the capital, he had taken the precaution to place Spanish garrisons in Antwerp and

Ghent. He established his own headquarters in the Culembourg Hotel, which had witnessed the Beggars' banquet, and he quartered his troops in the suburbs.

The arrival of Alva as Captain General, entrusted with the sole execution of Philip's policy, practically terminated the administration of Margaret of Parma. She had protested against the appointment of Alva when the news first reached her in the spring of the year, as she held herself entitled to the honour and glory of pacifying the Netherlands by herself. She also protested against the wisdom of his proposed policy of repression, to which Alva coldly replied "I have crushed men of iron in my day, shall I not easily crush these men of butter?" After some months, occupied with the endeavour to reconcile her position as Regent with that of Alva as Captain General, she resigned and quitted the Netherlands in December, 1567. But before that much had happened. The Netherlanders had learnt the full terror of Spanish rule. A few days after his arrival Alva produced his commission, dated as far back as January in the current year, ordering him to proceed against all who had in any way disputed or thwarted the royal authority. Egmont was warned on all sides to flee, even by Alva's own son, the Grand Prior Ferdinand, but he refused to believe in his peril. The blow was postponed until Horn had been induced to leave his castle for Brussels. On 9th September both were arrested in Alva's own house, and after a fortnight's detention there they were sent, for safe custody, to the Castle of Ghent. Other arrests followed, but none struck dismay to the hearts of the Netherlanders like that of the brilliant Egmont. His arrest was tantamount to a death-warrant against the whole nation. The next step taken by Alva was not of a nature to remove this impression. He appointed the Council of Troubles, which became known as the Blood-Council, that was to supersede all other jurisdictions so far as any question arising out of the late disputes and controversies was concerned. No time was lost in its formation, or in its beginning work. Ten days after the arrest of Egmont it sat for the first time. Finally Alva declared all charters and privileges to be null and void, and destitute of force or value. In this manner he cleared the ground for the arrest and speedy trial of all persons accused of participation in the late troubles. There was to be no appeal from the Council's decisions except to himself, and he was pitiless. Once the Council got to work wholesale executions followed. Alva himself reported that during a few days eight hundred persons had been executed by its order, and every day the victims might be counted by tens and twenties.

The sentenced were very far indeed from being all heretics. They were taken promiscuously, on no fixed plan, and put to death for the express purpose of terrorising the people of the Netherlands. To be accused meant condemnation, and without any form of trial or prospect of escape. Those who had taken shelter in the neighbouring states were condemned *in absentiâ* to loss of life and property. The estates of William of Orange were declared forfeit, the hotel of the Count de Culembourg was levelled with the ground. Alva, knowing his master's need of money, wrote gleefully that he could assure him an annual revenue of 500,000 ducats out of the confiscations. He also imposed heavy contributions on the cities for the purpose of building citadels for the maintenance of Spanish authority, of which that of Antwerp was the most important. The people of the Netherlands had thus to pay heavy taxes as well as to suffer in their own persons and those of their families. They were left in no state of ambiguity as to their fate, for the Spanish Inquisition passed a general sentence of death on the whole population of the Provinces.

Alva encountered no opposition from the Netherlanders. Their leaders were either in prison or across the frontier. The terrible measures of the Spanish dictator took the heart out of his opponents. The Provinces would have been reduced to absolute subjection without a shot being fired if the Prince of Orange had not collected the means of at least attempting its deliverance. He devoted such wealth as remained to him in Germany to the task of raising an army, and he employed all his influence and eloquence in inducing the electors of Hesse and Saxony to support his efforts on behalf of his distressed countrymen. In France the Huguenot party under Coligny, already in the death struggle with the League under the Guises, was willing to co-operate as far as possible with his efforts. In the spring of 1568 he was ready to make his first attempt, which was divided into several distinct enterprises. The most serious was that led by his brother, Louis of Nassau, who obtained some slight successes in Friesland. Alva sent 4,000 troops, under D'Aremberg, to oppose him, and the two forces came into collision near the petty town of Dam. Louis took up a strong and well-chosen position near a monastery called the Heiliger Lee, or Holy Lion. D'Aremberg, full of confidence through contempt of his adversary, attacked with little foresight, and when he realised the strength of the enemy's position it was too late to restrain his own men. Irritated by some remarks from his Spanish officers as to his excessive prudence D'Aremberg gave the signal for attack, and in a few moments the whole force was involved in the morass which covered the hostile position. Under such circumstances discipline counted for little and the Spanish cavalry fled ignominiously from the field. D'Aremberg exhibited the greatest courage, killing Adolphus of Nassau with his own hand, and falling himself some time later in the thickest of the fray. The Spanish lost several hundred killed, but notwithstanding this auspicious commencement, Louis of Nassau had no means of following it up, as there was no rising in the country to support his efforts. Alva decided to take the field in person, but before he did so he resolved to terrorise the population by some further acts of authority. Heiliger Lee was fought on 23rd May; on 1st June Alva caused eighteen nobles to be executed on the Grand Place at Brussels, and on the next day four more shared the same fate. On 3rd June Egmont and Horn were brought back to Brussels, and early on the 5th they also were executed at the same spot. By these extreme measures Alva showed that no obstacle would arrest him in his course of pacifying the Provinces according to his own fashion, and the horror and amazement of the people engendered a stupor that deprived them of the capacity of action. That Egmont, the prince of Belgian peers, whose military feats constituted the only glorious passages of Philip's reign, and whose Catholic fervour could not be suspected, should fall by the headsman's axe, without a crime committed, seemed to every one except Alva and the more fanatical of his Spanish officers an outrage that only a Nero could have perpetrated. At the same time it is beyond dispute that Alva not only had Philip's authority to act as he did in the matter, but that Philip expressly commanded him to execute Egmont and Horn as the sure way to "tranquillise the public." His personal part in the tragedy consisted in executing Horn's brother Montigny in his prison in Spain on the sentence passed by the Council at Brussels.

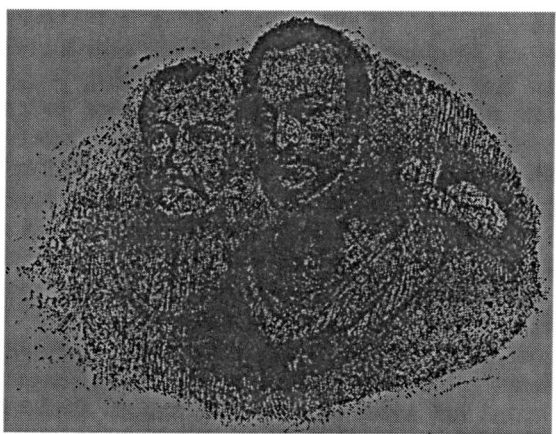

EGMONT AND HORN.

Having committed these deeds of a political butcher Alva turned to deal with Louis of Nassau, and the small ill-paid and ill-organised force with which he had gained the day at Heiliger Lee. In his arrangements he displayed the greatest prudence, leaving nothing to chance, and forbidding his lieutenants to open hostilities until he had concentrated 15,000 men within a short distance of Louis of Nassau's camp. Then the result was never in doubt. Alva gained one success outside Groningen, and another at Jemmingen which was decisive. In the latter action Louis's army was practically destroyed—seven thousand being left dead on the field. When the battle was clearly lost Count Louis swam across the river and made good his escape. The Spanish army followed up its victory by devastating the country, although it was undisputed that the inhabitants had been too timid to throw in their lot with those who had come to effect their deliverance.

The first blow for the expulsion of the Spaniards had failed. It remained to be seen if a second one, dealt by William in person, would succeed any better. The Prince of Orange, some time after the defeat of his brother, entered Limburg in the hope of being able to invade Brabant, or failing that to capture Liége. In neither object was he successful. There were no signs of any popular rising in the metropolitan Province of Belgium, and Alva hastened with his victorious army to bar his advance. The Prince-Bishop of Liége, Groesbeck, refused to allow any armed force to enter his jurisdiction, and made such preparations for a stout defence that both combatants respected his neutrality. The opposition of Liége compelled William to cross the Meuse by fording it— a feat of much peril, brilliantly accomplished on this occasion and scarcely credited. He then endeavoured to force Alva to accept battle, which that astute and calculating general as resolutely refused. Twenty-nine times in a month William moved his camp without bringing his cool antagonist to an engagement. Every day added to his embarrassment. The people dared not assist him, his own troops, chiefly German mercenaries, became mutinous, and supplies ran short. Only once did Alva depart from the strictly defensive tactics on which he had decided, and that was when he fell on the rearguard of William's army in crossing the Geta and destroyed it. A few weeks later the Protestant army, unable to cross the Meuse or to traverse Liége back to Germany, made its retreat into France, whence in due course it reached Strasburg and was disbanded. The great effort, made at immense personal sacrifices by William of Orange, for the deliverance of the Belgian provinces of the Netherlands thus failed completely. He could not win the battle which was necessary to produce any popular rising, and Alva had the satisfaction of seeing the whole country remain abjectly servile and submissive under his feet.

THE SEA BEGGARS.

With a small loyal body of the army he had raised, William and his two brothers, Louis and Henry, proceeded to France and linked their fortunes with those of the Huguenots under Coligny. The step was attended with important consequences, because it drew his attention to the possibility of renewing the struggle at sea, and establishing a base of operations in a new quarter. Coligny himself appears to have inspired him with the idea which resulted in the founding of "the Beggars of the Sea." William issued letters of marque to a certain number of privateers intended to prey on Spanish commerce, and for a time these carried on their operations from English ports. The chief of the Sea Beggars was William de la Marck, Count Lumen, a descendant of the Wild Boar of the Ardennes. Whether they would ever have accomplished anything important, without the incentive supplied by their expulsion in March, 1572, on Elizabeth's order, may be doubted. They had in consequence of that order to seek a place of shelter elsewhere, and they sought it, with pregnant consequences, on the coast of Holland

The small harbour of Brill at the mouth of the Meuse was captured and successfully held against an attempt by the Spanish Governor of the province to retake it. Brill became the base of the further operations of the "sea beggars," and the example set there was promptly followed at Flushing, which expelled the Spanish garrison, and celebrated the dawn of liberty by hanging Pacheco, Alva's best engineer and the constructor of Antwerp citadel. Reinforcements arrived from France and England, and the greater part of the island of Walcheren was soon occupied by a considerable force. The movement spread throughout the Batavian provinces. Zealand, Holland, Over Yssel, Utrecht cast down the Spanish authority and set up the jurisdiction of the Prince of Orange, who still, however, preserved the fiction that he was "stadtholder for the King." A few months later Louis of Nassau seized Mons, and almost at the same moment the "sea beggars" captured a rich fleet with sufficient treasure on board to pay the troops for two years. Alva had added to the hatred the people felt for him by imposing fresh taxes on them in the form of the tenth and twentieth penny. This attempted extortion was aggravated by the general depression of trade that followed from Alva's tyrannical proceedings. During the whole of this period he was engaged in a ceaseless struggle with the town councils on this subject and he encountered an opposition which he found it impossible to overcome. "Down with the tithe" was the cry to which Mons fell, and the townspeople rose to it most readily.

In July, 1572, the States of Holland met at Dort to recognise the authority of the Prince of Orange, and to promise the funds which would enable him to bring a considerable army out of Germany. Marnix de Ste. Aldegonde was his delegate on the occasion and succeeded in rousing sufficient enthusiasm among his audience to make them vote voluntarily a far larger sum than they had refused to Alva. With this pecuniary assistance the Prince of Orange was able to induce the large army he had recruited in Germany to march for Flanders. With thirty thousand men he made his way, via St. Trond, Louvain, Malines, Audenarde, and Nivelles, to the neighbourhood of Mons, where he hoped not merely to deliver his brother but to consolidate his conquest. That hope was the stronger because the Huguenots were at the moment in the ascendant with the King of France, and their co-operation was assured. On the capture of Mons, Alva had sent Frederick of Toledo, one of his sons, to besiege it with 10,000 men, and a Huguenot force coming to its relief was destroyed through the over-confidence of its commander. Before William could reach it the garrison had been reduced to very low straits, and then Alva's skill in avoiding a pitched battle once more placed William in a position of embarrassment, and deprived him of the fruits of all his labours. Still there can be no question that if the French King had even kept part of his promise "to employ all his forces to rescue the Netherlands from their oppressors" the fate of the Spanish garrison would have been sealed. There is evidence to show that Alva was alarmed at the outlook and that he thought of having recourse to moderation, equally foreign to his character and his instructions. At the very moment of assured success the tidings came of an event which destroyed all the hopes of the Prince of Orange, and as effectually removed Alva's fears. The event, it is scarcely necessary to say, was the Massacre of St. Bartholomew (25th August, 1572) which, by destroying the Huguenot party in Paris, swept away all hopes of that military co-operation with Coligny which would have been irresistible. The Prince of Orange, therefore, was beaten almost before a shot was fired, but a successful night surprise in which he lost six hundred men, and narrowly escaped himself,* hastened the dispersal of his army by discouraging it. He was compelled to order his brother to surrender Mons on the best terms he could obtain, and to retreat himself to the Rhine. Louis of Nassau obtained honourable terms —a rare event in that age—but Alva wreaked his vengeance on the citizens of Mons and Malines. The latter place was handed over to his army for three days to sack, and even in that terrible age the scenes enacted in the archiepiscopal city caused a shudder throughout Europe.

The failure of William of Orange's campaign in Hainaut, practically speaking, destroyed all his hopes of rescuing the Belgic provinces from Alva, for up to the point now reached the prince had been fighting in the name of Philip, not merely as King of Spain but as Count of Holland, and the justification of the rebellion was to put an end to the tyranny of Alva, not of Spain. There remained the possibility of saving the northern Provinces which were gathered round the central name of Holland, and thither the Prince of Orange betook himself after the events just described. Alva was determined to reassert his power as effectually over the northern Provinces as he had done over the southern, and thus to celebrate the conclusion of his viceroyalty, for he had already requested Philip's permission to resign. The security he was able to feel on the side of France, and through having cowed the Belgian people, enabled him to concentrate the whole of his military strength on the task. At first Alva met with several successes. Zutphen, Naarden and Harlem were captured after more or less resistance,

---

* Lovers of dogs will be interested in learning that on this occasion William of Orange was saved by his little spaniel, which heard the approaching foe and, knowing them to be strangers, awoke its master by scratching his face and barking. The prince had just the time to throw himself upon a horse and make his escape.

and at each place victory was celebrated with a ruthless massacre. Increased ferocity was imparted to the struggle on both sides, and the reformers, whenever they obtained the chance, emulated the example of their enemies by mutilating and slaying every priest or friar on whom they could lay their hands. The details of this struggle in the north belong, however, to the history of Holland rather than to that of Belgium.

It was after the successes of 1572 that Alva began the following campaign full of hope in a speedy issue by the siege of Alkmaar. The character of the man stands revealed for all time, and beyond the possibility of extenuation by any panegyrist, in his own letter to Philip, describing his intentions towards the inhabitants of this city—" If I take Alkmaar I am resolved not to leave a single creature alive; the knife shall be put to every throat. Since the example of Harlem has proved of no use, perhaps an example of cruelty will bring the other cities to their senses." Fortunately his plans on the subject of Alkmaar were confined to intentions by his inability to capture it, and perhaps the very ferocity of his intentions contributed to defeat them. The heroic defence of that place entailed the retreat of the Spaniards, and for the first time in his career Alva had to admit a defeat without the means of retrieving it. Outside politics also took a turn adverse to his schemes. St. Bartholomew's had saved Alva's position in 1572, but the vacancy on the throne of Poland, for which the King of France wished to nominate his brother, Henry of Anjou, led to that king's seeking, in 1573, the alliance of the Prince of Orange, whom the German princes would have put forward as their candidate. A year thus altered several of the conditions of the struggle, and altered them in a sense especially adverse to Alva. His reputation was diminished, his influence with Philip was shaken. His seven years of absolute power had not produced the results he had promised. He had turned the Provinces into a shambles, but the King's authority had been cast down in one half of them, and rendered hateful in the other. A costly war was in progress, the once productive revenues of the Netherlands had disappeared, and the army in the field could only be paid by subsidies from Spain herself, which were often not forthcoming at all, and sometimes went to enrich the hostile treasury by capture at sea. Alva's enemies at Madrid took advantage of all these circumstances to undermine his position, and at last Philip complied with his own request to be relieved by appointing Requesens Governor in his stead. Of "the hellish devil," the name given to Alva in the popular Flemish ballads which were all that represented their ineffectual patriotism, it is only possible to say that he represents for all time the incarnation of bloodthirsty cruelty, without a redeeming spark of human pity or weakness. The experiences of fifty years of warfare had turned his features to granite, the ferocious fanaticism of the most fanatical race and country Christendom has known had performed the same petrifaction on his heart.

Requesens, the new Governor General, was a man of temperate views, and of a character without any definite colour. In comparison with one of Alva's temperament and thoroughness he was a man of peace and humanity. His instructions might be summed up in the words, tranquillise the provinces, and obtain some revenue from them; but his experience was destined to be warlike in its course, and disappointing in the result. Perhaps his efforts were less successful than they might have been, because it was known that he held in reserve "a policy of extermination." The failure of his first military undertaking may also have embittered his feelings and diminished his hold on public sentiment. He came as an emissary of peace, but circumstances forced him to undertake military operations within a few months of his arrival at Brussels. The town of Middelburg was the last Spanish possession in the island of Walcheren, and it had been closely besieged for more than a year. The garrison was reduced to the lowest extremities, and unless aid came quickly it would have to surrender. Two Spanish fleets were accordingly fitted out to proceed to its rescue. One was completely routed off Bergen-op-Zoom; the other never fired a shot. A few days later Middelburg surrendered. This success was, however, heavily compensated for by the rude defeat which the Prince of Orange's brother, Louis of Nassau, suffered on land at the battle of Mook. The circumstances which brought this about were the arrangement made with France and the desire to raise the southern provinces which Louis hoped to accomplish by the capture of Maestricht. Instead of capturing that place he found himself compelled to accept battle in a highly disadvantageous position on the banks of the Meuse (14th April, 1574). The struggle was one of the most obstinate of the whole war, but it resulted in a complete Spanish victory, rendered more complete by the deaths of Louis of Nassau, and his brother Henry. The results of this victory were not great, because the Spanish soldiers mutinied for the arrears of their pay, and were only pacified when Requesens hypothecated his own plate for the satisfaction of their claim.

Having performed these necessary duties, Requesens turned to the fulfilment of the pacific instructions with which he had been charged Early in the June following the fight at Mook, Requesens published at Brussels the Pope's pardon to the peoples of the Netherlands and also the King's amnesty. The importance and practical value of these instruments have been derided, but there is no doubt that they produced a tranquillising effect on the Belgian population. They were a guarantee that the exactions of Alva in blood and property would not be renewed, and a pledge by the Church to overlook all minor delinquencies, and to afford an opportunity to all its members to re-enter the gates of orthodoxy. A definite significance was given to these measures by the abolition of the Blood Council and of the unpopular taxes known as the tenth and twentieth penny. The States General of the Belgic Provinces were also summoned to express their gratitude for these favours, but instead of doing so they boldly demanded more, pressing, among other things, for the restitution of all their old privileges, the cessation of the civil war in all the Provinces, north and south, and the stopping of the exactions of every kind practised by the Spanish soldiery. The letters of pardon were so limited as to have no effect in Holland, and the spirit of the Belgians, if it had not risen to the same height of obstinate opposition to the tyrant as the northern races who possessed the security of a watery barrier, at least induced them to reject proffers of peace which would not apply to those who had fought a strenuous and not wholly unsuccessful battle.

In face of this firmness Requesens turned again to military enterprise in the hope that it would facilitate his task. He had failed to relieve Middelburg, he might retrieve that and much else by the capture of Leyden. The siege of this place was pressed with all the available forces at his command. Walloon levies and German mercenaries co-operated with the regular Spanish regiments, now much reduced in number. On the other hand William of Orange concentrated his efforts on the relief of the place. While the siege was in progress Requesens published a second and ampler pardon to all who confessed themselves faithful members of the Church with the exception of a few individuals whose names were given. This pardon was accepted by the southern provinces, but rejected by the northern who thus plainly announced their final and complete severance from Rome. The Prince of Orange himself had anticipated this decision by joining the Calvinist body at Dort in October, 1573. So far as the capture of Leyden was concerned, the pardon of Requesens was a failure. To the summons to surrender on honourable terms there came back the proud reply, "When provisions fail us we will feed ourselves with our left arms and defend our liberties with our right." Still the garrison was reduced to the lowest ebb before the Prince of Orange was able to succour it by flooding the surrounding country, and introducing supplies into the place by means of his fleet. It was on this occasion that the memorable phrase was employed, "Better a drowned land than a lost land." The successful defence of Leyden was celebrated by the foundation of the University which has alike perpetuated the memory of the siege, and invested the place with imperishable lustre as a seat of learning.

Baffled at Leyden, as in the attempt to relieve Middelburg, Requesens again turned to pacific measures, but the Conference held at Breda produced no result, because the King's prerogative and the Catholic faith represented the irreducible minimum of the Spanish Governor's terms. Reinforcements were then summoned from Spain and, in order to assist the operation of landing them, Requesens despatched a force to seize the islands of Schouwen and Duveland. The undertaking was well and successfully accomplished, but immediately afterwards the death of Requesens threw the affairs of the Belgian provinces into confusion. But for a brief space it seemed as if the consequence might be beneficial to the liberties of the people, for the States of Brabant assumed the government of the country and succeeded in obtaining from Philip letters patent confirming their authority. Unfortunately the States did not prove equal to the occasion, and a mutiny among the Spanish troops clamouring for their arrears of pay was not quelled. While the States of Brabant were convoking the States General in defiance of Philip, and intriguing with William of Orange for a common union, the Spanish regiments took the law into their own hands, and anticipated the projects on foot for their expulsion. They seized Alost, and made it their headquarters, whereupon the Brabant Council declared the King's own soldiers to be "enemies, rebels, and outlaws," whom everybody might kill with impunity.

The Council had not the means of executing its own orders beyond arresting those members of its body, whose Spanish sympathies were too pronounced, for the Spanish veterans felt themselves secure against all the efforts of the civic levies. At first the Spanish generals held aloof from their mutinous troops, but when they found that the popular movement was taking an anti-Spanish form they supported their action and placed themselves at their head. The German regiments also threw themselves into the same movement. The Walloon troops were faithful to their salt, and not to their country. In November, 1576, the Spanish troops made themselves masters of the rich city of Antwerp, which they proceeded to sack during three days still known as "the Spanish fury." More than six thousand men, women, and children were butchered, eight hundred houses were destroyed by fire, and damage was done to the computed extent of two millions of our money. The Spanish troops holding the citadels of all the principal cities, except Brussels, became virtual masters of the country. Their supremacy was confirmed by such victories as that of Tisnacq, where a large body of raw levies was defeated with a loss of two thousand slain, while the Spaniards had only two men killed.

A congress was opened at Ghent between the States General and the representatives of the Prince of Orange, but its proceedings were slow and it was only after the loss of much valuable time that the signature of an agreement or alliance binding all the Provinces to combine together for the expulsion of the Spaniards from the Netherlands was effected. The settlement of all questions was to be left over until that object had been attained, when they were to be referred to the States General. The Pacification of Ghent was extremely popular for the moment, but, unfortunately, there was not available the military force to carry out its excellent provisions. The Spanish troops were masters of the country south of the Meuse, the forces obedient to the Prince north of it were not equal to the task of overthrowing the Spanish army, although they could very successfully defend the waterland of Holland and Friesland. There were also causes of disunion. Spanish tyranny and brutality had aroused a common hatred, but there was a gulf between the northern and southern provinces themselves that prevented any hearty or prolonged union. The northern had become Protestants of a pronounced and uncompromising type, the southern had been effectually cured of any inclination to venture into regions of theological disputation and conflict. They were quite content to leave those questions to the directors of the Church in which they had been brought up, and sought no higher object than a little security and tranquillity.

The ink on the deed of the Pacification of Ghent with its twenty-five articles was scarcely dry when the news came of the arrival of Philip's new Governor, Don John of Austria. At the moment of his arrival in Belgium Don John, a natural son of the Emperor Charles the Fifth, was perhaps the most celebrated man in Europe. His victory over the Turks at Lepanto, in 1571, had saved Christendom and made him famous for posterity. He was, however, more of a paladin of romance than of a great soldier or wise statesman. His manner of taking up his government in the Netherlands was typical of the man. He traversed France in disguise, and he announced his arrival at Luxembourg to the inhabitants of the disturbed country he had come to rule and pacify in the following words:

" I have just arrived so completely alone and so unprovided with everything that I am without a secretary." The policy which he pursued was in harmony with these facts. He had come to conciliate the Provinces, to restore tranquillity, and to rest satisfied with the formal recognition of the supremacy of the Church of Rome, and with the resumption of the payment of some contribution to Philip's exchequer. When the deputies, appointed after the Union of Brussels, which confirmed the Pacification of Ghent, named as one of their conditions the expulsion of the Spanish troops, he accepted it by what was called the Perpetual and Irrevocable Edict, signed at Marche in the district of Famene. The only condition made on his side was that the Provinces should bear the expense and provide without delay the sum of six hundred thousand florins. All the other terms were dictated by the national representatives, and there is no doubt that the extent of Don John's concessions embarrassed William of Orange for the moment and contributed materially to the subsequent cleavage between the northern and southern provinces. They were so agreeable to the Belgian representatives that they signed the deed without waiting for the Prince of Orange's assent, and in face of his agent's protest. The Perpetual Edict was consequently not accepted by William of Orange, and had no force in Holland. The one concession made, viz., the withdrawal of the Spanish garrisons, had already been obtained there by force of arms. However, the Spanish troops were removed from the country, and the event produced a tranquillising effect throughout Belgium, which again became Catholic and loyal.

So far Don John had succeeded beyond reasonable expectation, and his triumphant entry into Brussels on 1st of May, 1577, seemed to promise a long era of peace and popularity. Having won over, as he thought, one half of the lost territory, he hoped to gain the other by converting William of Orange into a friend and well wisher to Spain. He was quite confident that this could be done if only William's price could be ascertained, and with this object he sent the Duke of Aerschot, head of the House of Croy, to discover what it might be. He unfolded his plan in a letter to Philip—" The name of your

Majesty is as much abhorred and despised in the Netherlands as that of the Prince of Orange is loved and feared. I am negotiating with him and giving him every security, for I see that the establishment of peace, as well as the maintenance of the Catholic religion, and the obedience to your Majesty depend now upon him. Things have reached that pass that 'tis necessary to make a virtue of necessity. If he lend an ear to my proposals it will be only upon very advantageous conditions, but to these it will be necessary to submit rather than to lose everything." Don John's cajolery did not succeed. Orange remained aloof, distrustful of his intentions and preparing against all contingencies. He entered into negotiations, but with the avowed intention of making them abortive because, as he said, nothing less than the extirpation of himself and his followers would satisfy Philip.

In a little time Don John began to lose patience in the game of diplomacy when he found that his antagonist overmatched him in skill and firmness. He incited the southern states to take measures to coerce the northern, and at the same time he put forward his claim to command all the national troops and to make all appointments. These demands were rejected and Don John, alarmed as to the safety of his person in Brussels, suddenly seized Namur and made its citadel his headquarters. Here he ordered the regular troops to concentrate, for there still remained, after the departure of the Spaniards, not fewer than 10,000 German and Walloon mercenaries in Government pay. His policy had now veered round to the intention to "adopt extremities," although with reluctance, but the suddenness of his movements had produced such alarm at Brussels that an express was sent off begging the Prince of Orange to come at all hazards to their assistance. In a fit of petulance and by an impatient attempt at coercion Don John had lost all the advantages he had acquired. His seizure of Namur had been followed by an attempt to place a German garrison in the citadel of Antwerp, but it failed. At the instigation of William of Orange a step was taken which rendered future success in this direction impossible. The greater part of Antwerp citadel was demolished, and a similar work was accomplished at Ghent, thus removing two of the chief memorials of Alva's rule.

At this moment divided councils proved the ruin of the country in the sense of maintaining its united liberty. Some of the causes have been already indicated. To them must now be added the growing unpopularity of William with the nobles of the Belgian provinces, who remained staunch to the Catholic faith while he had become a heretic. Moreover, his masterful character was not calculated to make him popular among men who considered themselves in every way his equal. A party of the nobles, headed by the Duke of Aerschot and the Count de Lalaing, invited the Emperor of Germany to send his brother, the Archduke Mathias, to take over the Government and thus establish a loyal Catholic state between the Prince of Orange on one side and the Spaniards on the other. The former, by skilfully adapting himself to the arrangement, prevented its being turned to either his humiliation or more serious discomfiture. At the same moment Don John was declared to be deprived of all his offices, and a traitor to the country. As for King Philip the titular sovereign of the realm, his name was not so much as mentioned and his authority was completely ignored.

But the lull in the struggle was deceptive and unreal. The burghers were feasting and enjoying their newly gained responsibilities in Brussels, while Don John was making his preparations to deal them a heavy blow in return for the wrongs and insults they had piled upon him. He had succeeded in concentrating his German regiments. Considerable reinforcements reached him from Italy and Spain. His nephew, Alexander Farnese of Parma, the son of the Duchess Margaret who had so long ruled the Netherlands, brought him some picked regiments, and the aid of his own great military abilities. In this way he soon found himself at the head of twenty thousand men, and to stimulate their enthusiasm, as well as to make clear what they were fighting for, he designed a special banner bearing a Cross and the following inscription: "Under this sign I conquered the Turks, under it I will conquer the heretics."

The army of the States was numerically not inferior to that of Don John, but much of it was composed of fresh levies, and none of the troops could compare with the veterans of Spain and Italy. Still it advanced to Namur to oppose the Spaniards who, however, commanded the passage of the Meuse by the possession of the Citadel. Finding Don John stronger than was expected the national army, commanded by Antony de Goignies, retired in the direction of Brussels, but Don John pressed on with ardour and his cavalry caught up the rearguard near Gembloux. What was intended to be merely a skirmish developed into a general attack through the impetuosity of the cavalry and the easy success they obtained over their opponents, but the signal victory that followed was due to Alexander Farnese, who, traversing a marsh, came down on the flank of the Belgians and routed them. Only twelve hundred Spanish cavalry were engaged, and, at a quite insignificant loss to themselves, they destroyed ten thousand of the national army. After this victory the greater number of towns from Hainaut to Limburg opened their gates to the conqueror without resistance; those that did resist experienced all the cruelty of the Spanish victors. Antwerp, Brussels and Ghent were the only three places of any importance that did not fall.

The consequence of these military successes was that the confusion in the country became worse confounded. Orange and the Archduke Mathias fixed their headquarters at Antwerp, the States General at Brussels and Ghent summoned aid from any available quarter, the Catholics among them calling the Duke d' Alençon, brother of the King of France, to their assistance, the Calvinists appealing to the Count Palatine, John Casimir. Both came forward, Alençon capturing Maubeuge, and thence extending his authority over Hainaut, and John Casimir, bringing 12,000 Germans, largely paid by Queen Elizabeth, had the satisfaction of defeating Don John in person at Rymenam on the Dyle with the loss of nearly a thousand slain (1st August, 1578). This battle was fought against the advice of Alexander Farnese, who was fast gaining the reputation of the ablest military commander of the age. After this reverse Don John's spirit seemed to fail him. He retired to Bouges where he built a fortified camp on the heights above the town of Namur. Here he could accomplish nothing, and a lingering fever, produced as much by mental distress and disappointment as by bodily ailment, soon carried him off. He died on 1st October, two months after his defeat at Rymenam, and almost on the anniversary of the great victory of Lepanto which preserves his fame.

On his death-bed Don John left his authority to his nephew-in-blood, Alexander Farnese, Prince of Parma, and the choice could not have devolved on an abler man. As a military commander he was quite the equal of Alva, and he possessed one great superiority over him in being only thirty-three when called upon to guide the destinies of the Netherlands, whereas Alva was over sixty, in a period, too, when men aged rapidly. Parma was also far more of a statesman than Alva. Although he could be as cruel as his predecessor on occasion, he knew that cruelty alone is not statesmanship. It must also be allowed that circumstances were more in his favour. Alva had to deal with a solid opposition; more than one popular or powerful current was in Parma's favour. The excesses of the Calvinists at Ghent, where a small faction had seized authority and set up a republic that prohibited the practice of the Catholic religion, aroused deep resentment among the mass of the population. The churches were pillaged, image-breaking was turned into a popular amusement, and priests were maltreated. To crown their actions the Duke of Aerschot, the Governor of the Province, was thrown into prison. These excesses strengthened the feeling in the southern provinces in favour of a reconciliation with the legitimate sovereign. The Malcontents, as they called themselves, took up arms against the Ghent faction. Everywhere disunion, confusion, and faction fighting prevailed, except where north of the Meuse the Prince of Orange had further consolidated his position by the Union of Utrecht (23rd January, 1579) which practically founded the Netherlands or Dutch Republic. The name of Philip finally disappeared from the edicts in those Provinces, and in its place appeared that of " The States General of the United Provinces."

Parma perceived at a glance that the Spanish policy was to come to terms with the Malcontents, who were at least attached to their religion. The negotiations that followed between him and the Duke of Aerschot resulted in the Treaty of Arras, ratified at Maestricht on 28th June, 1579, stipulating once more for the withdrawal of the foreign soldiers, but also for the levy of a national army to be paid for by the country. The King of Spain was also to nominate as Governor-General a Prince or Princess of his own blood. The treaty of Arras was in a sense the reply to the Union of Utrecht* and marked more clearly the cleavage between north and south. The old seventeen Provinces divided into two groups represented to-day by the kingdoms of Belgium and Holland.

Notwithstanding these negotiations Parma did not remain inactive. He placed an army of thirty thousand men in the field resolving to employ the Spanish troops in two great enterprises before he suffered them to depart. One was to drive back all the scattered garrisons obeying the Prince of Orange into Antwerp, and the other was the capture of Maestricht held by a garrison under Count Schwartzenberg and recently strongly fortified by William's chief engineer, Sebastian Tappin. After a siege of more than three months and a half, during which nine assaults were repulsed, Maestricht was captured by surprise on 29th June, 1579. A horrible butchery followed, and for three days the town was given up to pillage. Before the siege began it contained 34,000 inhabitants, after the butchery it is said that only four hundred men, women or children survived, and that they were expelled to give place to new settlers. The blame for the fall of Maestricht, without an effort to save it, was very justly laid at the door of the Dutch States General, whose timidity, apathy and suspiciousness were destined to become a marked characteristic of their policy.

Philip, after the departure of the Spanish troops, tried to oust Parma from the Governor Generalship in favour of his mother the old Duchess Margaret, but Alexander was not to be so easily shunted, and after a brief contest it was the mother and not the son who took the road back to Italy. About this time Philip, on the advice of Cardinal Granvelle who had recovered his influence and become President of the Madrid Council, offered a large reward to whoever would assassinate

---

* Some Belgian towns joined the Union more or less temporarily, *e.g.*, Ghent, Ypres, Antwerp, Bruges, and the Frank of Bruges.

William of Orange. He had failed to beat him in war, or to worst him in diplomacy, but the assassin's blow would rid him of the presence of his rival. Let it be recorded in Parma's favour that he openly disapproved of the project, and that he said none of the inhabitants of the Provinces would make the attempt because they disapproved of such fashions. If the deed were to be done it must be accomplished by a foreigner, that is to say, by a Frenchman, Italian, or Spaniard. The reply of the Prince of Orange to these threats was to publish his famous apology, and at the same time the deposition of Philip as sovereign of the Netherlands (26th July, 1581).

The first attempt to slay the Prince and earn the King's reward was made at Antwerp in March, 1582, during the Duke of Anjou's visit. The assassin Jauregin, fired at him point blank with a pistol and wounded him seriously in the mouth. The assassin was immediately killed, and in the excitement the populace threatened to attack the Duke of Anjou and his French followers. The excitement was happily allayed, and the Duke of Anjou, abandoning the hope of becoming King of England by a marriage with Queen Elizabeth, allowed himself to be inaugurated as Count of Flanders at Bruges. The policy of the Prince of Orange at this moment was to create a French interest in the southern provinces as a set-off to the Spanish, but Parma was too strong for the realisation of such a policy even if Anjou had not been a silly worthless prince. His own brother said of him that he was only good for making a noise and that he accomplished nothing. At the same time Anjou wished to possess absolute power over his new Flemish subjects, and with the view of relieving himself from the fetters imposed by the civic privileges he had engaged to respect, he ordered his lieutenant to seize the towns in which they were garrisoned, while he undertook the capture of Antwerp. The task lightly undertaken in a reckless spirit failed ignominiously. At Bruges, Ostend, and other places the French garrisons were made prisoners; and from Antwerp, Anjou and his troops had to make an inglorious retreat. In June, 1583, Anjou left the Netherlands for good, and with his departure the French attempt to control them came to an end.

The feud between the Flemings and the French gave Parma his opportunity. He advanced into Flanders at the head of a large army, capturing town after town. He was engaged in the siege of Ghent when news arrived that William of Orange had been assassinated by the fanatic, Balthazar Gerard at Delft (10th July, 1584). Two months later Ghent surrendered through famine. The citizens were constrained to rebuild the citadel which they had destroyed a few years earlier, but Parma promised to respect their privileges, and granted Protestants a respite of two years before leaving the country, for it must be borne in mind that the point from which the King of Spain never swerved was the exclusive practice of the Roman creed. From Ghent, Parma hastened to besiege Brussels, where a Calvinist administration had been set up by Van den Tympel who raised a mercenary army of foreigners including a Scotch regiment. Having occupied the neighbouring towns Parma succeeded in cutting off all supplies and in reducing the garrison and inhabitants to such straits that they insisted on their leaders surrendering. On 10th March, 1585, Brussels opened its gates. To complete the triumph of Parma there remained only Antwerp to be recovered. He began his operations with that object before the capture of Ghent, but after the fall of Brussels he pressed the siege with redoubled vigour. It was bravely defended by Marnix de Ste. Aldegonde, but at last provisions failed, and no aid being apparent, he was compelled to sign a capitulation on 17th August, 1585. At Antwerp the sovereignty of King Philip and the Catholic religion were again set up, the Protestants being allowed, however, four years to realise their property before going into exile instead of the two years accorded at Ghent.

Marnix de Ste. Aldegonde, the friend and associate of William of Orange, and after him by far the ablest of the national leaders, was discredited by the surrender of Antwerp, although he had defended it with equal courage and ability. He retired from public life and died at Leyden in December, 1598. Somewhat tardily the tercentenary of this great patriot was made the first occasion of recognising his merit on the part at least of the city which he had so valiantly defended.

The army with which Parma had recovered the Belgian provinces was now destined by Philip for a greater enterprise. England had become by its insular position the true bulwark of Protestantism, and its subsidies, naval co-operation, and volunteers provided Holland with the means by which she preserved her independence. Philip proposed to complete his scheme for restoring the Catholic religion generally by invading England. On this adventure he concentrated the whole naval power of Spain, but Parma was to provide from the veteran and victorious force in Flanders the army of invasion. With this object he collected along the coast from Nieuport to Dunkirk an army of forty thousand men. It need only be said that Parma had everything in readiness to play his part in the ambitious scheme, but the Invincible Armada was unable to do its share against the less numerous but more active English fleet and the storms of the English Channel. Philip's grand scheme came to naught in the manner that everybody knows, but Parma had no part in the failure. Fortunately for Holland Philip also drew him off from the prey he had marked for his own, by ordering him to advance into France and save the League from Henry of Navarre. In these campaigns he added to his military reputation, but his career was cut short (December, 1592) by the fever which was then the scourge of camps. With the disappearance of Parma ended all possibility of reviving the policy which Alva had been directed to introduce nearly thirty years before. All that military skill could do had been done for its success, but an indefinite continuance in such a policy was simply impossible, for it signified gradual but certain extermination. Even if it had resulted in the uprooting of heresy in the southern provinces, it had entailed the disintegration of the possessions of the House of Burgundy cemented and aggrandised by the Emperor Charles. As a Belgian writer has said—" In vain might vestiges of the ancient prosperity of Belgium be sought for. The Belgian ports were blockaded by the cruisers of Holland and Zealand. Persecution and exile had emptied the workshops. England gathered in the industry of our ruined cities. Amsterdam, Rotterdam, and Middelburg inherited the commerce of Antwerp and

Bruges." These drawbacks and losses did not diminish the satisfaction of Philip because "the exclusive practice of the Catholic faith" was enforced everywhere under his rule.

One of the last acts of Philip's long reign was to appoint the Archduke Albert of Austria, son of Maximilian II., Governor General, and this Prince arrived in Belgium in February, 1596. Wearied in the task of government by the strain of forty years, Philip determined to lighten the burden for his successors, by assigning the seventeen provinces and the dominions of the House of Burgundy to his favourite daughter, Isabella, and by marrying her to the Archduke Albert. The act of cession was dated 6th May, 1598, and a few weeks after it was read to the States General Philip died at the Escurial in the 72nd year of his age (13th September, 1598). His name will always excite passionate controversy. His enemies will be implacable, his partizans luke-warm, thus affording evidence that he is generally regarded as a failure, and as having carried his tyranny too far. His influence on Belgian history is clear and incontestable. However terrible his measures, there is no gainsaying the fact that he stamped out all inclination towards the new religion in the bosoms of the Walloon and Flemish races, and in this way the impression left by the Inquisition, the Blood Council, and the Spanish Fury is not obliterated even to-day.

CHAPTER XII.

The Last Century of Spanish Rule.

The arrangement, assigning Belgium to the separate and independent government of the Infanta Isabella, had not been carried out at the moment of the death of Philip the Second, but it was ratified by his son and successor Philip the Third.

ENTRY OF ALBERT AND ISABELLA.

The marriage of this princess and the Archduke Albert was celebrated at Valencia in April, 1599, and the two new rulers made their "joyous entry" into Brussels in the following September amid popular rejoicings. After forty-five years of foreign rule it seemed as if the country had regained its national existence, and with it the hope of recovering its lost material prosperity. But the future contained no such agreeable facts in store for this cruelly used people who, without any contributory fault of their own, were about to become for two centuries the victim and plaything of the ambitious potentates by whom they were surrounded. The wars that had up to this been waged on their territory were, at least in some degree, national, affecting the interests and existence of the population, and representing issues for which Walloons and Flemings alike thought it worth while to give their lives. But those of the 17th and 18th centuries were wars forced upon the Belgian people against their will, often without their co-operation, and always in complete disregard of their rights and interest. If war devastated the country, Peace brought it no compensation in increased security, or in improved commercial and political conditions. Its opinion was ignored in the one case, its rights and interests were sacrificed in the other.

The new rulers, recognising the deplorable condition of the country, did devote their first efforts to its amelioration. They summoned the States General, which met at Brussels on 28th April, 1600, and the acts of this assembly revealed the extent of the misery afflicting the country. The situation was described in the following language, " The great cities of Flanders and Brabant had been abandoned by a large part of their inhabitants ; agriculture hardly in a less degree than commerce and industry had been ruined. Trade was diminished not more by the Government's prohibition of intercourse with Holland, Zealand, and their allies, than by the Dutch fleets which held the coast towns and the entrance of the Scheldt in close blockade. Industry, which had in the old days made other states tributary of this, had departed to England and Holland by the flight of the artizans who had supported it. The villages lay in ruins, the fields in desolation. Famine stalked through the land." This picture may be compared with that given of the country when Charles the Fifth laid down the sceptre. Albert and Isabella could not be blind to its terrible reality, and they even wished to remove its worst features, but unfortunately they had another aspiration that was uppermost, and this was to contribute to the overthrow of the United Provinces. They would do much for Belgian welfare afterwards, but this must be accomplished first. The most important matter they represented to the States General was the provision of the funds necessary for the continuance of the war with Maurice of Nassau. The assembly replied that they wished for peace, and that they were confident that an arrangement could be come to without having recourse to arms. In the meantime the troops were mutinous on account of long arrears in their pay, and Maurice was gradually acquiring possession of all the fortified places on the frontier. The hopes of the States General themselves must have been greatly diminished in a pacific solution when their delegates were dismissed summarily from the Hague with a curt intimation that there was nothing to be discussed unless the Southern Provinces were prepared to join the Northern in a common effort to put an end to the Spanish Yoke. When the Belgian representatives declared that Albert and Isabella intended to restore their national privileges and independence the Councillor-Pensionary, Barnevelt, replied that "those hopes were illusory seeing that all the strong places were held by Spanish garrisons." Under all these circumstances it was not surprising that the States General should be dismissed after a session of little more than six months, and that they should not meet again for a period of thirty-two years.

The struggle between Albert and Maurice continued with brief intervals of mutual exhaustion and fluctuating fortune during the nine years following the arrival of the Archduke and his wife in the Netherlands. It began with the battle of Nieuport in July, 1600, and terminated with the truce of Antwerp in April, 1609, that is to say, with a Spanish defeat and a Spanish humiliation. The German Empire poured forth its Catholic soldiers to crush the United Provinces, Spain sent her fleets under the brothers Spinola to assist in the task, but the Dutch more than held their own, although after a siege of over three years they were expelled from Ostend. The defence and attack on that place formed the most heroic episode in the long struggle. The garrison under Daniel Hartaing, constantly reinforced by adventurers from Holland and England, made one of the most obstinate defences recorded in history, and on surrender it was accorded the most honourable terms. The Archduke Albert embraced the courageous commandant, and entertained him and all his officers at a costly banquet. Something of the ancient chivalry of warfare was on this occasion imparted to this bitter religious struggle at what may be called the half way stage between the butcherings of Alva and those of Tilly and Pappenheim, between the Blood Council and the Treaty of Westphalia. The inhabitants of Ostend, too deeply compromised in the Reform movement, followed the garrison into exile, and the victor acquired only a mass of ruins without an inhabitant.*

Both sides were at last brought to a pacific frame of mind. Spain, impressed by the representations of Spinola, whose military skill had to some degree changed the fortune of the war, that tranquillity in the Spanish provinces was necessary at any cost, agreed to abate some of its haughtiness and to negotiate on the basis of the independence of the United Provinces. The Dutch Republic, on the recognition of its sovereign rights, was willing to enter into a treaty arrangement with the Power which it had denounced as "outside the bar of humanity" for the assassination of William the Silent. Such, however, were the mutual distrust and hatred that while these essential points were agreed upon in May, 1607, it was not for two years later that the definite result was obtained in a twelve years' truce, signed at Antwerp on 9th April, 1609. The Spanish negotiators, having pocketed their pride in recognising the Provinces as a Sovereign State and their representatives as Excellencies, sought to obtain compensation by the retention of some of the practical advantages claimed by Spain as her exclusive right. Among these was nothing less than the monopoly of the trade with the Indies. From the roar of protest that arose throughout the Provinces it might be imagined that a demand to submit themselves to the Pope would have

* Elizabeth died while the siege of Ostend was in progress and her successor, James I., two months before its close, signed the treaty with Spain which terminated the long struggle between England and that country.

been received with less disfavour. The Spanish diplomatists were haughtily informed, with excusable exaggeration, that the Provinces had 10,000 ships upon the sea manned by 120,000 of their countrymen, and that as they would not submit themselves to the King of Spain on land they certainly would not recognise his authority on the ocean which was free to all. For nearly two years this and other points were discussed, first at the Hague and afterwards at Antwerp. War was on the point of breaking out afresh when France and England intervened, and Spain was compelled to waive her pretensions. The natural demand put forward by the Belgian Provinces for the opening of the Scheldt was thrust aside in the competitions of the more powerful and determined rivals. The Twelve Years' truce bore the name of Antwerp, but that city derived no benefit from the arrangement. Its only outlet to the ocean remained closed in its face, and Amsterdam flourished by the grip it retained on the throat of Antwerp—not to be finally shaken off for the period of 250 years.

There is a little evidence to show that the twelve years' tranquillity thus secured for the country was turned to some profitable account, and at least it is on record that many churches were constructed during this period, and that several new religious orders established themselves in the country. A clerical writer exclaimed that in these few happy years there were more new foundations than in the previous two centuries. It is reasonable to deduce from these circumstances that there were at least indications of returning prosperity. If trade and industry languished, art and letters attained their highest points throughout Belgian history. Rubens, Jordaens, and Vandyke rendered famous this and the next generation. The Plantins and the Moretus placed the Antwerp press in the van of printing. Lipse, Heinsius, and Spiegel were among the foremost professors and thinkers of the age, and the Belgian Mercator traced the world which other than Belgian mariners were to conquer. Louvain displaced Padua as a seat of learning, and in Brussels was concentrated the splendour of that civic life which in earlier centuries had been diffused through all the cities of Flanders. The Perpetual Edict of Mariemont—dated 12th July, 1611—

DEATH OF ALBERT.

codified all the existing laws and customs* into what might be termed a National Constitution. There wanted two things to consolidate these auspicious movements, and to bring back departed prosperity, but these unfortunately were lacking. The weavers, and the handicraftsmen generally, who had made the prosperity of the country, had either emigrated or been exterminated during the days of trouble. The truce of twelve years was not an assured peace guaranteeing tranquillity in the land.

Thanks to the Truce, and to a subsequent tacit arrangement between the United Provinces and those to the south, Belgium was not involved in the first stages of the Thirty Years' War, although part of the Spanish garrison under Tilly entered Germany to support the Emperor. The death of Philip the Third of Spain, in March, 1621, was followed a few months later by that of the Archduke Albert—an event attended by important consequences for Belgium. Philip's deed of cession had stipulated that in the event of Albert and Isabella having no children the Spanish Netherlands were to revert to the Crown of Spain, and now this contingency had actually come to pass. In 1624 Belgium again passed formally under the Spanish Crown —Philip the Fourth being inaugurated as Sovereign from the steps of St. Gudule. Isabella, from the position of a sovereign, descended to that of Governor General for her nephew. The tie was drawn tighter by the revival of the Council of Flanders at Madrid in 1628. While these events were in progress south of the Meuse Maurice of Nassau had died in April, 1625, and was succeeded by his brother Frederick Henry, the third of the founders of Dutch Independence.

The restoration of Spanish rule was followed by the revival of its worst and most unpopular features. The officials of the country were ignored or superseded, the administration was impressed with a Spanish character, and the orders of government emanated from Madrid rather than from Brussels. The popular discontent was aggravated by a sense of danger when,

* Among these may be mentioned the establishment of the corporation of Brussels on its existing lines, and the subdivision of the trade guilds into the Nine Nations. Of course, this establishment was on the same model as that existing at the time of the Brabant Joyous Entry of Wenceslas.

in 1629, the capture of Bois-le-Duc by Frederick Henry seemed to expose the country to imminent invasion. So deep was the discontent that Isabella wrote to Madrid declaring that if the Prince of Orange advanced, the Belgians would certainly come to an arrangement with him. This result was only averted by the excesses and blundering policy of the Dutch themselves, who, on entering Brabant, treated the country as a conquest, and forbade the exercise of the Roman creed in all the districts they occupied. Intolerance had produced intolerance, but the Belgians willing enough to coalesce with the Dutch on political grounds were not prepared to alter their religious belief at a dictation scarcely less peremptory, if less bloodthirsty than that of Alva. The most favourable opportunity for reuniting all the Provinces of the Netherlands was thus lost, and the subsequent intrigues of some of the Belgian nobility, discontented at all the chief offices being assigned to Spaniards and other foreigners attached to Spain, with the object of coming to terms with Frederick Henry, produced no result because they aroused no responsive support from the mass of the people.

The opinion that the Belgians possessed too small a share in the government of their own country was too widely held to be wholly slighted, and with the view of appeasing the growing discontent the States General were summoned after an interval of more than thirty years to meet again at Brussels in September, 1632. This decision was very largely due to the refusal of the Provincial Councils to vote any further supplies, and to the continued military successes of Frederick Henry, who took Maestricht and added a close alliance with Gustavus Adolphus to that he and his brother before him had maintained with Richelieu. At the moment, too, the open defection of the Count de Berg, the ablest of the Belgian generals, whose claims had been ignored in favour of the Spanish Marquis de Santa Cruz and of the Count de Warfuzée, whose name is best remembered for the closing incident in his career, rendered it imperative in the eyes of the Infanta to do something to check the tide of what might develop into a popular movement. The fear of a general defection of the Belgian people, although not so acute as in 1629, was still an active force in the situation of 1632.

There were several who wished to negotiate on the basis of a federation of all the Provinces, but the most determined opponent of this scheme was Richelieu, who, although the supporter of the Dutch, had no wish to see a strong united State created on the northern frontier of France.

The delegates sent by the States General to the Hague with the view of establishing a peace with their "good neighbours and fellow countrymen" were accorded a very gratifying and honourable welcome, but when it became clear that nothing less than the repudiation of Spanish authority would content the Dutch, and that the Belgians were not disposed to go to that length a coolness supervened. The draft of a final agreement was presented to the Belgian representatives almost as an ultimatum with notice that it was to be accepted or refused within fourteen days. The intolerance displayed in this document may be realised from the fact that, while it demanded nothing but sacrifices from the Belgians, it insisted on the continued closing of the Scheldt, the only outlet left to Belgium since the sand of the ocean had filled up the ports of Flanders. In plain language the Dutch proposed to the Belgians to exchange the Spanish tyranny for theirs, at a moment, too, when the more terrible features of Spanish rule had become memories of the past. The Hague negotiations of 1632, which were intended to promote the federation of the Seventeen Provinces, showed up the obstacles to its realisation, and rendered it impossible. The Belgian States General replied to the ultimatum with a statement that they would give up neither their religion nor their king.

The death of the Infanta Isabella (30th November, 1633) followed close upon this consolidation of Spanish authority in the southern provinces. Her anxiety had been much diminished by the turn in public opinion in Belgium, and also by the death of Gustavus Adolphus (Lutzen, 16th November, 1632), which had deprived the Prince of Orange of his surest ally. During her 34 years' connection with the Netherlands she gained a certain amount of esteem from her close attention to the duties of her position, and from her consistent determination to avoid a collision with public opinion. She carried this decision to such an extent that she refused to order the arrest of even those members of the Belgian nobility who were known to be intriguing against her government. She was succeeded by a temporary Governor, in the person of the Marquis d' Aytona, who was in turn succeeded by the Archduke Ferdinand, brother of the King of Spain, but Aytona, before his withdrawal, arrested many of the nobles and dismissed (July,. 1634) the States General. The victory gained over the Swedes at Nordlingen (6th September, 1634) strengthened the Imperial position, and encouraged the Spanish Governor to adopt bolder measures against those accused of having secretly plotted against the King. A few months later the Archduke Ferdinand, the victor of Nordlingen, arrived at Brussels and took over the Governor Generalship (4th November, 1634). He was not much over twenty-five years of age when this event happened, and he was at once called upon to defend the Netherlands against a double invasion, from the north under Frederick Henry, and from the side of France by the Marshal Chatillon. The Confederates had formed a definite alliance for the expulsion of the Spaniards from the Netherlands, and their division between France and the United Provinces.

It proved easier to make the plan than to carry it out, for although Chatillon defeated the Spaniards at Awenne, and occupied Rochefort and Marche, the Archduke Ferdinand, by resorting to Fabian tactics and with the able assistance of Piccolomini, had brought the French army to such a state of distress at the end of the first campaign that it was no better off than if it had suffered a decisive overthrow. The outbreak of the plague in Holland also contributed to neutralise the successes of the field. But neither Richelieu nor the Prince of Orange was to be turned from a policy by the reverses of a single year, and the campaign of 1635 was renewed in every successive year, with varying fortune, down to 1641 without any absolutely decisive result. In the last named year the Archduke Ferdinand died (9th November, 1641) suddenly of fever, and the command of the Spanish forces passed to Don Francisco de Mello, who signalised his accession to power by defeating the French at Honnecourt (26th May, 1642). This was the last successful achievement of Spanish troops in the Netherlands for in 1643 the Spanish infantry, largely composed of Walloons, was overthrown at Rocroi by the French under the Duke d' Enghien, the famous Condé. While this brilliant soldier was destroying the reputation of the finest infantry of Europe, the negotiations for a definitive peace between the Papist and Protestant divisions of Europe had actually begun in the small town of Munster.

Both sides were exhausted by the long struggle of thirty years, but pride, prejudice, and religious antipathy delayed the conclusion of peace during five years passed in wearying negotiation. The death of Richelieu had brought fresh views into force at Paris, and a breach was made in the alliance with the United Provinces. Mazarin looked towards Spain and England for allies, and was already speculating on the advantages of a Spanish marriage for the young king Louis XIV. The idea seems to have been first put forward by Contarini, the Venetian envoy, who suggested that the dower of the Infanta chosen might be the Spanish Netherlands. Although destined to bear fruit at a later period its immediate consequence was to alarm the Dutch and to induce them to come to a separate understanding with Spain. It was immediately after the accomplishment of this arrangement that Frederick Henry died (14th March, 1647). He completed the work of consolidating the Dutch state which his father and brother had begun, and in so doing had established the claims of the House of Orange to the gratitude of the Dutch nation. His successor was his son, William II., a young prince of twenty-one years of age. The signature of the agreement between Spain and the United Provinces was not effected until January, 1648. The convention contained seventy-one articles, but of these the vital clause was the one containing the King of Spain's renunciation of all his claims and rights over the United Provinces. The Scheldt was to continue closed to all ships approaching from the ocean, and the injury inflicted thereby on the Belgian provinces became permanent. The fleet stationed along the coast, with its headquarters at Dunkirk, and officially known as that of Flanders, was withdrawn to Spain thus leaving Dutch naval supremacy undisputed, so far as that Power was concerned, in the Channel and North Sea. The arrangement at Munster between Spain and the United Provinces was supplemented by another, signed at the same place, between the Emperor and France, and by a separate treaty at Osnabruck between the Emperor and Sweden. All these arrangements were consolidated in the Treaty of Westphalia (24th October, 1648) which concluded the Thirty Years' War. But it is well to remember that the Dutch had had to struggle for eighty years to achieve their independence and to attain the position of a Sovereign State. Of all the states involved in that long struggle Belgium suffered most. Its dependence became more complete, its claim to a distinct national existence more obscured, and at the same time that it lost its civic and political rights its opportunities of material progress were curtailed and even cut off.

The two states left unaffected in their direct relations by these treaties were France and Spain. The former country was disturbed by the rivalry of Mazarin and the noblesse who formed the Fronde for his overthrow. In the latter Philip IV. still hoped that he might retrieve Rocroi, and overthrow the most formidable of his enemies. Philip accordingly determined to prosecute the war with greater vigour, and his Governor General in the Low Countries, the Archduke Leopold, son of the Emperor Ferdinand, succeeded in collecting there a miscellaneous army in which figured Prussians from Brandenburg, and Croats from the Banat. In the first campaign of 1648, Condé gained over the Spanish army at Lens a second victory, scarcely less signal than Rocroi, but very soon afterwards his hatred of Mazarin led him not only to join the Fronde, but even to enter openly the service of the King of Spain. His military genius might have turned the scale decisively if France had not found in Turenne his equal as a military leader. The war between France and Spain continued for more than ten years, and the Belgian provinces were the scene of this long struggle in the result of which they could scarcely feel any interest because their rights were certain to be ignored. The French Minister cleverly obtained the alliance of Oliver Cromwell, who fully realised the peril to English naval power from the Dutch fleet, and who actively participated in several of the campaigns on land while his Admiral Blake secured for that period at least the command of the seas. The United Provinces held aloof from the struggle except in so far as they were assailed at sea by the fleet of the Lord Protector, resolved to obtain redress for the massacre of Amboyna, and also an admission of equal trade rights for his countrymen in the Spice Islands. They were tied down to this inaction by the arrangements concluded at Munster, and also by the pacific policy of John de Witt, the Grand Pensionary.

William II. of Orange had died 6th November, 1650, and his widow the Princess Mary of England, daughter of Charles the First, had given birth a few days later to a son, destined to become famous as William the Third of Holland and of England. But his father's death was taken advantage of by the Dutch republicans to declare that the Stadtholdership was not hereditary, and all the services and sacrifices of the Orange family did not avail to obtain recognition for the claims of an infant in its cradle at the hands of an ungrateful people. John de Witt has been held up to general admiration, but his political views were narrow and his range of vision limited. If it had been otherwise he would never have stood aloof from the long struggle in Belgium which prepared the way for the subsequent direct attack on Holland herself. The struggle practically terminated with Turenne's great victory of the Dunes (4th June, 1658) for which Cromwell received, as his share of the reward, the temporary possession of Dunkirk. Don Juan of Austria, the natural son of Philip the Fourth, who had been entrusted with the task of pacifying the Netherlands, was so discouraged by this reverse that he voluntarily retired to Madrid, and recommended his father to make peace at any sacrifice. Negotiations were accordingly set on foot, and the Kings of France and Spain had a personal interview on an island in the Bidassoa. The Treaty of the Pyrenees was finally concluded and signed on 7th November, 1659, thus performing for France and Spain the same pacific work as had been accomplished for the other belligerents by the treaty of Westphalia eleven years earlier. But the most pregnant of its stipulations was the revival in a definite and practical form of Contarini's idea to marry the young king, Louis XIV., to a Spanish princess. That monarch was to marry the Infanta Maria Theresa, who was to bring him in dower 500,000 gold crowns, and a strip of territory cut off from the Low Countries, extending from Artois on the west to Thionville and Montmedy on the east. The Spanish marriage was thus accomplished, and it formed the crowning achievement of Mazarin's administration. The treaty of the Pyrenees was the recognition of Spain's decadence; it had been preceded by the death of Cromwell, and after him came thirty years of the unchecked decline of England, the most inglorious and contemptible epoch in her history. The decay of one neighbour and the corruption of another gave France an opportunity of which Louis and his ministers promptly availed themselves. If they had added moderation to perspicacity they would have permanently extended the frontiers of France, but an overweening presumption and ambition diminished the results and rendered them ephemeral.

If very little light from contemporary evidence can be thrown on the general condition of the country of Belgium which could not help being deplorable, there is curiously enough a vivid sketch of the city of Brussels at this very juncture and while Condé was residing there. Brussels had more than preserved the position it acquired under Maximilian, and in a still greater degree under Charles the Fifth, as the capital of the whole country. It is described in the account referred to[*] as " one of the finest, largest, and best situated cities, not only of Brabant, but of the whole of Europe. The old quarters which preserve in our time an aspect so singularly picturesque with their sloping and tortuous streets, the fine hotels of darkened stone, sculptured in the Spanish fashion, and the magnificence of the Place of the Hotel de Ville (then not yet destroyed by the French King) were buried in the 17th century behind an enceinte of walls pierced by eight lofty gates, flanked with one hundred and twenty-seven round towers at almost equal distance from each other, like the balls of a crown. At a distance of

[*] Colonel Duplessis l' Ecuyer in an unpublished work by the Count de Segur, Revue de Paris, 1899 (since published, I believe).

less than a mile commenced the forest of Soignes with great numbers of stags, red and roe deer, that were hunted on horseback even under the ramparts of the town. On the promenade of the Court there circulated in a long file, ceaselessly during fashionable hours, five or six hundred carriages, the servants in showy liveries. In the numerous churches the music was renowned, the Archduke Leopold being passionately given to the art, maintaining at his own cost forty or fifty musicians, the best of Italy and Germany. Under the windows of the Palace stretched the same park that we admire to-day, open all the year to respectable people and twice a year to the public, a park filled with trees of rare essences and the most delicious flowers, so artistically disposed and so refreshing to the eyes that M. de la Serre declared on leaving that if he had seen there an apple tree he would assuredly have taken it for an earthly Paradise." From this description it may be reasonably inferred that if Belgium was desolate by reason of the long wars, its capital possessed those attractive features which still make Brussels one of the most charming places of residence in Europe.

Although the Infanta Maria Theresa and her husband, Louis XIV., had renounced all their rights to succeed to the Spanish throne by the Pyrenees Treaty, the French King at once began to intrigue in anticipation of the day when he could conveniently repudiate the obligation. Of these preliminary measures the most important was a new treaty of mutual offence and defence with the United Provinces, dated 27th April, 1662, which was to remain in force for twenty-five years. This treaty was negotiated with John de Witt who, while he resented and opposed an hereditary stadtholdership, had established in his own person as complete a dictatorship as that of William the Silent or Oliver Cromwell. The grand problem still remained unsolved as to what was to be done with those ten Provinces of the South which were still bound fast to the decrepit realm of Spain. John de Witt favoured the policy of expelling the Spaniards, the King of France did not go to the length of openly opposing the project, but he instructed his representatives to the effect that his real policy was to extend his frontiers. The Belgians remained quite indifferent to these proposals for their assumed benefit, and then De Witt turned round and proposed that he and Louis should divide their territory, which was evidence that his true object was his own gain rather than the welfare of his neighbours. The scheme fell through because the Pensionary could not perform his part, and because Louis was not anxious that he should. The dislike of Amsterdam to see Antwerp incorporated in the same state, the naval war with England and the growing influence of the youthful Prince of Orange all gave De Witt much anxious thought, and his own position was too uncertain to enable him to embark on so adventurous a project as the conquest of Belgium. His inability to essay the feat harmonised with the view of his French ally, who had marked the spoil for his own. The difficulties of the Dutch in their contest with England inclined De Witt to promise Louis his moral support in making good his pretensions on the death of Philip IV., in defiance of the treaty of the Pyrenees. That event occurred in September, 1665, but Louis thought it politic to defer any attempt to secure "his rights" until the result of the war between the Provinces and England was clearly decided.

In May, 1667, Louis made his formal declaration to the effect that he was about to take possession of what belonged to him in the Netherlands by right of his wife. The only argument on which he attempted to base his claim was that an obsolete Brabant law, which could have no bearing on the Spanish succession, conferred superior rights on the children of a first marriage over those of a second, and Philip's son and successor, Charles II., came under the latter category. The only weapon that Louis could employ was that of force, and during the summer of this year his armies overran a great part of Belgium. The campaign was a mere promenade. The only resistance encountered was at Termonde, where the inhabitants cut the dykes and compelled the French to raise the siege, for which the townspeople were afterwards rewarded by exemption from taxes for twenty years.

The reception of the news of the French invasion in Holland was anything but favourable. It was sudden and unexpected, but the best arrangement De Witt could propose was that

France should define the limits of the part of Belgium she proposed to take so that as wide a gap as possible should be left between the two frontiers. The French made no reply to this suggestion and continued to make conquests. The Provinces hastened to sign the peace of Breda with England, and if Charles the Second had followed the advice of Sir William Temple he might have saved the Stuart dynasty by proclaiming a national policy against French aggression which would have been most popular. Even against the wishes of Charles II. some steps were taken in the right direction, and Sir William Temple was sent to the Hague to conclude the first memorable Triple Alliance with the Provinces and Sweden (23rd January, 1668). The practical outcome of this alliance was the presentation of an ultimatum requiring Louis to annex only a portion of the extensive territory he had overrun. Louis accepted the terms, and by the treaty of Aix-la-Chapelle (2nd May, 1668), he obtained among other places Lille, Douai, Courtrai, Charleroi, and Tournai. Lille and Douai, then detached from the old province of Artois, were destined never to return into the Belgian federation.

The triple alliance, before which he had been compelled to bow, turned Louis from the ally into the enemy of the Dutch Republic, and he declared that "the only way to conquer the Spanish Netherlands was by humbling the Dutch, and if possible destroying them." With that object in view he succeeded in detaching England, in the person of Charles the Second, from the Dutch alliance, and in concluding with him the secret treaty of Dover (1st June, 1670) for the conquest of the Dutch Provinces. France was to acquire the greater part of the territory, but England was to receive compensation in Walcheren. By this scandalous arrangement, directed against the interests of England herself, Charles obtained a large grant of French money for his own personal pleasures, and the condemnation of every historian who has to refer to the transaction. Sweden also abandoned the triple alliance leaving the United Provinces alone to withstand the greatest peril that had beset them since the time of Parma. In April, 1672, France and England jointly declared war on the Provinces, the former alleging no special grievances, the latter specifying the publication of some offensive prints about King Charles!

The war did not realise the expectations of those who brought it about. At sea De Ruyter made a good fight of it, and thanks to the defection of the French squadron during the battle off Yarmouth escaped destruction. On land Louis in person, with his great generals Turenne and Condé, who had returned to his allegiance, crossed the Rhine, and advanced to within a few miles of Amsterdam. In this emergency De Witt, still the head of the nominal government, although the young Prince of Orange was entrusted with the command of the army, could only suggest coming to terms with the French, and negotiations were begun with this object. But the terms that Louis offered were hard, and among them the hardest was the demand that the Roman Catholic religion should be again introduced, and that its members should be eligible for all offices. When this ultimatum became known at the Hague and Amsterdam the populace rose and proclaimed the Prince of Orange Stadtholder, attacking the De Witts, and wounding the younger of them. For a few weeks calm was restored, owing to the French army having come to a halt, and to the cessation of all hostile measures on the side of England. But the popular clamour against the brothers De Witt increased, and their fellow-townsmen, after subjecting one of them to torture in the supposed Spanish fashion, thus proving that neither Spain nor the Inquisition had a monopoly of cruelty, butchered them in the streets and hung up their mangled remains by the heels on the execution ground of the Hague. It was not an event of which the Dutch have any reason to feel proud.

The assumption of authority by the Prince of Orange was followed by a speedy alleviation of the situation. The German princes became alarmed at the consequences of a French conquest of Holland, and the ruler of Brandenburg, soon to be known as the great Elector, set an example of action in moving twenty thousand troops to the Rhine. The Emperor followed suit and the attitude of Spain became menacing. The courage of the Dutch themselves revived. They took the supreme step of preparing for an emigration *en masse* if the fortune of war deserted them. Ships were in readiness to convey the population to a new country in the East Indies. The necessity for executing this grave decision did not arrive, and the Prince of Orange enjoyed the honour by his skilful negotiations in every court of Europe, not less than by his dispositions for defence, of inflicting his first serious rebuff on the Grand Monarque. The campaign of 1673 saw Turenne checked on the Moselle by the Imperialists under Montecuculi, and the French compelled to abandon all the towns they had wrested from the Republic. Once more Belgium had to pay the penalty for the deliverance of the Dutch. Louis compensated himself for his disappointments in Holland in the Spanish Provinces. He secured the fortified places on the Meuse and the Sambre; his general Condé defeated the Prince of Orange at Seneffe, near Nivelles, in a battle (11th August, 1674) when the victorious commander said of his youthful opponent in a sentence which has become historic—" The Prince of Orange conducted himself in every way like an old general except in exposing himself like a young soldier." Every year from 1674 to 1678 was marked by a fresh campaign fought on Belgian soil, and out of which the victor took his reward. The Prince of Orange kept the field with admirable fortitude despite a succession of defeats, but the victors gained Ypres and Ghent on one side, and Huy and St. Trond on the other. In the year last named France and Spain came to a separate understanding, by the treaty of Nimeguen (17th September, 1678), which restored to the latter some part of the Netherlands then occupied by the French troops, and consigned to the former in permanence a further strip of Belgian territory.

The arrangement with Spain was intended to facilitate, not arrest, the northern expansion of his frontier on which Louis had set his heart, but he had recourse to more pacific means than he had previously employed for its attainment. He revived the claims of the three bishoprics of Metz, Toul, and Verdun, and he established two Chambers at Metz and Brisach for the purpose of defining them. These Chambers naturally took the most favourable view of the pretensions of their prince and assigned him the whole of Luxembourg, a great part of

Namur, and even a portion of Brabant. With this authorisation Louis sent troops to occupy the territories assigned to him, and as the Spanish garrison was far too weak for its immediate duties he experienced little or no opposition in carrying out his plans. But the French troops committed such excesses, pillaging and massacring wherever they went, and that, too, among a people of the same creed and language as themselves, that they incurred the bitter hatred of the whole population. Even the churches and convents were not spared during this inroad of licentious and sanguinary soldiery. The situation of affairs in Europe was especially unfortunate for the interests of the Belgian people. Spain was too weak, corrupt, and disorganised to defend her distant possession. England was represented by Charles who could always be bought over by a larger subsidy when the pressure of his own Parliament and people obliged him for a moment to separate from France. Austria was involved in that long struggle with the Sultan which closed under the walls of Vienna and Belgrade. No help, therefore, was available, and the French troops treated Belgium like a conquered country. The naturally strong town of Luxembourg was defended by the Prince de Chimay for a month, and then compelled to surrender by famine. With this exception no resistance was offered, and, as Spain could do nothing, the States General at Brussels negotiated, on their own behalf, a twenty years' truce with Louis (29th June, 1684). The treaty of Ratisbon (15th August) ratified this truce, and Germany and Spain became consenting parties to a further severance of territory from unhappy Belgium. It marked the completion of what may be termed the preliminary stage in Louis' designs on the Netherlands. The possession of Luxembourg, which Vauban hastened to strengthen as a fortress, protected his flank on the side of Germany whenever he felt inclined to renew them. A few weeks after the treaty of Ratisbon Louis assisted the Cardinal Prince de Furstenberg in putting down the democratic party at Liége, in reinstating the Bishop Maximilian Henry of Bavaria, and in curtailing the privileges of that ancient city. The guilds were deprived of their share in the government, and all the city officers became the nominees of the Prince Bishop for the time being. The semi-military associations of militia and cross-bowmen were also broken up, and the Liége constitution, which had survived so many storms after that of Ghent had been shattered in the dust, passed out of the pages of history.

The Grand Monarque signed during his long reign many Peaces without having his heart in any one of them, and he had no wish or intention to maintain that of Ratisbon. Its chief use was to enable him to deal with some of his minor enemies, and to plant friends as possible allies in different places, like Maximilian Henry and Furstenberg firmly attached to France at Liége. It also enabled him to carry out the sweeping measure against the Protestants of his own kingdom, known as the Revocation of the Edict of Nantes (22nd October, 1685), which was the completion of the St. Bartholomew's massacre a century earlier. The death of Charles the Second of England in February, 1685, had brought him a more staunch ally in his successor, James the Second, whose religious views were in complete harmony with those of the French ruler. The expulsion of the Huguenots enabled William of Orange to found the league of Augsburg but the defection of England from the anti-French party was a serious loss to those who were striving to maintain an equilibrium in Europe against French ambition.

Among the leaguers of Augsburg was the young Elector of Bavaria, Maximilian Emanuel, who had married the Emperor Leopold's daughter, the Archduchess Marie Antoinette. The mother of this Princess was the Infanta, now Empress Margaret, younger sister of Maria Theresa who had married Louis XIV., and their brother, Charles the Second, was the last King of Spain in the male descent from Charles the Fifth. The bodily infirmities of Charles made it certain that within a few years the Spanish throne would be left vacant, and as Maria Theresa and Louis XIV. had formally renounced their rights as already explained, the succession passed to the Empress Margaret, through whose daughter the Elector of Bavaria came on the scene as a formidable competitor. The Empress had confirmed these expectations by appointing her daughter her heir, but on her marriage with the Elector, the Emperor, her father, had insisted on her renouncing her claims. Notwithstanding this disqualification the blood claim was too clear and direct to be wholly ignored in the solution of a troublesome and difficult question. The Emperor, not indifferent to his daughter's claims to compensation, asked Charles to cede her the Spanish Netherlands, as had been done for the Infanta Isabella by Kings Philip II. and III. Charles would have acceded to this request but for the threats of France, and a new general war which Louis began by a sudden advance down the Moselle (known as the plundering of the Palatinate) altered the situation. The immediate cause of the French King's action was the failure of his nominee, the Cardinal Furstenberg, to gain either of the sees of Cologne and Liége, both rendered vacant by the death of that ambitious prelate's friend Maximilian Henry. The Pope and the Emperor conferred Cologne on Joseph Clement of Bavaria, younger brother of Maximilian Henry, and Liége on the Baron d' Elderen, Dean of its Cathedral. The Pope said with some irony that to put Furstenberg* in the chair of either would be tantamount to nominating Louis XIV. himself.

The directing mind in the leagues and coalitions formed against Louis XIV. was undoubtedly that of William of Orange, and he alone fully realised the consequences of the loss of English co-operation through the permanent defection of James and the triumph of Catholic influences in London. He saw that the financial and naval support of England was essential to the arrest of French domination throughout Western Europe, and this was the motive which led him to concentrate the military power at his immediate disposal on the task of

---

* Prince William Egon de Furstenberg, member of the great Austrian family of Furstenberg which has been among the devoted adherents of the House of Hapsburg from time immemorial, was one of eleven children—his mother being the Countess Anne of Hohenzollern. He and his elder brother, Francis Egon, entered the Bavarian service, and were school and college friends of Maximilian Henry. William, the Cardinal, proved himself one of the most skilful diplomatists in Europe, but the reverses of Louis XIV. prevented any of his schemes maturing. He died in 1704, in his 75th year, as Abbot of St. Germain-des-Prés. Consult M. Michel Huismann's *Maximilien Henri de Bavière, prince-évêque de Liége, 1899.*

wresting England from the influences under which it had momentarily passed. His scheme, however, was only rendered possible by the mistake of Louis in attacking Germany instead of the Netherlands in the autumn of 1688, a second plundering of the Palatinate being but a poor equivalent for William's bloodless conquest of England. When William returned to Holland in the spring of 1691, he had compelled James to flee from Ireland after the battle of the Boyne, and his plans for the expulsion of the Stuart adherents from that country were far advanced towards completion. The conferences held at the Hague in that year under the presidency of William of Orange, now generally called the King of England, concluded with the decision to place armies of 250,000 men in the field, and in that force figured for the first time a distinct and considerable English contingent. The policy of William had, in fact, isolated the French ruler.

One of the immediate consequences of the new league was that the King of Spain delegated his sovereign powers in the Spanish Netherlands to the Elector of Bavaria, and this step although not of the nature of a permanent cession was greeted throughout the country with general rejoicings, because it foreshadowed the return of a quasi-national existence and the severance of the disadvantageous connection with an ever absent ruler who took no interest in the country. The records of the time are full of the complaints of the States of Brabant at the neglect shown by the Spanish Government to the interests of the Provinces which had been ravaged by the passage of 200,000 soldiers. The nomination of the Elector Maximilian, whose reputation at the moment stood very high, seemed to open a new prospect for the much-tried Belgians, and if as the Marshal Count de Mérode says in his Memoirs "these felicities were far from being realised," it was because events proved too strong for the Elector's good intentions. It was inevitable that military operations directed from Holland and England against France should have as their scene of decision the plains of Belgium. On the other hand Louis looked to the conquest of the Belgian provinces as his recompense for a successful war.

It is unnecessary to give the details of the campaigns that

were fought during the four years from 1692 to 1695. They belong to the history of Europe, but of their general character it may be said that while they were marked by French victories through the military skill of Marshals Luxembourg and Catinat, worthy successors of Condé and Turenne, they brought Louis no nearer to the realisation of his hopes. The chief sufferers were the Belgians of whom none of the combatants took the least account. From one letter written to the nominal sovereign of the country, by a prominent citizen, may be taken these lines: "The French having seized Hainaut and Namur there remains but little of that fertile, populous, and illustrious Belgium so formidable in the past to its enemies." The ravages committed by the allied troops and by the unpaid Spanish

THE GRAND 'PLACE OF BRUSSELS AFTER THE BOMBARDMENT OF THE 13TH TO 15TH AUGUST, 1695.

garrison were scarcely less serious. The peasants deserted the country and sought refuge in the towns. Brigands frequented the high roads, and all trade was destroyed. To crown their misfortunes the French, under Marshal Villeroi, bombarded Brussels (August, 1695) with red hot bullets, which set fire to the town in several places. Sixteen churches, and four thousand houses were burnt down, and the buildings on the famous

Grand Place were seriously injured during this wanton destruction which exercised no influence on the fortune of the war, soon afterwards brought to a close by the peace of Ryswyck (May, 1697). Louis made many concessions, including the recognition of William as King of England, and the surrender of all the Belgian towns he had taken since the treaty of Nimeguen. His only compensation was the defection of the Duke of Savoy to his side, but at the same time it was perfectly clear that his only object was to obtain a breathing space prior to the more important struggle certain to begin on the death of the King of Spain.

After the bombardment of Brussels the Elector Maximilian devoted himself to the task of repairing, as far as possible, the damage in the capital, and also generally in the country caused by the war, and he even raised money in Bavaria for the purpose. This unwonted solicitude for their interests undoubtedly made him popular in Belgium. New churches and streets rose on the ruins of the old city, and a theatre displaced the old mint on the Place de le Monnaie. He also took steps to encourage trade, and he was the first ruler after the lapse of more than two centuries to take the national industries under his special protection. He had his eye fixed on the throne of the Netherlands, either for himself or his youthful son to whom the King of Spain had virtually promised the reversion of the Provinces. At this juncture, however, an important change took place in the policy of the Elector who began to gravitate towards France. The causes of this change are not altogether clear, and were probably inspired by several motives. A first indication of them was given in 1694, when hostilities were still in progress, on the occasion of the death of d' Elderen, Bishop of Liége, when he utilised French aid to secure the succession for his brother, Clement of Cologne, in the teeth of the Emperor's opposition. In anticipation of events he introduced Bavarian troops into the Provinces and despatched the Walloon or Belgian regiments still in the Spanish service to Spain. Both Louis and William seemed well inclined to the permanent establishment of the Elector in the Low Countries, and came to an agreement at the Hague (October, 1698) as to how the whole of his possessions should be distributed on the death of the King of Spain. Charles was informed of this transaction and with true Spanish pride made a new will appointing as his sole heir the infant son of the Elector Maximilian. This instrument was deprived of all significance by the death of the young Prince of Bavaria. The whole force of French diplomacy was then directed to the task of inducing Charles to select a French Prince in preference to the Austrian as his heir. The claims of the Dauphin were pressed on the ground that the renunciation of his parents did not debar him, while the fears of Europe were to be allayed by the selection of his younger son, the Duke of Anjou, to fill the Spanish throne. These schemes, strongly supported by the Elector Maximilian, whose aunt had married the Dauphin, and who was consequently Anjou's cousin, succeeded. Maximilian's reward was to be the government in permanence of the Netherlands. The death of Charles followed, in a few weeks, the signature of this fresh will, thus leaving him no time to change his mind again.

Louis, as soon as the King's death was known, did not hesitate to accept for his grandson the inheritance of the Spanish monarchy in spite of all his pledges and the formal renunciation by the Treaty of the Pyrenees. When William received the news he declared that "the King of France had forgotten himself in this matter, that he evidently knew neither his strength nor his true interests, and that, blinded by an exaggerated ambition, he justified the reproach so often made against him of following in his policy the maxims of Machiavelli." While Europe received the proclamation of Philip of Anjou in silence the Elector Maximilian ostentatiously proclaimed him at Brussels and as still further evidence of his French sympathies he co-operated in the measures of Louis for the expulsion of the Dutch troops left in "the Barrier" fortresses after the peace of Ryswyck. These measures were executed with such wonderful celerity and success that the garrisons were compelled to surrender almost simultaneously and without resistance, and they were detained as hostages until the States General of Holland recognised Philip as King of Spain. William was discouraged and alarmed by the loss, almost in a day and without a blow being struck, of that "barrier" which it had taken him twenty-eight years to construct. Clement of Cologne and Liége opened those cities to the French and a strong garrison was sent by Louis to the latter city.

William turned his attention to the formation of a new coalition, while Louis, who had defied Europe alone, felt now so strong in the alliances he had procured in Spain, with the Elector of Bavaria, the Duke of Savoy and the Archbishop of Cologne, that he did not hesitate to show his contempt for his chief opponent by an act of which he had not perhaps divined all the consequences. James the Second of England died in September, 1701, and Louis at once recognised his son King of England, Scotland and Ireland. This step caused great indignation in England, where William, who had never been very popular, became at once the national champion, and received without a dissentient voice the support necessary to form the Grand Alliance with the Emperor and the United Provinces. The two objects of that alliance were to prevent the Crowns of France and Spain ever being joined in the same sovereign, and to expel the French from the Netherlands so that they might again be converted into a barrier against French aggression. The Grand Alliance had scarcely been formed when the sudden death of William threatened to dissolve it. His successor Anne, swayed by the ambition of Marlborough, decided, however, to continue his policy, and the superior military genius of Marlborough was destined to humble the pride of Louis in a manner that all William's remarkable pertinacity had not sufficed to accomplish.

In the meantime Belgium, through the States of Brabant and Flanders, had accepted the French Prince, and proclaimed him as Philip V. The warmth of their language was due to the desire to propitiate the King of France, and to the hope of averting the evils of an open invasion.* The measures of the French ruler soon nipped this enthusiasm in the bud. While

---

* The Count de Mérode says that at that moment the Belgians would have accepted a Turk as a prince if they had only some reason to think he could protect them.

Maximilian hastened to Munich to look after his hereditary states which the Emperor was threatening, Louis took over the administration of the Netherlands, and introduced a new form of government which entirely ignored the old customs of the country and followed French lines of arbitrary rule. Among other innovations was the conscription for the army by lot. Compulsory military service was the particular horror of the Belgians, and before a shot had been fired in the new war the hold Louis had laid on the Netherlands was turned from that of an accepted prince into one of a conqueror, only sure of the ground he occupied.

In the meantime the war of the Spanish succession had begun, but it is not necessary to describe over again the well known battles and sieges which continued with scarcely a break during nine years. It is only incumbent on us to make clear how it affected the fortunes of Belgium in its progress, and introduced a new element into its government in the result. Maximilian, appointed Vicar General of the Netherlands by Philip, threw off the mask and invited two French armies to join him in the heart of Germany so that he might end the war in that quarter with the capture of Vienna. This scheme was baffled by the strategy of Marlborough and the decisive victory of Blenheim (13th August, 1704) when the Franco-Bavarian armies were overthrown. The Elector succeeded in escaping to Brussels, and it is recorded that on his way he accidentally met his brother Clement, the Archbishop of Cologne, who had just been expelled from that city. The Elector continued to hold a high command in the French army, and took a prominent part in the great battle of Ramillies (23rd May, 1706) when the French lost in the fight and the pursuit twenty thousand men. The Count de Mérode, whose criticisms of Marlborough are not always unjust, very rightly points out that if this victory had been properly followed up Mons could have been taken without a blow and Paris threatened in the following campaign. A few days after Ramillies the Brabant States, assembled at Brussels, recognised Charles III.—the Austrian Archduke Charles, put forward by the Allies to the Spanish throne in opposition to Philip V.—as King, and a new government was devised with the help of Marlborough and the Grand Pensionary* Heinsius.

After nine years' continual struggle all the belligerents were exhausted, but there was little or no agreement among them as to what the terms of peace should be. The jealousy and fears of the allies for one another were scarcely less than those they entertained for France. The French had been driven out of Italy and the Netherlands, but in Spain, thanks to the military ability of the Duke of Berwick, they more than held their own, and Philip's cause obtained more ready support† than that of his rival. Still the ostensible cause of the war was the Spanish succession, and the victors would have gone on fighting to prevent the French prince retaining the throne when the death of the Emperor Joseph summoned the Archduke Charles to succeed his brother. This event (April, 1711) made the governments regard the union of Austria and Spain under one crown with just as much apprehension as they had regarded the same possibility in the case of France and Spain. The French Government in the last distress from a military point of view made the most skilful use of its opportunities diplomatically. Philip, as King of Spain, made over the Spanish Netherlands, as a free gift, to the Elector of Bavaria. The deed was not likely to be maintained, but it showed that France assented to the Provinces being detached from Spain. At the moment its authority was only recognised in the provinces of Namur and Luxembourg into which Marlborough had not advanced.

The negotiations for a general peace were begun at Utrecht early in 1712 and the historic treaty bearing its name was signed on 11th April, 1713. Philip was left on the throne of Spain subject to the condition that that kingdom should never be joined to France. But Spain surrendered its Italian and Belgian possessions by way of compensation to the Emperor

* On the death of William III. the Stadtholdership again went into abeyance, and was not revived till 1747. In Belgium the supporters of Philip were called Cuirassiers, and of Charles Carabiniers.

† Curiously enough the chief part taken in this war by any Belgian soldiers was in Spain in support of Philip. The Walloon regiments, sent out of the country by the Elector, distinguished themselves especially at the battles of Almanza and Saragossa. They were commanded by Prince Charles de Croy, Duke d' Havré, killed in the latter battle.

Charles VI. Sardinia was assigned to the Elector Maximilian in compensation for the loss of his hereditary states, but by the subsequent treaty between the Empire and France at Rastadt (6th March, 1714), Sardinia was transferred to the Emperor on his reinstating the Elector of Bavaria and the Archbishop of Cologne in their territories. The Emperor was, by the Treaty of Utrecht, only to acquire possession of the Provinces on providing Holland with an effective barrier as against France. A conference was opened at Antwerp with the view of regulating this question which was rendered difficult by the excessive pretensions of the Dutch. A treaty was at last agreed upon after more than twelve months' discussion to the following effect—Austria received possession of the Spanish Netherlands on giving an undertaking (1) that they should form a single undivided and inalienable possession of the ruling House of Austria, and (2) that no part of this territory should ever be ceded to France. The pretensions of the Dutch Republic were not satisfied with promises alone. They required that two-fifths of the permanent garrison, fixed at from thirty to thirty-five thousand men, should be composed of Dutch troops, who were to have the exclusive right of garrisoning Namur and Tournai among other places. The cost of the garrison was to be borne by the Belgian provinces. The clause in the Treaty of Munster closing the Scheldt was to be made perpetual, thus strangling the external trade of Belgium. The conference of Antwerp resulted in what is known as the Treaty of the Barrier, the terms of which have just been cited. They were a compromise between the extreme demands of the Dutch and the revival of the hereditary rights of the Hapsburgs, representing the old House of Burgundy. But they ignored the special rights and interests of Belgium and her people. The best that can be said of these arrangements, as they affected the country that claims our attention, is that they restored peace to a realm whose domestic existence had been disturbed by more than a century and a half of such bloodshed, cruelty, injustice, and tyranny as had never in the whole range of history fallen upon any other people. If there are defects in Belgian character we shall do well to remember that no race has ever been more rudely tried without losing its territory and individuality; none has had the iron of adversity more ground into its blood and soul.

The Treaty of Utrecht and its complements brought to an end, after 160 years (1555-1715), the rule of Spain in the Netherlands. The connection cannot be described otherwise than as calamitous. When Phillip II. took from the stiff and powerless hands of his father the government, the Netherlands formed the most prosperous, the richest, and the most progressive of his many possessions. As an asset they were more valuable than the Indies. The industry of an intelligent community produced a larger revenue than the treasures wrested from the mines of Mexico and Peru, or torn from the persons and temples of Indian princes. The Seventeen Provinces formed a State that in power and importance ranked with the first kingdom of Europe. The union, tardily effected among them, seemed likely to prove stable and enduring as no one could have supposed that the Ruler, to whose power and pride they contributed, would, from a blind and reckless spirit of persecution, undermine and wreck the edifice that formed so conspicuous and glorious a part of his empire.

Yet such proved to be the case. Moved by a religious bigotry that has never been surpassed, Philip made an assault on the liberty and prosperity of the Netherlands with the express intention of stamping out all differences of religious opinion among his subjects. He treated them in precisely the same fashion that his Viceroys treated the gentle and helpless races of America. His inquisitors condemned without a hearing and on the flimsiest pretexts. A very sound Catholic writer said later that Roman Catholicism did not appear to have been much benefited by the Blood-Council, or St. Bartholomew's, or the Revocation of the Edict of Nantes. In the Belgian Provinces Philip indeed attained religious uniformity but at the price of their prosperity, while he permanently lost seven of the United Provinces. Those that remained suffered in more ways than by the direct loss incurred during the period of trouble. They remained tied to the Spanish monarchy, which paid no heed to their interests, and indeed had more than enough food for thought in its own troubles. They suffered from the common decrepitude evinced by everything dependent on the once splendid crowns of Castille and Aragon. War brought no remedy for their misfortunes, while peace aggravated them by tightening the fetters that bound them, and rendering the causes of their calamities more permanent. When the tyranny of Spain abated there remained the rivalry of the Dutch who, having asserted their rights to independence and a separate religion, proceeded to advance claims to a commercial monopoly at the expense of their southern neighbours. The narrow exclusiveness of Dutch policy was as evident as that of Spain, and the unfortunate Belgians, lying as it were between the upper and the nether millstone, experienced heavy blows on both sides. The termination of Spanish rule left Belgium a very different state from what it was when it began. The Seventeen Provinces were reduced to nine (Artois having been left to France at Utrecht), and these constituted the most wretched and depressed community in Europe. With a foreign garrison established on the soil, and the principal part of the revenue assigned for its maintenance, there would have been nothing surprising had the Belgian race finally disappeared from the roll of nations.*

* It will interest the curious to know that potatoes were introduced into Belgium about this period—the year 1704 being specifically mentioned as that in which they were planted near Bruges. An earlier attempt seems to have been made at Nieuport in 1620 by some English refugees, among whom figured Robert Clarke, the Christian Virgil.

369

CHAPTER XIII.

Austrian Rule.

AFTER one hundred and sixty years of perturbation and strife following the abdication of Charles the Fifth, Peace again settled down over the Low Countries. That the Belgian nation had not disappeared, that the public still clung to their civic privileges, and that alone of Continental States Belgium boasted of its Constitution—shared indeed by the severed provinces of the North—must always be considered one of the most remarkable instances of vitality in a people and a system to be found in history. The fact is rendered the more remarkable because the people clung faithfully to their old religion which in its teaching and policy is opposed to the popular privileges that it was the boast of the Belgians to have preserved.

Mr. Shaw in his *Letters on the Present State of the Austrian Netherlands*, written late in the 18th century, said " This is a monarchical State, but here the monarch is not absolute as in Spain, nor dependent as in England. There is between him and the people an intermediary power which does not govern, but which prevents tyrannical government in the name of the Prince. This power is called the States." Still more remarkable testimony to the same effect is furnished by the Count de Nény* who, although one of those illustrious Irishmen who did

---

* I cannot deprive myself of the satisfaction of mentioning that I have a common descent with the Count de Nény traced to his great grandfather, Sir Patrick Macmahon, one of whose daughters married the Count de Nény's grandfather and another Cormac O'Rourke, Prince of Breffny, whose daughter Lucy married my ancestor, Field Marshal Maurice de Kavanagh. The Sir Patrick Macmahon mentioned married Lady Helena Fitzmaurice, daughter of the Earl of Kerry (of the earlier creation) and was the ancestor of Marshal Macmahon, President of the French Republic. Patrick Mac Nény, the father of the Count and for many years War

Y

so much for the House of Hapsburg in the 18th century, had identified himself, in a very remarkable degree, with the interests of Belgium, and expounded the necessity of respecting its privileges. His efforts were especially directed towards the curtailment of the aggression of the clergy of the Church of Rome, which was by law the State religion but held in check by the limitations of the Constitution. The fundamental privilege of the country may be held to have been, that all cases of litigation with the Church were to be decided by the tribunals of the country without reference to Rome. While these privileges had been retained in the face of adversity and under immense difficulties, they had been lost in the neighbour country of France, where all the privileges of the towns had been swept away by the personal despotism of Louis the Fourteenth. When the Provinces became Austrian the new rulers encountered the one main privilege which struck at the root of the matter, viz., that of voting or refusing supplies.

The States which represented a Parliament were divided into three classes of nobles, clergy and the *tiers état*, but their exact composition and procedure varied among the provinces. In some the decision had to be unanimous, in others the nobles and clergy alone met in assembly but the adhesion of the *tiers état* was essential, for failing it whatever was passed by the upper orders was quashed. In Flanders there were no representatives of the Nobles, and in Gueldres none of the Church. The nobility of Flanders had either lost all their privileges or allowed them to lapse. On the other hand the noble class had fully held its own in Hainaut, where it was in actual possession of more than a third of the land of the province. The simple explanation of this seems to have been that the Flemish nobles were more deeply involved in the troubles of Philip's time, whereas those of Hainaut, by rallying to the side of Spain succeeded in preserving their estates. They had also

---

Minister to the States, was only 16 years of age when he left Ireland after the Boyne. He married a Belgian lady of the family of Peterbroeck. He dropped the use of Mac and became instead De Nény. The last of the Nénys died at Vienna in 1832, and the family is extinct; but I believe in the female line it is represented by the Belgian family of the Barons Fierlant.

preserved their ancient privilege of exemption from taxation. As a rule the states in the several provinces met twice in the year, but in Flanders only once, while those of Tournai and the surrounding district of Tournaisis sat in permanence. During the intervals the States generally delegated their powers to permanent deputations with, however, only a restricted right to commit the States. No subsidy could be granted by any one Province. All had separately to pass it to make it a general law. In their order of precedence at this period the Nine Provinces were: (1) The Duchy of Brabant, (2) the Duchy of Limburg and the country beyond the Meuse, (3) the Duchy of Luxembourg and the County of Chiny, (4) the Duchy of Gueldres, (5) the County of Flanders, (6) the County of Hainaut, (7) the County of Namur, (8) the lordship of Tournai and the Tournaisis and (9) the lordship of Malines.

The system on which the States were elected was essentially oligarchical, and exclusive. Privilege and not the popular voice decided the composition in each province. The priests, the nobles, and the commune chose their representatives on the narrowest lines by church discipline, by quarterings, and the possession of a specified estate, and by the office of sheriff or councillor. But even without the existence of a system of free public election Belgium enjoyed rare privileges in an age when monarchs, with the exception of the King of England, were absolute, and when Belgium itself had passed under the most absolute of them all. It is worth while citing the list* given of the privileges conferred by the charter known as the Joyous Entry of Brabant, which was indeed a little fuller than the charters of the other Provinces, but it will serve as a general illustration of what prevailed in Belgium. The chief of the privileges claimed under this Charter, which contained 59 articles, were as follows: (1) The catholic, apostolic and Roman religion was the only state religion; (2) The Council of Trent in matters of belief was recognised as the dogmatic authority or invariable rule of faith; (3) the people of each of the Provinces were represented by its States; (4) the nation could not be taxed without the express consent of the States; (5)

* Consult M. Charles Faider's *Etudes sur les Constitutions Nationales.*

citizens could not be tried except "by right and sentence" and before their ordinary and natural judge; (6) no inhabitant could be summoned before any court of justice outside the country, not even before the Court of Rome; (7) the laity could only be tried by a temporal Judge; (8) Belgium was a country of the common law, ruled by its laws and customs; (9) the establishments of mortmain could not acquire real property without the consent of the sovereign and the States, and only by accepting the burdens on it; (10) Belgium was a country with the right of passing judgment on all conditions of persons found in its territory; (11) legislative power belonged to the Prince, after having consulted and heard the States of the Provinces and the sovereign council of justice; (12) the Prince could change nothing, neither in the forms and rules established for the administration of justice, nor in the order of jurisdiction unless it were in common accord with the States and with their prior consent; (13) the rights of petition and of remonstrance were formally recognised both for constituted bodies and for individuals; (14) the States formed part of the sovereign power; (15) the existence and rights of the commune were recognised in all the Provinces; (16) the assembly of the States General was of constitutional right; (17) the Belgian Provinces although reunited under the same prince formed each a separate independent State, so that the inhabitants of one with certain exceptions are considered foreigners in another; (18) the sovereign should take the oath prior to his inauguration; (19) Belgium was a country of liberty, the slave who set his foot on its soil became free at once; (20) Belgium was a country of free tenure, and the presumption of franchise went with the soil; (21) each province had the right to make use of the language of its people in business and before the Tribunals; and (22) the right to refuse obedience, service and subsidies was vested in the States in case of the Constitution or the law being broken. As a valid constitution there was nothing superior in Europe and the remarkable feature about it was that it had been preserved through six generations of adversity, and that even without any striking display of patriotism, as had been shown in Holland.

The government had passed through as few changes as the constitution. The form given it of the three collateral Councils by Charles V., in 1531, endured down to 1702. It was then changed by Philip V. of Spain in accordance with his grandfather's wish and policy of a central control in the hands of the sovereign, and the Elector of Bavaria superseded the three Councils. The Allies after the battle of Ramillies, in 1706, revived the Council of State and the Council of Finance, but when the Low Countries were handed over to the Emperor Charles VI. only the latter remained. The Emperor soon revived the three Councils, and, in addition, established at Vienna a department called the Supreme Council of the Netherlands. It was thus intended that as little change as possible should be made in the mode of administering the affairs of the Provinces, and we shall see at a later period how a departure from this course entailed serious trouble.

When the Emperor took possession of the Provinces it was very natural that he should appoint his great military commander, Prince Eugéne of Savoy, Governor General, and it was a misfortune for them and for Austria that while he retained the name to the end of his life he never took any personal part in the administration, or even visited the country. It was a misfortune because Prince Eugéne had very clear views as to the importance of the Provinces, and had advised the Emperor to relax his hold on his possessions in Italy and to consolidate his position in Belgium. Had this advice been followed the history of Austria and Germany would have been very different, and the hearty support of the Belgic provinces might have turned the scale in the Seven Years' War.

On 4th February, 1716, Field-Marshal-Lieutenant Count Konigsegg took over the Netherlands in the name of the Emperor, but this soldier did not understand the situation for he represented that "the government should be endowed with much authority and power so that it should be able to make itself respected and feared." From that phrase it was quite clear that no thought of constitution or privileges entered the mind of Count Konigsegg. The Emperor favoured milder measures for he replied that all peoples could not be ruled in the same fashion and that regard must be paid to local customs and necessities. In a few months Count Konigsegg was displaced by the Marquis de Prié, who came as deputy of Prince Eugéne with the curious title of Minister Plenipotentiary. De Prié, whose family name was Turinetti, was an Italian of Piedmont, who owed all his fortune to the patronage of Prince Eugéne. He was a clever diplomatist, and an advocate of the divine right of Kings, on the understanding that he was to administer it. But he had no knowledge of the Low Countries, of their prescriptive rights, or of the tenacity shown in guarding them. With his views and convictions an early collision with the Belgians was inevitable. The distressful state of the country, aggravated by the heavy burdens* imposed on it under the Barrier Treaty, rendered public opinion doubly sensitive to the additional exactions imposed by an unsympathetic governor. During the nine years of his rule Prié, despite the good intentions of the Emperor and Prince Eugéne whose sole part in the affairs of Belgium consisted in receiving the reports of his deputy, succeeded in rendering Austrian rule unpopular and in irritating the people of all classes.

On arriving at Brussels Prié addressed himself to two distinct tasks, one was the conversion of the Belgians into obedient subjects of Austria, and the other was the obtaining of better terms from the Dutch by negotiations at the Hague. The latter he entrusted to Patrick Mac Nény, the Councillor of Finance and War Minister, who had left Ireland as a youth after the battle of the Boyne, and who was the father of the Count de Nény. Whether this was due to his assistant's skill it is certain that Prié experienced greater success in his latter object than in the former. A few months after his arrival at Brussels he was involved in a serious dispute with the representatives of the guilds or nations in that city. Before voting the subsidy for the year 1717 they claimed the abolition of certain laws and

* The Dutch received an annual subsidy of 1,250,000 florins. The revenues of Brabant and Flanders alone were hypothecated for more than half of this sum, the balance was levied on Tournai and other territory recovered from France. In addition two loans amounting to twelve million florins were attributed to Belgium. The financial burden thus imposed was so heavy that it had subsequently to be lightened.

orders, made in the stormy period of 1700-4, which they contended were an infraction of their privileges. In this indirect manner they combated the pretensions of Konigsegg and Prié to treat their country as if it were a province of the Austrian Empire. Prié showed a disposition at first to yield, but the obstinacy of the guilds aroused an equal resistance on his part, and he declared that he would "punish the insolence of these tradesmen." It was not until after the inauguration of the Emperor at Brussels, in October, 1717, that he felt able to show his real intentions. His strength and determination may be inferred from the fact that in what he did he acted in direct contravention of the Emperor's instructions which enjoined moderation and clemency. The Emperor's views were expressed in the following passages from a letter to his representative: "It has always been wise policy, in the beginning of a reign, to employ clemency and kindness so long as the respect and authority due to the sovereign are not thereby encroached upon. It is a maxim founded on reason, that of allowing each nation to be ruled in the manner appropriate to its character and spirit. It prescribes to us to prevent the disagreeable consequences that violent remedies would have in the Low Countries, where past examples recall many troubles."

Early in the year 1718 the Emperor sanctioned the substitution of a State Council for the Provisional Junta, and this single body possessed all the attributes of the previous three collateral councils. Its composition was somewhat elastic, and the representatives of the great families of D'Arenberg, de Ligne and Merode were entitled to sit on it whenever they happened to be at Brussels. This step taken, a decision was come to to compel the obedience of the Nations which still held out for the full letter of their rights, and had made their surrender the condition of their taking the oath to the Emperor. Prié summoned them on 24th May to the Hotel de Ville to take the oath. The burgomaster and forty others complied, but the majority refused, and left the building. Popular disturbances followed, the house of the burgomaster was sacked, and the Austrian garrison, too weak to overawe the citizens, was collected in the park on the brow of the hill overlooking the lower town.

At Malines a more serious collision occurred, and only the heroic intervention of the President of the Grand Council, Christopher de Baillet, prevented a sanguinary encounter. Tranquillity was only restored, however, by the departure of the Austrian garrison. The want of troops compelled Prié to temporise and make some nominal concessions, but as he gave way the demands of the guilds became more exacting. The Council of State advised compliance, and at last on 19th July he signed a letter assenting to all their requests, but at the same time he informed the Council that he did not consider himself bound in the least by this assent. Whether this statement became known or for some other cause beyond our information, the populace again broke out in disorder at Brussels. Several official buildings were plundered or destroyed, and only the opportune arrival of the cavalry regiment of De Ligne from Namur averted a serious outbreak.

The extent of the popular discontent aroused an equal resentment in the mind of the acting governor. He declared that "the country ought to lose its privileges, otherwise its privileges will make us lose it," and he drew up a plan of operations with the view of putting down Belgian independence. According to this scheme the capital was to be transferred from Brussels to Ghent, the constitution abolished, and a garrison of thirty thousand troops permanently maintained. Prié's policy, in short, was identical with that of Alva. In its full extent it did not have the Emperor's support, but opinion at Vienna had been irritated by the troubles in Belgium, which the Austrians had certainly had no intention of provoking. Spanish intrigues, under the direction of Cardinal Alberoni, were also a cause of anxiety, for there were still some partisans left of the old Spanish connection in the Low Countries. At this juncture the conclusion of the Peace of Passarowitz (21st July, 1718) with the Sultan freed the Imperial armies, and considerable reinforcements were sent to the Netherlands. Even before they arrived Prié had concentrated the bulk of the Austrian garrison in Brussels, and had felt sufficiently strong to issue a public notice to the effect that any further disorders would be suppressed by the employment of military force. The sheriffs and leaders of the city were cowed by this action, but there was at least one outbreak on the part of the mob, of whom about thirty were sabred by the Austrian cavalry—the Walloon regiment of De Ligne.

Such was the situation of affairs when Prié had to leave his administrative work in Belgium for that of diplomacy at the Hague. If the Austrian representatives had seriously devoted themselves to the removal of the harsh and unjust conditions imposed upon Belgium by the Barrier Treaty, they could not have failed to obtain some mitigation of them, and they would thus have earned the gratitude and loyalty of her people. But Prié paid no heed to the rights or wrongs of the Belgians. He only thought of securing the withdrawal of the Dutch troops from the country they continued to occupy into the towns which they were to garrison. The financial burden on the country remained undiminished, at the same time that its natural outlet by the Scheldt continued closed in its teeth. The treaty of the Hague left that of the Barrier intact, so far as the grievances and burdens of Belgium were concerned.

Prié returned to Brussels with the fixed determination of obtaining satisfaction at the expense of the persons who had defied him. The Emperor had in the meanwhile given his consent to a policy of firmness and severity by cancelling the decrees extracted from Prié, and by sanctioning judicial pursuits and adequate punishment in the case of known offenders. There was always a turbulent element in a great city like Brussels, and Prié took advantage of a street disturbance to banish four thousand strangers, and to make a house to house search, which resulted in the capture of forty persons in concealment. Some of these were whipped on the Grand Place, and then banished with the others. The next step was to obtain from the State Council a warrant authorising the arrest of the deans of the offending Guilds. In this matter Prié could plead that he acted under orders from Vienna, where some impatience began to be manifested at his slowness in giving effect to his new instructions. Prince Eugéne wrote to him to the following effect: "You have now under your orders sufficient troops not only to curb a few mischievous spirits, but to conquer a city like Brussels." Nevertheless a certain legality had to be observed.

The man on whom Prié had especially fixed his enmity was Francis Anneessens, syndic of the Guild of St. Nicholas. He was a man of much influence and reminded his fellow citizens of the great leaders that their ancestors had followed in the Middle Ages. Born in the year 1660 and a tiler by trade, he had read so much that Prié describes him in a contemptuous manner as "half a savant." The opposition of the guilds to the governor was considered, rightly or wrongly, to be due to his instigation and leading, and in the eyes of the Marquis de Prié he was the prime offender. On 14th March, 1719, the State Council passed an order for the arrest of Francis Anneessens and eight other syndics. As there was reason to fear a popular rising, the decision was kept secret, and Prié had recourse to a stratagem to capture his principal victim without a public scandal. Anneessens received a request to attend at the residence of Colonel Falck to carry out some work appertaining to his trade. He went without any suspicion, and was seized when inside the house by a party of soldiers. At the same time and place the Syndic of St. John was also seized, and the pair were conveyed under guard to the Sablon. Two other syndics were arrested and the four were lodged in the Steenporte prison before nightfall. No information was given to the prisoners' inquiries as to the reason for their arrest beyond the fact that it was done by the orders of the Marquis de Prié and the commandant of the garrison, Count Wrangel. When the news leaked out the town was filled with consternation. Fifty syndics fled from the city in panic, and de Prié, to show his confidence in himself and his contempt for his opponents, drove through the streets in an open carriage attended by only six lackeys instead of his usual twelve.

The interrogatories to which Anneessens was subjected elicited no striking facts. He admitted that he was one of those who had refused to take the oath because the privilege of direct appeal to the Prince had been withdrawn, but he represented that he had always done his utmost to restrain the violence of the towns-people and especially to save the burgomaster's house from pillage. The investigation or trial was allowed to proceed slowly. After two months' confinement in the Steenporte, Anneessens was subjected to a second examination, the object of which was to show that he had taken a leading part in inciting the mob to commit acts of plunder and incendiarism. De Prié was in favour of a brief trial and a short shrift, but the Council would not break the rules, and the trial continued its slow course. Notwithstanding that public opinion was in a state of ferment, and that many attempts were made to effect the release of the accused, Anneessens and his companions were kept in close confinement in the Steenporte throughout the summer, while even their request to employ counsel was rejected by the Council of Brabant. The Council, which showed itself servile in many things refused, however, to allow the application of torture for the purpose of extracting a confession. In the meantime some doubt appears to have arisen at Vienna as to the wisdom of carrying severity too far, and the Emperor sent early in August clear instructions that if the Council of Brabant found Anneessens and de Haeze, the principal of the other syndics accused, *equally* guilty the capital sentence was to be remitted, and that it was only to be carried out in the event of one being declared more guilty than the other. On 9th September the Council passed sentence, ordering Anneessens to be executed and the other syndics to be banished in perpetuity. The magistracy made an appeal to the Council for mitigation of sentence on the ground that the accused had done whatever they did by virtue of their office. Even the priests interceded on behalf of Anneessens, but in vain. De Prié was obdurate, and on 19th September the sentence was carried out on the Grand Place. As the executioner performed his task a voice in the crowd exclaimed "Adieu to our privileges! Their champion is gone." Anneessens became a public martyr,[*] and his name is still remembered as that of one of the champions of civic liberty in his country.

---

[*] Orders were given to throw his remains into the fosse, but a party of citizens seized them, and they were buried in the church of La Chapelle. De Prié wished to have them removed in defiance of the protection of the Church, but the Emperor intervened and forbade their removal.

Having thus removed his chief opponent, De Prié made short work of the Guilds. The oath was imposed on them under pain of banishment, and they were required to take it individually instead of as a body. There was consequently no possibility of evasion. By a similar procedure he coerced the opposition as effectually at Antwerp as he had done at Brussels. He also succeeded in resisting the desire of both the Emperor and Prince Eugéne to publish an amnesty, declaring that it was quite a mistake to suppose that the people of the Netherlands could be governed by kindness. His influence proved sufficient to obtain currency for an opinion that the least examination would have shown to be untenable.

Only one episode of the nine years' administration of the Marquis de Prié furnished ground for satisfaction in Belgium, and that was the development of Ostend as a commercial port and the founding of the Company for trade with the Indies which bore its name. The closing of the Scheldt had practically destroyed the maritime trade of Belgium and the only hope of reviving it lay in the creation and fostering of a new port on the main coast. Ostend was the only place possessing the necessary conditions. A ship-building yard was established there, the canal connecting Bruges and Ghent was extended to Antwerp, and finally, in 1722, a General Company was established at Ostend " for the purpose of navigating and trading to the East and West Indies and to the coasts of Africa, both on this and the other side of the Cape of Good Hope, in all ports, havens and places where other nations may freely traffic." The popularity of this undertaking may be gathered from the fact that its capital of six million florins was raised in forty-eight hours. Four ships a year were to be sent to India, and two factories were founded in India, one at Coblom on the coast of Coromandel and the other at Bankibazar on the Ganges. During the brief period of its existence the Ostend Company revived commercial enterprise among the Belgians and added to the national prosperity, but its creation alone could not make De Prié popular. Grave charges of peculation hung over his head, and the haughty Walloon aristocracy treated him as a parvenu. His patron Prince Eugéne withdrew his support, and the Marquis anticipated his dismissal by a prompt resignation. To his escape from a trial on the score of venality he was indebted to a sudden, but not less well-timed, attack of apoplexy. He was personally responsible for the fact that the introduction of Austrian rule into the Netherlands was less happy than it should have been. For such a task the inflexible and stern, not to say sinister, character of the Italian made De Prié unsuitable. The Belgians have always required a ruler whose strength was enveloped in a certain bonhomie or even levity of expression and demeanour. They found the happy medium of gravity and gaiety in Prince Charles of Lorraine.

The governor sent to replace De Prié was Field-Marshal Count Daun, father of the more famous Marshal who twice defeated Frederick the Great. His instructions were brief. He was to keep the Provinces quiet, to appease public opinion, and to obtain the sanction of the States to the Pragmatic Sanction.* A general amnesty was published and on 25th May, 1725, the States ratified the Pragmatic Sanction. As a mark of his Imperial pleasure Charles extended the pardon to the Syndics condemned with Anneessens, and appointed his sister the Archduchess Mary Elizabeth to the post of Governor General of the Netherlands.

The appointment of the Archduchess was hailed with much satisfaction in Belgium where female rule was associated with some of the happiest periods of its history, and the Emperor did all he could to complete the favourable impression, by the amnesty mentioned, and by restoring the old form of administration in the three Councils. This change was rendered necessary, as the Count de Nény explained in his Memoirs, by the confusion and delays that had sprung up in all departments, but the Archduchess made use of a Cabinet junta, composed of the chief court and military officers, which gradually super-

* The Pragmatic Sanction referred to was first published by the Emperor Charles in 1713. It was intended to give the succession in default of male issue to his daughter Maria Theresa, in preference to the daughter of his elder brother and predecessor Joseph I., as provided by the will of their father Leopold I. Twenty-five years passed before the last of the Powers signed the sanction in 1738.

seded the Council of State. The Archduchess was also invested with Imperial functions, and had the right of making all appointments. The sixteen years of her rule were marked by general tranquillity, and the only event of the period in which Belgium was directly concerned was the suspension, in 1727 for seven years, of the privileges possessed by the Ostend Company, and its definitive suppression in 1731 by the Treaty of Vienna as the equivalent paid for Great Britain's signature of the Pragmatic Sanction. The Archduchess* died in Belgium in 1741, twelve months after her brother, the Emperor Charles the Sixth. The Empress Queen Maria Theresa had succeeded to the dominions of Hapsburg and Burgundy, and on her aunt's death she appointed her brother-in-law, Prince Charles of Lorraine, to the Governor Generalship of the Netherlands, and with his arrival the second and happier part of Austrian rule in Belgium may be said to have commenced.

An interval of three years occurred between the nomination of Prince Charles of Lorraine and his arrival in Belgium. This was due to the war in which the Empress found herself engaged, immediately after her accession to the throne, through the ambitious designs of Frederick of Prussia. The treaty of Breslau (11th June, 1742) concluded the struggle between Austria and Prussia with the surrender to the latter of Lower Silesia after Frederick had refused to accept the north-east of Belgium as an equivalent, but the war continued with France and Bavaria. England came to the assistance of Austria, and in 1743 the Anglo-Austrian army defeated the French at Dettingen. This signal victory saved Austria by driving the French across the Rhine, but strangely enough it proved disadvantageous for Belgium by diverting French attack from Germany to the Provinces. In the thirty years following Malplaquet the Low Countries had enjoyed unbroken peace,

---

* One of the chief occurrences of her rule was the destruction by fire, in 1731, of the famous Palace of the Sovereigns of the Netherlands, which had been the scene of so many remarkable events, including the abdication of Charles the Fifth. The Grand Gallery with many of the chief works of Rubens was completely destroyed, and the Archduchess barely escaped in time. She then took up her residence in the Palace of Orange-Nassau, the home of William the Silent, which is now used as a Record Office and the Museum of Modern Pictures.

and there seemed to be a tacit understanding to leave them for once outside the field of battle, but the expulsion of the French troops from Germany led to a change of views and plans which coincided with the arrival of Prince Charles of Lorraine in the country.

On the eve of his departure from Vienna, Prince Charles married the Archduchess Mary Anne, sister of the Empress, and this princess was associated with him by name in the government of the Netherlands. They made their joint entry into Brussels on 26th March, 1744, and a few weeks later the Empress was formally inaugurated as Duchess of Brabant at Brussels, and Countess of Flanders at Ghent. The inauguration at Brussels was held amid the charred ruins of the ancient palace, which may have suggested to the prince the desirability of its reconstruction.*

A few weeks after these events the French invaded Belgium. By the Barrier Treaty the Dutch had been entrusted with the defence of the fortified places in Flanders. The long peace had rendered them negligent. The garrisons offered a very feeble resistance to the French who, in less than two months, captured all the fortified places in the west from Courtrai to Knocke. The divisions among the English, Dutch, and Belgian commanders would have entailed the complete occupation of the Netherlands if Charles of Lorraine had not hastened to Germany and led an Imperial army into Alsace. This diversion saved the greater part of the Netherlands by compelling the French to recall a considerable part of their army. The campaign of 1745 proved still more conclusively in favour of the French than that of the previous year. The great battle of Fontenoy, in which Marshal Saxe, thanks to the desperate courage of the Irish Brigade, won a signal victory over the Duke of Cumberland, was followed by the capture of all the principal towns of Flanders including Ghent. The descent of the Young Pretender on Scotland and his invasion of England necessitated the recall of the Duke of Cumberland and the

* Charles of Lorraine was the twelfth child of Leopold, Duke of Lorraine, and the Princess Charlotte, daughter of Philip d' Orleans, the only brother of Louis XIV. He was born at Luneville on 12th December, 1712.

English army. Marshal Saxe took advantage of this withdrawal to continue the campaign during the winter, and in January, 1746, he laid siege to Brussels. On 21st February the place capitulated, and some weeks later Louis XV. visited his victorious general at Brussels, and signalised his visit by the unopposed capture of Malines. The campaign of 1747 was also favourable to the French arms, despite the return of the Duke of Cumberland and an English army. Saxe gained another victory at Lawfeld (2nd July, 1747) not less decisive than Fontenoy, but of which the English at least had no reason to be ashamed. It was on that occasion that Louis XV., who was present, said "The English not only pay for all, but they fight for all." Here again it is doubtful if the French would have won if the Irish Brigade had not shown extraordinary intrepidity and indifference to loss. The capture of Bergen-op-Zoom, reputed impregnable, completed the triumphs of the French general.* The campaign of 1748 confirmed, by the French capture of Maestricht, the successes of 1747, but all the Powers were more or less disposed towards peace, and a congress was begun at Aix-la-Chapelle.

During this period of nearly two years Belgium was under a *de-facto* French Government, and its mode of carrying on the administration was not of a nature to make it popular. Marshal Saxe was appointed Governor General with an enormous salary, and other high officials were sent to batten on the country, while Princes of the Blood claimed monopolies and privileges unknown in the Netherlands, and repugnant to the sentiments of a people bred to believe in their free constitution even when subject to tyranny. One tax imposed was that on passports without which no one, not even the priests, could move out of the smallest village. Another tyrannical proceeding was to place the bells of all the churches and convents to ransom. Finally, the Intendant-in-Chief demanded one-sixth of the value of the property belonging to the church, and where it was refused he at once installed a party of soldiers whose

* Maréchal de Saxe was the son of Augustus the Strong of Saxony and Poland, and of Aurora Konigsmarck, sister of the Count Konigsmarck whose name is associated with that of Queen Sophia Dorothea of Zell, the wife of George 1st of England.

wants had to be provided for without payment. At the best the French could not have been anything but a hostile force in military occupation of the country, but they did everything possible to make their rule harsh and unpopular by extortionate demands and enforced requisitions.

The Treaty of Aix-la-Chapelle (7th October, 1748) restored the Low Countries to Austria, but it is beyond dispute that the Empress offered to cede them to France if that Power would induce or compel Prussia to restore Silesia. The secret negotiations of Count Kaunitz to that effect proved abortive, but they contained the germ of the alliance between Austria and France which was effected eight years later, on the eve of the Seven Years' War. The secrets of diplomacy were not then public property, and the return of the Austrians was hailed with trans-

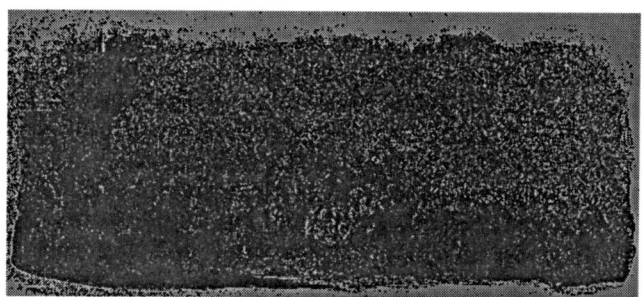

ENTRY OF PRINCE CHARLES OF LORRAINE INTO BRUSSELS.

ports of delight throughout Belgium. The entry of Prince Charles into Brussels on 23rd April, 1749, resembled a popular triumph, but it was not devoid of melancholy features, as in the interval the popular Archduchess Mary Anne had died. The weak point in the arrangement was that the custody of the barrier fortresses was again entrusted to the Dutch, although the French invasion had been only rendered possible by their negligence or inability to defend them. One other consequence of this war had been the downfall of the governmental system in Holland, where the family of Orange had been restored to the Stadtholdership in the person of William Henry, known as William the Fourth (May, 1747).*

The complete change in Austrian policy, which followed the treaty of Aix-la-Chapelle, averted from Belgian soil the horrors of war during the long struggle with Prussia from 1756 to 1763. Under the direction of Count Kaunitz the old alliance with England was abandoned, and in its place a new one was formed with France, the Empire's hereditary enemy. The arbitrary pretensions of Holland and England to stifle the trade of Belgium under the Barrier treaty were repelled, and when the representatives of those States at Vienna had recourse to threats the Empress gave a haughty and defiant reply that she was sovereign in her own States, and resolved that they should not be deprived of the privileges that belonged to them by inherent right. A more emphatic step was to decline to pay any longer the subvention stipulated for under the treaty of 1715. The treaty of Aix-la-Chapelle therefore brought Belgium the advantages of a long peace, and it entirely escaped from the ravages of the Seven Years' War. A contingent of Belgian troops formed part of the Imperial armies, and well sustained the high military reputation of the Walloon race.† Large subventions were also contributed to the exchequer of the Empress, but the undisturbed tranquillity and security of the country were more than an adequate compensation, and the Netherlands began to recover the prosperity they had lost two centuries before.

* He married a daughter of George the Second, and his disputes with his brother-in-law, the Duke of Cumberland, during the war on the ground of precedence were one of the causes of its barren result.

† At the battle of Kolin, 16th June, 1757, when Daun surprised and defeated Frederick of Prussia, the regiment of Latour Dragoons specially distinguished themselves. Their colonel, Prince Ferdinand de Ligne, asked permission to charge, but Count Daun, referring to their being young recruits, said "What can you do with these white beaks?" Prince Ferdinand, turning to his men, said "White Beaks, show that to bite one does not require moustaches, but teeth." The regiment charged with fury and showed conspicuous gallantry. The Latour regiment is now represented by the 14th Dragoons of the Austrian Army, who bear on their colours "Kolin. For the proved fidelity and valour of the Latour Dragoons," and enjoy the unique privilege among Austrian cavalry regiments of shaving their moustaches. They are still known as the "Blancs Becs," and in 1875 the Emperor Francis Joseph ratified the privilege.

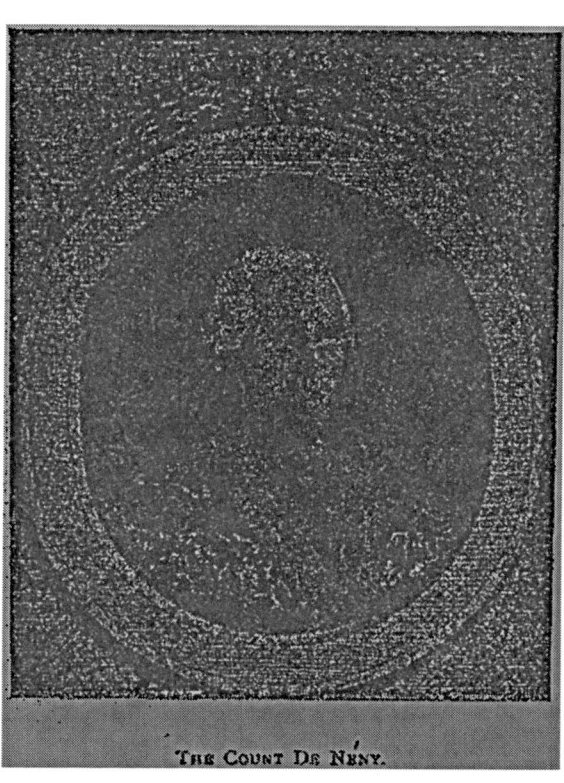

THE COUNT DE NÉNY.

For this result the credit must be largely given to Prince Charles of Lorraine who identified himself in a very special degree with the interests of Belgium, and who was supported by some ministers of exceptional merit. To assist the Governor General an official with the title of Minister Plenipotentiary was appointed from Vienna. In the time of Prince Eugéne he had been the acting Governor, but with Charles of Lorraine exercising the active functions for himself the Minister was merely a mouthpiece and reporter for the Vienna Government. It was not surprising, therefore, that he should sometimes advocate a policy more in accordance with the views of the general interests of Austria, whose one dominant view at this period was to humble Prussia, than with the local interests of Belgium. This charge could not, however, be made against the Marquis de Botta-Adorno who became Minister, in succession to Kaunitz, immediately after the treaty of Aix-la-Chapelle.

He associated himself with all the measures intended to restore to the country its long lost prosperity, and among these may be specifically mentioned the construction of the canal from Ghent to Bruges which, although it had been commenced as far back as the year 1379, had never been finished. Another canal with the construction of which he was closely associated was that between Louvain and the Scheldt. By the development of internal means of communication the prosperity of the country was increased, even although its natural outlet in the Scheldt remained closed. The Count de Nény, son of Patrick Mac Nény the War Secretary already referred to, was President of the Privy Council, and was quite the ablest man in the service, while his marriage with the daughter of the Viscount Wynants gave him special facilities for measuring Belgian feeling and studying its national requirements. He was entrusted with the control of the University at Louvain, which had fallen on evil days, and which he succeeded in making again the National University, although this was only accomplished by means of an order prohibiting all Austrian subjects from proceeding to a French College. When Botta-Adorno left Brussels he was succeeded by a still abler man in Count Cobenzl, of whose connection with Belgium more will have to be said.

The popularity of Austrian rule was, however, really due to the efforts of Prince Charles of Lorraine who devoted himself to his task, and represented in character and habits the typical governor of the Low Countries. He was frank, sincere and boisterous in manner, and addicted to the pleasures of the table. He was given to practical joking, and allowed much familiarity in his friends and associates. He showed a marked consideration for Belgian opinion and on several occasions he ranged himself on its side against the Imperialistic tendencies of Vienna. He identified himself so closely with his charge that he purchased the ancient palace of Orange-Nassau with his own money as a residence in Brussels, while he occupied the chateau in the beautiful park of Tervueren during the summer. Among his principal measures towards the embellishment of the city of Brussels was the planting of the elms and limes which line the boulevards of the upper town, flanked in his time by the old walls and gates of the city. In describing his mode of life to his sister-in-law* he said that it was very simple and unaccompanied by much state, as it was only on great occasions that he gave balls to the nobility.

With the exception of one raid, executed by the Duke of Brunswick in 1758, at the head of the Prusso-Hanoverian army victorious at Crefeld, Belgium remained happily outside the range of the European struggle for the seven years closing in 1763. The command of the Austrian armies was at first entrusted to Prince Charles of Lorraine, and for nearly two years he was obliged to be absent from Belgium, but his uniform bad success in the field led to his removal from the command. He then returned to his more congenial task of administration in the Low Countries. He devoted his attention specially to the improvement of agriculture, and a remarkable order was issued limiting the area that might be cultivated by any one man. This drastic measure seems to have been specially directed against the monasteries and convents, and ensured the frequent subdivision of the land. Moreover, the

* He was in a double sense her brother-in-law, as the Empress had married his brother Francis, elected Emperor of Germany in 1745. The Prussian Ambassador at Vienna, Count Podewils, has left on record a study of this prince's character.

cultivator in Belgium was a free agent, independent of feudal obligations as in France and Germany, and benefiting by his own toil. As the consequence the provinces of Belgium became exceedingly prosperous while the towns languished from the default of industry. The fields of Flanders and Brabant were compared to gardens, and many of the provincial districts were as populous as towns. On the other hand half the population of Bruges was composed of beggars, and the poor houses of Ghent and Liége counted their inmates by the thousand. On the whole Belgium was again becoming the happiest and most prosperous country of the continent with the exception of the sister provinces that had preserved their prosperity with their independence under the name of Holland.

Charles of Lorraine acquired much popularity by the consistent manner in which he respected and upheld the privileges of the country. But it must be allowed that some of the provisions under the grand charter of the Joyous Entry were a little out of date. Count Cobenzl wished to effect some material alterations therein, but the Council of Brabant clung tenaciously to every syllable of the old charter, even refusing to consider the removal of the sanction of "question by torture." And as the people of Brabant were so tenacious on one side, the Austrian Ministers began to be more assertive on the other, and to declare that the only way to obtain good government was to get rid of the whole of the Constitution that was the boast of the Netherlands. Cobenzl held these views because he found it to be an obstruction in his path, and Kaunitz the Chancellor, who had also had some practical experience of Belgian affairs, supported the view because a despotic system was more conducive than any other to the success of general and comprehensive schemes of policy. Prince Charles of Lorraine opposed this policy and made himself the champion of the rights of the Belgians, a course that naturally increased his local popularity. His personal representations to the Empress succeeded in thwarting the plans of Cobenzl and Kaunitz. In one letter he stated that "the great misfortune of these provinces is that they are too remote for your Majesty to know them personally, and that unfortunately those who are in a position to report to your Majesty about them and who think they know them do not really know them, and more than that are even prejudiced against them. For my part I dare to say that these provinces are very easily governed, and with the least degree of gentleness and goodness your Majesty can do whatever you wish in them, and to my way of thinking there is nothing more flattering for a sovereign than to reign in the hearts of the subjects. But the greater number of ministers, for their own personal aggrandisement, wish to rule despotically, and it is that which stops so many matters in this country."

After this correspondence the Empress allowed no further attempt to be made to interfere with the constitution of the Provinces. Their value as a revenue producing part of the Empire had perhaps as much to do with this decision as any tender regard for the rights wrested from the House of Burgundy. In twenty years, among which were those of the Prussian War, the Provinces contributed to the Imperial Exchequer in the form of subsidies, gifts, and loans, the enormous sum, for that age, of seventy-two million florins. The greater portion of the Austrian dominions consisted of poor undeveloped land, and the root cause of the decline of the old Empire was poverty. In respect of prosperity Belgium presented a striking contrast with the rest of the Empire. Fettered as it was in its external trade by the closing of the Scheldt, it still constituted the most remunerative portion of the wide-stretching dominions of the House of Hapsburg.

The government of Prince Charles of Lorraine deserves also to be remembered for its patronage of literature and the fine arts. By his generosity the famous library of the Dukes of Burgundy, which occupied and still occupies a wing of his palace at Brussels, was first made accessible to students, and although the censorship of the Church as well as the Government was still maintained in all its severity, the Imperial decree that a gentleman committed nothing derogatory in becoming an author or an artist marked a clear step forward. In the struggle to stifle knowledge and arrest progress all the arts had been lowered to the grade of mere trades. The intervention of the Church in secular affairs was also restrained, and the power of the civil law was asserted. The accumulation of lands and wealth in the hands of abbeys, monasteries, and convents had become a danger, and the restrictions placed on the acquisition of legacies by these bodies were only remarkable because they were the acts of the Apostolic sovereign.

The Belgians called Charles of Lorraine "the good governor," and they celebrated his jubilee by subscribing for a bronze statue which, originally placed on the Place Royale, then called Place de Lorraine, now stands in the little garden in front of the Royal Library at Brussels. The Prince died at Tervueren in 1780, and a few months later the Empress Maria Theresa followed him to the tomb, thus ending the first period of Austria's rule in the Provinces. With the exception of the French invasion, under Marshal Saxe, the sixty-five years had been marked by unbroken peace and steady progress.*

The next Austrian ruler was Joseph the Second, the best meaning of princes and the least fortunate. The son of Francis and Maria Theresa, he had, on his father's death in 1765, been elected Emperor of Germany, and he had accustomed himself to take a personal interest in the affairs of the people. Unlike any other prince of the time he sought knowledge in the lower walks of society, and found his chief amusement in mixing freely, and in a disguise which only deceived himself, with his subjects. He was simple and even severe in his mode of life. He slept on a hard bed, and his ordinary dress was a plain and often shabby military uniform. Penurious in his own life he was often generous towards others, and if his schemes for the welfare of his people had been put on a more practical basis, and better supported by ministers who were not in sympathy with them they might have borne fruit.

On the death of Charles of Lorraine the Empress had appointed, as Governor of the Low Countries, her daughter, the Archduchess Maria Christine, with whom was associated her husband, Duke Albert of Saxe Teschen. Joseph the Second confirmed this appointment, and at the same time

---

* The population of the provinces at this period was computed to be 2,272,892. The total seems excessive especially as Brussels contained only 74,000 inhabitants.

announced his intention of visiting the Low Countries himself. In his letter to the States announcing his accession he declared that he would make it his particular care to maintain his subjects of the Low Countries in the enjoyment of their rights and privileges. His reforming zeal and good intentions rendered him somewhat blind to the hard facts of the situation, and indifferent to the desire of the Belgians to be governed, not in a perfect, but in their own way.

Joseph carried out his intention of visiting the Provinces, and the Count de Nény drew up his remarkable memoir for the information of the sovereign. This sketch of the constitutional history and government of the Low Countries remains unsurpassed for clearness and accuracy in its statements of fact in regard to the intricate subject of which it treats, and it seems strange that the Emperor could have wandered from the track so clearly indicated by the Councillor whose very special acquaintance with the subject had led to his assistance being invoked for his guidance. It has been suggested that Joseph was so wedded to his own opinions and so convinced of the excellence of his own designs that he paid little or no attention to the special information provided for his benefit, and that he hoped to treat the Netherlands as a clean sheet on which he might trace what characters he pleased. But this theory is negatived by the very pronounced measures he took to promote Belgian interests in matters of which he could hardly have become aware if he had been either indifferent or unobservant. It is to those matters that attention may first be devoted, leaving for a fresh chapter the internal troubles that resulted in what was known as the Walloon Revolution.

When Joseph visited the Netherlands he found the greater number of the strong places garrisoned by Dutch troops, and he resented the arrangement, both on the ground of its being an infraction of his sovereign rights, and because it was a burden on his subjects. But at the same time the arrangement was in full accordance with the Treaty of the Barrier, ratified by several subsequent conventions. None the less Joseph decided on prompt and high-handed action which was rendered possible by the fact that at that moment Holland was engaged in a war with England which tasked all its strength. The excellence of the Emperor's relations with France, which had been strengthened by the marriage of his sister, Marie Antoinette, with Louis the Sixteenth, also enabled him to pursue a course which, under any other circumstances, would have produced hostilities. He ordered that all the strong places of Belgium should be dismantled, thus giving his policy a form that could not be regarded with disfavour by France, and which was destined as a matter of fact to greatly facilitate French plans during the Revolutionary Wars. The Dutch garrisons evacuated the places they held without any opposition, and before the end of the year 1782 the Dutch force, which had been quartered in the old Spanish Netherlands since the close of the War of the Spanish succession, was withdrawn. There is no doubt that this measure was popular in Belgium because it reduced the military burden upon it, but at the same time it is only fair to state that no charges were made against the Dutch troops, whose conduct in a somewhat difficult position seems to have been exemplary.

Emboldened by this first and easily obtained success Joseph turned his attention to the removal of the other impediments placed on Belgium by the treaties with Holland. He claimed the freedom of the Scheldt and the surrender of the forts commanding its navigation. He also claimed the surrender of Maestricht and the surrounding district. Putting into practice the same policy that he had employed in the matter of the fortresses, the Emperor hoped to carry the day by the simple assertion of what he considered to be his natural rights, notwithstanding that they had been surrendered by treaty. He accordingly ordered a small vessel to hoist the Imperial Flag at Antwerp and to sail for the open sea. When it arrived opposite the Dutch forts it was fired upon and compelled to turn back. At first it seemed as if the Emperor would resent this outrage to his flag by declaring war, but France declined to be a party to an attack on the United Provinces which would certainly have crippled them. A compromise was therefore proposed, and failing the alliance of France Joseph accepted her mediation. Even thus much permanent good might have been done if Joseph had adhered firmly to the policy originally marked out for himself of freeing the Scheldt, which was essentially a Belgian interest. But unfortunately there had always been a note of uncertainty in the Austrian policy towards Belgium. The Empress Maria Theresa had been willing to surrender it for Silesia, the Emperor Joseph was more than anxious to barter it for Bavaria, and if France could have been induced to abandon her historic ally in Germany the arrangement might have been concluded, notwithstanding the opposition of the aged Frederick. While the object of Joseph was to benefit the Provinces it cannot be contended that it was his exclusive or unselfish object. His main desire remained the rounding off of his proper Austrian dominions.

The uncertainty of his policy contributed to the meagreness of the result following the mediation of France in 1784. Louis XVI. could not oblige his Imperial brother-in-law so far as to abandon the House of Wittelsbach or to free the Scheldt. But he gave him possession of the two forts that had fired upon his flag, and awarded him compensation for the surrender of his claims over Maestricht. The Scheldt remained none the less closed for the Belgian nation. The well meaning but unfortunate Joseph may be credited with having made the best attempt to free it down to the successful effort of only forty years ago. The Emperor Charles VI. had sought to nullify the treaty provisions by patronising Ostend, Maria Theresa had been too much occupied to attend to it, and Joseph found consolation for his failure in improving the outlets of Austria by the Danube and through the port of Fiume. Among his minor enterprises should certainly be mentioned the acquisition of the Nicobar islands under a lease from Hyder Ali. There is some evidence among the India Office Records that this Imperial enterprise raised a flutter of anxiety in Leadenhall Street.

At the very moment when events were going to bring the Austrian rule to the verge of practical extinction, history shows that it was labouring for an improvement in the material condition of Belgium. The wholly sympathetic rule of Charles of Lorraine was over, and in its place was that of an interfering sovereign satisfied of his own good intentions but unpractical and indifferent to details. A reformer born before his time was specially unsuited to deal with the questions of the age in Belgium where liberty had been preserved by a rigid adherence to inherited privilege, and where the power of the Church had attained its summit by the absolute acquisition of the greater part of the real property in the country. The safest government was the one that left matters alone like that of Charles of Lorraine. The Emperor Joseph, with a far higher ideal, soon found himself involved in a hornets' nest. If there had been a close natural union between the two countries he might have succeeded in his plans, but the tie between Austria and the Netherlands was artificial, and his own external policy was not calculated to invest it with reality or strength. In order to be a popular ruler of the Netherlands it was necessary that the Emperor Joseph should realise their value, and this his tortuous policy at Versailles clearly showed he never did. None the less he was bent on laying a rough hand on the established order of things in the Provinces with a result that might well have been foreseen.

CHAPTER XIV.

The Brabant Revolution.

BELIEF in the immaculate merit of the Joyous Entry of old Duke Wenceslas was the first if not the only article of faith in the political conception of every native of Brabant. The Emperor Joseph, although he had visited the Netherlands, and had had a special memoir prepared for his enlightenment, recked nothing of this. At the most it was an antiquated charter, full of anachronisms and contradictions, to which his brand new constitution would soon provide a worthier and more acceptable successor. If he had had only popular convictions or prejudices to contend with, the plans of the Emperor might have succeeded, or at least incurred a less complete collapse. But they brought him into sharp collision with the Church whose privileges he assailed and whose property he diminished, and he thus left himself without any support in the task he imposed upon himself. His measures of religious reform and tolerance were passed immediately after his accession, and referred in the first place to his Austrian dominions, where the Church had acquired a control in secular matters that overshadowed the Imperial authority. He began, in 1780, with orders closing a considerable number of useless or excessive convents and monasteries, and assigning the funds derived from the sale of their property to the endowment of 400 parochial cures. In this reform he was supported by the Bishop of Laybach and other prelates who saw a peril to the Church in excessive monachism. In the following year he published his famous Edict of Tolerance, which opened the doors of the public service to others than members of the Church of Rome. The Edict which placed the Civil Law on a level with that of the Church declared that "His Imperial and Royal

Apostolic Majesty, convinced of the pernicious effect of all violence exercised on the conscience, and of the essential advantages of a truly Christian tolerance, decrees that the private exercise of their religion shall be permitted to all his subjects of the Helvetian confession, and of that of Augsbourg, as well as to all his subjects of the Greek religion in all parts of the Austrian monarchy where they are to be found in sufficient numbers. Those who do not profess the Catholic religion will be in no way constrained to take the oath with any formula contrary to the principles of their sect, nor to assist in the processions and ceremonies of the dominant religion. In conferring posts the sovereign will pay no regard to differences of religion, but will consider solely capacity and aptitude. Mixed marriages are permitted. No one can be punished on account of his religion unless he has also broken the civil law."

The publication of this Edict naturally caused a great flutter in Catholic countries where Protestants of all shades were ineligible for state employment. The Netherlands, first Spanish and now Austrian, were not less Catholic than the patrimonial dominions of the House of Hapsburg. The Inquisition had stamped out heresy, and left a deep-rooted terror in Belgian blood against any religious innovation or revolt from Rome. The power of the Bishops, and of the clergy, with the control they practically possessed in the States, rendered any encroachment on the rights of the Church especially hazardous. It became necessary to ask the States to sanction the promulgation of the Edict in the Netherlands, and the Governors, Maria Christine of Austria and her husband, Albert of Saxe-Teschen, proceeded in November, 1781, one year after it had become law in Austria, to bring the subject before them. In this matter they thought it advisable to follow a more apologetic procedure than was any part of the Emperor's instructions. They represented that the Edict was due to his charity and that it was not intended to detract from, or diminish in any way, the importance of the Catholic religion of which the Emperor remained a staunch and zealous champion. This explanation did not secure a better reception for the proposed measure. It was denounced, not only as a concession to heresy, but also as an infraction of the Joyous Entry, which had, of course, assumed as a question beyond dispute the predominance of the Church of Rome, there being at the time of that Charter no other. The University of Louvain put itself in the van of the opposition to the measure stating in its remonstrance that it had been specially founded to "form as a bulwark and support of Catholic piety and faith." The town councils in several of the chief cities roundly declared that the Edict was an infraction of their civic rights, a statement which could only be sustained on the theory that every syllable and letter of the Joyous Entry was to hold good for all time.

The Emperor was not to be turned aside by this kind of opposition from his intentions, and fortified by the admission of Pope Pius VI. that he was doing nothing contrary to religion, he proceeded to promulgate an order abolishing useless convents in Belgium. In this reform he did not encounter the same degree of opposition. It is quite true that the States of Brabant represented that "the Joyous Entry guaranteed their possessions to prelates, Houses of God, monasteries, etc.," but the Emperor brushed this objection aside with the observation that it "was not applicable to dispositions emanating from the sovereign authority for the good of religion and of humanity." The parish priests were by no means averse to a reform of the monasteries and abbeys which had gathered into their hands the greater part of the country's wealth, amounting to the then enormous sum, it was said, of three hundred million florins. The opposition of the church was, therefore, far less pronounced against the reduction in the number of monastical buildings than it had been against the Edict of Tolerance. The Council of Brabant passed the Edict on the subject of the Convents without much difficulty, the States ratified it, and the Governors General completed the work by ordering its publication within twenty-four hours under the threat of being declared disobedient.

If Joseph had stopped here no great harm would have been done, but in his reforming zeal he imagined evils and a state of things that did not in reality exist. His clerical reforms culminated in the order of 16th October, 1786, instituting general seminaries at Louvain and Luxembourg through which all candidates for the clergy were to pass, and he justified this step by alleging that it was taken with the view of bringing about a general reform in the prevailing corruption. There does not appear to have been any pressing need of reform, as there was in France, but that did not prevent the Emperor making an angry reply to the protesting Bishops to the effect that "there was a recognised need of reform as much in respect of habits and discipline as of instruction among the clergy." The measure completely upset the existing order of things, and as it depended for its success on the assistance of the clergy it is not surprising that this was not forthcoming.

Joseph's reforms were very far indeed from stopping with the Church. They extended throughout the civil administration as well. He suppressed the three collateral councils, which had been the most approved form of conducting the affairs of the country, and he substituted for them a single council bearing the title of the General Government of the Low Countries. All feudal and ecclesiastic judicial privileges were also abolished, and a regular order of Courts of First and Second Instance and of Revision was duly established. Finally the country was to be divided into nine circles, each controlled by an Intendant, and the circles were sub-divided into districts under Commissaries. It has never been seriously disputed that these alterations would have been improvements in the direction of simplicity and efficiency but the Belgians were not in a mood to give them a trial. The ecclesiastical and religious changes had disturbed them even when they partially approved of their drift, but these secular reforms alarmed them and seemed to have no end. They were well enough satisfied with their position and thought it better than any new-fangled constitution devised by a foreign Emperor could be. As a very competent authority (M. de Pradt) has observed "The transition from a conservative, methodical, and religious regime like that of Maria Theresa to another wholly set on reform and philosophy was too brusque not to excite general commotion. Men love fixity, and the protection of their habitudes often appears to them happiness itself. Joseph committed a moral anachronism. He proceeded to action before education. Enlightened and a philosopher himself he imagined that his people were his equals in that respect." He aimed at an ideal of perfect administration, and the Belgians preferred the Joyous Entry with all its irrelevancies and little details.

But although his measures were not popular he was still Emperor, with the hereditary titles of Duke of Brabant and Count of Flanders. If he had not offended the Church he might have succeeded in carrying out some part of his measures; if he had known how to withdraw them on the opposition becoming marked he might have saved himself the penalties that ensued. The opposition of the Church provided the national movement with leaders and an organisation that it might otherwise have lacked, while the Emperor's obstinacy prevented his drawing back.

The Brabant Council declined to pass the Imperial orders replacing the three Councils and rearranging the judicial tribunals on the ground that they were infractions of the Constitution. The States in their formal conclave not merely seconded this action, but announced that they would not vote the annual subsidy until the obnoxious decrees had been withdrawn. A general agitation spread throughout the country, and the war of pamphlets began between the two Parties who assumed the names of Royalists and Patriots. In face of this commotion and opposition the Emperor could think of nothing better than to give his subjects of the Netherlands a polite assurance that they were wrong and that he was right. He wrote in reply to their first protest "It has never been my intention to overthrow the constitution of my Belgian Provinces, and all the arrangements with which I have charged my Government aim solely, and without the least appearance of personal interest, at the greater advantage of my faithful subjects of the Netherlands, without my having wished thereby to deprive the legislative bodies of the nation of their ancient rights, liberties, and privileges. I only occupied myself with some reforms in the administration of justice upon the repeated instances mentioned in the numerous petitions presented to me, demanding a quicker and cheaper procedure. The Intendants

have no other function than to watch over the execution of the laws and to see that those charged with it fulfil their duties."
Notwithstanding this very reasonable letter the agitation continued and when the Patriots wished to be more offensive to the Royalists than usual they called them the Intendants.

The popular excitement had now become so great that it did not stop at words or writings. Volunteer corps were organised, every town raised its little company of civilians, and in the larger cities the trade guilds formed distinct regiments. The movement was only in its infancy when the mob attacked the residences of Joseph's officials and plundered or destroyed them. Worse might then have followed if the Governors General had not withdrawn the Imperial Decrees relating to the Administrative and Judicial changes on their own authority. This surrender was accepted and confirmed by the Emperor who, in return, insisted on the disbandment of the levies and the voting of the usual supplies. The Count de Murray who acted during the absence of the Governors General succeeded, by the display of much tact, in patching up an arrangement on this understanding, and he published a proclamation confirming all the old privileges and withdrawing the offensive measures excepting those relating to the convents and the University of Louvain. As the church was not satisfied there was nothing surprising in the fact that discontent continued to smoulder and that various proposals were made for breaking off the connection with Austria.

The Emperor, although he had given way, had not abandoned his plans. He had failed to carry them by argument and condescension. He hoped to have more success by having recourse to a little compulsion. He had somewhat strengthened the Austrian garrison which he placed under the command of a firm and uncompromising soldier, Count D'Alten, who thought nothing of constitutions and everything of his sovereign's orders. It has been said that Count D'Alten was personally responsible for the aggravation of the situation that followed, but it is clear that this was the inevitable result of the Emperor's decision to adhere to his policy.

The collision was not long deferred, for peremptory orders

were sent to the Brabant Council to publish the Imperial Edicts relating to the religious constitutions within twenty-four hours, failing which recourse would have to be made to "the sad means of bayonets and cannon." To give emphasis to the threat Austrian troops were drawn up on the Grand Place while the Brabant Council was deliberating inside the Hotel de Ville, and under this menace it gave its sanction to the publication of the Edicts. It accompanied its permission with certain reservations which left a loophole for the future explanation that its sanction had been given under compulsion, or that it had never been intended to violate the old charter. A week later the Governors General returned to Brussels, which they entered amid a sullen and silent population.

The Council had allowed the publication of the Edicts, but its attitude was the strongest encouragement to those who did not feel disposed to obey them. The clergy took up a still more pronounced attitude of opposition. They refused to attend the General Seminary appointed by the Emperor or to recognise its existence. Throughout the country the priests incited the people to disobedience of the Government orders, and the Patriots again brought out their red and yellow cockades as opposed to the black of the Austrians. The Count de Trauttmansdorff, the new Minister Plenipotentiary, was instructed to temporise and to only have recourse to military force when no other method was available, but he was hampered and over-ruled by his military colleague, Count D'Alten. The situation, to tell the truth, had got beyond diplomatic tact, and demanded nothing less than decisive action in the reversal of the policy adopted. Far from contemplating this step the Emperor was more pronounced in his determination to continue his course. He ordered the seminaries of the dioceses to be closed, so that there should be no rivals to his own grand seminaries of Louvain and Luxembourg, and when the States of Brabant refused to vote the subsidies he cancelled the general pardon issued when his civil reforms were withdrawn in return for the disbandment of the popular levies. The troubled situation, which had been composed in the autumn of 1787, was revived in an aggravated form in January, 1789, and the events occurring in France were of a nature to inflame the popular agitation. Joseph was a true and sincere reformer, but he was also Cæsar, and an Emperor thwarted and opposed in his schemes of popular government would naturally feel more irritated than one who only thought of playing the part of a despot.

The Emperor having failed to secure popular support in Belgium resolved to have recourse to strong measures, and to coerce where he could not obtain complete obedience. The States of Brabant were again summoned for 26th January, 1789, and on that day the bulk of the Austrian garrison was drawn up in the Grand Place, with its artillery ready for action. Under the shadow of this menace the three Estates met for a final decision, and the menace acquired a definite form when the Minister in his address to the assembly declared that failing assent his orders were "to turn Brussels into a desert and to let the grass grow in its streets." The threat did not answer, for while the nobles and clergy made humble protestations of obedience the third Estate absolutely refused to give way. In Hainaut the opposition was still more pronounced, the three Estates of that province combining in opposition to the Imperial orders. Joseph's reply was to send commissioners to Mons to announce that the constitution was annulled and that it was to be regarded as "a conquered state."

In Brabant the struggle took a different form. The Emperor concentrated his efforts on the suppression of the third Estate, while, with a dangerous irony in dealing with popular idols, he declared the Charter of the Joyous Entry "incomprehensible, shadowy, and incapable of execution." A little time was passed in idle discussion, and at last the delegates declared that their constitution might be annulled, but that they could not be forced to annul it themselves. An imperial order was thereupon issued to the following effect.

"From this day (6th June, 1789) all concessions made, accorded, and confirmed to the Province of Brabant, as well as the privileges of that Province, and the entire contents of the Joyous Entry are revoked, broken, and annulled; the intermediary committee of the States of Brabant, known under the name of Deputation of the States, as well as all receivers and employees of the same, are suppressed; the Council of Brabant is also suppressed, and the Grand Council of Malines will be entrusted with jurisdiction in the province of Brabant."

A general explosion of popular indignation followed this proclamation and all parties combined against the Austrians. The clause of the Joyous Entry permitting rebellion against the sovereign if he violated that constitution was triumphantly appealed to as sanctioning resistance. Definite form was given to it by the withdrawal of considerable numbers of young men to Breda in Holland, where they proceeded to train themselves as soldiers. The penalties of death and confiscation notified by Imperial Edict did not check the movement. Others, chiefly among the nobles, thought of importing a French Prince to found a new line of Dukes of Brabant, and the name of Philip of Orleans (Egalité) was mentioned for the vacancy. A remarkable man, the Count de la Marck,* left the French army and service to return to his natal country to push French interests and his own, for in the prevalent confusion and uncertainty the proposal to make the head of the princely D'Arenberg family chief of the state was as practical as any other. The crisis had also produced some popular leaders who became the true directors of the movement against Austrian rule.

While the nobility had formed among themselves a secret society, called after the motto " Pro aris et focis " of which the Duke D'Arenberg, his brother the Count de la Marck and his brother-in-law the Duke D'Ursel were the chief patrons, a more popular body had been drawn together at Breda under the direction of an advocate named Henri Van der Noot, and an ex-penitentiary of Antwerp Cathedral, named Van Eupen. Van der Noot was a noisy, vulgar, pushing demagogue without any real merit, but he had gained the ear of the people and was popular. On the other hand Van Eupen was a man of educa-

* Prince Augustus D'Arenberg, younger son of the Duke of that name, was induced by his maternal great uncle, Count de la Marck, to enter the French service as commander of his German regiment of De la Marck in the French service. He went to India with it and fought under Bussy at Gondalore where he was wounded. He also served in the American War of Independence under Lafayette. Afterwards he became the friend of Mirabeau and shared his political views. Mirabeau died in his arms.

tion and ability. They were both impregnated with the new French doctrines which, while these events were occurring in Belgium, had been translated into action by the destruction of the Bastille. They regarded the society of the Nobles with suspicion and dislike; when the Count de la Marck wrote offering his co-operation they took no notice of his letter. For the moment Van der Noot was supreme with a grandiloquent self-conferred title of Agent Plenipotentiary of the people of Brabant.

The situation had now grown so involved and critical that it is not surprising that the Powers became interested in it. In the summer of 1788 a triple alliance had been signed between Prussia, Holland, and Great Britain. The two first had a direct interest in promoting discontent in Belgium, and it was for this reason that the refugees were allowed to fix their headquarters near Breda. But when Van der Noot endeavoured to carry on negotiations with the Powers as diplomatic agent of his country he was not at all successful. The King of Prussia did indeed allow a minister to tell him verbally that, if Belgium succeeded in freeing herself, he would recognise her independence, but at the Hague he found very different and exclusively Dutch views prevailing, and in London he was snubbed by Pitt who refused to see him. Notwithstanding this failure Van der Noot continued to look mainly to foreign assistance for the success of his plans, which aimed at making Belgium a single independent state.

At this moment the noble society mentioned obtained a powerful ally in the person of Francis Vonck, an advocate surpassing Van der Noot in both ability and moderation. He proposed to the Breda Committee to join hands with him in organising a general insurrection, but although his proposals were at first rejected by Van der Noot circumstances brought about a temporary alliance. Vonck, having fled from Brussels on the failure of his plan to cause a general revolt, took refuge ·in Liége territory whence he had to retire on the approach of an Austrian army. A place of refuge at Breda could not, therefore, be refused him, although there was no friendship between the two leaders. All the faction being thus temporarily united at Breda, a decision was formed in favour of immediate action, but before this could be taken a leader to command the troops was necessary, and various names were put forward, among others those of the Count de la Marck and the Duke D' Ursel, both of whom were soldiers. The choice fell on Francis Van der Mersch, who had seen a good deal of service, and who had gained in the French service the name of "the brave Fleming." On 24th October, 1789, the Breda Committee issued a decree that the Emperor Joseph was no longer Duke of Brabant, and two days later Van der Mersch, at the head of his civilian army, drove the Austrian garrison out of Turnhout.

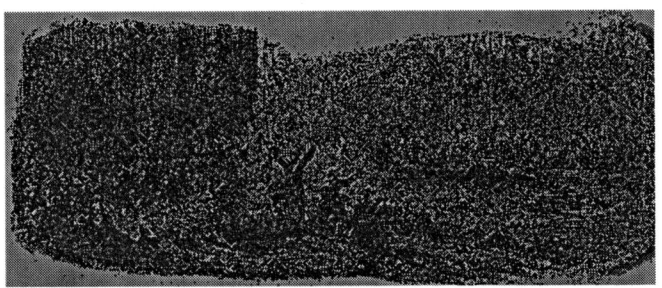

BATTLE OF TURNHOUT.

This was the signal for a general rising everywhere, not merely in Brabant but also in Flanders and Hainaut. The small and scattered Austrian garrisons were obliged to retire south of the Meuse. The Archduchess, Maria Christine, and her husband fled from Brussels on 18th November, and one month later Van der Noot entered the capital in triumph.

The defeat of his measures in a double sense had proved fatal to the Emperor Joseph. They had failed to obtain popular recognition and approval; they had failed to be carried into effect by force of arms. Never robust, a chest complaint turned to rapid consumption, and this amiable but impracticable prince died amid the wreck of his well-meant projects, exclaiming that "Belgium had killed him." The scene was graphically described in a letter* to the Empress Catherine of Russia by the Prince de Ligne, the favourite companion of the Emperor, from which the following passages are taken:—" He is no more, Madam, he is no more; the Prince who did honour to the man, the man who did the greatest honour to the Prince. This ardent genius is extinct like a light of which the envelope has been consumed, and his active body is between four planks which prevent his stirring. I was one of the four who carried him to the Capuchins. He died with firmness as he had lived, and himself arranged the order of the cortege bringing him the holy sacrament. The Emperor said to me a few days before his death, on my arrival after leading an army from Hungary to Silesia, 'Your country has killed me! Ghent taken was my agony, and Brussels abandoned, my death!'"

On 18th December, 1789, Van der Noot had entered Brussels in triumph, and for a brief space he became the virtual dictator of the country. But the triumph of this tribune, popular with the masses, was very far from ending the troubles of the country. It might rather be said to have begun a new series. Having expelled the Austrians, the question remained what was to be put in their place, and at once sharp differences were revealed between those who followed Van der Noot, and the party of Vonck and the nobles. The former wished to maintain the old system simply without a sovereign and to give the government an oligarchical form. The latter favoured reasonable reforms, with the idea of restoring the sovereignty of Austria, or some elected king after a brief interregnum. The Council of Brabant endorsed the policy of Van der Noot, and a few weeks later the States formally proclaimed a confederation of the country under the style of The Belgian United States. The government was to be carried on by committees, Van der Noot was made First Minister and his ally Van Eupen, Secretary of State. The followers of Vonck were rigidly excluded from office, and an oligarchy was founded out of the original members of the Committee of Breda. Those excluded

---

* The reader can consult the Memoirs of F.M. Prince de Ligne, a Belgian by birth and member of the famous family of Brabant of that name.

from office were left to form among themselves a Patriotic Society which was supported by the best elements in the country, including the soldier Van der Mersch, who had largely contributed to the expulsion of the Austrian garrison.

The Austrians had for the moment lost the Low Countries, with the exception of the province of Luxembourg, but they had not abandoned the hope of recovering them. The new Emperor Leopold II., as Grand Duke of Tuscany, had gained a reputation for ability and moderation which his brief reign as Emperor gave him no opportunity of establishing in a larger field. He at once devoted himself to the task of appeasing the excitement and disaffection in the Low Countries. Among the promises that he instructed the Governors General, then at Bonn, to give were a general amnesty, a full recognition of the authority of the States, and an undertaking that only natives of the Low Countries should be employed in the public service. He also condemned the policy of his predecessor, but he attributed the chief evils of the situation to the excesses of the military whose sole duty should be the defence of the country against foreign enemies. In a formal proclamation he declared that he had always regarded the Provinces as the most interesting and important portion of the Austrian Monarchy, and that their Constitution might well serve as a model to the rest. There was a time in the struggle when this language on the part of the sovereign would have commanded immediate obedience and restored calm to the country. At the time when it was spoken it produced only a partial effect. The men of substance and moderation were attracted and satisfied. The extreme party, which followed Van der Noot, having tasted the unusual sweets of power and encouraged by events in France refused to acquiesce in the restoration of Austrian rule, and adopted an attitude of insolence and defiance.

Taking no notice of the Imperial proclamations, Van der Noot devoted all his efforts to crushing the rival party under Vonck. The latter had certainly all the best chances of success. The influence of himself and the D'Arenbergs at Brussels might be held to outweigh that of the oligarchs; the greater part of the armed Volunteer force was attached to their side.

They lacked the audacity and resolution of Van der Noot, who had obtained the support, in military affairs, of a Prussian soldier, Von Schoenfeld, and who was still in touch with the cabinets of Berlin and the Hague. The intervention of the Church in the person of the Archbishop of Malines also tended to divide factions more sharply by placing clerical intolerance in opposition to popular aspirations. The proposals of the Emperor would restore to the Church its rights, and leave its privileges untouched. It could then denounce those reformers who, wishing to emulate the example of the French revolutionists, had threatened to seize church property. The moment for declaring such reformers "traitors to their country, and disturbers of public tranquillity" was badly chosen. It aggravated the difficulties of Vonck's position, and justified his description that it was the tocsin of persecution. His reasonable suggestions for a reform in the administration of Brabant were placed in the same category as the violent and revolutionary projects of Van der Noot.

At the same time it must be admitted that Vonck failed not through the intervention of the Church, but from his own want of courage and resolution. If he had acted on 9th of March, as some of the officers of the Brussels volunteers begged him, he could have overthrown Van der Noot, and averted his own downfall. Instead of acting, he and his partisans drew up a memorial in favour of an appeal to the people as to what should be the new form of government. Skilful advantage was taken of this act by Van der Noot who represented it as an insult to the States, while the Church fulminated its thunders against the signatories as innovators. Availing himself of the prevailing emotion Van der Noot caused Vonck's Patriotic Society to be dissolved, and its members to be denounced as disturbers of the public peace. It is not certain whether he purposely stirred up the mob to complete his work, but he certainly looked on at its excesses. From the 16th to the 19th of March the populace were allowed to plunder and destroy all the houses and other property of the Vonckists. Vonck succeeded in escaping to Namur, where Van der Mersch commanded a portion of the force with which he had freed the country. A decision was come to to march on Brussels and restore order; but unfortunate delays occurred in the execution. Van der Noot, while placing a force in the field under Schoenfeld to cover the approaches to Brussels, made some overtures for peace and promised concessions. The army of Van der Mersch left Namur not to fight but to fraternise with that of Schoenfeld. Advantage was taken of this false step by Van der Noot to stir up the populace in Namur. Three hundred determined men, well paid for the work, seized the place in Van der Mersch's absence and held it until Schoenfeld came to their help by a flank march. After this the Patriotic or Democratic party which had followed Vonck dissolved. Van der Mersch was thrown into prison in the Antwerp citadel, the Duke D' Ursel and others were also placed in confinement and suffered much ill treatment. Vonck and De la Marck, more fortunate, escaped to France. The "tyranny" of Van der Noot became firmly established, and the military skill and success of Schoenfeld confirmed it.

While Belgium was thus given over to be the prey of a faction which events showed was unable to control even the mob of the capital, where fresh disturbances had signalised the defeat of Vonck and Van der Mersch, the Powers began to look askance at Van der Noot. Aware of their change of sentiment Van der Noot attempted to establish an understanding with France. He wrote a letter with this object to Louis XVI., still King in name, but it was returned unopened. His subsequent overtures through the Foreign Minister were not more fortunate —the National Assembly passing an order of the day to the effect that the matter might be left to "the King's wisdom."

Negotiations between Prussia, Holland, and Great Britain occupied several months of the summer of 1790 and resulted in the conclusion of an arrangement (27th July, 1790) for the prompt restoration of the Low Countries to Austria, subject to the conditions that "the ancient constitution should be preserved, that a full amnesty and perfect wiping out of all that had happened during the trouble should be accorded, and that the whole arrangement should be made with the guarantee of the three Powers named." Brought face to face with this decision Van der Noot contemplated offering an armed opposition to the Austrians. He at all events ordered a *levée en masse* and he endeavoured to excite the people in his favour by alleging that there was an Austrian plot on foot for his assassination. The former measure resulted in the collection of twenty thousand ill-armed and worse drilled peasants, while the latter failed to arouse very much interest, for Van der Noot's popularity was very much on the wane. Events were gradually making the time ripe for a reassertion of Austrian power, while the Imperial garrisons in Luxembourg were brought up to a total of thirty thousand men.

In the autumn of 1790 Leopold made a further declaration to the people of Belgium, renewing his assurances of respect for its constitution and of a general pardon and act of oblivion. Instead of frankly accepting the situation, the States passed a Vote electing the Archduke Charles, the Emperor's younger son, Hereditary Grand Duke of Belgium. This was neither clever nor practical. It showed that the States no longer felt strong enough to defy the Emperor, at the same time that they usurped some of his functions. The real point at issue was whether the Provinces should return to the Austro-Burgundian family, and not as to the particular Austrian prince that should be its representative. The Emperor replied to the vote of the States by ordering his army to attack Namur and cross the Meuse. Marshal Bender carried out his instructions with equal celerity and success. He captured Namur on 25th November, and within a fortnight he had occupied Brussels and overcome all armed resistance. Van der Noot and Van Eupen were in their turn compelled to flee from the country, finding shelter in Holland. Schoenfeld benefited under the amnesty, expressing some surprise when he was told that his dismissal from the service was his only punishment. Vonck and Van der Mersch, who had honestly striven to benefit their country, sent in their allegiance to the Austrians, but they thought it prudent to continue to reside abroad. With the exception of Van der Noot the five leaders in the famous Brabant rebellion died a few years after these events. Van der Noot returned to Brussels during the French occupation and died there, in 1827, in obscurity, and forgotten by the populace of which he had been the idol, at the patriarchal age of 96.

Having recovered nominal possession of Belgium it remained to give consistency and strength to Austria's rule therein. The Emperor crowned his victory by evincing marked moderation, and he entrusted the task of conciliating Belgian opinion to one of his ablest diplomatists, the Count de Mercy-Argenteau, whose long residence at Versailles as the adviser of Marie Antoinette had gained for him a high reputation. It showed considerable grasp of the situation when Mercy began operations by inviting Vonck to come to Brussels and accept a post in the administration, but Vonck lay ill at Lille where he died soon afterwards, and there was no competent Belgian available at that moment to take his place. Mercy had accordingly to act on his own unaided knowledge and information, and his efforts were very much hampered and hindered by the intrigues and accusations of the French noble refugees who had made Brussels their headquarters. They found it amusing to denounce Mercy as "a philosopher," when he was merely endeavouring to carry out the difficult task entrusted to him by his sovereign by showing scrupulous regard for the charters and constitution of the country committed to his charge.

The Count de Mercy was very far indeed from meriting these insinuations. Immediately after his arrival he set himself to the difficult task of appeasing opinion and putting an end to political controversies. The excitement of the recent troubles had not died down, but it had passed into the form of pamphleteering. Every doctrinaire devised a constitution of his own, every one who could write and also pay the printer, rushed into print. A new society with the title of "Friends of the Public Good" claimed that the right to be a member of the States could only be established by "the qualification of a legal election." The recently established peace did not extend to the field of letters. Torrents of ink were shed, and anonymity provided a shelter against the persecution of the government. The aged Kaunitz in the last stage of his long career, which began where that of Mercy was to end, wrote asking "whether the authors and printers of inflammatory pamphlets could not be discovered by spies and properly punished?" Mercy wrote back in despair that, as far as he could see, "there was properly speaking no Belgian Nation, each of the Ten Provinces is different." It was a situation of the greatest difficulty, and it proved too heavy a task for the Count de Mercy.* Complimented by Kaunitz he resigned his post immediately after the re-entry of the Governors General, Maria Christine† and Albert of Saxe Teschen, into Brussels, and his successor was Count Metternich Winneberg, father of the celebrated Prince of that name.

The Prince-Bishopric of Liége, whose history was so often detached from that of the rest of Belgium, had had, during these years of trouble, a separate rebellion of its own, quite distinct from that in Brabant. The situation at Liége was peculiar. The authority of the Prince Bishop had been consolidated by a century's tranquillity, but at the same time the people had clung to and maintained their privileges which were considered by many superior to those of the rest of Belgium. They had always been subject to French influences, and the popular movement in France soon aroused imitators and emulators in the great city on the Meuse. Curiously enough the ostensible cause of the Liége revolution of 1789 related to the distribution of the proceeds of the gambling tables at Spa. The populace seized Bishop Hoensbroech, a man of merit and austere life, and compelled him to sign the appointment of two of their citizens as chief magistrates. The Bishop fled to Treves a few days later, and the German princes and counts took up his quarrel. The people of Liége based their demands on those of the French revolutionists, and affected no special regard for the Church. They claimed a free national assembly, and the rights of men and citizens. They placed themselves

* Count de Mercy died in London soon after and was buried in St. Pancras cemetery.

† During the long nominal rule of this Princess the event of most personal interest was the construction of the Palace at Laeken, which is famous as one of the favourite abodes of the great Napoleon, who wrote from that palace his celebrated order for the Russian campaign. Laeken is the winter residence of the Belgian Royal Family. Maria Christine's Palace was destroyed by fire in 1888, but a new Palace was erected on the same site by King Leopold II.

in an invidious light by certain excesses, and by disputes not unaccompanied by bloodshed as to the distribution of funds left in charity. The decrees of the Court of Wetzlar were entrusted to a Prussian army for execution, but the operations were carried on in a desultory manner. It was not until after the accession of Leopold that an end was put to the revolution by the active intervention of an Austrian army. The popular leaders were allowed to retire to France, and Bishop Hoensbroech was reinstated. He did not display after his return the moderation that had marked his earlier years, and the clerical rule of a Prince Bishop became more unpopular at Liége than ever, to bear fruit on a subsequent occasion.

Little or no success was experienced in the attempt to revive the popularity of Austrian rule. Metternich fared no better than Mercy in the task although he showed much skill in preserving an equilibrium, and playing one party against another. The dislike with which the constitutional pretensions of the Belgians had always been regarded became one of more or less intense hatred under the incentive of the object lessons provided in France. The States replied to the openly expressed hostility of the Archduchess Maria Christine by refusing to vote the necessary subsidies. The relations between Belgians and Austrians had become so acute that the former were impelled to appeal to the French to come to their aid. The part of the French programme promising to assist other nations in gaining their liberty appealed with special force to the Belgian people, which had a constitution that they only asked the right to enjoy in their own way. It is probable that the influence of Leopold, in name and character, might have kept things quiet a little longer, but his death on 1st March, 1792, followed by the declaration of war between France and Austria, precipitated events.

A plan of campaign was drawn up by the French General Dumouriez, with the express design of wresting Belgium from Austria. In this plan Belgium was quite correctly described as being full of malcontents and as being specially disposed at the moment to look to France for aid. Two French armies crossed the frontier, but retreated ignominiously at the first show of opposition. A second advance ended with equal ignominy. The campaign of the spring of 1792 seemed to improve Austria's position in the Low Countries. The Belgian generals, Clerfayt and Beaulieu, in her service more than held their own against the invaders. The success of the French arms in Lorraine against the Prussians, the cannonade of Valmy, left the Belgian frontier open to fresh attack, more especially as all the efforts of the Austrians to capture Lille were repulsed by the garrison, which was thus credited with having saved Paris. The second invasion of Belgium in the autumn of 1792 opened, therefore, with far better chances of success than that earlier in the year. The total Austrian garrison did not reach 40,000 men, while three French armies of nearly 90,000 men together invaded Belgium at as many different points. Dumouriez himself commanded the main force which marched direct on Mons. In the neighbourhood of that town it was opposed at Jemmappes by the Austrian army under Clerfayt. The battle (6th November) was stubbornly contested, and reflected much credit on the Austrians, who had only 16,000 men against the French 40,000. None the less the result was their decisive defeat, and the road was thus opened to Brussels. One week later Dumouriez entered the capital. Namur, Liége, and Antwerp surrendered to other French generals within a fortnight.

The Belgians welcomed the French because they relied on the statement in the French Constitution of 1791 that the French would never use their force against a people struggling to effect their own emancipation, while the declaration of war on 20th April, 1792, contained a special sentence that France took up arms for the liberty and independence of peoples among whom the Belgians by their position and associations with France naturally came first. These fine words were falsified by facts, and in a little time the conduct of the French made the Belgians regret even the government of Maria Christine, which fell far short in popular estimation of that of Charles of Lorraine. But the ease and rapidity with which the French conquest was effected in 1792 was due rather to the fact that all the fortresses had been dismantled at the time of the re-

BB

pudiation of the Barrier Treaty by the Emperor Joseph than to the enthusiastic sympathy of the Belgians as so often alleged. Beaten at Jemmappes the Austrian armies had to preserve their communications by retiring on Aix-la-Chapelle.

Dumouriez declared that the French entered Belgium "as allies and as brothers," but while he was in the north, carrying the French frontier to the Rhine, the troops left in Belgium, and especially those in Liége, committed many excesses. The Convention, in reply to the request of certain Belgian deputies, elected at Brussels and Tournai, declared that the Belgians were not yet entitled to complete freedom, because they retained certain prejudices which might prove dangerous for liberty. It was laid down by the extraordinary fanatics then in power at Paris that Belgium must undergo a preliminary process of plunder and spoliation before it would be entitled to enjoy republican liberty! Thirty commissaries were sent to the Low Countries to give effect to these decisions. The Church, the nobles, the wealthier citizens, who by a stretch of words could be included in the term aristocrats, were specially marked out as victims of republican fury. The Guillotine was erected on the Grand Place of Brussels. There descended on the abbeys and chateaux of Belgium a band of iconoclasts who worked more destruction than had marked any invasion since the time of the Valois. In a little time the French became an object of hatred, and all the efforts of Dumouriez to counteract this policy and to fulfil his promises proved futile. He paid the Belgians compliments by declaring that throughout history they had been "good, frank, brave, and impatient of any yoke," but he could not protect their lives and property against his own countrymen.

The year 1793 opened with the execution of Louis XVI., the declaration of war by England and the reappearance of Allied troops in the Netherlands. Dumouriez endeavoured to complete the conquest of Holland with the intention, it has been said, of creating a military power which would enable him to put down the Republic in France and establish there a constitutional monarchy, but although he gained some successes the defeat of the French round Liége, and the occupation of that city by an

AUSTRIAN RULE RESTORED.

Austro-Prussian army compelled the abandonment of his fanciful schemes for the practical work of securing his own retreat. He endeavoured also to propitiate Belgian opinion by promising the people protection, and his personal influence availed to arrest the popular rising that was being organised throughout Belgium. One week after his arrival in Brussels he risked a battle against the Allied army at Neerwinden, and was completely defeated by Prince Frederick of Saxe Coburg and Clerfayt. In this battle the Walloon or Belgian regiments* in the Austrian service specially distinguished themselves. The forbearance of the German commanders through their desire to promote the chimerical scheme of utilising Dumouriez for a restoration in France allowed the French army to make an unmolested retreat when it might have been destroyed. The French had thus only conquered Belgium in one year to lose it in the next.

The restoration of Austrian rule was rendered popular by contrast with French excesses, and if it had been maintained it might again have become consolidated, although the Austrian Government had begun to attach less value to the possession of the Low Countries. In fact, the Emperor Francis scarcely concealed his desire to exchange them for Bavaria. The recovery of Brussels was followed by the reassembly of the Council of Brabant to which Count Metternich repeated the old assurances of respecting the Constitution and received in return a subsidy of a million and a quarter florins towards the expenses of the War. But unfortunately Belgium was too much divided within itself to lend a solid support to any government. The movement which had begun for the raising of a national force to expel the French was not continued to prevent their return. The young Archduke Charles was hailed with some popular enthusiasm as Governor General, but Metternich, discouraged

---

* The story of the services of these regiments has been told at length by the (Belgian) General Guillaume. In 1792 they numbered eight regiments—five of infantry (Clerfayt, Ligne, Wurtemberg, Murray, and Vierset), one of cavalry (Dragoons of Latour), one of Chasseurs (Leloup), and one of garrison troops. The Prince de Ligne, son of the Marshal referred to, was killed at the head of his regiment during the 1792 campaign.

by the apathy of the people during the year 1793, decided to make a supreme effort by inducing the Emperor to come in person to visit his Belgian provinces. Francis arrived in April, 1794, at Brussels, where he was solemnly inaugurated as Duke of Brabant. An observer of the scene wrote these reflections upon it: "The buoyant joy of the people, the éclat and pomp of the ceremony, made a striking contrast with the circumstances which seemed to give warning that this solemnity would be the last of the kind that Belgium would ever see, and that the bonds with Austria were about to be broken for ever a few days after they appeared to be recemented in an indissoluble manner."

Francis prolonged his stay in Belgium until the beginning of June, by which time the fortune of war had declared itself in favour of the French. The divisions among the Allies, the insincerity of Austria's own policy, and the holding back of the Prussian army, were as responsible for French successes as the military skill of Pichegru, who succeeded to the command when Dumouriez, to save his head, crowned his intrigues by openly deserting the Republic. Clerfayt, with very inferior numbers, more than held his own against Pichegru, and if he had been properly supported the campaign of 1794 would have equalled that of 1793 in point of success. The only one of the Allies in earnest was the English, and their army was too small, and the military talent of their commander, the Duke of York, too mediocre, to obtain any satisfactory result. The Austrians, ostensibly the most interested persons in the question, came to the deliberate decision, in a Council at Tournai, presided over by the Emperor in person, to evacuate Belgium. On 26th June the last battle of the campaign was fought at Fleurus, when the Austrian army allowed itself to incur a nominal defeat. It was then withdrawn by Imperial orders to the Rhine. The Anglo-Dutch troops unable to continue the struggle alone retired by way of Antwerp into Holland. The French re-entered Brussels on 9th July, and before the end of the month Antwerp and Liége had received their garrisons. The war in the Low Countries was over, but a Belgian historian, M. Juste, has justly observed that his countrymen were indebted to the Emperor Francis for having saved them from the excesses of the Reign of Terror. During the despotic and bloody rule of Robespierre the Austrians occupied Belgium ; on the very day that the French recovered Liége Robespierre fell from power. The Netherlands were consequently spared on this occasion a repetition of the excesses which had marked the first French occupation of 1792-3.

CHAPTER XV.

French Rule in Belgium.

THE weak policy and relaxed energy of Austria rather than the victory of Fleurus brought about the establishment of the French government in Belgium for the first and only time in its long and chequered history. France had indeed given it the Burgundian dynasty, but that family had pursued a far more anti-French policy than any Belgian ruler. And now after the lapse of so many centuries, Belgium was declared to be united with France by the law of 9th Vendemiaire, in the 4th year of the Republic. We have seen how tenaciously the Belgians had clung to their old rights and constitution, on which they would not allow a reforming Emperor to lay a finger even by way of improvement. Their new experience must have given some of them reason to regret the change of masters, for without a moment's thought for "joyous entries" and "calfskins" the law mentioned abolished the constitutions of the Austrian Low Countries, Liége and Stavelot. A few days later the French Constitution of the year 3 was applied to Belgium by publication, and thenceforward for nearly twenty years Belgium changed its constitution with the changes in France as it passed from Directory to Consulate and from Consulate to Empire.*

Nor did the Austrian Provinces stand alone. Separated from the Northern Provinces at the time of the rising against Spain, they were now to be re-united in a common bondage under France. The bondage was not the less complete, because it bore the names of "liberty, fraternity, and equality." These

* An indispensable work to consult on the subject is *La Constitution Belge* by Gustave Beltjens, continued, after his death, by J. Godenne.

cries had fascinated a portion of the Dutch population as they had done the nations further south, and the desire to shake off the old regime was hardly less pronounced against Orange than it had been against Bourbon. The anti-Stadtholder party were the allies of the French Republic, and thought nothing of that patriotism which had glowed so brightly in the 16th century. They were fighting for an idea and a shadow, and not for national rights and the substantial privileges of independence. Their experience was to cure them of illusions, but while they lasted they contributed to the easy triumph of the French. The winter that followed the occupation of Belgium was among the most severe on record. The Meuse and the Rhine were frozen so hard that they provided a high road for the French armies into Holland. As Pichegru advanced the Dutch republicans revolted at Amsterdam, the Hague, and other cities, and did his work for him. The world had not to wait till the year 1795 for evidence of Dutch ingratitude to the House of Orange. The flight of William V. and his family in a herring boat from Scheveningen to England may be said to have been the consummation of the national ingratitude which had been first displayed when the States abolished the Stadtholdership in 1650, and again a second time in 1702. The establishment of the Batavian Republic, while it lasted, secured for Holland a superior position under the French domination than was possessed by Belgium, which was at once reduced to a state of complete dependence.

In Belgium the French declared that there were too many sympathies and ties with the aristocracy for it to be accorded the equal rights of a republican government, and in consequence an ingenious and terrible form of human tyranny was introduced with the ostensible purpose of improving the principles of the unfortunate Belgian people. Improving the principles of the Belgians meant wholesale confiscations, summary arrests and the ruthless destruction of its chateaux and abbeys. Then the incendiary and the robber laid their hands on the beautiful church and convent of Orval, and on many stately castles too numerous to name, but it is only right to record that all the breakers of images were not French, and that some of them were Belgian zealots, and furious political doctrinaires. Protest was as much out of the question as resistance, for there sat at Brussels a criminal tribunal whose special mission was to judge and punish summarily any opponents or critics of the Republican administration. For the first year after Fleurus the Belgians suffered a more odious tyranny than they had experienced since the time of Alva. They were compelled to accept assignats at their full face value, and at the same time to pay their own taxes and subsidies in money. When the taxes were not forthcoming the heads of families were summarily arrested and interned in a fortress. It is said that the forced levies of the French in the first seven months of their rule were not less than eighty million francs, and these " military contributions," as they were termed, were raised in a country barely recovered from a civil war and two foreign invasions. The export of specie to France practically drained the country of its currency, and at last even the Convention had to listen to the complaints poured into its ears from municipalities as well as private citizens. Having squeezed the sponge dry, the French were willing to assume that Belgium had purged itself of its royalist proclivities, and was worthy to be enrolled in the ranks of Republics. Some members wished it to be a separate Belgian Republic, but the Committee of Public Safety opposed this project on the ground that it would be dangerous for Belgium, because it could not hold its own against the power of its late tyrants, and dangerous for France, because it might join the Batavian Republic at some future time against her. The Act of 9th Vendémiaire, 1795, settled the question as stated in the first lines of this chapter by incorporating Belgium in the French Republic.

Europe was unable to interfere with an arrangement which disturbed the balance of power and made France preponderant. The ruler of Austria had of settled purpose withdrawn from the Netherlands; by the Treaty of Campo Formio, which closed the unfortunate campaign of 1797, he formally surrendered the rights he had never valued to France. This confirmation of the conquest stifled whatever hopes the Belgians may have entertained of establishing an independent administration of their own. French military power could no longer be denied and was moving rapidly towards absolute supremacy on the Continent, while England was devoting herself more resolutely to the acquisition of colonies, including the Dutch, and of the mastery of the seas. Pitt looked elsewhere than the Low Countries in his wish to humble France, and no outside aid or encouragement was ever vouchsafed to the Belgian people in their efforts to free themselves from a tyranny that bore so heavily upon them. The want of patriotism of the Belgians became a favourite phrase, and a belief in the accuracy of the charge produced a certain impression in diplomatic circles, but a closer examination of the facts will show that the accusation is unjust, and that the Belgians, abandoned by Europe, did make an effort to recover their lost liberties.

The first ebullitions of popular discontent were due to the terrible distress caused throughout the country by French exactions, and by the cessation of trade with England. Holland had lost some of her colonies, and communications with the rest were controlled by the operations of British cruisers. The connection with France brought all the Provinces nothing but loss and inconvenience, but it weighed most heavily on Belgium which had no outlets, for the formal proclamation of the freedom of the Scheldt under French protection meant nothing, as the river was effectually closed by the British fleet. Driven by distress, caused by the absence of work and the interruption of the country's trade, large bodies of men took to the forests with which the country was then covered, and in the famous wood of Soignies, which extended from Brussels to Waterloo without a break in those days, one of the largest bands had its headquarters. They terrorised the whole country. Travellers were not safe, small parties of French soldiers were cut off, and what these desperate men could not get by work they got by pillage. That they were badly armed goes without saying, and may be inferred from the name of garrotters by which they were best known. They were a public evil and menace; they were also a proof of the evils under which the whole country was suffering.

Matters were in this pass when a new act of the French

Government added fuel to the flame. In 1798 orders were issued to enforce the law of military conscription. Even if French rule had been popular and of a character to command appreciation and respect, the conscription would have been unpopular in Belgium, where the objection to a standing army was deep rooted and found a place in the constitutional rights of the country. But as French rule was deeply unpopular—all the romance of the rights of man and human equality having been dispelled by a very brief experience of the reality of Republican government—the new law was openly resented and opposed. It was the signal for a popular rising which, if it had found leaders and outside support, might have made the Peasants' War of 1798 historically important and epoch-making. In north Brabant, especially in the region of moors and marshes called Campine, the insurrection may have been termed general, but it was always confined to the villagers, farmers, and farm labourers. Only one man of superior birth, the Baron de Meer de Moorsel, associated himself with the movement, and he was captured soon after the outbreak began and shot by the French. Notwithstanding the absence of leaders, and the scarcity of arms, the insurgents offered a stout resistance to the French forces. They even captured Malines, but had to evacuate it. At Louvain, Diest, and Hasselt they fought engagements which might almost be termed battles, but their rude and untrained courage was no match for the discipline of the French regulars, who classed the Belgian peasants under the common head of brigands, and shot them down indiscriminately. Hundreds were slain on the field of battle, hundreds more were shot when the fighting was over, and if the Belgian magistrates had not made a stand on behalf of their unfortunate fellow-countrymen hundreds more would have been handed over to the executioner. One Judge protested that he would not be a party to any assassination, and another, Deswerte, summoned to Paris to explain before the Five Hundred why he had acquitted a priest accused of inciting his people to rebellion, proudly declared that "We Belgian Judges have learnt in our courts of justice that Judges before applying the law should examine if it has been published in the form decreed by the Constitution of our country. We applied that principle to the present case. This opinion is erroneous in the Republican constitution, but it was not in that of Belgium." Deswerte was fortunate enough to save his head where a less open defiance had often entailed decapitation.

But even his courageous effort did not greatly avail his unfortunate countrymen, who continued to be shot on sight within what was termed the disturbed area, until at last, in 1799, it was declared that an end had been made of the brigands.* The Conscription was then accepted and enforced throughout Belgium, and shortly afterwards the Walloon regiments† in the Austrian army were disbanded under the Treaty of Luneville, leaving Belgium entirely free as a recruiting ground for the French.

The two years between the treaty of Luneville and the rupture of that of Amiens were the most prosperous for Belgium during the whole period of the French occupation. The opening of the Scheldt, however temporary, sufficed to revive the waning prosperity of Antwerp where in a single year of peace (1802) nearly a thousand ships entered from the sea as against a single ship in the year 1798. At this period the population of Antwerp was 54,000, while that of Brussels reached 66,000, and of Ghent 55,000. Brussels, although it had lost its pride of place as a capital, being included in the Department of Jemmappes, was still one of the gayest cities of northern Europe. Even the state of siege established during the continuance of the Peasants' War did not rob it of its gaiety. The advent of Napoleon to power undoubtedly increased the popularity of the French in Belgium, and it cannot be disputed that his appreciation of the importance of their country was very gratifying to Belgian self love. At the time of the Treaty of Luneville, and before he had even set foot in Belgium, Napoleon, then General Bonaparte, declared that "France would never cede her rights in, nor renounce the possession of Belgium." The course of history showed clearly that she had

* Consult *La Guerre des Paysans*, par A. Orts.

† These regiments were reincorporated in the French army, and took a prominent part in the Spanish and Prussian campaigns of the Emperor. Consult General Guillaume's works on the subject.

no rights, and that her possession, established for the first time since Cæsar, was upheld by the sword alone.

None the less, Napoleon's appreciation of the importance of Belgium was gratifying to its people and promised them a return of prosperity. Soon after assuming the title of First Consul he paid his first visit to Belgium, and he proceeded direct to Antwerp, which he had declared he would make the metropolis of Europe. His progress through Belgium resembled a triumph. The people acclaimed him with enthusiasm, partly due, no doubt, to the brilliant reputation he had gained by so many military triumphs culminating in Marengo, but chiefly to be attributed to the popular expectation that a ruler had appeared at last who was desirous to promote the true interests of the country. It would be absurd to see in the welcome of the young French conqueror any deficiency of patriotism among Belgians. Who had a claim on their loyalty? Certainly not the Austrian rulers whose policy, for fifty years before their disappearance, had always contained, like a card up their sleeve, a project for exchanging the Low Countries with Prussia or with France for a province or a kingdom in Germany. Any hopes that the Belgians might entertain in the year 1803 centred in the person of the First Consul, and the realisation of his schemes.

Napoleon passed three days at Antwerp, examining the fortress and the port with the greatest care. He laid the foundation of the Arsenal, he ordered the construction of a dock which was to bear his name, and he also gave instructions for the making of a road between Antwerp and Amsterdam, thus decreeing that the two commercial rivals should be allies. His intentions with regard to Antwerp were far more vast than what he actually accomplished. The plans that were only partially realised formed the substance of many of his conversations later on at St. Helena. They aimed at making Antwerp a base for defensive and offensive measures, and on extending the city to the left bank of the Scheldt, and its quays down the river to the sea. The enceinte of the fortress was to be extended so as to enable an army of one hundred thousand men to be sheltered behind it. These projects, conceived as early as 1803, enlarged in 1808, were never executed in their entirety, although the official description of the Empire given by Count Montalivet, in 1813, recorded that over two millions sterling had been expended on Antwerp, and that a further outlay of the same amount had been sanctioned. Napoleon's schemes for the extension of the city to the left bank have been revived in recent years by the distinguished engineer officer, General Brialmont, who has proposed to connect the new city on the left bank with that on the right by a tunnel under the Scheldt.

After concluding his visit to Antwerp Napoleon, accompanied by his wife Josephine, proceeded to Brussels, where he was received with much enthusiasm. The crowd extended for a league outside the Gate of Laeken, along the Antwerp highway, to witness the passage of the First Consul, and of his escort composed of 12,000 veterans of the Italian campaigns. Brussels was still a walled city, and the *Allée verte* formed the principal approach to the lower town. Here a triumphal arch was erected in imitation of that of Titus at Rome, and on the stage and in the gazettes the French General was openly compared with the Roman hero. The façade of Ste. Gudule bore a placard with the words "He restored with his triumphant hands the ruins of the sanctuary." In the First Consul the Belgian people saw what they had long been seeking, the restorer of their decayed fortunes and prosperity. When he entered the city, riding on horseback in a plain uniform, dusk had fallen (21th July), and every house along the route promptly illuminated. The clergy of the Cathedral in full canonicals received him at the steps of Ste. Gudule. During the period of his stay in Brussels fête succeeded fête, and the whole city gave itself up to popular rejoicings. Actors, including the famous Talma, were brought from Paris to amuse the gay citizens, and a topical play entitled "The Joyous Entry" was performed at the Monnaie Theatre to give special distinction to the occasion, and perhaps to remind the French general of the past glories of Brabant. Napoleon's first visit to Belgium was brought to a conclusion under the most agreeable circumstances, and he left the country more than ever determined that it should remain an integral part of France.

A few months after his return from Brussels Napoleon became Emperor, and his brief popularity in Belgium began to fade very soon after, through the increased exactions rendered necessary by the enlargement of his ambitious schemes, and also through the disastrous consequences, especially to Belgium, of the continental blockade. The grandiose projects for making Antwerp the port of the Continent were idle and abortive so long as the British fleet commanded the high seas. But the chief cause of the decline of Napoleon's popularity in Belgium was the opposition of the priests, irritated and rendered hostile by Napoleon's treatment of the Pope. But if his reputation waned in Belgium, it disappeared in Holland, where a succession of important events had occurred that must be passed in review.

After the French military success, in 1795, Holland had retained a large measure of independence under the name of the Batavian Republic. Its external history was represented by the loss of its fleet, trade, and all its colonies excepting the island of Java, which it was destined to lose at a later stage of the question. Its internal history somewhat resembled that of France in showing the progress from a free republic to a dictatorship. The Pensionary Schimmelpenninck emulated on a small scale the example and rise of Napoleon. Napoleon did not wish for imitators, and having broken up the Third Coalition at Austerlitz, despite the annihilation of his fleet at Trafalgar, he began a series of intrigues intended to create another kingdom for his family in Holland. Brantsen, the Dutch ambassador at Paris, seems to have been the intermediary chosen by the Emperor for the subversion of the Batavian Republic, and with characteristic reticence he kept the plot concealed from his brother Louis on whom he had fixed in his mind for the occupant of the new throne. A deputation composed of representatives of the French faction at the Hague came to Paris to solicit a monarch at the hands of the World's conqueror, and Louis was informed that the Emperor had decided to place him at the head of a new Dutch kingdom. Louis, the favourite of his brother and "the best of the Bonapartes," would have refused the offer, and he even went so far as to say that a member of his family was not qualified to play the part of a King, but Napoleon cut short these objections by declaring that "a subject should obey." It was as a subject of the French despot, therefore, that Louis Napoleon ascended the throne of Holland in the year 1806, soon after the second and final occupation of the Cape of Good Hope by the British. In the Treaty of June, 1806, it was stated among other things that "only an hereditary government could guarantee the tranquil possession of all that is dear to the Dutch people." Deferring to the wish of the High Powers, the Emperor allowed his brother Louis to accept the dignity of hereditary and constitutional King of Holland. In order to demonstrate that the Constitutional kingdom of Holland was to be none the less a vassal kingdom of the French Empire its King was to be in perpetuity "Constable of France."

Louis had been forced into accepting the throne of Holland, but he satisfied his conscience by deciding with himself to spare no effort to be a model king, and his success can hardly be disputed seeing that he left in Holland the best impressions, and that he is called in popular histories "the gentle King Louis." He began his reign with declarations of a patriotic character and indicated his wish and intention to be a national sovereign, and not a mere nominee of his brother. He adopted the Dutch cockade, refused a French escort in favour of a Dutch, and made all his officers declare that they had become Dutchmen in sentiment and interests. The vehemence of his reply to the States General on taking the oath that he had not only become Dutch but would always remain Dutch, carried conviction with it, but notwithstanding this sincerity his reception, by his own description, was cold and reserved. It could not well have been otherwise. The connection with France had destroyed the commerce of the country, and in a state which had been notoriously prosperous, and among a people who valued material prosperity more than any other possession, there was much distress and suffering. Louis turned his attention to the remedy of those evils. He began by inducing his brother to remove the French garrison, and he commenced the organisation of a National Dutch army. But he very soon came into collision with the Emperor, who wished the Dutch army and fleet to be of far greater numerical strength than Louis thought the finances of the State could bear. Pending the coercion of Louis to his views by moral or physical pressure, the Emperor retained the French garrison in Walcheren. Perhaps he foresaw the possibility of an English expedition to the Scheldt.

More serious differences arose between the two brothers when war broke out with Prussia at the close of 1806. Louis wished to remain neutral because Dutch interests were not affected. The Emperor ordered him to send his troops to the Wesel, and when there he placed them under French generals. Still greater dissension was caused when Louis flatly refused to become a party to the famous blockade of the British Isles with which Napoleon endeavoured to crush their power and prosperity. The King of Holland had the courage to declare that this measure would complete the ruin of his country, and as the maximum of concession he could only be induced to give the order partial effect. But Napoleon was not the man to brook opposition from any one, and especially from a relative whom he had set upon a throne. He told the Dutch representative at Paris that "Your King wishes then to favour the English," and in his private letters he declared that it was clear that Louis had ceased to be a Frenchman in becoming a Dutchman. Resenting the partial manner in which his orders were carried out he inflicted personal slights on the King for having created the grade of Marshal in the Dutch army, and an Order of his own. Louis offered to abdicate, but the Emperor would not allow him to do so, because his plans for the incorporation of Holland with France were not yet ripe. But a few months later he offered to transfer Louis to the throne of Spain. Louis made a proud reply to this effect: "I am not the Governor of a Province. There is no promotion possible for a King except to Heaven. How could I ask another nation to give me its oaths of allegiance when I had not kept my own to the Dutch?" This reply, creditable to Louis's right feeling, was not palatable to the Emperor; but, as a Dutch historian has remarked, it evinced a misconception of Louis about his own position in

Holland. The only reason for his being there was the command and power of Napoleon. The Dutch did not want him at all.

An interruption was caused in the progress of the question by the campaign of 1809, when Austria made a supreme effort against Napoleon. The English undertook to throw a large expedition on the continent, and Antwerp, where the Emperor's projects had begun to appear formidable, was selected as its object. How lamentably this expedition, associated with the name of Walcheren, failed is matter of history, while there can be no difference of opinion that, if it had been properly led, it would have captured Antwerp with little difficulty. The delays of the commanders gave the French time to bring up troops and prepare their defences; the English fleet sailed away after capturing Flushing, and throwing a few shot into one of the forts on the Scheldt. Yet it was well known that, if Antwerp had been taken, Holland would have risen the next week.

The consequences of the 1809 campaign were to make Napoleon feel secure in Austria, and more resolute towards Holland. He summoned Louis to Paris, and in one of his first conversations the Emperor declared "Holland is altogether an English colony, and a greater enemy to France than England is. I wish to swallow up Holland." He developed this idea by declaring that "in reality Holland is only a portion of France—the alluvion of the Rhine, Meuse, and Scheldt which are the great arteries of the Empire." In the hands of the tyrant, Louis still remained true to his duty towards his adopted country and he sent his ministers warning of what was impending. The Emperor had decided to unite Holland with France as he had done in the case of Belgium. In March, 1810, Louis signed a treaty surrendering the southern part of his kingdom, including North Brabant and Zealand. These concessions did not satisfy Napoleon, who was irritated by the cool reception shown him during a visit to the ceded provinces by the Dutch population, and he decided to place a French garrison in Amsterdam which Louis had made his capital. This brought matters to a climax. Louis abdicated in favour of his son Louis, long afterwards the restorer of the Second Empire, and fled secretly from Amsterdam to Bohemia on 3rd July. Six days later the remaining provinces of Holland were united with France.*

The time had not arrived for Napoleon to feel all the consequences of irritating the nations subjected for a moment by his military power, and he reproached the Dutch representatives and people with ingratitude for not having appreciated his efforts to conciliate their interests and those of the Empire. Silence was the only possible reply to the despot who, with all his power and with the Continent at his feet, could not protect the only interests in which the Dutch felt any concern, colonies and trade. Napoleon said with a truth that is of permanent force and application:—"Holland could not retain her independence after the annexation of Belgium to France." The Dutch saw their colonies follow their independence; the very year of the proclamation of the Empire at the Hague and Amsterdam, Java, the pearl of her possessions, was taken from its Franco-Dutch garrison by the British. The French occupation of their country brought the Dutch nothing but loss. It could not but create a bitter feeling of resentment which at the first outside encouragement broke forth in open insurrection.

In the meantime French rule had become fairly consolidated in Belgium. There was throughout the greater part of the country a common language. Both peoples held the same religious belief, and the Emperor had modified his anti-Papal policy. He was no longer aggressively anti-religious, and he constantly urged his brother in Holland to employ Roman Catholics and not Protestants. Moreover, a very considerable Belgian contingent served in his armies. How numerous it was may be gathered from the fact that after the abdication of Fontainebleau over 2,000 Belgians, decorated with the Legion of Honour, returned to their homes. The fascination of the Emperor's military glory was consequently felt in Belgium scarcely less than in France. Moreover, the French occupation

* In a very characteristic letter Napoleon replied as follows to the representations of General Lebrun as to the distress and discontent in Holland. "You speak to me of the complaints of the citizens of Amsterdam, of their disquietude, their discontent. Do the Dutch take me for their Grand Pensionary Barneveldt? I will do what is proper for the good of my Empire, and the clamour of senseless men who think they know better than I what is proper inspire me only with contempt."

had not entailed any direct loss on Belgium. She had no colonies to lose, her external trade had been cut off by the closing of the Scheldt, and so far as words went France had removed that impediment. Then Belgium had no tangible, definite independence to lose like that of Holland. She possessed no national family such as that of Orange to personify her history. There was no reason why French rule in Belgium should not have been popular, and if it was not it must have been largely due to its own shortcomings.

Up to a certain point, then, it is true to say that the French occupation of Belgium excited no active hostility as was the case in Holland. Napoleon personally enjoyed the popularity due to his military success and reputation, and this sentiment was in full force when he paid his second visit to Brussels in 1810. On this occasion he was accompanied by the Empress Marie Louise, and no doubt the presence of the Austrian princess evoked some loyal memories to the House of Austria, especially among the aristocracy. The Emperor's residence in Brussels was marked by a succession of fêtes, including gala performances at the old Monnaie theatre, and he affected a special partiality for the palace of Laeken, where he conceived the fatal design of invading Russia. His second visit to Belgium marked the highest point of his popularity in that country, and it soon afterwards began to decline.

Circumstances made the rule of France oppressive. The showy Empire was at the heart rotten. There was an absolute dearth of money, the taxes were crushing, and trade practically did not exist. Belgium had been drained of its specie and resources; yet the exactions continued, and of all the burdens none was so severely felt or bitterly resented as the unpaid-for maintenance of the very considerable French garrison retained in a country that, after the Peasants' War, had not attempted the least opposition. The necessities of the Empire, the drain on its resources in Spain, and the preparations for the war with Russia led to an increase in the demands for men and money from which Belgium escaped no more than France. A little military glory was not distasteful to the Belgians, but when they found that every other interest was sacrificed to it the glamour of the Imperial legend wore off, and everybody became more or less discontented. The Belgians had some special grounds for dissatisfaction. They had become part of the French Empire, but they liked to preserve their national individuality. This natural sentiment was one that the Emperor could not understand, and it certainly ran counter to all his plans of amalgamation between the two peoples. Among the most unpopular of all his measures with this object was that requiring the Belgians of the upper and middle classes to send their eldest sons to receive their education for the army at St. Cyr and other military schools in France. The resentment of the Belgians towards the French was increasing. It was less apparent than that of the Dutch, but it was none the less genuine and deep. Far from there being a prospect of amalgamation, the sentiment of cleavage and difference had acquired fresh force between Belgians and Frenchmen.

But if the Belgians were getting ripe for revolt they also realised very clearly the strength of the French position and their own weakness, which was indisputable. Rapsaet, a contemporary writer, puts the difference between Holland and Belgium very clearly in the following passages from his Memoirs. "If Belgium had revolted it would infallibly have been put to fire and sword by the French. French armies, more or less considerable, pressed back from all sides, bordered our frontiers, and all of them had to traverse Belgium in their retreat. Strong places held by numerous garrisons were in our midst, and would have suppressed or crushed our least efforts. Besides, the French system of deception and perfidy only let us know what it was impossible to conceal, and deceived us equally by its silence and its lies. We knew not the details of the rising in Holland. We felt our impotence."

Evidence of the failure of French rule to benefit the country was found in the decline of the population, especially marked in the chief cities. With the exception of Antwerp these showed a decline of from twenty to twenty-five per cent. for the period of the French occupation. During the last two years of its existence French rule in Belgium became an absolute tyranny. The situation was aggravated by the importation of the religious question. In 1813, after the Russian expedition, when Napoleon's military reputation was shaken, he took a step which profoundly irritated the Belgians. He nominated himself, without reference to his prisoner the Pope, Bishops of Tournai and Ghent. The priests and congregations of those bishoprics refused to recognise them, and when the Bishops forced their way to the altars of their cathedrals everyone left the building. Napoleon ordered the arrest of some of the priests, the banishment of others, and the seizure of all young men over 18 among the congregations to form a regiment at Magdeburg. These measures were carried out, and increased the bitter feeling in the country, but the Belgians were helpless. They could, however, show indirectly the state of their feelings. Several officers of the customs at Antwerp were accused of peculation, and there seems to have been little or no doubt of their guilt, but the jury of that city acquitted them amid popular acclamations. Napoleon ignored the verdict and imprisoned the accused, a breach of the fundamental principle of his own laws which produced an immense impression in the country. Thiers in his history has given a striking picture of the sufferings of the Belgians at the hands of his countrymen. He specially denounces "the violent acts of the Prefets carrying off the children of the people for the conscription, those of the upper classes to the so-called schools of honour, torturing the families of those who did not answer the appeal by quartering troops on them, employing movable columns against the refractory, taking provisions, horses, cattle, under the name of requisitions. Added to these exactions were those of the secret police, collecting and magnifying the smallest gossip, and arbitrarily imprisoning on the least suspicion." All the Belgians could do was to offer a passive opposition. Taxes were only paid under extreme military pressure, of the thousands of conscripts seized to swell the Imperial armies the majority escaped en route. Belgium was ready to hail the arrival of a deliverer, although not ready or able to deliver itself.

The battle of Leipsig (16-19th October, 1813) was accepted in Holland as a signal for the recovery of its lost independence. Napoleon had deceived himself into believing that Holland was loyal to him. Curiously enough two of the chief administrators of Holland, Count de Celles and Baron de Stassart, were Belgians thoroughly devoted to Napoleon. The Dutch of all parties were irreconcilable towards the French Government, and before Leipsig the most influential among them had begun to plot for the restoration of the Prince of Orange, who had sought and found refuge in England nearly twenty years before. The chief of the plotters were Counts Van Hogendorp and de Limburg Stirum,* but it was the former who organised the whole movement. The total French garrison under Marshal Molitor towards the end of 1813 did not exceed ten thousand men, while the whole of the National Guard and a large number of volunteers had been organised for an insurrection. The withdrawal of the French garrison from Amsterdam for the purpose of a concentration at Utrecht encouraged the patriots to strike the first blow. Fifteen hundred national guards rose, and assumed the yellow cockade amid cries of "Long live Orange!" the Imperial ensigns were torn down and displaced, and the French Governor General made a precipitate escape. The Dutch with characteristic prudence became alarmed at their own success, for the rising at Amsterdam was premature, and it was fresh in their memory that a precipitate insurrection at Hamburg had recently led to the recapture of that town with severe reprisals. The French garrison was, however, thinking only of retreat, and a second rising at the Hague led to a general revolt throughout the country.

A provisional administration was formed in the name of the Prince of Orange, and delegates were sent to invite him back to his country. These were charged to say that they "counted on the generous help of England, which, if demanded by the prince, would be rendered more willingly and in greater force." Other delegates hastened to Munster to invite the Prusso-Russian corps under Bulow to come to the assistance of Holland. The Prince of Orange wrote from London expressing his gratification at the news and his intention to proceed to Holland without delay. A few days later an English frigate

* Here the rising of Holland is only briefly summarised, see for details *A Narrative of the late Revolution in Holland*, by G. W. Chad.

brought him to the Dutch coast, and he made his formal entry into the Hague on 1st December, 1813, when he was proclaimed Prince Sovereign of the Low Countries at both the Hague and Amsterdam. On the same date small detachments of the Allied troops had entered Amsterdam, and Bulow crossed the Rhine with his main force. The French garrison under Molitor retired to Naarden which, with Bergen-op-Zoom and Flushing, was held till the end of the war. About six thousand troops were sent from England to Holland, and the Prince of Orange* occupied himself with the task of raising a national army of twenty-five thousand men.

In the meantime Belgium, for the reasons given, had not attempted to emulate the Dutch rising. The French were too strong and the Belgians too weak, and Napoleon made peace overtures to the Powers on the basis of his retaining Belgium and surrendering Holland. England would not listen to this proposal, and it was rejected. The Ultimatum of Chatillon in January, 1814, called upon the French to evacute Belgium, and a few days later the battle of Hoogstraeten, in which the French were defeated, opened the road to the heart of Belgium. Bulow then issued a proclamation to the peoples of Flanders and Brabant, calling upon them to rise and "drive out the foreign hordes which occupy your hearths." On 21st January Liége was taken, but Antwerp, well defended by Carnot, repulsed a combined attack by Bulow and an English squadron under Graham. This repulse did not prevent the occupation of Brussels on 1st February, followed by that of Ghent, Mons, Courtrai, Tournai, and other towns in the course of the month. The French retained possession of five or six fortified places, of which Antwerp, Ostend, Maestricht, and Namur were the principal. Immediately after the occupation of Brussels, where the Allied troops were received with demonstrations of joy, the following Proclamation was issued in the name of General Bulow:—

* William Frederick, Prince of Orange, afterwards and, in history, best known as William I. of the Netherlands, was born in 1772. He was the son of William V., Stadtholder of the Provinces, and the Princess Sophia of Prussia, niece of Frederick the Great. He was also connected with Prussia by marriage, having married the daughter of King Frederick William the Second.

"All the nations of whom we have been the liberators have up to now shown a desire to participate in the great cause. Everywhere they have taken up arms, they organise, they march forward. Deputies arrived from all the Departments of Belgium prove to me that the inhabitants of these fine provinces are animated by the same spirit. The hope of shaking off the insupportable yoke of foreign tyranny gives them the necessary courage to become, following the example of their ancestors, their own liberators. I will reciprocate this fine spirit, and I will support this disposition with all my power as I advance. May that Belgium, once so flourishing, be again revived, but may it revive under the ægis of peace and tranquillity. Its independence is no longer doubtful, but hasten to merit it by the preservation of internal order, and by the organisation of military levies, which will fight for liberty and honour."

The representatives of the thirty-two principal families of Brussels were summoned to report on the subject of a provisional government, and they selected three of their number, the Duke de Beaufort-Spontin, the Marquis d' Assche, and the Marquis de Chasteler, to act as their spokesmen. All these were in favour of the restoration of Austrian rule and, indeed, the whole of the Belgian aristocracy was of this opinion. The Duke d' Ursel was, however, suspected of French leanings, and he was sent to Germany. The Duke d' Arenberg* was also suspected, but he was only placed under supervision. The Duke de Beaufort was made Acting Governor General, and in Belgium no one doubted that the Austrian rule would be restored. It was also thought that the old laws in favour of the Church, before the reforms introduced by Joseph II., would be revived, and colour was given to this belief by a letter to the Bishops and Vicars General from the Count de Robiano, the representative of the government in the absence of the Duke de Beaufort. In March, however, the Belgian nobles were superseded by the Dutch Baron de Horst on the nomination of the celebrated Prussian minister De Stein. Stein was in favour, not of the Austrian restoration nor yet of Belgian independence, but of the

---

* He married a niece of the Empress Josephine, raised a regiment for Napoleon, and was taken prisoner by the British in Spain. Several of the D'Arenberg family distinguished themselves in the French Imperial service.

union of Holland and Belgium under the House of Orange. He wrote—"My objection to little sovereign princes is known by everybody, but I make an exception in favour of the House of Orange."

In May, 1814, a step was taken which seemed to herald the certain return of Austria. Baron de Horst handed over the reins of government to Lieut.-General Baron de Vincent, of the Austrian service. Baron Vincent was another of the men, whose ancestors had gone to Austria from Ireland. At the same time the remaining French garrisons in Belgium surrendered on the removal of Napoleon to Elba. But the course of diplomacy did not favour Austrian pretensions. England, Prussia and even France, in the person of Talleyrand, favoured the extension of Holland so as to embrace Belgium. The Prince of Orange had even larger ideas wishing to create a perfect barrier state, subject to his sway, between France and Prussia. The Protocol of London—20th June, 1814—settled the question. Austria's claims were not to be revived, Holland and Belgium were to form one kingdom, and the fate of the Belgians was decided without their assent, "because they had not done enough on their own behalf to justify independence being conferred upon them." Yet there never has been any question that, so far as there was any opinion or wish in Belgium, it favoured an Austrian restoration. All the faults and shortcomings of the old regime would have been forgiven in a wave of revived loyalty to the heirs of Burgundy and Flanders. The Church also, ever powerful in Belgium, strongly favoured the return of Apostolic rule as against union with a Protestant State. Its members knew well that equality of rights to all meant a loss of position and privileges to them, especially as they had been counting on a return to the position of half a century earlier. A few partisans declared that the Belgians would never accept the Dutch rule, but the supporters of Austria confined their efforts to a war of pamphlets, harmless at the time and now forgotten. Of all the champions of Austria the most unexpected was Van der Noot, who reappeared upon the scene for a few weeks as the ardent supporter of the cause he had done so much to injure and destroy more than twenty years before.

The will of the Powers was a law more powerful than any local considerations, even if they had been more pronounced and generally held than the representations of the rather exclusive Austrian faction could claim to be. The Austrian Government was less keen about taking over the Belgian provinces than those who wished to bestow them upon it. The Petition of eighty members of the old nobility demanded the restoration of the ancient privileges under the rule of an Austrian Prince, to be nominated by the Powers. It was replied with some point that the Batavian Constitution would assure to the Belgians precisely the same privileges, because the Dutch had successfully upheld them in the 16th century with their blood. An end was put to all uncertainty when, on 31st July, the Baron de Vincent handed over to the Prince of Orange the government of the country as Prince Sovereign of the United Provinces of the Low Countries. A Privy Council was formed, many of the nobles favourable to Austria rallied to Holland. Baron Capellen was appointed Secretary of State, and Baron de Tindal, who had served Napoleon and created the Young Guard, became High Commissioner for War. A separate arrangement was come to between England and Holland, by which some of the Dutch colonies were to be restored, and some were to be purchased. Java, Surinam, the Moluccas, and Curaçao were given back; the Cape of Good Hope, Demerara, Essequibo and Berbice were bought for two millions sterling. On 1st August the Prince, whose title was still indefinite, issued the following address to the Belgians on his arrival at Brussels:—

"Europe owes its deliverance to the magnanimity of the Allied Sovereigns, very shortly it will owe to their wisdom a political system which will assure to the disturbed nations long years of calm and prosperity. The new destinies of your fine provinces are a necessary element of this system, and the negotiations about to commence at Vienna will have as an object their recognition, and to consolidate the aggrandisement of Belgium in your interest, and in the interest of your neighbours, and that of the whole of Europe. Called to the government of your country during the short interval that still separates us from a future so long desired, I bring amongst you the wish to be useful to you, and all the sentiments of a friend, of a father. It is by the most enlightened, the most respected among you, that I wish to be surrounded in the honourable task imposed upon me by the confidence of the Allied Monarchs, and which I hasten in person to undertake. Cause the evils to cease which still weigh on the Belgians, despite the wise, firm, and loyal conduct of Baron de Vincent during the difficult period when he acted as Governor General! Honour and protect your religion! Surround the nobility with the distinction due to its antiquity and merit! Encourage agriculture, commerce, and all kinds of industry! Such are my duties, the most agreeable to me, and the cares which will occupy me unceasingly. Happy if in multiplying my titles to your esteem, I succeed in preparing and facilitating the union which should fix our fate, and which will permit me to join you in the same love with those people whom nature herself seems to have destined to form with the Belgians a powerful and prosperous state."

While the more intelligent members of the community were not indisposed to accept the new government, the mass of the people remained more or less indifferent, and the clergy headed by Prince Maurice de Broglie, Bishop of Ghent, showed themselves actively hostile. It was said that a spark would have sufficed to cause an explosion, but the progress of events and the return of Napoleon prevented its being applied. A large part of the garrison of Brussels was composed of British Guards and Hanoverian troops during the winter of 1814-5, and their presence contributed to the maintenance of peace and good order. The growing popularity of the Hereditary Prince, who was soon to receive the title of Prince of Orange by which he is known in history, also contributed to the preservation of tranquillity, but the causes that produced separation in 1830, and the dissolution of the Kingdom of the Netherlands were just as apparent in 1815, before it had even been created. On 24th February, 1815, the constitution of the Kingdom of the Netherlands was formally announced at Brussels amid considerable popular rejoicings. It had at least the merit of ending a period of tension and uncertainty, and a few days later the news of the return and landing of Napoleon turned every one's thoughts into a new channel.

Curiously enough the uncertainty as to what would be done with Belgium, and the perhaps exaggerated hopes raised by the opposition of the Prince de Broglie and his clerical friends, had encouraged the French to think that they might get a slice of the country or at least retain some influence over it. Their press began to ask the Belgians from what they had been delivered by the expulsion of the French, and to paint the French rule in attractive colours. The *Oracle*, the leading Brussels journal of the day, replied—"You ask from what we Belgians have been delivered? We reply, from chains, from prisons, from flying columns carrying despair across our country, from the prescription of our venerable bishops, from the horrible abuse of all power!" Whatever tendencies there might be in Belgium in other directions there were certainly none towards the restoration of a French Government. Whatever its merits might have been under a different set of circumstances, it presented in the eyes of the Belgians of 1815 a recent and real tyranny.

In the first phase of the French domination the excesses of the Republican zealots had stained the history of the country with deeds of blood, rapine, and destruction. In the second phase the Empire had constituted an organised tyranny, beginning with the heavy taxation necessary to support the ambitious schemes of Napoleon, and culminating in the violent appropriation of all the available wealth in the country, and its resources in men and money, for the salvation of an Empire built upon an insatiable lust of conquest until the inevitable moment of exhaustion and peril arrived. In the default of regular statistics it is difficult to arrive at the absolute truth, but the statement that France drew twelve millions sterling by way of subsidies and enforced loans from Holland, which was never so completely under her authority as Belgium was, strengthens the conclusion, formed on such evidence as is available, that Belgium contributed to the French Exchequer a total sum of twenty-five millions sterling. To appreciate the burden that that sum represented on a small country with a population which did not much exceed two millions of people, and without any foreign trade at all, is not difficult. Even the thrift and endurance of the Belgian agriculturist could not bear up under the burden of Imperial rapacity and extortion, and at the moment when French rule came to an end popular dissatisfaction even without national leaders was on the point of breaking forth in a fresh Peasants' War. This explains the readiness, if not enthusiasm, with which the Belgians co-operated in the opposition offered to Napoleon after his return from Elba, and the really extraordinary and undeniable fact that very few Belgians* amongst the thousands of old soldiers and officials in the country joined him after crossing the frontier in June, 1815. Briefly put, French rule in Belgium was not from any point of view a success. For all their sacrifices and sufferings the Belgians could only show that two thousand and sixty of their countrymen had received the Legion of Honour in fighting Napoleon's battles. It was a poor return for the loss of independence and national existence during twenty years of virtual slavery.

* It is said that 347 Belgians, who were ex-French soldiers, joined the Emperor and were formed into half a battalion at Lille. Nearly 4,500 Belgians fought at Quatre Bras and Waterloo.

CHAPTER XVI.

The Waterloo Campaign.

WHEN Napoleon landed from Elba the Powers in conference at Vienna had decided in principle on the enlargement of Holland by the addition of the Belgian provinces, and the old Seventeen Provinces, thus reunited after a separation of more than two hundred and thirty years, were to form a single Kingdom of the Netherlands under the descendant of William the Silent who might have anticipated this result if the Walloons and Flemings had supported him with the ardour and obstinacy displayed by the Batavians and Frisians. This new creation was still in an informal stage when the return of Napoleon brought Europe face to face with the peril from which she thought that she had finally escaped. Prompt action became necessary, and without waiting William caused himself to be proclaimed King simultaneously at Amsterdam and Brussels. This event occurred on 17th March, 1815, and contributed much to calm public opinion in Belgium and to give its people a definite object to fight for. In England the creation of the Kingdom of the Netherlands was hailed with special satisfaction. Lord Castlereagh declared that "We saw in a kingdom of the Netherlands a means of strengthening the balance of power in Europe. It is a kingdom powerful by all the resources of soil, commerce, and navigation. Art and nature must be united in placing it in a position to resist attack until other Powers can come to its aid."

The new kingdom, scarcely created, was at once exposed to all the perils of an imminent invasion. Belgium had granted shelter and hospitality to the fugitive King, Louis XVIII., whose court was established at Ghent after the withdrawal from Paris. The fallen Government had consequently fixed its abode at the door of France in the conviction that Europe would soon restore it; but Napoleon was convinced that in the Belgians he would find an ally and not a foe. Shortly after his arrival in Paris he wrote thus to Davoust, his War Minister: " Cause to be published on our frontiers from Lille to Landau a proclamation stating that all former soldiers of the left bank of the Rhine and of Belgium who served under our Eagles are taken back into our service, and are to rejoin the regiments that will be formed to receive them. This notice can be circulated by little hand-bills, and we shall very soon get from eight to ten thousand soldiers" It was, therefore, quite evident that the storm would burst in the first place over Belgium, where the political situation was far from consolidated, and where no absolute certainty could be felt as to the real tendency of popular opinion. Napoleon counted on the return of his old soldiers. Experience could alone prove that his expectation was not to be realised. As far as Belgian records show, not a single Belgian joined him, and this was very remarkable when we remember that there were over two thousand veterans wearing the Legion of Honour in the country, but the French claim that three hundred and forty-seven of these latter did rally to their old colours. Perhaps a still more remarkable proof of patriotism was furnished by the fact that all the generals and most of the regimental officers, Dutch as well as Belgian, who took part in the Waterloo campaign had acquired their military knowledge in the French service. To Napoleon's invitation to the Belgians to desert, the Brussels journals made a firm reply to this effect: " When the sword is drawn, and if the Orange flag leads us in the field, they will see on whose side there will be defection." The political firmness of King William, and the popularity of his son, the Prince of Orange, furnished the main explanation of the solidity shown by Belgium opinion in face of French blandishments.

But the storm approaching from the side of France required an army to repel it, and it was clear that the Powers would expect the Netherlands to take their share in resisting the common danger. The Dutch army had been raised to an effective strength of about twenty-seven thousand men, and as it had been under arms for nearly eighteen months it was far better organised, and in a condition of better cohesion than the Belgian portion of the Netherlands forces could be. The creation of a Belgian force was begun in the summer of 1814 by the Austrian Commissioners, Count de Murray and Baron Vincent, when it was thought that the authority of the old Empire would be restored. Two cavalry regiments, carabiniers and hussars, and two infantry regiments, linesmen and chasseurs, were raised from men who had served in the old Walloon regiments, first in the Austrian and latterly in the French service. A very considerable portion of these regiments were thus trained soldiers, and by the battle of Waterloo the recruits had had ten or twelve months' training. These regiments were the 2nd Carabiniers, the 8th Hussars, the 7th of the Line, and the 35th Chasseurs. At the time of William's proclamation as King another cavalry regiment—the 5th Light Horse—and several foot regiments had been raised, but the total regular regiments of Belgian composition did not, at the end of March, muster more than five thousand men.

This force was obviously quite inadequate for the occasion, and on 1st April, 1815, the King issued a proclamation stating that, "circumstances necessitating increase of forces, to assure the independence of the country and its security against invasion" a national militia of twenty-five thousand men was to be formed. The order was very well responded to, and the great cities like Liége stimulated patriotism by offering rewards to the first hundred or so who came forward to form a regiment, On 25th April King William entered into an engagement with England and Prussia to place fifty thousand men in the field and his efforts were greatly assisted by the zeal and cordiality with which the Belgians responded to his appeal. An indication of the awakening of Belgian national sentiment was furnished at Liége when the Saxon troops, probably worked upon by Napoleon's agents, mutinied and would have murdered Marshal Blucher, if he had not escaped by jumping out of the window of his hotel. During this disturbance the people of Liége, whose French sympathies had been suspected, rendered the Prussians the greatest assistance, and thus prevented a very serious outbreak that might have produced a disastrous effect on the fortune of the campaign. Two Saxon officers were shot, the Royal regiment of Guards was disbanded and the rest of the Saxon regiments were sent back to Dresden.

By the end of May the Netherlander army, divided into three Divisions, was drawn up a short distance north of the French frontier from the neighbourhood of Mons on the west to Genappe and Fleurus on the east, where it came into touch with the pickets of the Prussian army, Blucher having transferred his quarters from Liége to Namur early in that month. The three divisions were in order of rotation under the commands of Generals, Prince Frederick of Orange, Baron de Perponcher, and Baron Chassé. The chief command of the Netherlands army was held by the Prince of Orange, whose chief of the staff was Baron de Constant de Rebecque, an officer of much ability. The strength of the three Divisions was rather less than thirty thousand men, divided as follows: 23,440 infantry, 3,405 cavalry, 2,725 artillery with nine batteries of eight guns each.* It will thus be noted that the King of the Netherlands was not able to provide as large a contingent as he had engaged to do, but neither were the English. We had undertaken to supply an army of fifty thousand men for the defence of Belgium, but when Quatre Bras was fought only thirty-three thousand five hundred British troops had landed in the country, and of these not more than twenty-seven thousand reached the front in time for the fighting. The total force placed under the supreme orders of the Duke of Wellington numbered, with the Hanoverians, German Legion, Brunswickers and Nassauers totalling twenty-four thousand, a little more than eighty thousand men, and out of these must be deducted the First Division of the Netherlands army, numbering from twelve to thirteen thousand men, which by Wellington's

* Van Loben Sels. Another authority divides the army as follows:—Line infantry 8,684, Nassau Rifles 3,560, Militia Infantry 9,928, Cavalry 2,466, Artillery 2,000 and Militia Artillery 1,534, or a total of 28,172, as against 29,570 of Van Loben Sels. Another Dutch authority, Van Knoop, gives 31,499 officers and men, 7,450 horses, and 80 guns as the strength of the army. He divides the guns as follows:—48 6-pounders, 12 12-pounders, and 20 howitzers.

DD

orders and disposition was assigned an inactive rôle at Hal. This was the greater loss because it contained some of the best Dutch regiments, among others the Indian Brigade, a force of picked men intended to effect the reoccupation of Java. Two minor details deserve mention. The Duke of Wellington was made a Marshal in the Netherlands army at the time of his taking over the command of the Allied armies, and the King founded the William Order in order to stimulate the military spirit of his peoples.

Three months had nearly expired since the almost concurrent return of Napoleon and the proclamation of the Kingdom of the Netherlands, and not a shot had been fired on the frontier. Napoleon's efforts in that period were devoted to the collection and equipment of an army, while those of Europe were directed to the accumulation of an overwhelming force to deal finally with the deposed Emperor who by an extraordinary effort had regained France. These preparations on both sides demanded time, and when the Emperor was ready to begin his task at the commencement of June neither Austria nor Russia had been able to bring any of their troops close to the French frontier. In Belgium there were disposed for the defence of the country two distinct armies, one of eighty thousand men under Wellington, and another of one hundred and ten thousand men under Blucher. Of the latter army ten thousand were employed in holding Liége, and the line of communication with it. On the other hand Napoleon had succeeded in gathering together an efficient army of nearly one hundred and twenty thousand men besides providing garrisons for Paris and the fortified places on the northern frontier. Owing to Napoleon's belief that the Belgians would greet him with open arms strict orders had been given to abstain from all hostilities on the borders and to do nothing to irritate the Belgians. Up to the day after Quatre Bras Napoleon was fully convinced that the Belgians would join him, and described them as "brothers." Confident in his coming victory he even drew up a Proclamation to the Belgian people, calling on them to rise *en masse* against their Princes and tyrants, and he proposed to issue it from his "Imperial Castle at Laeken."

This document was captured in his coach after Waterloo. Some incidents had happened on the frontier that ought to have undeceived him as to Belgian sentiment. When the Duke de Berri escaped into Belgium he was closely pursued by a patrol of French cavalry which would certainly have captured him if a small body of the 7th regiment (Belgian) under the command of Lieut. Carrondal had not intervened and compelled the French to retire. The French officer offered Carrondal a captain's commission in the French army and the Legion of Honour if he would surrender the Duke de Berri, a proposal which was indignantly rejected. The gallant Carrondal was afterwards killed at Waterloo. Another incident occurred in the neighbourhood of Dunkirk, when a Customs officers named Piton, hearing that twenty cannon were being removed from that place to Lille, made a swoop upon them, and carried them off. The refusal of a trooper of the Marechaussé to be bribed by the younger Cambacéres, after he had been taken prisoner on 15th June, was further evidence that the spirit of the Belgians was aroused against the French. His retort, "I am a Belgian soldier, not a traitor" was a far more faithful expression of the views of his countrymen than the few shouts of "Vive l' Empereur" raised at Charleroi as the Emperor passed through the town after his cavalry had driven the Prussians back from the Sambre. The moment of disillusionment had not then arrived, although it was very near at hand.

Relying on the information of his spies, the principal of whom was a Parisian lady, the Duke of Wellington believed that the main French attack would be made by Mons and Nivelles, and his nervousness for his right flank is the only reasonable explanation that has ever been offered for his keeping the Division of Prince Frederick unutilised during the critical fighting of 18th June, when its arrival at Mon Plaisir, for instance, would have determined the discomfiture of the French army, even if Blucher had not been able to arrive as soon as he did. The same belief was responsible for Wellington's whole disposition of his force which made its concentration at Nivelles or Hal easy, but invested with difficulty the same operation at any point of the Charleroi route south of

Mont St. Jean. It is probable that Wellington would not have attempted to move his main body further south but for the necessity of keeping in touch with and covering the exposed right flank of the Prussian army, when Napoleon made his brilliant advance from Charleroi. Napoleon's strategy has been admired by every careful and unbiassed chronicler of the campaign. Here it is only necessary to make clear that the disposition of the Netherlander troops was such as to throw a tremendous strain on them alone, without the support of a single British regiment until half-past three in the afternoon of 16th June, the day of Quatre Bras.

Napoleon having reached Beaumont on the 14th June, orders were issued for the immediate advance of the French army on Charleroi. At three in the following morning the Prussian vedettes were driven off at Ham-sur-Heure, a few hours later a second cavalry fight occurred at Courcelles, and by eight o'clock the French army was marching through the streets of Charleroi. The Belgian Light Cavalry Brigade, considerably to the west at St. Symphorien aux Bergen, watching the Mons road, knew nothing of these events until the next morning when it received an order to retire as rapidly as possible on Nivelles. Having driven back the Prussian outposts, the main French army, under Napoleon, marched towards Fleurus, while the left wing, passing by Gosselies and Courcelles, aimed at capturing the position of Quatre Bras, the achievement of which object would keep the two portions of the French army in communication by the excellent chaussée from Nivelles to Namur, passing through Quatre Bras and Ligny.

No definite arrangements had been made by the Duke of Wellington for holding the position of Quatre Bras, but one of the brigades of the Perponcher Division, that commanded by Prince Bernard of Saxe Weimar, was bivouacked in the vicinity of those cross roads, or, to be more exact, along the high road from Charleroi to Brussels, between the villages of Frasne on the south and Genappe on the north. This brigade consisted of four battalions of infantry and one battery of artillery, without cavalry. One battalion and the battery were posted in advance on the slight acclivity above the village of Frasne. At

POSITION AT QUATRE BRAS.

six o'clock in the evening of 15th June Ney's advance guard reached Frasne, and the battalion—Nassau rifles of the Dutch army—began to retire on Quatre Bras, the battery helping very materially in keeping off the French cavalry. The two miles between Frasne and Quatre Bras were covered without any material loss, and the French made no attempt on the position which was held by Prince Bernard's three other battalions. At nine o'clock Prince Bernard sent the following account to his Divisional Commander, General de Perponcher, at Nivelles, distant six-and-a-quarter miles west of Quatre Bras:—

"I must confess to your Excellency that I am too weak to hold out here long. The two Orange-Nassau battalions have French guns, and each man has only ten cartridges. The Volunteer Chasseurs have carabines of four different calibres, and only ten cartridges per carabine. I will defend as well and as long as possible the posts entrusted to me. I expect an attack by the enemy at day-break. The troops are animated by the best spirit. The battery has no infantry cartridges."

Such was the force holding Quatre Bras on the night of 15th and 16th June, when Ney with an army of at least eighteen thousand men had reached Frasne, while his advance guard was in close contact with Prince Bernard's pickets at Quatre Bras. If he had pushed on at sunrise he would have swept Prince Bernard's force out of Quatre Bras, seriously compromised the concentration of Wellington's army, and completed the effect of Napoleon's victory at Ligny. Even Ney's dilatoriness would not have lost this advantage if General de Perponcher had not resolved to promptly reinforce his brigadier with the rest of his Division, and to make a determined effort to hold Quatre Bras until Wellington, with the English troops, could come to the rescue. News of the cavalry fights on the Sambre seems to have reached both Perponcher at Nivelles and Chassé at Binche about midday, and expresses were at once sent to Brussels, where Wellington appears to have received the first message as early as three o'clock. Nothing, however, could be done until more certain news had been received, and this certain news only reached Nivelles a little before ten on the night of 15th June.

Wellington's orders had been that, in the event of a French advance, the army was to concentrate at Nivelles and Hal. Had these instructions been obeyed Prince Bernard's force would have retired on the former place, Quatre Bras would have fallen into Ney's hands, and the Prussian right would have been at the mercy of the French. The credit of disobeying them must be divided between Perponcher at Nivelles and Constant de Rebecque at Braine le Comte. The latter writing to his commander-in-chief, the Prince of Orange, late at night on 15th June, said:—

"At this moment Captain Baron de Gagern has arrived from Nivelles reporting that the enemy has shown himself at Quatre Bras. I have thought it my duty to take it on myself to instruct General de Perponcher to support his 2nd Brigade with the 1st, and to warn the 3rd division and the cavalry in order to support them if necessary."

This document clearly shows that the major credit was due to Baron Constant de Rebecque. It was one of the happiest instances of disobeying superior orders on record, and obtained the special praise and gratitude of Gneisenau, Blucher's chief of the staff. We learn from the report of Baron Van Delen, chief of the staff of General Chassé, that the 3rd division, which had been moved from Fay to la Haine during the afternoon of 15th, on receipt of this order, began its march at daybreak to Nivelles, leaving a small force at Arquennes to cover the retreat of Van Merlen's cavalry, summoned in all haste from its position near Mons. Perponcher was unable to reinforce Prince Bernard as early in the morning of 16th as was desirable, because he could not abandon Nivelles until fresh troops were near enough to fill up the gap. The five battalions constituting his first Brigade—that of Van Bylandt—were moved to Quatre Bras gradually, the first reaching their destination at 10 o'clock, but the 7th Belgian regiment did not arrive till 3 o'clock having been detained at Nivelles till the absolute arrival there of part of the 3rd Division. Until that hour there were only eight battalions and two batteries holding Quatre Bras, where the Prince of Orange arrived at seven in the morning, and took command of the position.

BELGIAN CAVALRY.

Firing began at Quatre Bras about 9 o'clock, but it was only the firing of the advanced pickets, Ney's main force remaining two miles in the rear at Frasne during the earlier hours of the morning. It is impossible to explain Ney's inaction, but the fact remains that his serious attack on Quatre Bras did not commence before two o'clock, although slight skirmishing went on during the morning. Ney then endeavoured to make up for the loss of time by delivering his attack with exceptional fury. He directed upon the Netherland force the fire of fifty guns, and within a quarter of an hour of his arrival his attacks with both cavalry and infantry were repeated. The 5th Dutch militia suffered a good deal from the artillery fire, and while thus shaken were charged by the French cavalry. They broke and only escaped annihilation by finding shelter in the buildings of the farm of St. Pierre. The Prince of Orange sought to check the ardour of the French by leading a battalion to the charge. His horse was shot under him, he narrowly escaped being taken prisoner, and the effect was only momentary. It was now three o'clock, and it was perfectly clear to everyone that if aid did not come from somewhere the Perponcher division would be driven out of Quatre Bras, and once on the level ground from that place to the southern side of Genappe the numerous French cavalry could have easily cut it up. At this desperate moment aid did come in the almost simultaneous arrival of the seventh Belgian regiment and the cavalry under Van Merlen. The probability is that the seventh regiment arrived first, but some time was lost in establishing it in the wood of Boussu, and it is certain that the cavalry came soonest into action, and exercised the influence that saved the day.

The Van Merlen brigade consisted of two regiments—the 6th Hussars, a Dutch regiment, and the fifth Light Horse or Dragoons, a Belgian corps. Van Merlen had received the summons from Constant de Rebecque later than any of the other detached commanders, probably not before six o'clock in the morning of 16th June, and thirty-six English miles lay between him and Quatre Bras. Some troops were posted en vedette, and had to march forty miles, and passage through Nivelles was much impeded by the baggage of the third division. Still at three o'clock the cavalry came trotting along the chaussée from Nivelles. The present condition of Quatre Bras gives but an erroneous idea of what it was like on the day of the battle, for all the woods have been cut down. The Prince of Orange, seeing that the battle was lost in the centre, determined to employ this cavalry in a last effort to gain time by arresting the advance of the French along the main chaussée and across the

GENERAL VAN MERLEN.

fields between it and the road to Namur. Forming up on the Nivelles chaussée, but at the point of the cross roads, the leading regiment, which happened to be the Dutch Hussars, was ordered to charge down the slope in an oblique direction, parallel in fact with the Namur road, on the French who were pressing home their attack by overlapping the wood of Boussu, the last key of the position, behind the ground on which now stands the Brunswick monument. No hesitation was shown in making the charge, but it was wildly delivered as the horses were blown by their long march. It was described as being made *en fourrageurs*, and it was quite impossible for it to achieve any success beyond the immediate object of gaining time. As the regiment charged, it was exposed to the fire of the French guns, and before it reached the French infantry it was taken in flank by the French sixth Hussars, under Colonel de Faudoas, and badly cut up.

The Belgian fifth Light Horse were then ordered to charge in support of the brother corps, and they did so with considerable effect. There is an improbable legend about the French cavalrymen recognising them as Belgians, and inviting them to ride through their ranks. We will content ourselves with stating that a desperate melée took place, that the Belgians inflicted considerable loss on the French, and did not retreat until they were assailed by the Cuirassiers forming part of the cavalry division of Lefebvre Desnouettes.* As they rode back to cover in the woods the English troops of Pack's Brigade had just arrived, and mistaking them for French cavalry, greeted them with a volley. The losses of the two regiments were as follows. The Sixth Hussars lost three officers and one hundred and forty-one men killed, and six officers and sixty-four men wounded. The Fifth Dragoons lost eighty-one men killed, and two officers and seventy-four men wounded. Captain Crooy killed a French officer, Captain Van Remortére wounded another, Colonel de Merx was wounded in four places, and Captain Brion especially distinguished himself. All these officers were Belgians. The importance and the value of the double charge of Van Merlen's brigade was that it checked the French advance

---

* Colonel Van Zuylen van Nyevelt in his remarkable report of the campaign first published in my *Belgians at Waterloo*. The light cavalry "carried away by their impetuosity rushed too far forward and fell upon the 8th and 11th Regiments of Cuirassiers who, being far superior in numbers and arms, routed them completely with heavy loss."

and thus saved the day. General Van Merlen took part in it himself, and escaped without a wound only to meet with a more glorious death at Waterloo.

Up to the arrival of Picton's division shortly afterwards and probably at half-past three o'clock, and during the final passages of the charge thus described Quatre Bras had been held by Dutch and Belgian troops alone. The successive arrivals of Picton, nine thousand seven hundred men; the Brunswickers, seven thousand eight hundred men; and of Cooke's, Alten's, and other British troops, seventeen thousand five hundred, raised the Allied force to an equality with that of Ney, who was then driven back to his original position at Frasne. The Belgian battery of Stievenaar suffered very heavily in the fighting during the morning. Stievenaar himself was killed. Two of the guns were lost, one gun was disabled, the horses of three others were killed so that the guns had to be abandoned, and only two guns were saved by Lieutenant Winzinger to take part in the battle of Waterloo. The total loss of the Netherlands army at Quatre Bras was given at 1,031 men. Wellington writing to Lady Frances Webster advising her and her father, Earl of Mountnorres, to prepare to remove from Brussels to Antwerp as he might have to "uncover Brussels temporarily," described Quatre Bras "as a desperate battle in which I was successful."

The following is the official report of the Prince of Orange written to his father the King:—

Headquarters at Nivelles,
17th June, 1815, 2 o'clock in the morning.

The Prussian army was attacked on the 15th very early in the morning in its positions which it abandoned, and retired from Charleroi by Gosselies to the neighbourhood of Fleurus. As soon as I had knowledge of that attack I gave the necessary orders to the army corps under my command. The result of what had happened to the Prussian army was that the battalion of Orange-Nassau, which occupied the village of Fraisne (*sic* Frasne) with a battery of light artillery, was attacked on the 15th at five in the evening. The troops maintained themselves in the position on the heights of that village at a short distance from the road called Quatre Bras. Skirmishing ceased at this point at eight in the evening. As soon as I was informed of the attack I ordered the 3rd division, as well as the cavalry and two English divisions to advance to Nivelles, and the 2nd division to support the position of Quatre Bras. Only a part of the 2nd division could move at once, seeing that the brigade of Major-General De Bylandt could not leave Nivelles before the arrival of the other divisions there. The fire of the *tirailleurs* commenced yesterday morning at five o'clock at this point, and we carried it on on both sides till twelve o'clock without result. About two o'clock the attack became fierce, especially by the cavalry and artillery. The brigade of light cavalry under General Van Merlen could not arrive till nearly four o'clock. I had before this no cavalry to oppose the enemy. Seeing how important it was to preserve the position on the height of the road called Quatre Bras, I was fortunate enough to hold it against an enemy very superior in every respect. Having been attacked by the two army corps of D'Erlon and Reille and having succeeded in holding them in check, the Duke of Wellington had enough time to reunite sufficient forces to baffle the designs of the enemy. The result of this attack was that after an obstinate fight which continued till nine in the evening we not only stopped the enemy but even drove him back. . . . . I experience a keen pleasure in being able to inform Your Majesty that his troops, the infantry and artillery particularly, fought with much courage.

William, Prince of Orange.

Finally it may be stated that Gneisenau not only paid a special compliment to the quick strategical insight of Constant de Rebecque, but praised " the steadiness of the Belgian-Netherlands troops." At least one English officer who was present, Carmichael Smith, testified to the latter fact.

Early in the morning of the 17th Wellington learnt of Blucher's defeat at Ligny and that his own left flank was thus left exposed to attack by Napoleon. He accordingly withdrew by the main route to Mont St. Jean, where he had fixed on what he considered a good position for a battle, and at the same time he sent orders for Chassé's division to retire from Nivelles to Braine L'Alleud. The Belgians took no part in the skirmishing during the retirement of the 17th through Genappe to the position south of Waterloo, and consequently there is no need to attempt to describe their withdrawal with the rest of the allied army. When the allied army under Wellington was arrayed in its full strength on the morning of the 18th from Braine L'Alleud to the farm of La Haie near Frichermont the Netherlands part of that army consisted of the 3rd division, and the cavalry brigades of Generals Trip and Ghigny, all of which had not been under fire, as well as Perponcher's division from Quatre Bras and the remains of Van Merlen's brigade. The first division under Prince Frederick remained as explained at Hal. Sir Charles Colville, the English general with this division, was during the whole of the 18th at Tubise, $3\frac{1}{2}$ miles south of Hal, and 10 miles from the field of battle. Prince Frederick himself and the Dutch Generals Stedman and Anthing were further off at Clabbeck and Braine le Chateau. Anthing commanded the Indian Brigade, and the total strength of this division seems to have been 12,700 men, 2,906 horses, and 40 guns, with in addition a field park of artillery.

The Chassé division passed the night of 17th-18th in and round Braine L'Alleud where is now the nearest railway station to the field. As it did not come into action until late in the afternoon it will be better to pass on to the other sections of the force. The brigade of Prince Bernard of Saxe Weimar, which had suffered most at Quatre Bras, was posted on the extreme left, in the least exposed position, near Papelotte and Frichermont. Of the four battalions one—that of the Orange-Nassau rifles—was detached and placed in the wood of Hougomont (more correctly Gomont) on the extreme right of the front line. With Prince Bernard were the two guns left of the Stievenaar battery, commanded by Lieutenant Winzinger, and strengthened by the addition of a howitzer. The other brigade of the Perponcher division, that of General Count van Bylandt, which had also participated in the defence of Quatre Bras, was assigned a place of honour and danger in the front rank of the left centre. Here it was brigaded with Picton's Division, composed of the Brigades of Kempt and Pack, which included two of the best Highland regiments, viz., the Black Watch and the Camerons.

The Bylandt brigade was made up of five battalions. All of these had fought at Quatre Bras, where the 7th regiment had lost one hundred men, and the 5th Militia nearly half its numbers. Of these five battalions three were Dutch militia, 5th, 7th, and 8th. The two regular battalions were 7th Belgian regiment and 27th Dutch Chasseurs. It had also attached to it the Dutch battery of Byleweldt. Four battalions were drawn up parallel with each other, and in the rear was the diminished 5th Militia. We now come to the much discussed question as to the exact position occupied on this spot by the Bylandt brigade which was accused of having behaved in a cowardly manner, but considering the very precise information there is on the subject it is remarkable that authorities should entertain any further doubt on the subject. The line of the Allied position was marked here by the famous sunken road of Ohaim—the route from Nivelles to Wavre—and the Belgian or rather the Netherlander troops were originally placed south of it, or in plain words in an exposed position. Wellington has been blamed for this arrangement, and several English writers have expressed their surprise at such an unfair and unnecessary exposure. They might have spared themselves the pains because the evidence is conclusive that the error was repaired, not in the first place by Wellington's order, but undoubtedly to his subsequent knowledge and satisfaction. It was one of those errors that was only made one, or at least apparent, by the measures taken by the assailant. If Napoleon had not established the Grand Battery opposite this point it would not have been an error at all.

The same dilatoriness that had characterised Ney's movements on the morning of Quatre Bras marked those of Napoleon during the morning of Waterloo. The wet weather, which had made the clayey soil exceedingly heavy, might be pleaded as an excuse in his case, and the early hours were employed in arranging the Grand Battery of seventy-eight twelve-pounders which were to cover the great attack of the divisions of D'Erlon, Reille and Lobau, the last of which was held in reserve and not used. In his cool way of giving personally pleasant assumptions as facts, Napoleon in his subsequent description of the battle says that "one of the English divisions was entirely destroyed by the shot and shell of this artillery fire." Such very possibly would have been the case if the Bylandt brigade had remained in its first position. Baron Constant de Rebecque saw the collection of the French guns being made on the opposite hill at a distance of half-a-mile, and he at once realised the havoc their fire would work among the Bylandt brigade. He promptly withdrew the brigade behind the sunken road, and any one who cares to examine Craan's* plan, made at the time, will see that the Bylandt brigade is shown *behind* the road on a line with the English regiments. The ground the Belgians are accused of abandoning as an act of cowardice was therefore evacuated by them in good time, under superior and prudent orders, and to avoid an absolutely destructive fire. Napoleon either wilfully or ignorantly cherished a delusion. Far from "entirely destroying a division" the volleys from his seventy-eight guns did comparatively little harm. At half-past one Napoleon gave the order for the D'Erlon division of fifteen thousand infantry, led by Ney in person, to assault the left centre of the Allied position. With the exception of one brigade which advanced to attack La Haie Sainte by the main chaussée, the whole of this huge force in serried columns proceeded to assail the part of the plateau held by Picton's division. The French force drove back the sharpshooters on the southern side of the Ohaim road, and they made their way across that road and through the hedges by which it was lined, but in doing so they suffered heavily, and were thrown into confusion. It is probable that the Netherlands troops, and especially the two Dutch militia regiments, were forced back as Captain Arthur Gore describes : "The Belgians (*i.e.* Dutch-Belgians) gave way because they could not resist that formidable mass, and retired with great loss. They immediately reformed behind the 5th battalion and again advanced." But this giving way was in no way disgraceful, especially when it is borne in mind that the regiments were only militia. If the evidence points to a temporary yielding on the part of some of the regiments, it is also conclusive on the point that the one Belgian regiment in the

* M. Craan was an engineer on the Cadastral Survey of Brabant, and his plan of the battlefield showing the positions and movements of the troops, together with an explanatory statement, was first issued at Brussels in September, 1816. It was republished in London with an English description by Captain Arthur Gore in 1817. Captain Gore served at Waterloo in the 30th regiment, which was helped by Van der Smissen and Detmers under the direction of General de Chassé. The Van Zuylen van Nyevelt report furnishes conclusive evidence of the retirement behind the hollow way.

Brigade, the 7th of the Line recruited at Ghent, did not cede ground at all. The English historian of Picton's Division, who is one of the chief critics of the conduct of the Bylandt Brigade, specially " exonerates a Belgian Colonel and his little body of troops, who held firm under the heaviest fire throughout the day." There cannot be any doubt that Colonel Van den Sanden and 7th regiment is here referred to. A personal account of what took place by an eye witness and participant in the fight is that given by Colonel Scheltens, who was Adjutant of this regiment at Waterloo.

"The battalion remained lying down *behind the road* until the head of the French column was at a distance of a pistol shot. The line then received the order to rise and commence firing. The French column, which was crossing the hollow road, committed the fault of halting in order to reply to our fire. We were firing at such close quarters that Captain L'Olivier received the wad of a cartridge with the ball in his wound. The fire of the English very soon enveloped the column which endeavoured to deploy instead of pushing on. The English cavalry arrived to take part in the fray. It passed like a whirlwind along the wings of our battalion, several of our men being knocked down by the horsemen. The battalion, which had to cease firing, for the cavalry were in front, immediately crossed the road and advanced. The enemy, taken in flank by Picton's regiments, and in reverse by the cavalry, was compelled to retreat leaving behind a good many prisoners. The battalion then took up again its first position where it remained to the end of the battle. There was no further serious attack on this side, only fighting between *tirailleurs*. In the evening we bivouacked on the very position we had held throughout the day. We were no more than three hundred men all included; all the rest had been killed or wounded in this terrible affair—it was about half the effective. In a review held in the Bois de Boulogne by the Duke of Wellington that general stopped before the battalion and complimented it on its fine conduct at Waterloo."

Two officers and one hundred men were killed, six officers, and one hundred and thirty-four men wounded. At Quatre

Bras the regiment also lost more than one hundred men. Lieut. Carrondal, who saved the Duke de Berri, was killed, and Colonel Van den Sanden was seriously wounded in several places. In this struggle Baron de Perponcher had three horses shot under him, Bylandt was wounded, and the colonels of the three militia regiments were all wounded. The total loss of the Perponcher Division at Waterloo was nearly one thousand five hundred killed and wounded, while at Quatre Bras it had lost six hundred and sixty-seven. The exact figures for the two days fighting were twelve officers, and one thousand and twenty-four men killed, and sixty-six officers and one thousand and thirty-nine men wounded. These facts and figures should in themselves finally dispose of all allegations of cowardice against the Bylandt Brigade. But apparently there are those who deem it a point of honour to uphold at all cost the calumnies of Siborne. A recent writer* has passed the comment on these figures, that there is no distinction between the killed and missing, and he very uncharitably suggests that the missing or "*disparus*" ran away. Never did an English writer expose himself to a more crushing rejoinder. Of British troops alone at Waterloo ten officers and five hundred and eighty-two men were missing, as against eighty-five officers and one thousand three hundred and thirty-four men killed. How should we like it if some foreign critic were to insinuate that these five hundred and ninety-two missing Englishmen ran away? Missing means simply absent at roll call from any cause. In all the corps of the Prussian army the missing actually exceeded the killed.

The Netherlands cavalry furnished three brigades at Waterloo, forming a division under Baron Collaert. The Heavy brigade composed of three Carabinier regiments, two Dutch and one Belgian, was commanded by Baron Trip, one light cavalry brigade, consisting of the 4th Dragoons (Dutch) and 8th Croy Hussars (Belgian), was commanded by Baron Ghigny, and the second brigade of light cavalry was that of Van Merlen which had fought at Quatre Bras. The last had suffered so severely in the first action that it was scarcely

* Mr. Oman in *Nineteenth Century* of October, 1900.

stronger than a single regiment, but the Belgian 5th Dragoons had more officers left, and was in better heart generally than the Dutch 6th Dragoons. The total strength of the cavalry Division was given at three thousand six hundred and forty-six, and attached to it was Captain Petter's battery of Horse Artillery. The position of the Netherlands cavalry was in front of the farm of Mont St. Jean, on the right of the Brussels chaussée, and directly behind the English Heavy Cavalry.

It is impossible to disentangle from the numerous cavalry fights in the course of the battle all the deeds of the Belgian cavalry. There seems little or no doubt of the three following main incidents. Trip's heavy cavalry moved forward in support of Ponsonby's brigade, but apparently did not charge on this occasion, Dutch historians stating merely that Trip supported Ponsonby. It would be more correct to say that he supported Somerset. The principal charge of the Carabiniers was that made in conjunction with Somerset and Dornberg, when Captain Batty of the Grenadier Guards "saw a Belgian cavalry regiment fight valiantly with the cuirassiers in a manner never to be forgotten." The Carabiniers made several charges, and in one of them General Barnes, the Adjutant General, was severely wounded.* Both the Ghigny and Van Merlen brigades assisted Vandeleur's 12th Dragoons in driving back Jacquinot's Red Lancers when they had almost annihilated the relics of the Union Brigade. These same brigades also took a prominent part in the repulse of the successive charges of Kellermann's Cuirassiers late in the day. It was at this period that the gallant Van Merlen was killed by a cannon shot at the head of his brigade. The survivors of the Ghigny brigade, especially the 8th Croy Hussars, took part in the final charges of Vivian and Vandeleur, when Wellington gave the signal for the general advance. The only charge made against any Belgian or Dutch cavalry at Waterloo was that "at one

* In one of the charges against Milhaud's cuirassiers Count D'Hane of the 2nd Carabiniers fought a French cuirassier officer, wounding and disabling him, but himself receiving some wounds. Baron Trip states in his report that his regiments took some French cuirassiers prisoners during the afternoon, and that he continued the pursuit of the beaten French army till midnight.

EE

moment Trip showed hesitation." So vague a statement scarcely merits notice. Perhaps the following incident may have been the basis of the story. At seven in the evening immediately before receiving his wound, the Prince of Orange, who had been entrusted with the command of the Allied centre by Wellington, thus addressed the 2nd Carabiniers (Belgians)— " Resume your position, brave Carabiniers! You have done enough for to-day," at the same time seizing the Colonel's hand.

PRINCE OF ORANGE AT WATERLOO.

No one has ever thrown a doubt on the courage of the Prince of Orange. The losses of the three Carabinier regiments in the battle were as follows: 1st Carabiniers, three officers killed, twenty-five men killed, eight officers and sixty-six men wounded; 2nd Carabiniers, one officer killed, eighty-seven men killed, four officers and sixty-four men wounded; 3rd Carabiniers, thirty-two men killed, two officers and twenty-nine men wounded. The Colonels of the 1st and 3rd regiments died subsequently of their wounds. Wellington specially mentioned the assistance rendered by Baron Trip whose brigade was close to him, and under his immediate eye.

The light cavalry suffered even more heavily than the heavy. The Croy Hussars lost more than half their number, one officer, Count Camille du Chastel de la Howarderie, killed, one hundred and thirty-two men killed, seven officers and one hundred and forty-five men wounded. The total loss of the whole Cavalry division was one thousand two hundred and sixty-two, or one-third of the number present, Baron Collaert commanding the Division was wounded.

The incident of the Cumberland Hussars, who were confounded by Alison with the Belgian cavalry, may here be referred to. This regiment was a Landwehr cavalry regiment of the Hanoverian army. The men provided their own horses, and Siborne quotes some officer who told him that they refused to charge because they did not wish to risk their horses. The report of the Court Martial, subsequently held at Hanover, does not bear out this story. The regiment was formally acquitted by the Court of the charge made against it of "having disordered the ranks of the army at Waterloo," but Colonel Hake was cashiered and degraded, and Major Mellzing, the second in command, was severely reprimanded. This was one of those cases covered by a passage in Wellington's despatch of 8th August, 1815. It is "better to pass these portions of history in silence than to tell all the truth." The Cumberland Hussars incident might have been suffered to pass into oblivion if it had not been perverted to the support of a false charge against the Belgians.

We come now to the part taken by the 3rd Division of the Netherlands army under Lieut.-General Baron Chassé.* The movements of this Division between the 15th, and the morning of the 18th June are set forth in full detail in the report of

---

* David Henri Chassé, born at Tiel, Gueldres, 18th March, 1767, son of a Major in the Regiment de Munster. Baron of Holland 1809, Baron of Empire 1811, distinguished in French army in Peninsular War, called General Baionnette. Afterwards famous as the heroic defender of Antwerp Citadel in 1830-1.

Major Baron Van Delen, Chassé's Chief of the Staff, dated Montmorency, 11th November, 1815. It had had no fighting during the retrograde movements which brought it from Peronne and Binche, near the frontier, viâ Nivelles to Braine L'Alleud. The division consisted of two brigades—the first commanded by Colonel Detmers, the second by Major-General D'Aubrémé. The Detmers brigade consisted of 2nd Dutch line regiment, 35th Chasseurs Belgian, and four battalions Dutch Militia, viz., 4th, 6th, 17th, and 19th. The other brigade contained 3rd Belgian Line, 36th Chasseurs Belgian, 12th and 13th Dutch Line, and 3rd and 10th Dutch Militia. The Division contained no cavalry, but attached to the twelve infantry battalions—six regulars and six militia—were two batteries of sixteen guns. One battery was Horse artillery six-pounders and the other foot artillery twelve-pounders. The total strength of the Division was six thousand six hundred and seventy-nine men. The Horse Artillery battery was commanded by Captain Krahmer, a Dutch officer, but the personnel was Belgian. The foot battery, commanded by Captain Lux, was Dutch. The command of the two batteries was held by Major Van der Smissen, a Belgian who had served under Napoleon and gained the Legion of Honour.*

As the Prince of Orange was entrusted by Wellington with the command of the centre of the army the Chassé Division was placed under the orders of Lord Hill, who commanded the right. Before three o'clock orders came from the Duke of Wellington for the Division to advance from Braine L'Alleud and take up a position along the Nivelles road behind the English army, whose second division had been moved forward to strengthen the first line. It was while executing this movement that the Belgians were nearly fired upon by the English troops. General Mercer, who commanded a battery at Waterloo, the only battery whose men did not retire into the infantry squares during the French cavalry charges throughout the day, thus describes the incident.

* After the campaign Major Van der Smissen married an English lady, a relative of the Duke of Richmond, and their son was the second General Van der Smissen who commanded the Belgian Legion in Mexico in 1864-5.

"Suddenly loud and repeated shouts, not English hurrahs, drew our attention. There we saw two dense columns of infantry pushing forward at a quick pace towards us. Crossing the fields as if they had come from Merke Braine, everyone pronounced them French, yet still we lingered opening fire on them. Shouting, yelling, and singing, on they came right for us and being now not above eight hundred or one thousand yards distant it seemed a folly allowing them to come nearer unmolested. The commanding officer of the 14th, to end our doubts, rode forward and endeavoured to ascertain who they were, but soon returned assuring us they were French. The order was already being given to fire when luckily Colonel Gould, R.A., who was standing near me recognised them as Belgians."

For four hours General Chassé remained in this position having several times to form his men into squares as the French cavalry passing through the British lines reached his force. Captain John Pringle describes this part of the battle—"They (Chassé) remained firm against the attacks of the French cavalry, and repulsed it. Perhaps they even suffered more from the enemy's artillery than those in the first line, and yet at the end of the action they advanced with much firmness and regularity in order to support the first line."

Chassé's real chance did not come till late in the day, in fact, not before Napoleon's final attack with the ten battalions of the Middle Guard, two of which remained in reserve. It was at this supreme moment that the Chassé Division came directly into action. The first incidents of this despairing attack, which Ney led on foot, were the wounding of the Prince of Orange and the retirement of the Nassau and Brunswick troops whom he was rallying behind the English Guards. At that critical moment Chassé came into action in support of Colin Halkett's brigade to the right of the Guards. This brigade consisted of the 30th, 33rd, 69th, and 73rd regiments, and it has been declared that the 69th regiment broke, but there does not appear to be any valid ground to believe this statement which was denied by all the officers present. The moment was undoubtedly critical, and it was rendered more so by the fact that the ammunition of the English batteries was giving out. Chassé noticed this in good time and on ascertaining its cause he moved up his horse battery under Major Van der Smissen to the first line. The effective fire of this fresh battery of eight guns proved very destructive. A French officer of the Guard in the charge said that they failed in their attack "through the fire of the masked battery in reserve," and an English officer bore testimony to "the very officious and very opportune aid of Van der Smissen's battery. It literally cut lanes through the columns in our front. His guns were served most gloriously and their grand metallic bang, bang, with the rushing showers of grape that followed, were the most welcome sounds that ever struck my ears." Van der Smissen had three horses shot under him, and his battery lost twenty-seven men killed and twenty-one men wounded. In a letter to the Duke of Wellington, written at Roye sur les Mats on 28th June, 1815, General Chassé said—" It was he who so well directed the light artillery of the 3rd division which in the battle of the 18th had the good fortune to attract the attention of your Excellency and of Lord Hill. At the moment when I attacked with the bayonet the French Guard, he seconded me in a manner above all expectation." No passage stands out clearer from the confusion of this great battle than the service rendered by the battery led by Van der Smissen.

The repulse of the Guard was ensured by the simultaneous attack with the bayonet of the Maitland, Adams, Colin Halkett and Detmers brigades. Chassé led the last in person to shouts of "Long live the House of Orange! Long live the King!" The advance was not arrested, for immediately afterwards it became clear that the battle was won, and Wellington gave his memorable order "the whole line will advance." There was fighting all the way down the slope, and it was renewed with increased desperation in the dip below La Haie Sainte where there were not only the two battalions of the Middle Guard but four battalions of the Old Guard whom Napoleon had brought up to save the retreat. The story of that final struggle which raged from eight until after nine has never been told. The most lurid light of all is perhaps cast upon it in the following rough letter of a sergeant-major of the 35th Chasseurs—Bruges battalion—published in the Flemish journal *Nieuwe Gazette van Brugge* of 6th July, 1815.

Compans, 3 leagues from Meaux,
1st July, 1815.

The bloody battle of the 18th, where Napoleon commanded in person, commenced at seven in the morning, and at eight in the evening the whole French army fled in disorder. It was we Belgian Chasseurs who in the evening after seven o'clock attacked a square and pursued it to Charleroi. This square was composed of *vieilles moustaches* of the Guard. We commenced firing square against square, but that irritated us chasseurs, and we called out for an attack with cold steel. This order we were happy enough to obtain from our General. It was then that you should have seen how that fine Guard fled at full speed. Never in my life shall I see again such a carnage. Not one of that Guard, nor of the few cuirassiers who tried to help it, escaped. All perished by the bayonet. We only saw before and around us corpses of men and horses, guns, helmets and shakoes. Napoleon thought that all the Belgians would range themselves on his side, but he very soon found that he was mistaken. We fought as if we were possessed. Our battalion had one hundred and fifty killed and wounded. My Captain Guyot was wounded in the side. Captain Dullart was slightly wounded. All we Bruges chasseurs made a great booty out of the Imperial Guard.*

The Colonel of the 6th Militia, Arnauld Tilli, or Van Thielen according to another spelling, was killed in this charge, and the total loss of the Chassé division in the battle was given

---

* The returns of killed and wounded for this regiment are variously given. Van Loben Sels mentions Roberti and Guyot as wounded among the officers, but says nothing about the men. Knoop says seventy were killed. Another official document gives Guyot, Dullaert and Roberti wounded, of whom the last died, and seventy-one men killed and wounded. The battalion mustered twenty-two officers and five hundred and eighty-one men. The sergeant-major's account must not be all set down to boasting. Ney in his account of the battle refers to the annihilation of four battalions of the Old Guard late in the evening, and the 35th Chasseurs bivouacked for the night, 18th and 19th June, at Rossomme, the furthest point occupied by any of Wellington's troops. His reference to Charleroi is not to be taken *au pied de la lettre*, but it may serve to introduce the following incident. On 17th June, Lieutenant Van Uchelen, quartermaster of the 4th (Dutch) Hussars, was taken prisoner by a French patrol, and sent in to Charleroi. When the French fugitives poured through the town in the early morning of the 19th he raised the townspeople, organised them into a police force and restored order. When Prince Frederick's corps entered Charleroi on 21st June it found Van Uchelen installed as provisional governor.

as one officer and four hundred and two men killed and thirteen officers and two hundred and fifty-one men wounded. General Chassé wrote in his official report, which I published for the first time: "I am in the highest degree satisfied with the conduct of the whole of my division, particularly with those soldiers who were only a few months in our ranks and whom we could only look upon as recruits. They gave the best proof that the blood of their ancestors flows strongly in their veins." The part taken by the Van der Smissen battery and the Detmers brigade in deciding the battle might have passed out of history, but for the subsequent correspondence between General Chassé and Lord Hill. Siborne, whom we are asked to accept as the standard English authority on the battle, makes no reference to this subject. Wellington in his report to Lord Bathurst has not a word about it, and if Lord Hill had not explained that Wellington's report was sent off before his own, praising "the steady conduct of the 3rd division of the troops of the Netherlands under the command of Major-General Chassé," had been received, this omission would have been accepted as proof positive that the Chassé division did nothing. The following correspondence puts the matter straight. General Chassé's letter and Lord Hill's reply are documents that should not be omitted from any description of the battle of Waterloo.

Bourget, 5th July, 1815.

Your Excellency,

It was only yesterday that I read the report which H.E. the Duke of Wellington has made on the subject of the battle of the 18th ultimo. On that day I had the honour to serve with my division under the orders of Your Excellency. As no mention is made in the report of that division, I must presume that its conduct entirely escaped the attention of Your Excellency when making your Report to the Duke of Wellington. I find myself under the hard necessity of stating myself to Your Excellency the facts as they took place and the part which I believe my Division had in the success of the day.

Towards evening, seeing that the fire of the artillery on the right slackened, I proceeded there to learn the cause. I was informed that ammunition was wanting. I saw very distinctly that the French Guard was advancing towards these guns; foreseeing the consequences, I caused my artillery to advance to the crest, and ordered it to keep up the liveliest fire possible. At the same time leaving the second brigade, commanded by Major-General D'Aubremé in reserve, and in the formation of two squares in echelon, I formed the first brigade, commanded by Colonel Detmers, in close column and charged the French Guard. I had the happiness to see it give way before me. Through delicacy I did not make a report of this fact, being entirely persuaded that Your Excellency would mention it in your Report, and that with so much the more confidence because Your Excellency honoured me two days after the battle (being then at Nivelles) with the expression of your contentment with the conduct of my artillery as well as with that of my infantry. But seeing my error I should deem myself wanting in my duty towards the brave men that I had the satisfaction of commanding, and even towards the whole of my nation, if I dd not make it my task to remedy this omission by begging Your Excellency to be so good as to render the justice to these brave troops which I am persuaded that they deserved. They attach the greatest value to the matter and are deeply sensible of the honour of having contributed to so glorious a victory, etc., etc.,

Chassé.

Lord Hill made the following reply to this letter:—

Paris, 11th July, 1815.

Your Excellency,

I have the honour to acknowledge the receipt of your letter of the 5th instant, which only reached me yesterday.

In the report that I had the honour to make to H.E. the Duke of Wellington on the battle of 18th June, I made special mention of the conduct of your Division during that day, and I did not omit to mention that it advanced to repulse the attack of the French Imperial Guard. Unfortunately, the Report of H.E. the Duke of Wellington was already sent to London before the arrival of my own Report. Nevertheless I am well assured that His Excellency is informed of the fine conduct of the troops under your orders on that glorious day, and I beg Your Excellency to feel convinced that it will always afford me great pleasure to show how sensible I am of it. Accept the assurance of the high consideration with which I have the honour to be your very obedient servant.

Hill (General).

The Duke of Wellington went to Brussels early on the 19th, and not having time to write a full report for King William, requested Baron de Capellen to say to the king: "that it was impossible to gain a victory more complete than that of the 18th, and that he had never taken part in a battle like it, that the result remained doubtful until six o'clock, that he could not sufficiently praise the conduct of his troops, nor find eulogiums great enough for the Prince of Orange, who had so well directed the movements throughout all the day, that from the commencement to the end he had not had any need to send him a single order." In August, during a subsequent visit to Brussels, Wellington personally complimented the officers of the 2nd Carabiniers on their conduct at Waterloo. In the same month he wrote thanking the Mayor and people of Brussels for their kindness to the wounded which he said would "never be forgotten." Finally in his order of 9th December, 1815, issued at Paris Wellington praised "the conduct of the troops of the Netherlands throughout the campaign." An English officer, General XX, writing to his friend Colonel XXX, from Paris, 10th July, 1815, said, among other things: "The battle was glorious for the conqueror and for the conquered. The young Belgians did honour to their nation and themselves. They lost a third of their number."*

The total loss of the Netherlands army at Quatre Bras and Waterloo was two thousand and sixty-eight killed and two thousand and eight wounded, and that fact alone should suffice to silence the voice of calumny. The Dutch and Belgians shared equally in the Prince Regent's Grant for Waterloo with their English comrades—a remarkable tribute on which every English historian had observed silence until I drew attention to the fact

As evidence of what was thought of the Belgians at the time the following Proclamation of 21st June, 1815, issued by

---

* The following note, written in the King's anteroom at Brussels to his wife by Baron Constant de Rebecque who had so distinguished himself in the four days' campaign, is of interest.

"19th June, 1815.

Hurrah! Victoria! At last he is utterly beaten by the genius and perseverance of the chief (*patron*—Wellington). Boney was put to rout last evening. I have received three contusions but no blood lost, except that of my pretty mare which received first a ball in her leg and then one in the head which killed her." He also describes the ride of Wellington, whom he accompanied in the evening of the battle to as far as the farm of Caillou, and their return, meeting Blucher and Bulow near La Belle Alliance after 10 at night, and their reaching Waterloo at 11. It may be worth stating that the cabaret did not receive its name from this incident as commonly supposed. It was built as far back as 1760, and was named after the marriage of its pretty hostess with a handsome ostler.

Prince Blucher at the moment of his departure from the country, provides a striking and sufficient tribute. It was written at Merbes le Chateau and contains the first employment of the alliterative phrase *les braves Belges* which was probably suggested by Cæsar's line *fortissimi sunt Belgæ*.

"Brave Belgians! We have had an opportunity of appreciating your virtues. You are a brave, noble and loyal people. In the moment of danger which seemed to threaten you we were summoned to your assistance. We answered the summons, and it has been very much against our wish that we saw the commencement of the struggle so long delayed. The presence of our troops has been onerous for your country; but we have paid with our blood the tribute of gratitude we owed you, and a benevolent Government will find the means of compensating those who have suffered most from having to meet military exactions. Adieu Brave Belgians! the memory of the hospitable reception you have offered us as well as that of your virtues will be eternally engraved on our hearts. May the God of Peace protect your beautiful country, and banish from it for a long time the troubles of war. Be as happy as you merit to be."

Blucher was not the only German general to express a laudatory opinion of the Belgians. General Pirch II., who fought at Waterloo and also in the stiff fight with Grouchy at Namur on 21st June, published the following order of the day when leaving that city to march up the Meuse into France. "Namur, 24th June, 1815. At all times the Belgians have shown themselves a brave, generous, and valiant people. They have sustained this brilliant reputation especially at the battle of La Belle Alliance, where they fought with such intrepidity as to astonish the Allied armies. The recollection of their invincible courage will not quit the minds of our warriors."

The troops who had fought at Waterloo were so exhausted by the arduous labours of the four days following the French invasion of Belgium that they were given some time to rest, to repair the material, and to receive reinforcements. The first division under Prince Frederick, which had remained inactive at Hal, was now brought to the front, and, with the light cavalry of the Netherlands army reformed into a single brigade under

General Ghigny, was converted into the advance guard of the Allied army and was pushed on into France, where a considerable French force garrisoned the border towns from Lille to Givet. Le Quesnoy, with a garrison of two thousand eight hundred men, surrendered to this force after a night attack on 27th June. Peronne and Condé also surrendered. Valenciennes, stoutly held by General Rey, did not surrender until 15th July. Cambrai was taken by assault, and Wellington, always chary of praise, went out of his way to praise a Belgian battery. At Valenciennes, Colonel de Man of the 4th regiment was seriously wounded and died a few weeks later in Brussels.

Down to the end of the Campaign the Netherlands army continued to take a prominent and honourable part in the operations, and after the conclusion of peace and the restoration of the Bourbons, it was entrusted with the garrisoning of Picardy. When the Division left there under the command of General Stedman was withdrawn in 1817, the inhabitants made a public manifestation in its honour, in recognition of its good conduct, and efforts to make a foreign occupation as light and agreeable as possible. As a recompense for her sacrifices eight French cantons, of which the most important was Bouillon, were added to the Netherlands by the Treaty of Paris, and now form part of the modern kingdom of Belgium. Sixty million francs out of the indemnity exacted from France were assigned to the purpose of constructing a number of fortresses intended to provide for the easy defence of the Low Countries. The Duke of Wellington* was entrusted with the task of superintending

* King William conferred on the Duke and his male heirs in perpetuity the title of Prince of Waterloo, and an estate of five thousand acres in the forest of Soignies not far from the battle field was also bestowed on him. The value of the estate, which consisted of wood, was very small during the Duke's lifetime and on his death the question was raised whether the gift was for the Duke's life alone. Holland and Belgium having separated in the interval there was some uncertainty on the subject, but the Belgian authorities decided to treat the matter in a large spirit, and the gift was placed on the same level as the title of Prince of Waterloo, viz., heirs male in perpetuity. The second Duke once remarked to the distinguished Belgian statesman, Baron Lambermont, on the little value of his property and was advised to place the estate in the hands of the regisseur of the Duke D'Arenberg of the day. This was done with the result that the timber was cut down, farms were established in the place of the forest, and a fair income was derived from a previously valueless property.

their construction, and in a few years the old barrier of the 17th and 18th centuries had been restored.

Looking back at the records of the Waterloo campaign and the highly honourable part taken in it by the Belgian soldiers, it must surely seem one of the strangest perversions of history that it should be cited to establish the cowardice of the Belgians. Curiously enough there is not a trace of any such allegation in any of the contemporary accounts of the battle. On the contrary there is nothing but praise. It was not till twenty years after the battle that an imaginative writer discovered that "two thousand Belgian cavalry bolted at Quatre Bras and nearly carried the Duke of Wellington off with them in their flight." The Van Merlen brigade mustered one thousand one hundred sabres and it left nearly half of them on the ground. The survivors charged several times at Waterloo with Van Merlen at their head, and Van Merlen was killed there. If Thackeray were living to-day I am sure he would remove Regulus Van Cutsum from the pages of Vanity Fair. Siborne's silly stories were refuted at the time, and have been disposed of over and over again by foreign experts. The hitherto unrecognised part of Chassé's division in the victory cannot be disputed, and affords legitimate ground for pride to the peoples of the Netherlands. The admission that the Belgians showed the courage to be expected from their history and antecedents does not diminish in the least the credit and glory of the British troops at Waterloo, or detract from their imperishable fame. What it does accomplish is to relieve the English reputation from a charge of ingratitude and injustice in not merely refusing to accord the Belgians what is their due, but in advancing against them charges of cowardice and misconduct of which they were demonstrably innocent, and which were never so much as heard of until nearly a generation after the battle.

The accusations levelled at the Belgians of having run away at Waterloo, and too readily believed in this country, have operated in another direction besides spreading an undeserved calumny. They have created a belief that the Belgians are by nature an unwarlike and craven people. This is absolutely contrary to the truth. The Belgians are by their Constitution a neutral people for whom the costly luxury of War has no reality, but no one can live in the country without seeing that they still possess special military aptitudes that only good organisation and strict discipline are needed to develop. The record of the Belgians in the armies of Spain, Austria and France is a notable one. They were always ranked among the élite of the army to which they belonged. General Thiébault, one of Napoleon's best but least appreciated officers, says in his interesting *Memoirs of the Empire*: " As for the Belgian soldiers in the Imperial army, they were what Belgians, when well commanded, always will be—men combining with the dash of Frenchmen a tenacity and an energy which, when in large numbers, we have not—soldiers that are inferior to none in the World." The true story of Waterloo confirmed this opinion, and it is very unfortunate that a false impression should have led Englishmen to come to conclusions opposed to the facts and calculated to prejudice them against the Belgians in matters about which there should be no dispute, and which have a direct bearing on the relations of the two peoples.*

* Since this chapter was written the Duke of Wellington's Report to King William of the Netherlands has been discovered at the Hague by Colonel de Bas. Substantially, it is identical with the Duke's letter to Lord Bathurst. There are four variations of more or less importance (1) The hour of the arrival of Picton's division at Quatre Bras is given at half-past three, instead of half-past two in the letter; (2) the name of Bylandt, the brigade commander, is substituted for that of Perponcher, the divisional commander; (3) the name of the non-existent General Van Hope disappears, and in its place that of General D'Aubrémé is given; and (4) there is a fresh closing sentence mentioning the capture of seven thousand prisoners, including Generals Lobau and Cambrone.

The Belgians at Waterloo

By the same Author.

In this work were published for the first time the reports of the Belgian and Dutch commanders present at Quatre Bras and Waterloo.

"Mr. Boulger's important pamphlet."—*Athenæum*.

Four Plans and Eight Illustrations.

Copies, price One Shilling, post free, will be sent on application to the Author at 11 Edwardes Square, Kensington, W.

Made in the USA